Rome's Great Soldiers

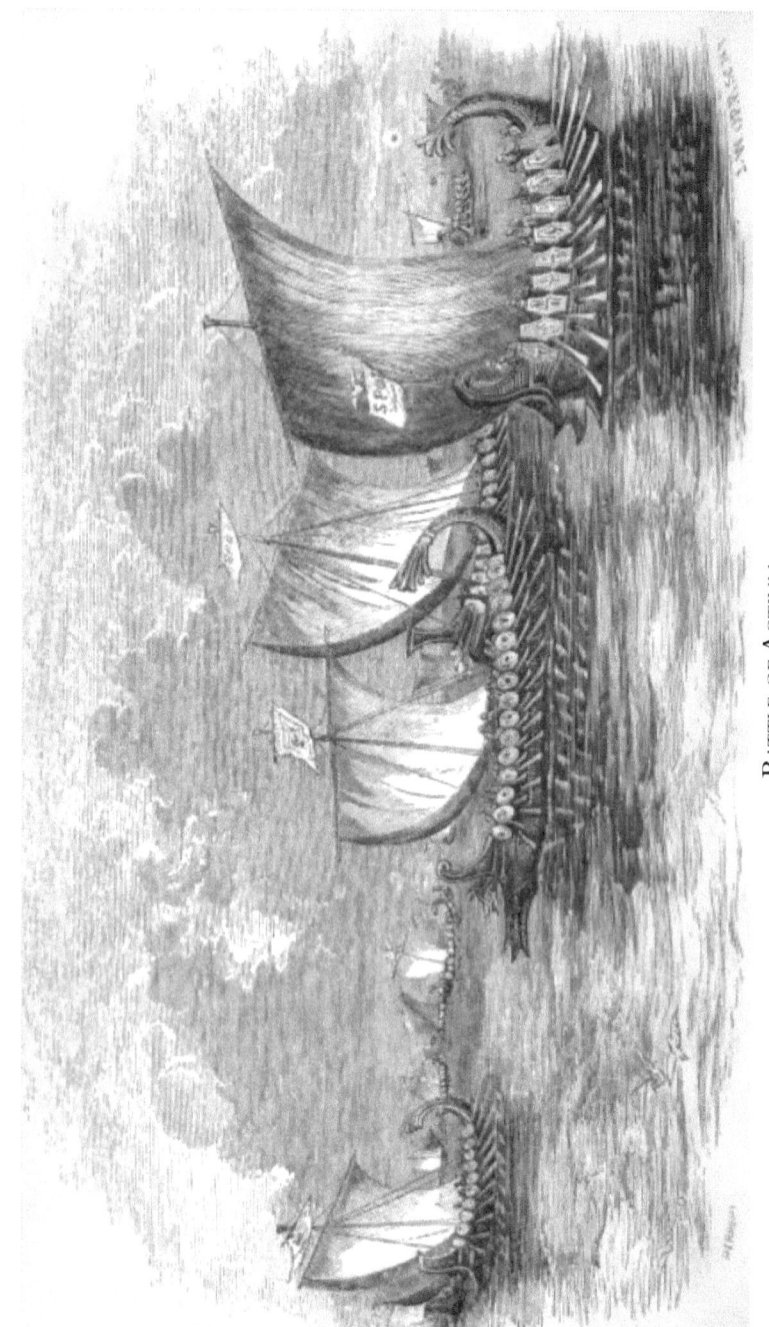

BATTLE OF ACTIUM

Rome's Great Soldiers
The Campaigns of Six of the Roman Republic's
Notable Military Commanders

Henry William Herbert

Rome's Great Soldiers
The Campaigns of Six of the Roman Republic's Notable Military Commanders
by Henry William Herbert

First published under the title
The Captains of the Roman Republic

Leonaur is an imprint of Oakpast Ltd
Copyright in this form © 2015 Oakpast Ltd

ISBN: 978-1-78282-447-3 (hardcover)
ISBN: 978-1-78282-448-0 (softcover)

http://www.leonaur.com

Publisher's Notes

The views expressed in this book are not necessarily those of the publisher.

Contents

Preface	9
Publius Cornelius Scipio, Africanus	15
Titus Quinctius Flamininus	98
Lucius Æmilius Paullus	126
Caius Marius of Arpinum	186
Lucius Cornelius Sylla, Felix	261
Caius Julius Caesar	317

To C. C. Felton
Regent of Harvard University
&c., &c., &c.,
In Memory
Of Many Pleasant Hours Heretofore Spent Together,
And Hope of More Such Hereafter,
Nor Less in Token
Of Cordial Regard for Himself,
And Sincere Respect for His Talents and Attainments,
This Volume
Is Dedicated, by His Friend,
The Author.

Preface

My Dear Felton;

Nearly two years have elapsed since I had the pleasure of dedicating to you my *Captains of the Old World*, and as you will, I know, be gratified to hear, I feel myself justified, by the cordial kindness with which that work was received, in proceeding to offer to the public its next successor, *The Captains of the Roman Republic*.

I believe, I stated in my former preface with sufficient clearness, to render many words on this occasion unnecessary, what are my views, and what the principle on which I propose to act in this system of works.

I use the word system, you will observe, because I choose to avoid the word, series; and for this reason—that I notice, and do not wonder at, a daily growing disinclination on the part of the reading public to engage in the purchase, or even the perusal of works ostensibly serial; from the very natural and reasonable apprehension that the series will never be concluded at all; or, if at all, not within the lifetime of the present generation—as seems likely to be the case with M. Thiers' brilliant history of the Consulate and Empire; or, Mr. Macaulay's no less brilliant history of England.

It is for this reason, then, that I have eschewed not to call, but to *make* my work *serial*. In as much as I propose that each volume shall contain the military history of the truly great captains of one distinct period, in itself complete, disconnected from any preceding work, and perfectly intelligible in itself, without reference to that which has gone before, or which shall follow it.

In one sense, *serial* these volumes unquestionably are and will be; that they are intended to follow one another, and in some sort to grow out of one another, naturally, in the course of time, and in the current of events; so that, of course, he who has read one will better understand the gist of arguments, and the narrative of events contained in the next succeeding it, than he who is wholly inexpert in my method of dealing with antique strategy and tactics.

Beyond this, each volume has its own interest, self-contained, and undivided; and possesses its own subject in itself unmingled and complete.

To what length this system of volumes may be carried is, as on its face must needs appear, uncertain in the highest; for to insure its continuation, the continuation of all things else, and those the least insurable, as life, health, leisur, means, ability, and, last in place though first in importance, popular favour must be insured likewise. Suffice it to say, that it is my plan, other things granted, to persevere in my undertaking until I have reached the period within which men may write partisan declamation, but cannot write history; and that were I permitted to announce a termination so remote to my labours, I would announce the close of the Thirty Years' War, as the most recent date of which I would in any event desire to treat.

For, in the first place, I do not believe that all the documents and archives, which are hereafter to throw light on the true history of subsequent events, are as yet attainable; and, in the second, I am of opinion that personal, that patriotical, that political prejudices are not fully extinguished in families, or individuals, within a century at least; and that no man, while influenced by prejudices of party or even national friendship or hatred, can so write history as to leave it worth the reading. In order to descend, however, to the subject of my present volume, I would remind you of a principle which I laid down to myself in my last, and to which I ought perhaps to refer, as explaining the cause of my passing over so many years of the Republic in total silence, before treating of a single captain. In the preface to that volume I used these words:

> I have not, of course, dreamed of including in my list of captains, all the men who set battalions in the field, and fought gallantly, whether for patriotism or ambition; but have selected those only who were, in my opinion, really eminent, really worthy of continued remembrance, really entitled to be enrolled in the annals of all time as great generals.

And by these words I propose to myself still to be governed. It is for this reason, therefore, that, while treating especially of *The Captains of the Roman Republic*, I have entirely omitted the continually warlike, and almost continually victorious, magistrates of that republic, during the first three centuries of its existence; and that I commence only with . Publius Cornelius Scipio, subsequently surnamed Africanus, in the 545th year from the foundation of the city of Rome, the 301st of the Republic, and the 208th before the Christian era; being in fact little more than a century and a half previous to the extinction of the Commonwealth, and the erection of the long dynasty of Caesars on its ruins. For this reason, I mean—that I do not intend to deal with successful soldiers, who conquered by brute valour, or by the inborn superiority of the men they led; and that before Scipio, the conqueror of Hannibal, there was no Roman, who at all merited the style of a great captain.

This will doubtless astonish many of my readers, who have been wont to believe as implicitly in the fabulous exploits of the Camilli, the Curii, and the Decii, as in the authentic campaigns of Julius Caesar; and who have been taught that the subjugation of all northern and middle Italy to the arms of Rome, a little prior to the date at which I commence, was due to the individual science and prowess of her generals, and not to the extraordinary constitution and peculiar organisation of her people.

In this respect, it is admirably remarked by the lamented Arnold in the *exordium* to his 53rd chapter on the second Punic war, that:

> If Hannibal's genius may be likened to some Homeric God, who in his hatred of the Trojans rises from the deep to rally the fainting Greeks and to lead them against the enemy; so the calm courage with which Hector met his more than human adversary, is no unworthy image of the unyielding magnanimity displayed by the aristocracy of Come. As Hannibal utterly eclipses Carthage, so on the contrary Fabius, Marcellus, Claudius Nero, nay Scipio himself, are as nothing when compared to the spirit and wisdom and power of Home. The senate which voted its thanks to its political enemy Varro, after his disastrous defeat, 'because he had not despaired of the Commonwealth,' and which disdained to solicit, or to reprove, or to threaten, or in any way to notice the twelve colonies, which had refused their accustomed supplies of men to the army, is far more to be honoured than the conqueror of Zama.

And if this be true—as true it is to the letter—of the great Scipio, of whom Niebuhr said in the preface to his third volume that he "towers as far above his nation, as Hannibal above all nations," so much the more correct is it of all those who preceded him, and who, whether they conquered or fell, alike in their duty to their country, fought and fell, lived and died, by the genius of Rome, and by no peculiar virtue or inspiration of their own.

I do not precisely mean to say that no Roman prior to Scipio, known as Africanus, displayed any high soldierly qualities, or merited any praise either for strategy or tactics; since several had done so during that very second Punic war, which he was born to terminate,— especially his own father, Publius Scipio, whose persistency in sending his army into Spain after Hannibal had already passed the Alps, was, it may well be, ultimately the cause of Home's salvation; and, secondly, Claudius Nero, whose forced march from Venosa in La, Puglia, to the banks, of the Metro in the marches of Ancona, and defeat of Hasdrubal, is the solitary specimen of true generalship on the part of the Romans during Hannibal's seventeen campaigns in Italy. But I do assert that prior to the conqueror at Zama, no single man displayed such qualities, in so high a degree, or in instances so numerous, as to justify us in attributing to him the praise of decided military genius.

In my last volume, *The Captains of the Old World*, you will remember that I included Hannibal, whom I regard, and whom a far better judge than I, Napoleon the Great, regarded as the general unequalled of all ages, and this I did, rather perhaps for the sake of uniformity, than in order consistently to close an epoch.

The pages of this, work will relate exclusively to Romans, unless in so far as the generals opposed to them are incidentally concerned; and will contain accounts of the campaigns of all those, whom I hold worthy to be deemed captains, from the time of Scipio to that of Marc Antony.

Nor, if I have heretofore dealt with some of the greatest and most splendid heroes and leaders of antiquity, such as Miltiades, Xenophon, Epaminondas, Alexander, Hannibal, must my readers imagine that the tale of great men or mighty generals is nearly exhausted, or that the interest attached to the growth, the grandeur, and the decline of the Roman Commonwealth is in any degree inferior to that which clung around the immortal isles of Greece, until "all except their sun was set?"

Scipio, the conqueror of Hannibal, Flaminius, and Paullus, conquerors of Philip and Perseus, who first demonstrated the superiority of the Roman legion to the far-famed Macedonian phalanx, Marius, the mighty democrat, Sylla, the last of the Patricians, the princely pride of Pompey, and the wondrous versatility of Caesar, should furnish ample topics for a more spacious margin and a more puissant pen than mine.

Yet I fear not, that in depicting the close of the last struggle Rome was ever compelled to maintain on her own soil, fighting not for empire but existence; in tracing the successive steps by which she subjugated, West and East, the known world, until, weary with victory and seeing nothing more to vanquish, she turned her suicidal arms against her own unconquered bosom, I shall fail to offer something of more than common interest to such as choose to follow me.

It will seem strange—not to you of course—but to many of my readers, that I should apologise at this period, for the scantiness of the material from which I have now got to draw—for the many believe, doubtless, that the farther we descend the stream of time, the stronger shine the lights of knowledge, the clearer beams the lamp of veritable history. You know, however, too well that I should need repeat it to you, that the descent from the clear, luminous and truthful histories of Herodotus, Thucydides, Xenophon and Arrian, to the brilliant and beautiful but inexact romancings of the credulous and unquestioning Livy, to the bald, skeleton narratives of the partisan Polybius, and the cold condensations of Appian, is something similar to a return from the demonstrations of Newton or Laplace to the wild dreams of the Astronomers of old.

I have, moreover, from this time forth—so soon at least as I shall have conducted Scipio to his victory at Zama—no guide in our own language, by whose intuitive skill in deciphering the mysteries of ancient history, even suggestively, to profit. The history of Home in its most interesting periods is yet to be written; for it seems indeed that an especial and peculiar fate cuts off untimely all who possess that singular combination of qualities natural, and abilities acquired, which fits them for so arduous an undertaking.

Twice within our own age, persons so qualified have come upon the stage, Niebuhr, the discoverer, and Arnold, the handler, of the key which might have unlocked to us, at least by close approximation, the hidden sense of that unfathomable mystery of historic treasures, among which, as yet, the most patient and laborious of us grope our way ignorant and darkling.

Twice have our hopes been raised to the highest, of having the veil lifted from before our eyes—twice have they been cast down—yet in neither case wholly prostrated. Since the first great discoverer not only succeeded in making plain to our comprehension much of what seemed the dimmest and most incomprehensible in Rome's darkest ages, but dying left to us the knowledge of his method, and the hope at least of in some sort applying it. Since the second great improver, advancing on *his* plan and progress, has converted what he left difficult and profound disquisition into easy and patent narrative; and, his guidance ceasing, has given us in the history of Hannibal and the Second Punic War, the ablest, most accurate, most impartial, and most eloquent relation of events long since entombed in falsehood, worse almost than oblivion, that ever has graced our English language.

The times, to which I am coming in this volume, the struggles no longer between the ancient people and the ancient fathers, but between the proletarian populace and the moneyed nobility of Rome; the secret workings of the rival factions, aristocratic and democratic, as they were self-styled, from the days of Marius and Sylla, to those of Brutus and Octavius, are confessedly the most painful, I will not say desperate, to be unravelled, of all truly historic ages.

It is true, that, in my work, confining itself in the main to military history, political strife bears but a secondary interest; but when the principles of war itself are political and partisan, politics and the secrets of partisanship must form an integral part of the narrative of the wars.

Feeling, therefore, that I am entering perhaps upon too bold an enterprise, with nothing whereon to depend but diligent research to the extent of my own unassisted powers, and nothing which to promise to my readers but the candid and faithful use of such authorities as I can command, with my own best deductions from the same—premising always that I have no preconcerted theories, with regard either to men or measures, to be bolstered by manufactured facts, or misinterpreted quotations—I lay my work before you and the public, in the hope, at least, that if of little value itself, it may contain something suggestive, to other and abler minds, of what may prove advantageous to the elucidation of historic truth hereafter.

    Pray believe me, my dear Felton,
        Ever and most faithfully yours,
                Henry William Herbert.

The Cedars, April 20, 1854.

1
Publius Cornelius Scipio, Africanus

Than the Scipios, whether by descent from most illustrious blood, or by renown of most illustrious actions, there was no family in Rome more noble. Between the years of the city 359 and 545, no less than ten persons, all of this name, and all in the direct male line, held *curule* magistracies, and served their country with distinction, both in the field and in the forum. A branch of the great Cornelian house, the proudest, haughtiest, and almost the oldest of the old patrician houses, the Scipios were by blood, by tradition, by temperament, the most unbending of the ancient aristocracy; and as such, although, by something of prescriptive right, which yet prevailed in Rome, and much more, be it said, by right of native virtue, they obtained, during two centuries and upward, all the highest offices in the gift of the people, they never held even for a time the people's favour.

With the Punic wars from their commencement they were so immediately and, so to speak, hereditarily connected, that when service was to be taken against Carthage, that service appeared almost, as a matter of course, to belong to a Scipio. When in the First Punic War, the Romans by one of those gigantic efforts of energy and enterprise, unequalled in the annals of the world, created a fleet as it were in a single day, won with it their first naval battle, and thenceforth disputed the empire of the seas on even terms against the greatest maritime power the world at that time had ever seen, a Scipio superintended its construction; and, although beaten and made a prisoner in his first encounter with the enemy, subsequently well redeemed his laurels, and well avenged his disaster, by the conquest of the greater part of Sicily from the Carthaginian arms.

When it was known that the terrible—already terrible—Hannibal had passed the hitherto inaccessible ramparts of the Pyrenees, and was advancing with giant strides across the unexplored wilderness of central Gaul, a Scipio, the father of him who is the subject of this sketch, was elected Consul, and sent by sea to Marseilles with an army to encounter the boy general, and dispute with him the passage of the Rhone, and the entrance of the Alps, whose icy fastnesses he was the first to conquer.

That Scipio was too late to intercept the bold invader on the Rhone is not attributable to any neglect or miscalculation on his part, but rather to the extraordinary energy and speed with which the great commander opposed to him had pressed onward, setting difficulties at naught, and holding nothing to be impossible which it was requisite for him to do. But that, on finding all his combinations thus overthrown, and his plans anticipated, he had the truly Roman hardihood and perseverance to forward his consular army into Spain, its proper destination, while he himself returned by sea to Italy, there to make head, as best he might, against the enemy on his descent from the mountains, is a proof of judgment so sound, generalship at once so prudent and so daring, that it compels me to pronounce him a man of no ordinary abilities, and a soldier second to no Roman who preceded him.

The wise and cautious Arnold says:

> As a mere military question, his calculation, though baffled by the event, was sound: but if we view it in a higher light, the importance to the Romans of retaining their hold on Spain would have justified a far greater hazard; for if the Carthaginians were suffered to consolidate their dominion in Spain, and to avail themselves of its immense resources, not in money only, but in men, the hardiest and steadiest of Barbarians, and under the training of such generals as Hannibal and his brother equal to the best soldiers in the world, the Romans would hardly have been able to maintain the contest. Had not Publius Scipio then dispatched his army to Spain at this critical moment, instead of carrying it home to Italy, his son in all probability would never have won the Battle of Zama.

In the sharp cavalry action on the banks of the Tesino, which was the first combat on Italian soil—wherein the Roman horse and the allies fought well against the Carthaginian *cuirassiers* in front, until the wild Numidians thundered on both their flanks and their rear, with the unbridled shock of their desert barbs, and routed them with fearful carnage—Scipio was himself severely wounded; and was rescued from inevitable death, only by the exertions and devotion of his son, then eighteen years of age, serving in the cavalry, or as others say of a faithful Ligurian slave. Arnold at once discards this relation of the young hero's early exploit, as a fabrication of Polybius, from whom it is probable that the other writers borrowed the legend, or rather of Caius Laelius, the personal friend and lieutenant of the elder Africanus, who related it to him, says the historian, with his own lips; and it must be admitted that some considerable suspicion does attach to such portions of his narrative as relate to this great and noble family, the writer having been himself a near personal friend and tent-companion of the younger Africanus, and as such certainly liable in some degree to the charge of having seen historical events with the eyes, and related them with the tongues of the Scipios.

I confess, however, that I cannot see wherefore so direct an assertion of an author, not proved to be unveracious, and speaking, as he asserts, on the authority of a very competent witness, should be absolutely rejected as a falsehood; the rather that in the tale itself there is nothing to startle the least credulous, nothing in short which is contrary to probabilities, as regards the character of the man, or the nature of the case. And I might perhaps here observe that Dr. Arnold appears to me to have carried his usual caution somewhat too far in respect to the traditions relative to Scipio, refusing to give credit to him for deeds positively attributed to him by many writers, while he unhesitatingly gives the credit of them to others on no discoverable authority, as in the case of Varro, to which I shall come hereafter.

Shortly after the cavalry action on the Tesino, Sempronius the other consul, coming up with his army, effected a junction with that of Scipio, which after the disaster of its horse had fallen back upon Placentia, and lay a few miles thence among the hills inactive, owing to the unhealed wound of its own commander. In consequence of the disability of that officer, he took command of the united force of the two consular armies, delivered battle on the banks of the Trebbia, and received a defeat so terribly crushing and complete, as gave the Romans their first foretaste of what was likely to befall them from the qualities of Hannibal as a general, and of the men whom he had formed to conquest.

This battle was fought in the midwinter, which in the marshy plains of the Po, directly exposed to the cold blasts sweeping down from the eternal snows of the Alps, is still of unusual severity; and the loss of the Carthaginians, in their high-blooded African horses and in their elephants, to which the cold was intolerable, having been heavy, both armies went at once into winter quarters, and the operations of Hannibal's first campaign on the Italian soil were closed triumphantly in the last days of the 537th year of Rome, and the 217th before the Christian aera.

In the following year, the new consuls, Caius Flaminius and Cneius Servilius Geminus, came into office, the former succeeding Sempronius in Etruria, while his colleague took the leading of Scipio's army at Arminum; but so little were the Roman aristocracy discontented with the conduct of Scipio, that he was immediately appointed proconsul, and sent to command his own original forces in Spain, whither he had sent them with his brother Cneius, as his lieutenant, in the preceding year; and where they had already done good service against the two Hasdrubals and Mago, whom thus far they had held in check.

There, during those terrible succeeding years, which shook the power and tried the constancy of Rome to the utmost; the years of the awful earthquake-shocks of Thrasymene and Cannae; when the unbridled coursers of the fierce Numidians swept like a hurricane, with fire and sword, over the half of Italy; when, beyond the confines of the old Latin colonies, Rome had neither ally, nor friend, nor well-wisher on the peninsula; and when even of those ancient colonies twelve at the least were wavering in their faith, the Scipios maintained the war, unwearied and undaunted. Cneius had already, before his brother's arrival, defeated Hanno [1] and made him prisoner, driving the Carthaginians back beyond the Ebro. In the following year Hasdrubal, in full march to reinforce his brother Hannibal in Italy, for which purpose he had been strengthened by a large force of Carthaginian veterans and Numidian horse, was encountered by those two strenuous brothers, and beaten so signally, "that all hope was lost to him not only of advancing into Italy, but even of holding securely his occupation of Spain." (*Livy XXIII.*)

What the effect of the addition of twenty thousand fresh troops, largely provided with the formidable Numidian horse and with elephants, to the already all-victorious camp of Hannibal, would have produced on the fortunes of Rome had it been launched against them in that appalling crisis which succeeded the unparalleled carnage of Cannae, may readily be estimated; nor will it be too much, I think, to say, that by this action beyond the Ebro, the Scipios did more to-

---

1. Polybius III. 76; though this is denied by Appian, VI. 15.

ward the salvation of Rome, than Fabius with all his politic delays, or Marcellus with all his headlong daring, all his real successes and pretended victories. For several succeeding years, they certainly did well, by ably maintaining their ground, and so far neutralised the efforts of the Carthaginians, that they entirely cut off the supply of Spanish auxiliaries not only from the Italian, but from the African armies of their enemy.

Publius Scipio moreover acquired so much popularity and influence among the Spanish tribes, particularly the Celtiberians, that he not only gradually diverted them from Mago and the Hasdrubals, but annexed them as auxiliaries not only to his own two original legions, which had never been reinforced, nor had received any pay from home, since he sent them out six years before, and to have supported which as he did in an enemy's country, making war maintain war, is not the smallest proof of his strategetical conduct and capacity.

In the latter part of the year of the city 452, after having maintained the credit and character of Rome with ability for nearly six years, the Scipios felt themselves strong enough to assume the offensive; and laying a careful plan of the campaign by which they hoped entirely to clear Spain of the Carthaginians, they crossed the River Iberus with divided forces, and, pushing forward into the middle of Southern Spain, wintered, (*Livy*), at the towns of Castulo, now Cazlona, and Orso, in the valley of the Baetis or Guadalquivir.

Here, it appears that the influence of Hasdrubal, the son of Hamilcar, was still too great over the minds of the natives for the hopes of the Roman leaders; for no sooner were those fickle and treacherous barbarians brought within the immediate sphere of his fascination, than they melted like snow, (*Livy*), from the standard of the Scipios, and left them with inferior powers, and divided forces, at a great distance from their resources, and in the presence of three superior Carthaginian armies. These speedily forming a junction attacked the Roman commanders in detail, and almost utterly destroyed both armies, killing the leaders, either in the actions or in the carnage that followed, for they were not defeats but total and irreparable routs. A miserable remnant only under Titus Fonteius, one of Scipio's lieutenants, and Lucius Marcius, a Roman knight elected to command in that emergency by the *legionaries*, maintained themselves within the Ebro, until they were relieved by the army of Claudius Nero, which could now be spared from home duty in consequence of the fall of Capua before the Roman fortune.

Livy has a whole tissue, (*Appian VI.*), woven from the deliberate falsehoods of the Roman annalists, concerning pretended victories won from Hasdrubal the son of Gisco, by this most illustrious youth, who, he says, alone and single-handed restored the affairs of Rome. Not a particle of credit is to be attached, however, to these barefaced fictions; nor can much more be attributed to the tale related by Livy of the advance of Claudius Nero, who had only brought out six thousand foot and three hundred horse, to the aid of the broken and disheartened remnant cooped up within the Ebro, so far as to Iliturgi, now Andujar, on the frontiers of Jaen and Cordova, in the valley of the Guadalquivir; yet there he is reported to have gained signal advantages over Hasdrubal, and to have been robbed only of a perfect victory by the wonted Punic Faith, or that treachery of which the Carthaginians are continually accused by the Romans, without there existing the smallest visible cause for the accusation.

One thing is certain, that when the subject of my present sketch was appointed to the office and command of his late father, and relieved Claudius Nero with a considerable fleet and army in the year 545 of Rome, he found him still within the Ebro unassailed indeed, and in full possession of that ancient territory, of which in fact during the last eight years, and after the defeat and capture of Hanno, the Romans had never lost the occupation. But as no permanent progress had been made beyond this line, even by the two Scipios at the head of there powerful legions, augmented by twenty thousand Celtiberian allies, it is little probable that Nero, with less than a fourth part of their power, should have attempted a foray at once so useless and so rash.

In the meantime the son of Publius Scipio, whether or not he was the preserver of his father's life on the banks of the Tesino, had distinguished himself singularly during the progress of the war, and especially at Canusium, when he was present at the tumultuous and terror-stricken councils which succeeded the overwhelming disaster, and almost incredible carnage of Cannae. Arnold says:

> The scene, at that place was like the disorder of a ship going to pieces, when fear makes men desperate, and the instinct of self-preservation swallows up every other feeling.

And so general and despairing was this panic, that a conspiracy was set on foot among the principal young men, mostly of equestrian rank, which had already perverted the minds of nearly one half the soldiers who had escaped from the slaughter, with the intent to cut their way to the coast, seize shipping, and forsaking Italy for ever and the fortunes of Rome as hopeless, sell their swords to some foreign king, and make their camp their country.

The extent to which this plot was carried appears at once when we consider that in the first instance only four thousand men of the infantry and two hundred, (*Livy*), knights were collected at Canusium, previous to the arrival of Varro, who was at this time lying at Venusia, (*Livy*), with a somewhat larger body of dispirited and disorganised fugitives of all arms; and that two years afterward, the censors judging an extraordinary punishment necessary for an offence so extraordinary, degraded every knight concerned in this affair, besides depriving no less than two thousand citizens of their elective *franchise*, who had misconducted themselves on this occasion or avoided military duty on frivolous pretexts within the last four years, and sentencing them to serve unto the termination of the war in Sicily, as common legionaries in the ranks.

It appears that, with the men rallied at Canusium, there were four tribunes of the soldiers in command—Fabius Maximus, son of the dictator, of the first legion, Lucius Publicius Bibulus and Publius Cornelius Scipio, both of the second, and Appius Claudius Pulcher of the third, who had recently been *aedile*; and that, by the unanimous consent of all the men present, the supreme command was temporarily conferred on Scipio, who was an exceedingly young man scarcely yet in his twentieth year, and Appius Claudius.

To these, (*Livy*), while they were holding council, with a few leading men, as to what steps should be first taken, arose Publius Furius Philus, son of a consular, and disclosed to them the secret of the plot, at the head of which he said was Lucius Caecilius Metellus, of whose views he was himself a participant.

Fearful as had been the event of the day, and almost hopeless as appeared the state of the Republic, spirit-broken and demoralised as they were by the last most lamentable issue of their arms, that little band was not yet prepared to desert their country or dishonour the high name of Romans. For a moment, they were thunderstruck and stood aghast at the mere suggestion, and then desired to refer it to a general council of war. There is, I believe, scarcely an instance on record, in which a council of war has determined on the bolder line of conduct, when the alternative has been directly submitted to it; but fortunately for Rome, for Europe, for the world, there was one present, who, though but a boy in years, was a man already in forecast and wisdom, a leader by virtue of that instinct which, in some singularly endowed characters, at once and from the first, supplies the place of experience.

Livy says, and I do not hesitate here to quote him as full and credible authority—being confirmed to the letter by Dio Cassius and Valerius Maximus, and indirectly by Appian, nor less because, from the silence of Polybius, it is clear he has followed some other historian:—

> The youthful Scipio predestined to be the victorious general in this war, exclaimed, 'That in such disasters as this, audacity and action are .the two things requisite, not consultation. That all who wished well to the Republic should take up arms and follow him, for that in no place of a truth are any camps so hostile as where such treason is contemplated.' Thence, followed only by a few, he went direct to the quarters of Metellus, and there finding that council of youths in session, of which he had been informed, he drew his sword in their faces, and exclaimed, 'From the resolve of my own mind I swear, that I will not forsake the republic of the Roman people, nor will suffer any other Roman citizen to forsake it. If knowingly I fail in this, Jupiter, best and greatest, smite me, my house, my family, and all that belongs to me, with death in its direst form. To these words of mine, Lucius Caecilius, I insist that thou must swear, and all the rest of you here present. Who will not swear, let him know that against him this sword is naked.' And thereupon, fearful no less than if they had seen Hannibal himself among them, they all swore and submitted themselves to Scipio's protection.

This vigorous and energetic course, worthy a hero of the older days of Greece when heroes were, undoubtedly saved Rome. Appian says:—

> Within the last two years the Romans had lost, warring in Italy against Hannibal, not less than one hundred thousand men, of their own citizens and their allies.

Now in Roman armies the force of the *legions* and of the allies of the Latin name was always equal, so that the actual Roman loss cannot have amounted to less than fifty thousand citizens, from a state the whole population of which could furnish only two hundred and seventy thousand, (*Livy*), two hundred and thirteen male citizens, above seventeen years of age.

Or otherwise: Within the space of less than two years, one fifth part of her men had fallen, and that without one transient gleam of success, one accidental stroke of fortune, which might lead them to hope for better things in future. The second city of Italy, Capua, (*Livy*), which had heretofore remained true to Rome in her most perilous trials, which, according to the requisition of the Roman commissioners themselves, was capable of raising without unusual effort an army of thirty thousand foot and four thousand horse, had opened her gates to the enemy, and formed with him a close alliance, offensive and defensive.

It cannot be doubted, that if, in addition to all these calamities, enough in themselves to shake the resolution of the bravest state, the despairing counsels of these young men, the very flower of Rome's youthful nobility, had been adopted, a universal revolt of all the colonies and the destruction of the republic must have followed. But Scipio's ready wit and brave devotion met with the success they merited, and harbingered, if they did not arouse, that indomitable spirit of the Roman aristocracy, which never blenched, never wavered, never hesitated at any sacrifice, never counted the loss of anything a loss, so long as that loss might be a gain to Rome, until their almost superhuman enemy was summoned homeward to defend his country's hearths and altars against the young antagonist, whom on that night of his greatest victory Rome's destiny evoked against him.

On the following morning Varro came up from Venusia with the remainder of the army, which raised the whole effective force of those who had rallied from the field to about ten thousand men, beat off the cavalry of Hannibal as it rode up in all its confidence and daring to the very gates of the town, and then:

> Neither despairing nor in consternation, but with sound judgment, as if no disaster had befallen him, ordered and carried out everything most advisable in that crisis. (*Dio Cassius*).

This done, he resigned his command to Marcus Marcellus, one of the *praetors* for the year, who, lying at Ostia, was commanded to march up his single *legion* whereupon to rally the relics of the two consular armies; and then returned to Rome, calmly to meet the judgment of the Senate, which, as being of *plebeian* origin and elected by the popular party, he had every reason to expect condemnatory in the last degree.

It is remarkable that Dr. Arnold ascribes to Terentius Varro, the whole merit of suppressing this conspiracy, while no author who has been yet discovered by the diligence of Professor Hare, Arnold's posthumous editor and candid expositor, makes any praiseworthy mention whatever of that unfortunate general, with the exception of Dio, in the short passage quoted above, and Appian, who briefly states that "he endeavoured to infuse spirit into the army" before returning to Rome. I do not, however, regard this as any error, much less want of candour, of the great historian, but rather as an instance of that singular and instinctive shrewdness which enabled him and his predecessor, Niebuhr, to arrive suddenly from the slightest hints at true conclusions.

The two brief paragraphs above quoted, together with the fact that the Senate came out to meet the defeated consul, their own political enemy, moreover, and thanked him "for that he had not despaired of the republic," was confirmation strong as proof to the clear mind of Arnold.

The thanks of the Senate to the fugitive leader have never been explained at all, or explained, literally *ad absurdum*, by other writers, who have grossly told us that the "not despairing" consisted in giving battle with an overwhelming superiority of numbers; when in fact he was under direct orders to fight, and was in command of not less than eighty-nine thousand six hundred horse and foot, [2] while Hannibal was certainly inferior by nearly one half, in force, (*Arnold*).

To suppose, therefore, that for simply obeying orders and not showing himself a palpable coward, he received the thanks of the Senate, is so plainly absurd, that it proves clearly that he did receive them for something done not in, but after, the battle. And what was there to be done thereafter, but to repress the mutinous spirit of despair which had manifested itself, and to reorganise the disorganised fugitives from that field of blood? This he did, and did so effectually and so well, that he merited and received honours, rarely granted by a Roman Senate to an unsuccessful general, and by the same Senate be it noticed, which so piteously punished and disgraced the authors of the meeting.

But if Dr. Arnold's judgment is perfectly satisfactory to me in the case of Varro, it is by no means equally so in the case of the young

---

[2] Polybius III. 107. The Consuls, Paulus and Varro, had each four Roman *legions*, each of 5,000 foot and 300 horse, = 20,000 foot and 1,200 horse, united, 42,400 men; besides four *legions* of the Latin name, each of 5,000 foot and 900 horse, singly 20,000 foot and 9,600 horse, = 47,200 men; 42,400 Romans and 47,200 allies = 89,600 men.

Scipio; for while I admit his right to conclude from facts, wanting authorities, in the one case, I cannot admit the propriety of rejecting or doubting positive authorities, facts likewise coinciding, in the other.

It is true, that at a very early age he was with his brother Lucius created Curule Ædile; the very earliest doubtless at which he was legally eligible—Polybius says in the very year in which his father sailed for Spain, that is to say according to his own synchronism, for in the preceding chapter he makes him save his father's life at the Tesino—that is in the preceding year—when only seventeen. But this is absurd—for no one ever heard, during the Republic, of a boy of eighteen holding a Curule office—and it is very clear that there is some error in the Roman chronology, as relating to the life of this distinguished man; for if he had been seventeen as Polybius states in the winter of 437, he could have been but twenty-four in the spring of 445, when he was elected proconsul—at which age Livy rates him—whereas Arnold, with both these authorities before him, reckons his age, at this time, as twenty-seven; and, to prove that the error is not textual, draws a parallel between his years and those of Napoleon, when appointed to the leading of the army of Italy, in view doubtless of some farther authority which I cannot discover.

Be this, however, as it may, it cannot be denied that, having been elected Curule Ædile at the earliest lawful moment, through some casual popular favour—obtained as Polybius says by his beauty, his courteous address, and his large liberality, as Livy by a repute of sanctity and mystical semi-divine inspirations—having filled no higher office than that of Ædile, and—if not at Canusium, after Cannae—never having distinguished himself at all, he was appointed proconsul by unanimous acclamation, and entrusted, an untried boy, with the command of a war, next to that raging in the heart of Italy, the most vital to Rome.

Who believes this of Rome, at a period too when the Dictator Fabius actually refused to receive the free vote of the first century in the Consular Comitia, but called it back and bade it vote over again, telling the people that it was not for them now to elect ordinary magistrates, and charging them:

> This day to elect consuls, as they would, if standing under arms, in array for present battle, elect two generals, under whose conduct and auspices they would fight, to whom their sons should swear the oath of military service, to whose summons they

should gather to the field, under whose care and safeguard they should give battle to the enemy.

Who, I say, believes this of Rome, will believe anything.

But it is clear to me, that no man in that year, nor in any subsequent year of Rome, previous to the abandonment of Italy by Hannibal, could possibly have been elected to any office, involving the command of any army—much less of one so important as that of Spain—unless the Senate, and above all, the wise and patriotic men who were then its leading members, as Fabius, Quintus Fulvius, and Titus Manlius, had been perfectly satisfied with the fitness of the choice. For, henceforth to the end of the war, the officers of each year were indubitably agreed on by the Senate beforehand, and submitted merely to the ratification of the people; who in their wisdom submitted to such unconstitutional dictation, satisfied that it was done for the best by the Senate, and that it was for the best that they should do so themselves.

Nor does the story, which we find in all the authors of the time, to the effect that no candidates would offer themselves for those two proconsulships—for the filling of which especial comitia were held—on account of the disastrous state of the Spanish war, and their unwillingness to hazard the risk of reputation, amount to anything more than this—if it be true at all—that it was a preconcerted and settled matter that Scipio should be the man to whom the prosecution of his father's and his uncle's war must be assigned. This being known, of course, no one opposed him.

Had it not been so, there would have been no lack of eager candidates for the post of honour; since, however disastrous the Spanish war might be, and however great the hazard of being matched against Mago and the two Asdrubals, yet more disastrous was the war of Italy, and yet greater the hazard of encountering Hannibal, the invincible. Yet not for that, had there been any hesitancy of the patricians or the people to offer themselves for any office from the highest to the lowest.

Therefore, I regard it as a fact, beyond the necessity of argument, that Scipio, who served at Cannae in a rank equivalent to that of a lieutenant colonel in the present day, if not superior, had proved himself sufficiently a soldier before that disaster; and did, on that occasion, by his own energy and force of character suppress the incipient mutiny, which would have been his country's destruction if unchecked;

displaying not the mere soldier's qualities of daring and devotion, but the forecast, the intuitive perception, and the instinctive action, which presage in the man, the statesman and the general.

Thus far, I have lagged somewhat on my way, yet I trust not unprofitably, and must request my readers to bear with me; for had I rushed at once *in medias res*, and taken up my hero at the date of his election only, that which is to follow must needs have been perplexed and indistinct; and neither the importance of the war, which we shall soon find him waging in an obscure, remote, and barbarous corner of the world, the last spot of Europe, and the extremity, as men then believed, of the universe, nor the real greatness of his genius and his deeds, would have been perceptible.

Henceforth, we have to do with himself alone; and, if I cannot promise to lay before my readers the picture of a perfect and unselfish patriot such as Epaminondas; of a truly honest man and consistent philosopher, such as Xenophon; or of a thunderbolt of war such as Hannibal or Alexander, I can at least present to them the portraiture of a great general, and very great man.

As a general, if his campaigns are less magnificently bold and dashing than those of others who might be named, they present fewer faults than those of almost any. Indeed I know not where from his first to his last battle to look for a single error of judgment, or failure of execution.

As a man, he was, in my eyes, very far from perfect; yet his very imperfections are of that strange and half-fascinating nature, which rather add interest and attractiveness to a character, than the reverse; even as shadows, in a striking landscape, if not unduly dark or numerous, render the lights more brilliant and effective by the contrast.

There is a general desire in almost every breast to know something concerning the personal appearance and habits, nay even the dress and daily deportment of historical personages, with whom we are about to become more intimately acquainted; nor is this desire so frivolous and absurd as it would on the first impression strike us to be. For all men are in some degree, more or less, physiognomists, and form their first opinions at sight, which perhaps are never entirely eradicated; nor is this true of men only; for children, before they are capable of speech, and dogs to a very high degree, will show symptoms of attraction to one stranger, and repugnance toward another, on a first interview; and what is more remarkable, they are very rarely deceived in their *prima facie* judgments.

Nor is this tendency to attribute good qualities to the good mien and noble person, and the reverse to the down-looking and deformed, confined to those whom we see, to admire or to shrink from, with our outward eyes. On the contrary, I believe that it often influences, perhaps I should say prejudices, our opinions concerning those of whom we merely read in history or fiction. I will believe, for instance, that the pretended deformity, the withered arm and distorted shoulder of him whom we know chiefly as the humpbacked tyrant has done as much to render him odious for ever, as the alleged slaughter of his infant nephew, the facts being, that he was as straight and well-made a man as any of his court; and the strong probability, that he was wholly guiltless of the pretended murders in the Tower. And, in the case of Mary Stuart, of Scotland, it cannot be disputed that we are swayed from true judgment of her character and crimes by the mere report of her loveliness, in a scarcely less degree than were her contemporaries by its present reality.

I do not think it, therefore, beneath the dignity of history to relate, as it stands on sure record, that the remarkable influence which Scipio possessed over the minds of men, was owing not a little to his singular personal beauty, to his unusual dignity of deportment, to his great conversational talents, and great suavity of demeanour. There was in him, says Cicero:

> A certain princely grace and majesty. Furthermore he was marvellous gentle and courteous unto them that came to him, and had an eloquent tongue, and a passing gift to win every man. He was very grave in his gesture and behaviour, and ever wore long hair. In fine, he was a truly noble captain, worthy of all commendation, and excelled in all virtues, which did so delight his mind that he was wont to say that he was never less idle than when at leisure, or less alone than when alone.[3]

To come from the person to the mind of this very remarkable man, we shall find the character of the latter no less peculiar and abnormal, than of the former striking as un-Roman. But in regard to this we shall have much more difficulty in coming to any certain or tangible conclusion.

We find, in the first place, that from the period of his first assuming the dress of manhood, he put forward pretensions to a peculiar

---

[3]. Cicero Off. III. 1, quoted in Anthon's *Class. Dic.* I presume as translated in Berwick's *Life of Scip. Afr.*

sanctity, affecting never to engage in any business, whether of a private or public nature, until he had ascended into the Capitol, and there remained shut up alone in the sanctuary with the god, (Dio Cassius, *Frag. Peireso*).

Livy says:

> And this practice, which was kept up through his whole life, whether by design or accident, gave credit among many to the popular belief, that he was a man of divine descent; and produced the same fable, which had been previously circulated concerning Alexander the Great, and of the same absurdity and falsehood, that he had been conceived of an enormous serpent, and that the vision of that prodigious thing had been frequently seen in his mother's chamber, but ever glided away on the entrance of men, and vanished from their eyes.

The historian adds, that he never directly attempted to deceive anyone by such fables as this, but rather increased his belief in their truth, by a peculiar art which he possessed, of exciting wonder and admiration without either affirmation or denial.

It will be observed, that in the word sanctity, which I purposely employed in speaking of his pretensions, something totally different is intended, from what we mean, when we say piety.

To the ancients prayer and self-humiliation, or the seeking of pardon through penitence, were things unknown, so that the superstition or hypocrisy, be it which it might, of Scipio, when he shut himself up alone to commune with Jupiter in the Capitol, was a totally different thing from the superstition or hypocrisy of Louis the XIth of France, when he grovelled on his knees, before a pewter image of the Virgin in his hatband, imploring her pardon in advance for crimes which he was resolved to commit thereafter.

The superstition or hypocrisy of Scipio claimed that he was in direct communication with the god; the hearer of divine sorrows, the seer of prophetic visions, the one emphatically guided by the counsels of the ruler of the universe.

The superstition or hypocrisy of Louis XI., claimed nothing but the right, possessed by every human being, of imploring pardon, whence his religion, such as it was, taught him that pardon was to be attained.

The superstition or hypocrisy of the one might possibly deceive himself, but was certainly calculated eminently to cheat, and did in truth cheat others.

The superstition or hypocrisy of the other must certainly have deceived himself, for he never applied it to any other end; but could assuredly cheat no one else, unless it were the pewter image of the Virgin in his hat-band. And this, absurd as it may seem—far be it from me to write irreverently of any creed—it almost appears, from some of his extant prayers, he thought to do; as if the Virgin worshipped at one shrine, were not aware of crimes confessed to the Virgin at another. Mistaken or assumed piety, as of an erring man, was the characteristic of the one.

Mistaken or assumed sanctity, as of an admitted saint and seer, that of the other.

It is therefore to Cromwell, or yet more to Mahomet, that Scipio is to be compared; and by nearly the same tests with them is he to be tried, as enthusiast or hypocrite.

Accordingly, it is to Cromwell that Dr. Arnold has compared him; and that so eloquently and ably, although I cannot agree with his verdict in many points, which I shall take the liberty to refer to hereafter, that I shall quote this fine passage without hesitation or apology. He says, after stating what I have told above regarding the visits to the temple of Jupiter:—

> But Polybius, by temper and circumstances a rationalist, is at great pains to assure his readers that Scipio owed no part of his greatness to the gods, and that his true oracle was the clear judgment of his own mind. According to him, Scipio did but impose upon and laugh at the credulity of the vulgar; speaking of the favour shown him by the gods, while he knew the gods to be nothing. Livy, with a truer feeling, which taught him that a hero cannot be a hypocrite, suggests a doubt, though timidly, as if in fear of the scepticism of his age, whether the great Scipio was not really touched by some feelings of superstition, whether he did not in some degree speak what he himself believed.
> A mind like Scipio's, working its way under peculiar influences of time and country, cannot but move irregularly; it cannot but be full of contradictions. Two hundred years later, the mind of the dictator Caesar acquiesced contentedly in Epicureanism; he retained no more of enthusiasm than was inseparable from the intensity of his intellectual power, and the fervour of his courage, even amid his utter moral degradation. But Scipio

could not be like Caesar. His mind rose above the state of things around him; his spirit was solitary and kingly; he was cramped by living among those as his equals, whom he felt fitted to guide as from some higher sphere; and he retired at last to Liternum, to breathe freely, to enjoy the simplicity of childhood, since he could not fulfil his national calling to be a hero king.

So far he stood apart from his countrymen, admired, reverenced, but not loved. But he could not shake off all the influences of his time; the virtue, public and private, which still existed at Rome, the reverence paid by the wisest and best men to the religion of their fathers, were elements too congenial to his nature, not to retain their hold on it; they cherished that nobleness of soul in him, and that faith in the invisible and divine, which two centuries of growing unbelief rendered almost impossible in the days of Caesar.

Yet how strange must the conflict be, when faith is combined with the highest intellectual power, and its appointed object is no better than Paganism. Longing to believe, yet repelled by palpable falsehood, crossed inevitably by snatches of unbelief, in which hypocrisy is ever close at the door, it breaks out desperately, as it may seem, into the region of dreams and visions, and mysterious communings with the invisible, as if longing to find that food in its own creations, which no outward objective truth offers to it. The proportions of belief and unbelief in the human mind in such cases, no human judgment can determine; they are the wonders of history; characters inevitably misrepresented by the vulgar, and viewed even by those who have in some sense the key to them as a mystery, not fully to be comprehended, and still less explained to others. The genius which conceived the incomprehensible character of Hamlet would alone be able to describe with intuitive truth the character of Scipio or of Cromwell.

In both these great men, the enthusiastic element which clearly existed in them, did but inspire a resistless energy into their actions, while it in no way interfered with the calmest and keenest judgment in the choice of their means; nor in the case of Scipio did it suggest any other ends of life than such as were appreciated by ordinary human views of good. When religion contained no revelation of new truth, it naturally left men's estimate of the end of their being exactly what it had been before, and only furnished encouragement to the pursuit of it. It so far bore the character of magic, that it applied superhuman power to the furtherance of human purposes; the gods aided man's work; they did not teach him and enable him to do theirs.

The charge of early dissoluteness brought against Scipio by his enemies is likely to have been exaggerated, like the stories of our Henry V. (And he might have added, as a case more in point, our Cromwell.)

Yet the sternest and firmest manhood has sometimes followed a youth marked with many excesses of passion; and what was considered as unbecoming interruption to the cares of public business, was held to be in itself nothing blameable. That sanction of inherited custom, which at Rome was, at this period, the best safe-guard of youthful purity, Scipio was not inclined implicitly to regard.

With all his greatness there was a waywardness in him which seems often to accompany genius; a self-idolatry, natural enough where there is so keen a consciousness of power and of lofty designs; a self-dependence, which feels even the most sacred external relations to be unessential to its own perfection. Such is the Achilles of Homer, the highest conception of the individual hero, relying on himself, and sufficient to himself. But the same poet who conceived the character of Achilles, has also drawn that of Hector; of the truly noble, because unselfish hero, who subdues his genius to make it minister to the good of others; who lives for his relations, his friends, and his country.

And as Scipio lived in himself and for himself, so the virtue of Hector was worthily represented in the life of his great rival Hannibal, who, from his childhood to his latest hour, through glory and through obloquy, amid victories and amid disappointments, ever remembered to what purpose his father had devoted him, and withdrew no thought, or desire, or deed, from their pledged service to his country.

This is amazingly fine writing; nor is it deniable that the writer, if his view of Scipio's character be correct in the first instance, had, in a great sense, the key to his mystery. I cannot deny, much less controvert, the truth of that view; for it is evident that we lack sufficient data, as to his private and individual life, whereby to arrive at any positive conclusion. So that, to all time, he must probably remain a mystery.

And yet I would fain indicate two or three salient points of difference between the characters of Scipio, Mahomet, Joan of Arc, and Cromwell, all of whom in some sort put forward the same pretensions; which differences, it appears to me, until they can be reconciled, must prevent us from assigning to him the same imaginative or superstitious temperament, the same fanatical, enthusiastic sincerity of belief and purpose, which we may ascribe to the others.

The extreme paucity of extant authorities, the very doubtful character of these as to veracity and judgment, and the extreme meagreness of the skeleton-like historical abstracts, which alone they have left to us, render it in the highest degree difficult to attain anything like a correct knowledge of the individual habits and private lives of the great men of this period; and of none perhaps more so than of Scipio, the elder Africanus.

We have, in fact, no method of learning their character, except by a close consideration of their authenticated actions, and a laborious scrutiny into the circumstances and motives of those actions. Now it is palpably true, that the greatest recorded actions of these greatest men are not so well authenticated, that we can receive them as facts on the bare statement of any one or more author or authors, of that day. On the contrary, we must apply the test of analysis, we must examine whether the subsequent known events are such as would consequentially follow the doubtful events stated to have preceded them; we must count times and measure distances; and not till we have satisfied ourselves that what is stated to have happened is both physically and morally possible, that it is consistent with what went before and followed it, and with the characters of the persons concerned, may we venture to accept it as the truth.

Now it appears to me, that Dr. Arnold has founded his argument concerning the sincerity of Scipio's conviction in his own sanctity and inspiration, or second-sight, on two presumptions; neither of which is sustained by history, nor in my opinion borne out by the circumstances of the case, as compared with those of Cromwell or the other persons named.

These assumptions are: first, that he was a hero, in the truest and highest sense of the word—not taken merely as a strong and brave fighting man; and, second, that he was an enthusiast. Granted that he was hero and enthusiast, and it follows that he was not hypocrite.

That Cromwell was thoroughly an enthusiast, and from his very boyhood of the most gloomily, perhaps morbidly, imaginative character, no one can have carefully studied his life without discovering. The story, well-known to all of his contemporaries, years before he seemed likely to attain any eminence, of the Shape which drew his bed-curtains at midnight, telling him that he should be the "Greatest man in England, but not king;" the very inconsistencies of his conduct, especially at the signing of the king's death-warrant; and, most of all, that extraordinary prayer uttered by him on his death-bed, when he thought no human ear was listening, prove this beyond a peradventure.

Wise, prudent, crafty, shrewd, as all his enterprises and all his successes show him to have been; yet it would not, I think, be difficult to show that all his actions were impulsive, and almost all his great successes achieved by giving the full swing and sweep to his genuine impulses.

In some sort, too, he was a hero—probably felt himself to be one altogether. Surely, there must have been a strong element of the heroical in that man, who, finding his country the very lowest in the scale of European nations, boasted that he would make the name of Englishman as safe a passport as ever was the name of Roman citizen, the world over—nor so boasted vainly; in that Protestant, who, when Rome, France, Austria, Spain, the world, Holland excepted, were banded to suppress the faith of Calvin and of Luther, made cease the persecutions of the saints, as he termed them, by one brief threat, that, if another drop of Christian blood were shed for religion's sake, "the English guns should wake an echo in the Vatican."

That Mahomet was an enthusiast, a zealot, imaginative to the very verge of inspiration, if his entire career, which without conviction he never could have run; if that almost miraculous work, the *Koran*, of his composition do not prove; at least the history of the religion which he founded, and from which, I believe, there has never been an honest convert, proves it beyond all argument.

That Joan of Arc was an enthusiast, witness the almost madness of her military successes, of her military errors—such as the wild and fruitless march to Rheims, through the very centre of an enemy's country, with no object beyond an empty pageant—witness, above all, her unchanged constancy and most heroic martyrdom.

Who believes that these were vulgar impostors, that such things as they accomplished through the very spirit which is termed imposture, could be accomplished by impostors, must be themselves so narrow and so vulgar-minded, that what they believe, or not believe, can concern no one.

All these three lived, too, more or less in transition periods, when religious questions were disturbing and perplexing the minds of the whole world, and actually driving the weaker spirits into insanity and blasphemy.

Mahomet, the originator and inventor of a new system of religion, and himself its prophet.

Cromwell, the propagandist and enforcer of a new code of morality and church discipline, the asserter of the right of self-government and self-responsibility, and himself its champion.

Joan of Arc, the ordained instrument of her country's salvation, the one supernaturally instructed of the will of Heaven, and herself Heaven's minister unto freedom.

But of this, or similar to this, I can find nothing written in the annals of the day, as pertaining to the character of Scipio, to the nature of the circumstances, to the genius of the times.

In no act of Scipio's life, except the gratuitous assertion that he saw visions, and dreamed dreams, can I detect a single feature of the enthusiast, of the impulsive man, the imaginative man, the poet, the visionary, or the dreamer.

Nowhere, from beneath the heterogeneous costume which he affected to wear, half warrior's *sagum*, half stoic's blanket, can I espy one limb or lineament of the true hero.

Nowhere do I see inconsistency, nowhere perplexity of mind, nowhere fits of gloom and despondency, like those of Saul and of Cromwell; nowhere do I see gleams of almost supernatural vividness and splendour.

Far from it: I see an equable, self-consistent, self-confident, self-righteous man—a great, calm, steady, unmoved soldier, reasoning sagaciously, divining profoundly, judging almost unerringly, and acting rapidly, strenuously, energetically, thoroughly—but not in the least degree impulsively or energetically—that which he had determined to act out.

His intellect appears to me to have been entirely rational, logical, intellectual—not in the least sensuous, ideal, or imaginative.

His temperament, I think, was cold, unimpassioned, unexcitable, and solid. Nor this, the less on account of his imputed irregularities of life and early orgies, whether real or pretended—although indeed I lay but little stress on them at all, as unconfirmed by credible authorities—for the nature of man is far too well known at present, that we should doubt the existence of cold-blooded and unimpassioned sensualists and voluptuaries.

Nor do I perceive anything in the nature of the times to produce such a frame or constitution of mind as Dr. Arnold has attributed to Scipio. That age was an acting, not a thinking age. Neither religious nor philosophical questions; no, nor as yet even political questions in the abstract; had hitherto much begun to distract the minds of men. The old religion of Rome still prevailed, still reigned paramount in. the minds of the many, and in the minds of the vulgar. Within a year or two of this very date, four human victims had been entombed alive in a vault beneath the forum; and scarce an election passed, or had passed for two centuries, in which some religious juggle—which, had strong-minded men believed in that religion, would have been most irreligious blasphemy—was not practised by one party or other, but especially by that of the nobles, Scipio's own party, to whom by right belonged the sacred things and the sacred laws of Rome.

I conceive, therefore, that it may be taken almost for granted, that among the upper class of Romans, not excluding even the ministers of religion, there was, so early as this period, no distinct religious belief, nothing of genuine and lively faith in the personifications, characteristics, or authenticity of the numerous deities of their mystical and poetical polytheism. This infidelity had not undoubtedly yet become so widely diffused as at a later date, when senators and men of the highest rank openly disavowed their belief in the monstrous and incredible fictions of paganism, beneath the very roofs of the temples in which their councils were convened; but still so utterly inconsistent with common sense were the legends concerning the gods, so utterly at variance with all natural principles of virtue, piety, and morality, that it is hardly conceivable that any man possessed of ordinary reasoning powers, much more of high and enlightened intellect, could hold them in anything but absolute contempt.

Accordingly as men were constituted, therefore, they would naturally fall into one or other form of schism and disbelief; those who were born with reverential and religious tendencies, would have recourse, as Plato, Cicero, Socrates, Lucan, and others of the best and wisest Greeks and Romans, to a pure Deism, or faith in one self-existent, omnipresent, and all overruling principle and power, whether they called it God, or Spirit of the World, or First Great Cause, or Soul of Nature; while those of lower intellects and more debased temperaments would blindly rush into the abyss of atheism, or wallow in the sty of Epicurus.

By neither of these classes, however, is it probable that the ancient polytheism was openly assailed or denied; as the former portion conceiving the Spirit of Deity to be ubiquitous and existent more or less in everything, from stocks and stones through all animate nature up to the azure vault of heaven and the everlasting stars, would see no desirable result to be attained in demolishing the ignorant creed of the many, not caring to propagate their own among the masses, to whom it would be unintelligible from its immateriality. While both classes would regard the pompous, sensuous ceremonials and processions, so fascinating to vulgar minds, as an admirable system for the continued government and subjugation of the people to their own caste; since the nobles were, *ex officio*, the *pontiffs* and priests of Rome.

Lastly, we find Polybius, who was born in the year succeeding the elder Scipio's crowning victory at Zama, who was the contemporary and friend of his lieutenant, Laelius, and the tent-companion of his grandson, the younger Africanus, as Arnold terms him "by temper and circumstances a rationalist" evidently disbelieving the very existence of the gods, and holding it incredible and absurd that Scipio could have believed those gods, whom he professed to worship and consult, to be anything beyond creations of the human fancy. Now if Polybius attained this stage of disbelief within some thirty years at farthest from Scipio's own day, no change having occurred in the condition of religious worship, or in the state of religious belief and feeling among the masses, it is no argument to say that Scipio could not possibly have arrived at the same stage, because Sylla, Caesar, Catiline, and other Epicurean atheists, did not carry out their scepticism and moral debasement to the lowest depth, until another century had passed.

And for many reasons, it appears to me more probable and consistent with the spirit of his times, and, so far as known, the temper of the man, that fully believing in the existence of some powerful and overruling influence or essence somewhere, but utterly incredulous as to the myths which it is difficult to convince oneself that any reasonable man ever did believe, of Jupiter, Apollo, and the rest of their compeers, Scipio made use of the machinery still believed by the vulgar and superstitious, to work out his own end, and to control and guide the masses to their own good.

Such pious frauds—as they are impiously termed—have been resorted to with effect by demagogues and ambitious rulers of all times and all religions; and by many, I doubt not, with a sincere sense that they were justifiable and even virtuous methods of bringing about justifiable and desirable ends.

Wherefore, contrary to Dr. Arnold's opinion, I must hold it less probable that a man of Scipio's cool, phlegmatic, cautious temperament, and clear high intellect, should have believed fables so absurd and childish, than that he should have laid hold of the superstitions of the weak and credulous yet well intentioned masses, in order to conduct them by those means to victory, independence and glory.

Be this, however, as it may, in regard to his character theoretically, or to the alleged exploits of his early life, we come to his actual historical career in the end of the year 545 of the city of Rome, or B. C. 217. In this year the Roman people being somewhat relieved from their instant terrors by the fall of Capua, resolved to send large reinforcements into Spain; and called a general assembly for the election of a proconsul and *propraetor* for its prosecution.

Now, for the well understanding of what follows, it must be borne in mind, that the office of Proconsul conferred the second military rank in the Roman armies, and was usually held by men who had previously occupied the Consular office itself, after their term had expired, as was the case of Publius Scipio, our hero's father.

To confer it, therefore, on one who had not gone through the regular grades, or attained the just age for holding it, was so unusual, that the historians who related the facts, have endeavoured to account for it, by framing the most absurd and untenable fictions.

By all, however, it is admitted that at these *comitia*, the high elective assemblage of the people, Publius Cornelius Scipio, certainly not being above twenty-seven, but according to general report only twenty-four, offered himself candidate for this elevated station, to which neither his years, nor his previous offices, in the least degree entitled him.

In the course of his canvassing he declared himself to be not only the natural and kindred avenger of his father and his uncle, but the heaven-raised champion and restorer of Rome's greatness. Nor did he content himself with proclaiming to the people, that he was the destined conqueror of Spain alone, but of Libya and Carthage likewise, (*Appian* and *Livy*).

Whereat so greatly were the people moved—for he spoke eloquently, and with vehement enthusiasm, so that he seemed even as one inspired, and moreover no one offered himself as a rival candidate—that they forthwith elected him by an unanimous vote, not of the centuries only, but of the individual voters.

The fact that he had no rival candidate is undoubted; that he was unanimously chosen of the centuries may be granted; that he was so chosen of the individual voices must be untrue. But the very tale proves how generally he was accepted by all classes as the fittest, and only fit, man for the prosecution of the war in Spain.

That he would have had rival candidates in abundance, had he not been so esteemed by the Senate and its wisest members, is directly proved by the fact of their refusal to receive the votes in favour of worthy men, who were not proved generals, on two occasions even at Consular elections, through Fabius Maximus and Titus Manlius, the latter in this very year; and is strongly confirmed by the appointment of the very Nero, whose command he superseded in Spain, to be consul in the year next succeeding his return, (*Appian* and *Livy*).

The unanimity of the centuries in his favour as clearly disproves the statements that his pretensions were ridiculed, his qualifications doubted, and himself derided as a vain, boyish braggart, by the elders and leading men of the city; for there was an actual majority of centuries under the direct control of these very elders and leading men. To render this, if needful more obvious, Livy states that he was unanimously chosen in the first instance, but that the elders immediately repented, until he had cheered them by a second speech of such art as:

> To rekindle an excitement greater than that which had subsided, and to fill all men with a hope more certain, than any which trust in the promises of humanity, or reasoning on the circumstances of the case, could justify.

Now it was never, at any time, the character of the Roman aristocracy—the steadiest, most obstinate, most enduring of all aristocracies—and at no time less than this—to hesitate, to waver, to change, or to repent. At no time, within a century previous to this date, did they attach any very serious faith even to the established canons of their religion, though they used them to command others, when it suited their purpose so to do; much less would they now be like to trust to the assumed personal sanctity of a young man, wholly unconnected with their priesthood, and nearly new to the affairs of state.

Forty years before this time Publius Claudius, then consul, and as such priest, being in command of the fleet off Drepanum in Sicily and desiring to engage, was told by the Augurs that he must on no account do so, "because the sacred chickens would not eat."

"Let them drink then," exclaimed the consul, threw the sacred chickens overboard, engaged, and got terribly defeated.

Him the Senate severely reprimanded, and never entirely forgave; not because any of them believed in the sacred chickens one *iota* more than Appius Claudius; but because he dispirited the minds of the superstitious soldiers on the eve of battle; and might easily have brought discredit on that excellent patrician religion, which was so capital an instrument for managing the ignorant plebeians.

If Appius Claudius had led Adherbal in triumph home to Rome, he would no more have been punished for drowning the sacred chickens, than was Sir Horatio Nelson for not seeing Sir Hyde Parker's signal through a glass applied to his blind eye at Copenhagen.

The defeat in the one case caused the punishment; the success in the other the impunity. In neither instance was the act, in both were the consequences regarded. Such is the way of men and nations.

Unquestionably, the elders of Rome did laugh in their sleeves at the credulity of the people, at the cleverness of their own man, at the success of their own machinery.

But they were far too clever to laugh openly; or if they did laugh, it was with that rare art which conceals art, in order to dissemble their collusion with one, in fact their own, but ostensibly the people's, candidate; and to enable him to carry his dissimulation, or his fanaticism, whichever it might be, yet farther, since they had already found it so useful, and expected to find it yet more so thereafter. And this I, in truth, consider the probable history of this unconstitutional and strange election, not, however, as settling one way or other the question of Scipio's personal hypocrisy or fanaticism, but as accounting for the conduct of the magnates on the occasion.

They had already, certainly wisely, but as certainly unconstitutionally, refused to receive votes in favour of T. M. Otacilius, and forced two consuls of their own choosing on the centuries, and naturally would shun directly interfering with the people's choice of a proconsul for Spain also.

I cannot say that they did this—though it very nearly resembles their course on many other occasions—but I do say, if they did not desire to risk a struggle for power with the people, there was no better method of retaining it without a struggle, than to set up their own man—personally unknown to be such, while known to themselves as possessing rare arts of fascination—as the popular candidate; to hold back all rival candidates against him; to oppose him just so far as to conceal all collusion, bringing out all his art and eloquence, and then to affect contentment, and concession to the popular voice. He was elected, at all events, if not unanimously, by an overwhelming majority; Marcus Junius Silanus was chosen his *propraetor*, and the two generals set sail almost immediately for the city of Tarraco, now Tarragona, and famed in the yet bloodier and more eventful annals of the modern Peninsular War. It was at that time the headquarters of the Roman forces, and the capital of all the land they occupied in Spain, the narrow strip, namely, situate between the Pyrenees and the Iberus, or Ebro.

They took with them, (*Appian*), in thirty ships of war, all *quinqueremes*, the line-of-battle-ships of that day, (*Livy*), ten thousand legionary foot and one thousand horse, all incomparable veterans, tempered in the fires of that fierce war-furnace which had "tried men's souls," now for so many years, in the heart of Italy. These men had stood face to face with Hannibal himself, and having come off unscathed and without dishonour, were little like to flinch from any weaker adversary. With arms, with military chest, clothing and provisions, they were so well furnished as Rome's exigencies would permit; and on their landing at Tarragona, they found eighteen thousand capital infantry and fifteen hundred veteran cavalry.

Many of these had fought under Scipio's father and his uncle, and now rapturously hailed his arrival; some of them, the troops brought over by Nero, had assisted at the first reverse of Hannibal, and taken Capua under his very eyes; all of them had, for the last two years, held their ground defiantly against Mago and the two Hasdrubals. These were men versed in Iberian warfare, who had learned to dread neither Spanish foot nor Numidian horse, neither Punic skill nor Barbarian force; men who had need to dread no equal force on the face of earth, when under equal leaders. And now they had a leader second to none but Hannibal, the greatest of all ages.

And Scipio, scarcely as yet beyond the gristle of his earliest manhood, was surely in a proud and high position; for even at this present day, a general, with an independent command of thirty thousand superb veterans, of whom two thousand were tried horse, and thirty line-of-battle-ships to back him, would hardly care to change places with the most favoured of mankind.

When we consider, that his land forces, alone, were superior, as ten to one, to those with which Clive [4] dethroned Surajee Dowlah,

---

[4]. Clive took the camp of Surajee Dowlah, and subsequently dethroned him, with 2,900 men, of whom 900 only were Europeans, and six guns, against 58,000 horse and foot with 50 guns—Alison III.

and laid the foundations of an empire larger than the civilized world of those days; as four to one, to that with which Lake and Wellesley [5] secured its superstructure—When we consider that they nearly equalled in numbers, and infinitely excelled in every other particular, that army with which the young Bonaparte [6]—not as yet Napoleon, but how much greater—beat down the arms of Austria, conquering all Northern Italy, and Scipio's Rome herself, in one miraculous campaign—we shall be perhaps better able to estimate the greatness and brilliancy of his position, than by any opinion drawn from a dry estimate of numbers.

Nor if his position was brilliant and commanding, were his own abilities less commanding, his own career less brilliant.

He is perhaps the only commander on record, in no one of whose campaigns can we discover any error of judgment, any failure of execution. Nor can it be said of him, with truth, that he conquered by caution only; for he knew, as well as any, how at times the most desperate daring is the most real prudence. On him, as on the general of modern times whom he most resembles in his military career—as he resembles him the least in his moral character—caution was imposed as a necessity by the circumstances of the war they were waging, of the country in which they were waging it, and in the character or condition of the governments they served; I mean of course the Duke of Wellington.

Both warred in the same country, Spain, although for the most part their operations were on the different sides of the peninsula; both were opposed to the ablest marshals or lieutenants of the greatest general then existing; both were surrounded by allies, on whose faith and firmness in the field no reliance could be placed; both were compelled to rely on their ships as a basis of their operations.

Each knew that the existence of the war depended on the preservation of the army he then led; since, that lost, his country could by no possibility send out another. Each, after every blow he struck,

---

5. Wellesley won the Battle of Assaye, with 8,000 men, of whom 1500 only were Europeans, against 50,000 men and 100 guns; Lake stormed Delhi, and won Laswaree, with 5,000 soldiers.—Alison III.

6 The army of Italy, when Bonaparte took command of it nearly at Scipio's age, was forty-two thousand strong, but had no magazines, no rations, pay, shoes, clothing, tents, nor shelter. Yet with this material he fought four pitched battles all triumphantly, and conquered the whole of Northern Italy, including the Eternal City, remaining master of all from the Tyrol to the Tiber, in one magnificent campaign of a few months' duration.—Alison I.

was cramped in his future movements by want of supplies and reinforcements, wants of cordial co-operation or energetical support from home; the one, owing to the jealousy and parsimony of the democratic branch of the government, ever adverse to the war, in England; the other in consequence of the absolute inability of Rome, bleeding at every pore under the puissant blows of Hannibal, to spare a single soldier from the war that was raging in her vitals.

Each, after his best fought actions, his most brilliant exploits, was more than once compelled to retreat before a beaten enemy. Each, ever vastly inferior to the combined forces of his adversary, contrived always, partly owing to the inferior skill of the generals opposed to him, partly to their mutual jealousies and dissensions, ever to be equal, at least, at the actual delivery of battle.

Each, cautious as to the general plan of his campaigns, not of choice but of necessity, dealt some of the most daring blows, and the rashest, had not the success justified the daring, that have been ever dealt by an inferior in face of a superior army.

Each succeeded at the last, the one by disciplining and converting into soldiers, the other by bringing over to his banners, the unsteady or faithless natives, in sweeping every vestige of the enemy from the confines of the land on which at first he had scarce a foothold.

Neither was ever conquered in a pitched battle, nor ever committed any material military error; and both, to complete this extraordinary parallel, after beating every lieutenant of their country's gigantic enemy, terminated the war and ended the career of that enemy with a thunderbolt on the confines, or in the heart, of his native land.

Never was there a parallel more singularly close and well-defined, unless it be that between their colossal adversaries, the masters of all strategy of all ages, Hannibal and Napoleon [7] the great.

As we proceed with the narrative of the five campaigns of Scipio, we shall perceive more clearly how similar was the conduct of these two great men under similar circumstances; and with what equal steps, equal fortune followed on equal conduct.

Nor will it be incurious to observe how, his wars ended, either general was met at home, after his return, by the basest injustice and ingratitude; and how by his tranquil fortitude and undeviating obedience to duty the one disarmed his enemies, and lived to fill at home the highest offices of state, to win the deepest love of all classes; while the other by his petulance, his insolent defiance of the legal tribunals,

---

7 See *Captains of the Old World,*—art. Hannibal, for this parallel.

and his intolerable arrogance, estranged his very nearest friends, and died self-exiled among the shades of Liternum; not, in my thoughts, a hero king baffled of his true vocation, nor yet an enthusiast philosopher, but an untamed, undisciplined, selfish, moody soldier, who, though he could govern others nobly, could in no sort govern his own soul.

It was, as it appears, late in the Autumn of the year of Rome 245, that Scipio disembarked his troops at Emporiae, now Ampurias, a colony from Marseilles just within the Pyrenaean promontory—or Cap de Creus—the first town in the Hispano-Roman province, and his thirty line-of-battle-ships shoreward to Taragona. On them he relied, I presume, as well for his subsistence as to cover his march; since the road doubtless, then as now, ran close along the coast through a mountainous, wild, and sterile country; marched thither himself by land at the head of his army, and established his headquarters in that ancient city, famous no more for its antique splendour, than for the glorious and immortal resistance, characteristic of Spanish cities from Numantia to Saragossa, it offered to the arms of Suchet.

And here, it may be worth a moment's pause, to cast a glimpse over the map of Spain, since to do so now will save much time and reference hereafter. The form of this vast and mountainous peninsula is, of course, generally familiar to my readers, a huge irregular parallelogram, jutting out from the south-western extremity of Europe into the Atlantic ocean, and connected with the continent only by a comparatively narrow Isthmus walled by the almost impregnable Pyrenees, less difficult of access only, if less difficult, than the eternal snows of the Alps.

Along the northern coast, for seven degrees of distance, nearly parallel to the sea, these massive and stupendous barriers are prolonged in the Cantabrian ridges, now the Asturian and Santillana mountains. Among the latter, near the modern town of Reynosa, rises the noble River Iberus, or Ebro, flowing south-easterly into the Mediterranean and forming with the Pyrenees and the sea-coast, a long narrow-based acute triangle, which at this period was every foot of land the Romans owned in Spain, being less than a twelfth part of its superficial area, while all the rest was more or less under the control of the Carthaginians.

It is uncertain, how far northward their actual dominion extended; nor does it concern us much to know, since all the operations of this war lay along the eastern and southern coasts, from Tarragona to

Cadiz, beyond the straits of Gibraltar, and the pillars of Hercules, Abyla and Calpe.

Clearly, however, their influence extended far inland, even to the shores of the Bay of Biscay; since it was by the passes of St. Jean pied de Port, and the Adour, by which Wellington entered France in 1813, that Hasdrubal made his bold and almost successful attempt to reinforce his brother, in the extreme south of Italy.

How far soever it extended, from east to west, from north to south, the power of the Carthaginians was immense, the influence of their Generals unlimited. Three generations of the wonderful family of Barcas had succeeded each to the other, living almost as independent princes among the natives, many of them marrying, some of them born, yet more of them dying on its soil, until they were regarded by the Spaniards almost as their natural sovereigns. Hanno, the father of Hamilcar, Hamilcan Hasdrubal, his son-in-law, Hannibal his son, son also it is said of a Spanish lady, and now Hannibal's brethren, Hasdrubal and Mago, had successively held sway, and maintained splendid courts among them.

For it must be remembered that Spain was then the richest auriferous country in the known world; that its precious mines were believed to be inexhaustible. Spain was to Carthage, in a word, what her Indian empire was to England, in the days of Clive and Hastings; and the family of the Barcas were Spain's East India Company, her merchant princes, her invincible dominators, her *nabobs* and her sovereigns. And nearly by the same method as England governs and conquers the Orient, did Carthage sway and subdue Spain. For, in both instances, the native troops of the foreign governments were disproportionately small, while their armies were kept up to an almost fabulous amount by the voluntary or mercenary swords of the natives themselves. In both instances, though the intrusive governments were military and in some sort despotical, yet their violences were mildness to the clan cruelties of the petty princes of the ever-warring tribes, their rapacity equal-handed justice as compared to the barbarous extortion of the native rulers.

In both instances, the natives had come to love their masters, to be proud of being fellow-soldiers to their conquerors. In one respect, however, Carthage was in advance of England in the profit she derived from her foreign domain, that she used her Spaniards habitually, not against the natives of Spain only, but as the bulk of her home and foreign armies, the bravest, firmest, steadiest of her mercenary soldiers. Whereas England has never but on one occasion made use of her Hindoo troops in extra-Indian warfare; when with 3,600 British troops she landed 2,800 sepoys [8] at Cosseir, under Sir David Baird, and marched them across the desert to the Nile, in order to cooperate with their European brothers in arms, in the reduction of the French under Menou.

It was against this extraordinary influence, commanding the richest gold mines in the known world, and governing the bravest and fiercest barbarians, that the Romans were now set to struggle, unaided except by the fortitude of their own dauntless hearts, and now for the first time by the genius of a truly great leader.

But to resume our view of Spain, we shall find that the eastern coast of the peninsula running southerly with a trending toward the west, and terminated by Cape Charidenum, now Capo del Gata, is broken into three great wavy recesses, not deep enough to be called bays, by the promontories Dianium and Scombraria, now Capes Marlin et d'Escombrera, close to the latter of which was situated the stronghold and fortress, as well as the capital, of the Hispano-Carthaginian Empire, known then as New Carthage, and to this day a fine and flourishing city, under the name of Carthagena.

Westward of Capo del Gata, the coast runs nearly due east and west, but for the protrusion of the great bastion-like mass of Gibraltar, to the Sacrum Promontorium, Cape St. Vincent, famous thereafter for Sir John Jervis's celebrated Battle of St. Valentine's Day, over the Spanish fleet; and between this point and the city of Tarragona, near the mouth of the Ebro, occurred all the events of this memorable war, especially after the first campaign, along the valley of the Batis or Guadalquiver which falls into the Atlantic a little distance beyond the straits, near the lovely city of Cadiz. A glance, therefore, at the map of the provinces of Catalonia, Valencia, Murcia, and Andalusia, the fairest and richest part of Spain, will enable the reader to follow all the operations of the war with precision and facility.

Having arrived in Spain, after the troops had already gone into winter quarters, Scipio was, of course, unable to set any expedition on foot until the opening of the next spring. He did not fail, however, to

---

8. Alison. *Hist. Eur.* I. 137. In connection with this fact I find a note so curious, that although it has no bearing on the text above, I cannot resist quoting it. "A singular incident occurred on this occasion. When the *sepoy* regiments came to the monuments of ancient Egypt, they fell down and worshipped the images; another proof among the many which exist of the common origin of these early nations."

profit by this period of compulsory inaction, by thoroughly exercising, disciplining, and encouraging his troops, and by putting everything as regards arms, armour, military engines, entrenching tools, and the like, on the most complete and serviceable footing.

Nor was he long ere he had an opportunity of seeing the good effects of his care and providence. During the winter, he had meditated a blow which, he readily perceived, would not only give him the advantage of the initiative, always of vast importance in war, but if successful would give such a prestige to his arms, as could scarcely fail to demoralise in a great degree the Carthaginian forces, to perplex their generals, and to prevent, at least for that campaign, the threatened irruption of Hasdrubal into Italy, a movement which it was especially his mission to counteract and frustrate. This blow, was the taking of Carthagena, the great magazine and treasury of the Punic leaders, and the place of confinement of all the Spanish hostages.

The ancient town of Carthagena was situated on a bold peninsula, jutting out to the southward into a large bay, the mouth of which is sheltered from all winds but the south, by a small narrow island. The peninsula itself was formed by a deep inner gulf, cutting far into the land on its western side, which forms the interior harbour of the modern city, and by a large lagoon on the eastern and part of the northern faces. The town is situated at the southern extremity, with an easy ascent from the sea; but, toward the rear and the two flanks, it stands on several difficult and craggy eminences, on the easternmost of which was perched the temple of Æsculapius, while on the western stood the magnificent palace of Hasdrubal. Between these principal heights were three lesser hills sacred to Æsculapius, Kaletus reputed to be the discoverer of the gold mines, and Saturn.

It was strongly fortified to the northward by lofty walls and towel's, which were commanded by the heights within, and farther strengthened by a canal cut across the isthmus connecting the lagoon with the sea, although this was bridged in several places for the convenience of the citizens. The front and flanks were defended by strong sea walls, yet of inferior height and strength to the landward ramparts, as relying mainly for their protection on the waters, those of the lagoon not being of sufficient depth to allow ships of war to be brought against the defences.

The reader, who chances to be acquainted with the modern city of Carthagena, will at first hardly recognise this description, for the lagoon has vanished since that time; but on closer examination he will discover traces of it in a large tract of marshy land on the north and east of the city, which even yet after unusually heavy rains is at times converted into an inundation; but at the period of Scipio's daring *coup de main*, it was open to the slight rise and fall of the gentle Mediterranean tides, (*Polybius* and *Livy*).

At the opening of this campaign, the three Carthaginian generals had most injudiciously divided their forces, which united were sufficient to have crushed the Romans at a blow; just as Napoleon's marshals did at a later day with a greater than Scipio, and in like manner suffered their opponents to strike a deadly blow at their heart, and gain a central position, enabling him to act in force against either of them disunited with superior strength.

Never were circumstances more nearly identical than those of the sieges of New Carthage by Scipio, and of Ciudad Rodrigo by Wellington, the dispersion of the hostile armies in moderately distant quarters, leaving both towns exposed to a rapid and sudden attack, while their vicinity rendered it absolutely indispensable that the fortresses must be attacked with the utmost secrecy, and carried with a rapidity, which in neither case could be fairly anticipated.

In both cases, however, the audacity and—as it may almost be termed—rashness of the generals were justified by the indomitable strength and intrepidity of the veterans they commanded, and by the triumph which crowned either enterprise.

Early in the spring of the year of the city 545, having learned that Mago, with his army, was lying at a place called Conii, near the pillars of Hercules, that Hasdrubal, the son of Gisco, was on the River Tagus in Lusitania, and Hasdrubal Barca besieging a city in Carpetania, now New Castile, so that none of them were within ten days' march of Carthagena, Scipio broke up from his cantonments, leaving Marcus Silanus with three thousand foot and five hundred horse to defend the Roman province, called out the contingent of the few native allies Rome then possessed, ordered the army and fleet to rendezvous at the mouth of the Iberus, and communicating his intentions to no one but Caius Laelius, his favourite lieutenant, set on foot his long premeditated design.

On joining his troops, as was usual, he delivered a long and eloquent harangue, in which, according to Livy, he directly promised and prophesied to the soldiers that he would eradicate the very name of Carthage out of Spain; and I conceive that in this instance far more than usual credit attaches to the relation, since it is perfectly in character with the genius of the man; although in general, the speeches attributed by ancient authors to the generals of whom they are treating, are to be regarded as little more than their own views of the arguments, which influenced the conduct of the actors.

This done, he sent off Laelius with the fleet, instructed so to time its movements that the army and the ships should arrive at the same moment under the city walls, and marched himself on the same day, at the head of his land forces. With such unwearied diligence did he press forward that he is stated by Polybius to have arrived at the isthmus within which the city stands, on the seventh day, having marched 325 Roman miles, and at the very moment when his fleet sailed into the outer harbour; so that the investiture of the town was in the same point of time commenced and completed. His work being so far accomplished, the Roman general lost no time, but established his camp across the whole breadth of the isthmus on the edge of the mainland, with his flanks resting on the sea and the lagoon, and his rear strongly fortified by an earthen work and palisade. The port he left open, in order, as Polybius says, to terrify the enemy by his boldness, as well as to give his own men room enough to deploy on advancing to the attack, but probably because it was sufficiently defended by the canal.

On the following morning, having already during the winter fully examined into the topography of the city and ascertained everything that it was desirable for him to know, particularly that at low ebb the lagoon was so shallow as to be fordable, Scipio advanced to the front of his army with a smiling face, fully armed for battle with his scarlet *sagum* over his corselet, and addressing the soldiers, bade them:

> Be of good cheer, since that day they should surely conquer, for Neptune had appeared to him in a vision of the night, and promised him that, should the Romans need his aid, he would give it to them in a manner so clear and evident that the minds of the most unbelieving should be convinced.

And this he said, well knowing that the ebb would be at its lowest on that day late in the afternoon, and having determined, if not previously victorious, to ford it with a body of picked men, and escalade the walls, which were lower on that side, while the attention of the enemy should be occupied by the direct attack in front.

Surely such juggling as this does not much savour of that heroic simplicity of heart, that enthusiastical sincerity of faith, for which Dr. Arnold gives him credit. Men who believe deeply in religious doctrines, are not apt to play tricks or conjure with them for temporal expediency; and he who falsifies them for his own advantage, must needs be a hypocrite and an impostor.

Sincere however, or otherwise, this trick was not without its immediate and favourable results, for the minds of the men were singularly impressed by his words, and they advanced to the attack with unusual spirit and excitement.

At nine o'clock in the morning, the fleet received instructions to lay the ships as nearly alongside the western walls as possible, and to sweep them with their powerful artillery of javelins, shafts, and stones, so as to make a strong diversion in favour of the storming parties, which consisted of two thousand picked soldiers, the strongest, bravest, and most able-bodied men of his whole army, bearing long scaling ladders, and equipped only with their shields and the tremendous stabbing broadswords, used from the earliest period by the Roman infantry.

Just, however, as the stern and thrilling notes of the straight trumpets made the hills ring around, and fired every warrior heart with their fierce brazen clangour, the city gates flew open, while the eastern heights and the palace hill were occupied by regular guards of five hundred men each, the armed citizens manning the walls, and Mago rushed out at the head of two thousand of his most valiant men, in a desperate and daring sortie.

At the first, they were partially successful from the impetuosity of their charge, and they appeared to be yet more so than they were in reality; for Scipio, wishing to entice the enemy as far as possible from their supports and fortifications, drew back his men, facing about from time to time, and fighting gallantly; while the Carthaginians, encouraged by this semblance of success, and animated by the cheers of their comrades on the walls, pressed fiercely forward on the retreating legionaries, shouting victory, of which they felt themselves already secure, and charging so impetuously, and with a spirit so daring, as to deserve it.

In the meantime, both parties were continually reinforced by detachments from the city and the camp, but the Romans far more effectually, as well as more rapidly, since the Carthaginians had but one narrow gate from which to debouch, and that above a quarter of a mile distant, while the absence of palisades in front of the Roman lines allowed them egress everywhere, and Scipio had withdrawn his men so far that they were close to their own lines.

Still, in spite of this disadvantage, the conflict was fierce and terrible, being in fact little other than a series of individual single combats along the whole front, between men well matched in personal strength, courage, and activity, and similarly armed with bucklers, and short two-edged broadswords—the most deadly and destructive weapons that can be used at close quarters.

For above an hour, the mass struggled thus in blind and reeling fury, swaying to and fro like billows tossed by a tumultuous wind, now one side now the other pushing forward or beaten back, and the Roman or Punic war-cries alternately rising loud and triumphant above the dreadful diapason of shouts, and shrieks, and groans, and the clash and clang of the steel blades on the bronze casques and bucklers, and the maddening clangour of the brazen trumpets.

But, at length, bringing up his reserves, and ordering a sudden charge at all points, Scipio gained his end, and the enemy were borne back bodily for some distance, by the mere weight and brunt of numbers, before they broke and fled; which they did not, until they were very near the walls of the town.

Many fell in the first close encounter, but far more—as was invariably the case in battles previous to the invention of gunpowder, where men fought personally with short weapons, and where individual hostility and. inveterate rage and vengeance were added to the natural ardour of the soldier—in the hot pursuit that followed it.

Most of all fell by their own weapons, or perished miserably trampled under foot by their own comrades, entangled, a weltering and helpless mass, on whose rear the bloody broadswords of the Romans were doing merciless execution, in the narrow gateway, which was entirely insufficient to admit the tumultuous and panic-stricken mass.

So great was the consternation within, that the defenders even fled from the ramparts; and the cry went through the streets that the city was taken; and the shrill wail of miserable women, who knew too well the fate of cities stormed by the Romans, to hope for anything but dishonour and death, already *"smote heaven in the face."*

And indeed it was scarce too soon; for so terrible was the confusion, that the pursuers almost forced their way in pell-mell with the pursued; and would assuredly have done so, had not Mago resorted to the terrible alternative of closing his gates against his own fugitives, and leaving them to the mercy of the swords that, once fleshed, never spared a living foeman.

The massacre before the gates ended, Scipio gave the word to advance and assault the walls, at all points, in great force; not attempting to make approaches in form, or to shake the ramparts with the ram—for to do so would have occupied so much time as to have permitted the Carthaginian armies to attempt, and perhaps to effect, a relief—but resolutely to carry the place, at whatever loss of life, by sudden escalade.

Meantime, the fleet had got alongside of the walls, and blockading the harbor mouth, was maintaining a distant but severe discharge of artillery against the sea-bastions and the Carthaginian galleys, which acted rather as a diversion to the principal attack, dividing and distracting the attention of the defenders of the city, than as itself an effective onslaught.

It will be of course remembered, that in those days there was no incessant booming of ordnance, no continuous roll of musketry, deafening the ears and stunning the senses, to the exclusion of all lesser sounds, by its interminable thunder—that there were no volumes of murky smoke-cloud covering the deeds of darkness done within its shadow, as with an impenetrable pall—but it is probable that the absence of these, instead of detracting from the horrible sublimity of the battlefield, added to its terrors, and increased its magnificence.

Then, every individual cry, from the heroic shout of some leading champion to the cheer of charging thousands, from the sharp shriek extorted from some bold heart by sudden and intolerable anguish, to the sick gasping groan of the death agony, all rose to the ear distinct and audible. Then every manoeuvre of troops, of squadrons, every brave blow, every gallant exploit of individual heroism, was seen by the leader's eye; and the whole field of action was one unclouded blaze of brazen casques and brazen corselets, flashing and lightening in the sunbeams, with blood-red banners rustling over head, and the tall black and scarlet plumes of the legionaries tossing in the air, and the bright crimson cassocks of the leaders conspicuous among the *manipules*.

And now, as the assault commenced, the air was literally rent asunder by missiles of every description, from the vast *falaricae*, huge beams of wood steel-shod, sent hurtling against the Roman lines, from the gigantic cross-bows; great stones, ton weight, launched high, like modern shells, into the atmosphere, to crush whole files by their fall; and volleys of ponderous javelins driven with mighty force from the catapults, down to darts cast from the hand, close flights of arrows, and sling-shot falling like hail into the advancing *cohorts*.

The eye was dazzled by the incessant stream of missiles, gleaming and rushing through the half-darkened sunshine; and the sharp twang of the bow-strings, the whizzing of the shafts, and the deep resonant hurtling of the heavier missiles were blended strangely and fearfully with the barbaric shouts of the defenders of the walls, and the long stern blasts of the trumpets "that bid the Romans close."

So fearful, indeed, was the incessant stream of arrow-shots, sling-shots, and javelins, and so fast did the men fall, that as is ever the case when troops waver, the officers rushed to the front to encourage them, and Scipio himself, (*Polybius* and *Livy*), covered by the large oblong shields of three powerful young men, formed *in testudo* before him, advanced in front of the extreme right, and greatly comforted his men, by his presence and encouragement.

And now the ladders were set up against every coigne and flank of the walls, and the shouts of the assault waxed wild and furious, as up swarmed, sword in hand, the daring Romans. But many of the ladders were too short, and the assailants were overwhelmed with stones and javelins from above, frantic at their own inability to come to thrust of *pilum*, or stroke of sword, with the enemy; many broke sheer in twain under the weight of the numbers, clad in full panoply, who struggled up them; many were hurled bodily backward, stormers and all, by the defenders, so that the brave men, who still rushed upon what seemed certain death undaunted, lay in piles, maimed, broken, crushed, and grovelling like worms, at the foot of the insurmountable walls, or perished miserably transfixed by the spears of their comrades.

Nor were those who ascended to the battlements more fortunate; for so vast was the height of the ramparts, that many, when within sword's length of the defenders, became helplessly giddy, lost their heads, and their foothold, and plunged sheer down, to be dashed to atoms; and many more were dragged forcibly from the ladders with barbed hooks, and either cast headlong, or upheld to writhe out their agonies in mid air.

None gained the summit of the walls—not one.

But still raved on the maddening trumpets, still pealed the fierce shouts, now of personal vindictiveness and vengeance; still up went ladder after ladder; up went, undeterred, the eagles and the cohorts.

By this time the day had advanced to nearly three in the afternoon, and beside the frightful loss of life which the Romans had endured, and their total want of success, the extraordinary heat of the mid-day in the south of Spain, even in early springtime, overpowered alike defenders and assailants.

So that when Scipio commanded the trumpets to sound a recall, the discomfited and shattered, but not dispirited, Romans gladly drew off their forces. And yet more gladly did the defenders quit the walls, proud of their success, believing that their day's work was over, and confident in their ability to maintain themselves, until the siege should be raised by the arrival of Hasdrubal or Mago with one of their armies.

Nothing, however, was less in Scipio's intention than to give them more than a temporary respite. He had learned from his watchers that the tide had begun to turn; and, while the enemy, with the exception of a few tired and drowsy sentinels, had retired to their houses to refresh themselves and sleep after the fatigues of the assault, he had already detached a party of five hundred picked men, led by guides well acquainted with the waters and the bottom of the lagoon, to turn its northern extremity, follow its eastern shore, and attack the walls with their ladders, where they were low and wholly undefended, so soon as the ebb should be at the lowest.

In the meantime, within his camp, he had formed his best men with all his reserves, provided new ladders, longer and stronger—at which the artificers of his corps had been incessantly employed—equipped them in the best manner for the assault, and prepared powerful covering parties of javelineers, slingers, and bowmen, to protect the advance of the stormers, while the weary Carthaginians were thinking only of solacing the inward man, after the labours of the day.

And now the ebb had fallen so low, that where in the morning the waters of the lagoon would have reached fully to a tall man's armpits, they would now scarcely wet his knees; and Scipio, seeing that his time had arrived, rushed to the head of his storming parties—

Now, my men, now! The time hath come! Lo! the God fights for us, the God Neptune, even as he promised! To the walls! to the walls! the sea retreats before us—to the walls, forward! forward! (*Appian*).

Out spoke again the trumpets, shriller and madder than before; up went the mighty cheer of twenty thousand men to the astonished firmament, and forth rushed the forlorn hopes with their ladders, followed by their stormers, and covered by their light infantry with clouds of arrows and sling-shot.

Taken by surprise, and dispirited already, having thought their work done for the day, the Carthaginians hurried to their walls, but not with the same vigour and determination as before. Their stock of artillery and missiles were failing, their hearts failing also.

Still they resisted manfully in front, and held the Romans at bay stoutly, though these now forced their way bodily up the ladders, and at the head of each fought desperately blow and thrust, another enemy coming up hand to hand, when the one above him fell. Others crowded to the great gates, on the leaves of which their axes began to clang ominous of speedy ruins.

But while the conflict was still balanced, and the Romans were unable to force their way over the battlements, or through the massive portals, a fearful sound fell upon the ears of the defenders.

A fierce Roman shout, a shout of victory, harbingered by an exulting burst of horns and trumpets from the sea wall in their rear.

Neptune had kept his promise.

Without the loss of a single man, the stormers had forded the lagoon, mounted the undefended walls, and establishing themselves in force on the esplanade, now gave this note of dismay and havoc to the enemy, of triumphant encouragement to their countrymen.

The next moment a fierce rush cleared the rampart, the street—the bars and bolts of the gates were hewn asunder; in rushed, like an entered tide, the merciless assailants of the gates; and, encouraged beyond measure by the shouts of their comrades, the escaladers overflowed the walls at fifty points at once, a torrent of living "sound and fury!" Mago still did his duty as a governor, as a soldier. He drew back and concentrated the remains of his force in the market-place; but these being overwhelmed by numbers, and cut to pieces, as it were, in a moment, he shut himself up with a handful of men in the citadel, (*Appian*), where being able to effect nothing more, he shortly after surrendered himself to Scipio.

Thereupon began the saddest, cruellest, most revolting and inhuman spectacle that even horrid war has ever witnessed—the sacking of a captured city by a Roman army, (*Polybius*). The fate of taken towns is always cruel, lamentable enough, at all times, even under the milder usages of civilized nations under the light of Christian dispensation. But there is this wide distinction between the most terrible excesses of a modern army, and the deliberate barbarity of victorious Romans; in the former the outrages are, as it were, casual, consequent on the passions of a fierce soldiery, infuriate from loss and resistance, on the bonds of discipline broken for a moment in the tumult of the storm, and are in every case resisted, checked, and punished by the officers.

In a Roman sack, on the contrary, the word was given by the general, as it was in this case by Scipio himself, to go in and kill, to spare no living thing, man, woman, child, even the dumb beasts of the doomed city; to hold not back the hand for mercy, nor for ransom, no, nor for plunder, until the signal should be given by the trumpets to turn from massacre to robbery and worse license. Polybius, their friend and panegyrist, says:

> And this they do, I think, for the sake of striking consternation into their enemies. Wherefore it is of frequent occurrence to see in cities stormed by the Romans, not only men and women butchered, but even the dogs cloven asunder, and the limbs of other domestic animals hewn off and mutilated.

It would appear, however, that on this occasion the coldblooded massacre was scarcely continued so long as usual, for it ceased so soon as Mago laid down his arms and surrendered himself; and thereafter commenced the systematic and thorough ransacking and plundering of every house in the city, which lasted until nightfall, when the centurions called off the soldiers, and assembled them with all the booty and the captives, without exception, on the market-place, where they rallied under their respective banners in perfect discipline and order, and bivouacked there among their miserable victims.

Then, as night fell, guards were appointed to keep the camp; a force of a thousand *field* of heavy infantry was posted on the palace hill, and all the javelineers were brought in from the camp and arrayed on the eastern hillock, which is called that of Æsculapius.

"Thus it was that the Romans became masters of Carthage, which is in Spain;" and so night sunk down friendly and grateful, and bringing temporary quiet both to the cruel and triumphant victors, and to the helpless and exhausted captives, a quiet, to endure only to the morning's dawn, and then to be succeeded, as they would naturally expect, by new agonies, new insults, and new horrors.

On the following morning a regular examination into the number of the captives and the amount of plunder followed; when it appeared that about ten thousand Spanish citizens and denizens were prisoners of New Carthage; to the former of whom, with their families, Scipio immediately granted their freedom, their political rights, and the enjoyment of whatever property remained to them, after the sack of the preceding day—a clemency most unusual in a Roman commander, and in this instance unquestionably a line of conduct originating rather in a wise and far-sighted policy, than in any sentiments of mercy or of humanity.

The artificers and mechanics, to the number of two thousand, he retained for the present, as public slaves of the Roman people, with the promise of their freedom at the conclusion of the war, in case of their being found loyal to their new masters; and these he caused report themselves to the *quaestor*, and divided them into gangs of thirty, and under a Roman inspector. This done, he set them instantly to work at their several trades, some to increase the height of the sea-walls, over which he had forced his way, and to reinforce them with buttresses, flanks, and parapets; others to repair and furbish arms and armor; to provide store of missiles for the powerful artillery he had captured; and to place everything, within and without the fortress, on the most complete war-footing. From the remaining prisoners of the lower classes, sailors, fishermen, and the like, he selected all the youngest, finest-looking, and most vigorous of the men, whom he introduced among the crews of his own ships of war, in the ratio of about one to two; and thus having increased his marine forces by about a third, he manned the eighteen Carthaginian galleys, which he had taken in the docks, and added them to his own fleet, of thirty *quinqueremes*, which were the line-of-battle-ships of that day.

Thereafter he entreated the Spanish hostages, who were detained by the Carthaginians in the city, with all honour and respect, loaded them with gifts, and restored them to their several tribes well pleased, and gratefully contrasting the justice and clemency of their Roman conquerors, with the insolence and violences of their Punic masters or allies. On his army he lavished the highest praises, liberally bestowed crowns and decorations on those who had the most distinguished themselves, and reviewed the whole of his forces on the several successive days, so that, in lieu of being relaxed in discipline, as is frequently the case by the indulgences and license which are so apt to follow the sack of a rich and luxurious city, they were actually in better condition for the resumption of hostilities than they had been in the first instance to commence them.

On the following day, Laelius, his lieutenant, set sail for Rome, carrying with him Mago, the commander of the garrison, two members of Supreme Council, and fifteen senators of Carthage, with all the Punic captives; the bearer also of tidings the most grateful and glorious that Rome had received, since Hannibal's descent from the icy ramparts of the Alps into the rich plains of Lombardy and Piedmont.

The consequences of the taking of New Carthage were not less important, than the circumstances were creditable to the soldiery, and glorious to the general, who had commenced his first campaign by delivering a stroke so brilliant, that while confounding all the combinations of the enemy, and throwing him back upon a timid and cautious defensive, it doubled in a single day the moral strength of his own army, and made his soldiers hold themselves at once invincible.

In eleven days, (*Appian*), from breaking up his cantonments at Tarragona, in four from his investment of New Carthage, and in a brief but bloody storm of a few hours, he had made himself master of the strongest fortress of the enemy in all Spain; had released all the hostages, by holding whom he held the native tribes less as allies than as subjects; had taken all his arsenals, with a vast artillery, and munitions of war almost incalculable; all his naval docks and storehouses, with eighteen ships of war, and above sixty sail of merchant vessels loaded with cargoes so rich as no other land than Spain then exported; and, last, not least, all his principal treasuries, filled with the produce of the goldmines of Tarshish and Ophir, in coined money to the amount of six hundred talents, or nearly a million of dollars, besides a far greater sum in rude ingots, in plate and vessels, statues and sacrificing utensils of pure bullion; so that, in one word, so vast was the amount of public property taken from the enemy, that Carthage itself appeared the least valuable of all the rewards of this remarkable victory, (*Livy*).

The conduct of Scipio in this memorable storm bore a strong resemblance to that of Lord Wellington, at the opening of his fourth Peninsular campaign, when the dissensions between the French marshals and the unsoldierly dispersion of their armies, enabled him to strike the two deadly blows at the strongholds of Ciudad Rodrigo and Badajos, both of which he captured in an incomparably short space of time, thereby seizing the initiative, which he was enabled to maintain until the final expulsion of the invaders from the peninsula of Spain. But the immediate consequences are not precisely similar, inasmuch as Scipio was not as yet sufficiently strong, nor his influence and authority with the natives so firmly established, as to justify his advancing at once into the heart of the country, where be would be opposed to the combined attack of three Punic armies, each singly superior to his own, and led by three generals at that time unsurpassed by any except Hannibal himself.

Contented, therefore, with the great and brilliant exploit he had performed, and the immense moral influence he had gained over the

Spanish mind by his treatment of the hostages and the native population of the captured city, he resolved to attempt no farther active operations during the present season; the rather that his soldiers, who had been now several years abroad, with out receiving pay or supplies from home, were suffering sorely from the want of shoes and clothing.

So soon, therefore, as he had seen the new defences of the place completed, and the whole fortress re-established in a perfect position of defence, in fact far more capable of resistance—independent even of the admitted superiority of Roman legionaries when fighting behind walls, to any troops that could be brought against them—than it had been previous to his storming it, he garrisoned it very strongly with both horse and foot and returned leisurely to Tarragona; where he laboured assiduously at the perfect organisation of his army, and the conciliation of the allies, until he might hope to be equal again to assume the aggressive.

In the meantime, it is very difficult to understand or account for the strange want of co-operation among the Punic leaders, and their inactivity at a moment when by a combined motion of their three armies, they might possibly have retaken New Carthage, and at all events might have shut up their youthful adversary within the Ebro, and so deprived him of a portion of the prestige of success, and prevented him from extending his influence over the fickle barbarians.

This conduct is the more remarkable, when we consider the fact, that of the three Carthaginian leaders two were brothers of Hannibal, and therefore, one would imagine, committed to his policy—that Hasdrubal was under orders both from his brother in Italy, and from the Senate at home, to cross the Alps immediately and reinforce him—and lastly that Mago was appointed by Hannibal himself to command in chief in his brother's absence; and was, moreover, as he afterward approved himself, a soldier of undoubted ability, and fully able to appreciate the advantage of time and the value of combined operations.

What was the nature of Hasdrubal Gisco's command, or how far it was independent of the others, we have no means of ascertaining, since no Carthaginian accounts have reached us; and, as Dr. Arnold has well observed:

> The interior of a Carthaginian camp, and still more the real characters and feelings of the Carthaginian generals are utterly unknown to us.

It cannot be, however, that at this instant, the very crisis of the Hannibalic war in Italy—when for the first time the fidelity of the Latin name was wavering, when twelve out of the thirty Roman colonies had declared their inability to send in their contingents either of men or money—mere jealousies between the officers should have defeated the attempting of a movement, vociferously demanded by Hannibal as of the first importance, and enjoined on the leaders by the home government. Thus much only is evident at a glance; that Hasdrubal Barca lay all the remainder of this year, and till late in the next campaign, at a town variously named Elinga, Tlipa, and Silpia, the site of which cannot be satisfactorily identified, although it is known to have been adjacent to the silver-mines in the Sierra Morena, and to have stood on the lower Guadalquivir. Perhaps it was Alcolea.

Again, the route by which Hasdrubal did actually penetrate into Italy on the following year, across the central table-land of Spain, and by the western passes of the Pyrenees, was entirely open to him at this very period; since the position of Scipio at Tarragona, on the extreme eastern coast of Spain, could not have disquieted him for a moment as to his line of march through the interior; and it is far more than doubtful, from the operations of the ensuing campaign, whether the Roman leader was aware of the existence of any passes, by which the Pyrenees could be surmounted, to the north-westward.

Hence, I conceive that, whatever meaning we may attach to the want of combined action between Mago and Hasdrubal Barca in the following year, 546 of Rome, we may assume it as a fact, that some causes, wholly separate from jealousy, or absence of the desire to cooperate, rendered it impossible for Hasdrubal to attempt the invasion of Italy during this eventful autumn.

That cause I presume to have been simply this; that the great blow of Scipio at the heart of the Punic Empire in Spain, deprived Hasdrubal in one day, of the very treasures, stores, and supplies, on which he had relied for the prosecution of his intended effort. That, seeing the probability of a long siege, and the great doubtfulness of complete success, in case of an attempt to recover New Carthage, he judged it better, and probably so judged wisely, to fill a new military chest from the mines under his control, and to collect fresh supplies and munitions of war in his own winter quarters, than to risk the defeat and disorganisation of the forces destined to deal the fatal blow and close the war in Italy with a thunderbolt, in attacking an enemy of no importance, should that blow be struck against Rome's vitals.

It is very possible, moreover, that the Punic armies were purposely scattered widely asunder, in order to give them facilities of foraging in a barren and sparsely cultivated country, and to enable Hasdrubal to gather in the undivided crops of the rich valley of the Guadalquivir, for the sole benefit of his own division.

Lastly, it appears to me that the sudden and unexpected treason and defection of Mandonius and Indibilis, with the southern Spaniards who had not fallen personally into the sphere of Scipio's fascination, which is scarcely explicable on the grounds of the wonted fickleness of barbarians, must be attributed to some recent acts of oppression and violence on the part of the Carthaginians; which they would not naturally have been like to commit, unless on the plea of absolute necessity, at such a crisis, when it was all-important to them to hold their allies steady in their allegiance.

But if they were so straitened by the capture of their magazines, treasures, and military stores at Carthagena, as to render the utmost exertions needful for the opening of the ensuing campaign, the unavoidable necessity would have arrived. Nor is it otherwise than highly probable, compelled as the Carthaginians were by their circumstances and unsupported position to make war support war, that they should have recourse to the use of forced labour in the mines, forced levies of provisions and munitions of war, and forced impositions of all kinds, to provide themselves at all points for the emergencies of the ensuing year.

Thus it appears to me, we have a clear solution of what Arnold sets down almost as an insoluble mystery, the non-combination of the Punic armies, and the inactivity of Hasdrubal Barca, at the moment when activity was most required of him. And so far are the causes, to which I attribute the conduct of the Carthaginian leaders, from seeming to me improbable; that I am at a loss to discover how they should not have occurred, as themselves consequences of what had preceded them, in the capture of the arsenals of Carthagena.

In this view of the case, the same causes fought for Scipio against the Barca, which fought afterward for Wellington against the marshals of Napoleon; and it was then first demonstrated, as it has been a dozen times since then, that large combined armies can only be kept together in the Peninsula by means of supplies brought up from the rear, based on the cooperation of a powerful marine; and that a small army occupying a central position must succeed in the end, against very superior dispersed forces; which the nature of the country and the necessities of warfare will not allow to act, for any considerable length of time, in unison.

Let this, however, be explained, or remain unexplained, as it may, Scipio lay during the whole autumn and winter in his quarters at Tarragona entirely unmolested, even by a demonstration against his new conquest; and the three Punic generals lay as tranquilly at the head of their several armies in the districts they had occupied, and from which they had not moved, during the assault, or since the capture of Carthagena.

How they were employed, we can but hazard a conjecture; but Scipio, as we know, besides distributing the clothing and pay, which he received from Rome during the winter, among his own soldiers, and keeping them in admirable discipline, had succeeded so largely in conciliating the Spanish chiefs, principally through the intervention of Edeco, whose wife and sons he had restored to him unransomed, after their being made prisoners in New Carthage, that he not only combined all the tribes eastward of the Ebro in league against Carthage; but gained an influence, through his envoys, over the more distant clans and leaders, which manifested itself almost immediately on the opening of the next campaign.

He had, moreover, sent off, (*Livy*), the greater part of his warships to assist the Praetor Veturius in Sardinia; all, it is probable, except such as he found necessary to protect his convoys, and maintain his communications with Italy—since the enemy had no longer in those waters any naval force with which to oppose him—and drafting from the crews all the fighting men, and the flower of the mariners, had intermixed them, as new levies, with the best and steadiest of his legionaries, thus making a very considerable addition to his command.

It would appear, that the campaign of the year 546 of Rome began immediately on the breaking up of winter; and it is very natural that Scipio should have earnestly desired to strike a blow against Hasdrubal Barca, at the earliest possible moment; since to detain him in Spain at all hazards, and prevent his invasion of Italy, was his especial mission. He had, moreover, received intelligence that Mandonius and Indibilis, two of the most influential of all the Spanish chieftains, had already separated themselves with their clans, from the forces of Hasdrubal; had taken post on a very strong height between the Carthaginian and Roman camps; and were awaiting only the advance of the legions to throw aside their quasi neutrality, and join him in force.

Why Hasdrubal should have been willing to await Scipio's advance, and to give him battle, when his route was already determined, by the passes of the Sierra Morena, northward to the Western Pyrenees, by which he might have been hundreds of miles out of the Roman's reach, before a single eagle should be on the Guadalquivir, is less explicable; the rather that, so far as concerned his own peculiar duty, he had all to lose, and nothing to gain by lighting even a victorious action.

We find, however, that he was looking for Spanish levies, recruited by his brother Mago on the Oceanic shores unaffected as yet by Roman influence; and that he also expected large reinforcements of the terrible Numidian horse under Masinissa, son of Gala, a tributary African king, without which he did not care to break up from his winter quarters. Again, it may be that he had hopes of once more bringing over the disaffected and deserted Spaniards from Scipio the son, as he had previously brought them over from the father, before his defeat and death; and, once more, it may have been, and I think it *was* the case, that the whole question was one of time; and that Scipio's march upon the valley of the Guadalquivir in 546, as had been that on New Carthage in 545, was effected with such celerity, as in some sort to effect a surprise, and defeat the proposed combination of the Punic leaders.

Now, although it is stated by Appian, that Mago and Massinissa were present at the affair and operations about Baecula, it is very certain from the silence of Poly bins, Scipio's own mouthpiece, and from the narrative of Livy, that Mago had not joined when Scipio came upon the ground. And when we find that Massinissa, who had been especially sent to reinforce Hasdrubal with a view to Italian operations, did not accompany that general to the Pyrenees, but remained in Spain, doing no service of any moment, when he might have turned the tide of victory, and determined the fate of Rome herself, at the Metaurus, we may, I think, hold it proved that the Numidian succours had not come up, any more than Mago's levies, when Hasdrubal, finding his hopes vain of bringing back the Spaniards to their allegiance, judged it better to decamp and make the best of his way northward, with what power he had, than to run the risk of defeat and dispersion, by giving battle in the absence of his supports.

The operations that follow occurred in the valley of the Guadalquivir, at a strong position and town called Baecula, the site or modern name of which cannot now be ascertained; though, from its vicinity to Andujar and Cazlona, it is supposed by many to have been at, or very near to, Baylen; where occurred the solitary victory of the Spanish armies over the French, in the Peninsular war of the present century.

Here Scipio found Hasdrubal strongly encamped in a retrenched position, fortified with ditch and *palisadoes*, and evidently desirous of maintaining himself there as long as possible; in order, past doubt, to enable his tardy colleagues to join him when the three united armies would be superior to the Romans in such ratio as to render an overwhelming route and carnage probable, if not certain.

The same considerations, which had lent wings already to Scipio's advance, induced him now to attack at once, before he should be outnumbered, and overpowered. He, therefore, displayed his army without delay, and having, it would seem, gained some advantages in a cavalry affair of outposts, threatened a general attack, manoeuvring his legions with such skill and promptitude, that Hasdrubal judged it better to evacuate his entrenchments at once, and fall back steadily on the Pyrenees, than to fight even behind his defences.

This, he evidently effected skilfully and thoroughly; bringing off all his elephants, his baggage, stores and military chest, without any material loss, either of men or means. So that Scipio's or Laelius' narrative, as delivered by Polybius, of the storming of the Punic lines at Baecula, with a Carthaginian loss of twelve thousand prisoners, beside the killed and wounded, must be set down as an impudent exaggeration—too common, alas! in the annals of the great Roman Houses—if not a yet more impudent fiction.

The truth is, that, except a few Spanish prisoners—more or less, it matters not—Scipio had taken no trophies, and gained no positive results whatsoever by his action at this place, if any *bona fide* action there were. Hasdrubal, on the contrary, succeeded in carrying off the whole of the treasures, for which he had been tarrying so long, and decamped so skilfully and secretly that Scipio knew not which route he had taken, or in which direction to pursue him, even if he had dared to pursue; which he did not, owing to the concentration of the armies of Mago and Hasdrubal Gisco, a few days after Hasdrubal Barca's march, or retreat, if it may be so termed.

The pretence of a decided victory gained by Scipio is therefore absurd; but I conceive it is fairly to be deduced, from a thorough examination of the circumstances, that Scipio, by his splendid coup de main against Carthagena in 545, rendered Hasdrubal's march on Italy impossible for that year; and that by the extreme celerity of his descent from Tarragona north of the Ebro, to Andujar on the lower Guadalquivir, in the Spring of 546, he prevented the concentration of the Punic forces, and compelled Hasdrubal to set forth on his perilous expedition without Mago's new levies, and without the invincible Numidian horse, whom he had so long and anxiously awaited, as the most important arm of his service.

If, therefore, this were the case—and the fact, that in Hasdrubal's fatal action on the Metaurus no mention is made of his African horse, goes far to prove it—the Roman leader had already won enough of glory, perhaps acquired the right of being styled the saviour of Rome.

For, had it been possible to Hasdrubal to create a diversion in the North of Italy, previous to the surrender of Tarentum, and at the moment when the twelve colonies fell off from Rome, it would have produced a crisis most fearful if not fatal; and if, in the following year, his want of Numidian horse prevented him from opening up communications with his brother, and ultimately lost him his battle on the Metaurus, he who caused that want, contributed no less than Claudius Nero, by his marvellous Italian forced-march, to the ultimate downfall of Hannibal.

In the meantime, on Hasdrubal's evacuation of his lines at Baecula, Scipio had occupied them; and lay there calmly on the defensive, observing the operations of Mago and Hasdrubal Gisco, who had now, when it was too late, come up in force against him.

From this strong post, he had sent detachments to guard the lower passes of the Pyrenees, so far northward, perhaps, as to the valleys of the Aran above Lerida, and eastward to the shores of the Mediterranean above Perpignan. These watchers sat in vain, however, on their lofty stations, while he for whom they looked was toiling through unsuspected defiles, far to the westward, and making his way, through the dark forests and morasses of central Gaul, to descend upon the Rhone, and scale the Alps, "far inland, where the river was unknown even to the Roman traders of Massilia."

Soon after this, Scipio felt himself so strong in the ascendancy he had gained over the barbarians—who would have made him their king, even as they had recognised for such the first Hasdrubal, Hamilcar's son-in-law and founder of New Carthage—that he drafted ten thousand infantry, and a thousand horse, all picked men, part Roman veterans, part Spanish and Gaulish allies, from his army, whom he countermarched to Tarragona. Thence they took ship, (*Livy*), for Etruria, to co-operate with the consular and praetorian armies already there, in the destruction of this new and formidable enemy.

So well aware were the Carthaginian leaders in Spain of the extraordinary power and fascination which Scipio had now gained, and still exercised, over the Spanish mind, that they not only ventured not to make any attempt on his lines with their dispirited Africans and half-disaffected Spaniards, but scarcely even trusted their native troops within the sphere of his influence, which spread through the barbarians like a contagion.

The secret of this wonderful power of fascination, Arnold thus eloquently explains:

> Everything in him was at once attractive and imposing; his youth, and the mingled beauty and majesty of his aspect; his humanity and courtesy to the Spanish hostages and to their friends: his ability and energy at the head of his army. Above all, there was manifested in him that consciousness of greatness, and that spirit, at once ardent, lofty, and profound, which naturally bows the hearts and minds of ordinary men, not to obedience only and respect, but to admiration and almost to worship.

To this, all of which is doubtless true, may be added, that his pretensions to wisdom and ability greater than human, his supernatural visions and communications with the gods, which had of course spread far and wide among the superstitious Celts and Celtiberians, naturally prone to mysticism, to the ghostly and the superhuman, would of course obtain full credence, and command implicit reverence among them.

So manifest was this leaning of the Spaniards toward the youthful Roman, especially after he had sent back unransomed to Massinissa his nephew, Massiva, taken at Baecula, that the Punic leaders determined immediately to remove all their barbarians beyond the reach of his contact. Mago surrendered his command to Hasdrubal, who fell back at once, without fighting, to the frontiers of Lusitania, beyond the Tagus, and going in person to the Balearic Isles, Majorca, Minorca, and Ivica, renowned for their incomparable slingers, proceeded there to raise large reinforcements of hardier barbarians, who had never heard of Rome, or heard of her only to detest her very name.

The cities were all strongly garrisoned, each by each, as Hasdrubal fell back; and Massinissa was alone left in the field, with three thousand incomparable Numidian horse, to which the Romans had nothing to oppose, under orders to relieve all friends wherever attacked or threatened by the enemy, to skirr the country on all sides and devastate with fire and the sword all districts which had fallen off from their fidelity to Carthage.

Thus ended the second campaign of Scipio in Spain; in which, by again anticipating the Carthaginians, and assuming the initiative before they had concentrated their forces, or combined a plan of operation, he deprived Hasdrubal of a very effective portion of his forces, thus materially contributing to his defeat in Italy, if he could not prevent his march thither. So completely also did he paralyze the movements, and demoralise the armies of that general's successors, that he was enabled to send most important succours at the very point of time to Etruria, without weakening himself or endangering his own position.

It must be admitted, however, that after being surprised, as they surely were in the first instance, the Punic chiefs displayed rare ability in recovering themselves from their dilemma, and in enforcing on Scipio an inactivity, which was more necessary to themselves than to him, until they should restore the morale of their troops, collect new levies on whom they could better rely, and recommence the war under, perhaps, better auspices.

The whole strategy of Hasdrubal Barca in this campaign, and in his advance far toward the heart of Italy, is beyond all praise; nor can it be disputed that, had Scipio given him the leisure to carry with him Mago's new Spanish levies and Massinissa's wild Numidians, the result of the year's operations, perhaps of the whole war, might have been vastly different.

In the beginning of the 547th year of Rome, and of Scipio's third campaign, while Hasdrubal Gisco yet lay at Cadiz, and the Romans were still in winter-quarters within the Ebro, a new general was dispatched from Carthage, with reinforcements, to supply the place of the force carried into Italy by Hasdrubal Barca; and to attempt, if he might do so, to raise the Spaniards of the interior against the Romans.

It would seem, that, in the first instance, Scipio was in some sort surprised; for Hanno having landed, as it would appear, without the fact of his arrival being known, contrived to penetrate into Celtiberia, now Arragon, nearly in the centre of Spain, where he effected his junction with Mago, who had returned from the Balearic Islands, and at a very early period levied a considerable body of raw troops. The information, that a new Carthaginian army was forming in the heart of Spain, with intent to operate against his right flank and rear, in the event of his moving southward against Hasdrubal Gisco, was brought to the proconsul by some Spanish deserters, just in time that he might anticipate and avert the danger.

Perceiving at once the fatal consequences, which would arise from his allowing the Punic leaders leisure to organise and discipline a force in so central a position, Scipio lost not a moment of time. Acting with all his wonted decision of character, he at once dispatched Marcus Silanus, with a division of ten thousand infantry and five hundred horse, to crush the movement and anticipate the coming peril.

Following the example of his superior, and marching with such speed and secrecy through wild crags and deep cork forests of the difficult Celtiberian country, that he outstripped not only all direct tidings, but all rumours of his advance, Silanus came upon the enemy, wholly unprovided, and expecting nothing less than action.

They occupied two camps on adjacent eminences, the new Spanish levies under Mago to the left, promiscuously hutted on the open hill-top—the Carthaginians and Numidian horse, well entrenched on the right, under Hanno, (*Livy*).

Mago, on the approach of the Romans, sallied at once with his whole force, which could not, however, sustain for a moment the sword-in-hand charge of the Roman legionaries. The Numidians and Punic veterans came pouring down from the fortified camp to the rescue; and these, seeing the fortunes of the day adverse, and unwilling to sacrifice the nucleus and flower of the army in a vain attempt to cover allies so unsteady, Mago at once carried off unbroken, and preserved them for a future conflict. Hanno, less fortunate, having taken command of the broken Celtiberians who had retired to a strong knoll, while endeavouring to retrieve the day, (*Appian*), was treasonably surrendered to the Romans by his own fickle barbarians, not, it would seem, without something strongly savouring of treachery on the part of Silanus.

All the new Spanish levies dispersed at once into their native fastnesses of rock and wilderness, not easily or soon to be again collected under the Carthaginian standards; and by this single blow the fate of the campaign was decided; for the Carthaginians had no longer any force on foot capable of encountering the Romans in the field, unless it were that of Hasdrubal Gisco, which for some cause, unknown to us, was not available.

The Punic leaders thereupon determined, with true soldierly prudence, to risk no decisive actions, which would probably be fatal to themselves, but to convert the war into one of sieges, on the Roman part, and thus indefinitely protract it. For indeed, by this method, considering the proverbial stubbornness of tenacity and desperate valour with which Spaniards have in all ages held out in places most untenable, they might well hope to weary out even Roman energy and daring.

But the chief to whom they were opposed, though on the success of Silanus he had resolved on assuming a vigorous offensive, and striking a blow at Hasdrubal Gisco, who lay far beyond Andalusia and the valley of the Guadalquiver, was far too politic to engage his victorious army in a series of harassing and useless operations against petty walled towns and hill-forts, which, he well knew, must surrender instantly in consequence of one more victorious battle.

So soon, therefore, as he ascertained that the enemy, after provisioning and garrisoning every place capable of resistance, had retreated at his leisure, with all his powers, and concentrated them within the powerful fortifications of Cadiz, Scipio deferred all active operations to the ensuing season, withdrew the bulk of his army, and retired to near Carthage, and thence with all his prisoners to headquarters at Tarragona.

He did not, however, entirely evacuate the valley of the Guadalquiver, or permit the enemy to reoccupy that already twice-conquered district; but detached his brother, Lucius Scipio, with ten thousand foot and a thousand horse, to make himself master of Oringis, a strong and important town, situate in a very fertile region, and commanding the site of the silver mines. It had been much used by Hasdrubal as a base for his operations against the inland tribes of central Spain.

This place Lucius surrounded with lines of circumvallation and contravallation; and then assaulted it so vigorously by escalade, that, although the first storming parties were beaten back from the ramparts with severe slaughter, on the second onslaught the townsmen fled in a panic from the walls, and the Punic garrison, supposing themselves betrayed, drew off and retired to the citadel. That movement led the Spaniards, in their turn, to impute treachery to their allies; and in their anxiety to obtain terms, before the city should be won, they flung away their offensive weapons, threw open one of the gates, and streamed out in a tumultuous crowd, showing their unarmed right hands, though still covering themselves with their shields, and crying to the enemy for quarter.

Naturally enough, the Romans mistook so turbulent and precipitate a surrender for a sortie in force, and charging home with their broadswords drove the fugitives back, massacring them unresisted, and entered the gate with them pell-mell. For some time longer a horrible carnage prevailed through the streets, but as the other gates were hewn down from within with axes, a strong body of horse and the *triarii* of the reserve marched in, and occupied the forum, when the officers, learning the true state of the facts, quickly restored order, received all to mercy who surrendered, and put a stop to the pillaging and confusion.

The Carthaginian garrison laid down its arms on the first summons, and Lucius Scipio, adhering to the wise policy of his brother, restored the city and all that it contained, together with their personal freedom, to the Spanish citizens.

Of this exploit Publius Scipio affected to speak, anxious to gratify his elder brother who served under him, as not inferior to his own at the storming of New Carthage, though in truth there was no similarity between them, the capture of Oringis being the result of a mere accident; and honoured him personally, as he had previously honoured Caius Laelius, by sending him with dispatches to Rome, in charge of Hanno and the trophies of victory. This done he went into winter-quarters, as usual, at Tarragona.

It is probable that during the period of inactivity, while he lay on his arms within the Ebro, the tidings of Hasdrubal's defeat and death on the banks of the Metaurus, and the relief of Rome's most urgent apprehensions, reached him; and it may be taken for granted, though we no where find it distinctly stated, that, this imminent peril being fortunately overpassed, the large detachments which Scipio had sent home from Tarragona by sea in the preceding year, to cooperate in the defence of Rome, were now restored to him. At all events, we find him in sufficient force at an early season of the following year to take the field, and commence operations with greater vigor than he had previously exerted.

Many arguments would suggest themselves why he should strenuously press the war. Nero, whom he had superseded in his present command, had performed the great achievement and gained the only great renown which had fallen to any Roman General during the war; if, therefore, Scipio would still hve in the mouths of his countrymen, he too must strike such a blow as should leave as bright a mark on the page of history, as the grand forced march and decisive victory of his rival.

The Carthaginian leaders, Hasdrubal Gisco, and Hannibal's youngest brother, Mago, had likewise drawn together, whether by reinforcements from Africa or by Spanish levies, does not appear, a very formidable army, and were no less willing than their antagonist to risk a battle.

Their forces are stated by Polybius and Appian to have amounted to seventy thousand foot, with four or five thousand horse and two and thirty elephants; against which Scipio, after having mustered all his allies, and gained over some auxiliaries from a Spanish prince, Colchas or Colichas by name, could bring no more than forty-five thousand infantry with three thousand horse.

The Carthaginians lay at a town variously called Ilipa and Silpia, the locality or true name of which cannot readily be ascertained; which seems, however, to have commanded the mining districts and not to have been very far distant from Baecula, the scene of their unsuccessful operations of the previous campaign. They were advantageously posted along the lower and last ridges of the hill country, with open plains in their front.

On the approach of Scipio, the Carthaginian cavalry and Massinissa's Numidian horse sallied out and made a vigorous attack on the Romans, as they were engaged in entrenching themselves; nor was it without some sharp fighting, and ultimately calling out the legionary foot, that they were repulsed.

For several days, the armies faced each other in battle array; Hasdrubal leading out first in the morning, and usually recalling his men the first at evening, while the light troops and horse skirmished sharply in the interval between the hues, with little result and no marked superiority.

During the whole of these indecisive days, the two armies were regularly arrayed in the same manner, with the native Roman and Carthaginian foot forming the centres, and the Spanish allies on the wings; but such was not the order in which Scipio had determined to fight.

It was his plan on the day of battle to throw the whole weight of his unrivalled Roman legionaries against the Spaniards of the Punic army; and to retire his own allies, so as to keep the Carthaginian veterans out of action, until the day should be far spent and the decisive impression made.

This is unquestionably his finest battle, and that on which his reputation must depend as a tactician; and it is not to be denied that the plan itself was masterly, that it was admirably executed, and that the sagacity and perseverance with which the Roman general availed himself of every point of advantage, can scarce be praised too highly.

Desiring to turn against Hasdrubal the same advantage which Hannibal had so successfully adopted against his father, Scipio gave notice to the *tribunes* of the soldiers that he meant to deliver battle on the following day, and made the men arm themselves betimes and breakfast well at an unusually early hour. This done, he advanced into the plain, leaving his centre, contrary wise to his order of battle on the previous days, composed of his Spanish allies and auxiliaries, and his wings formed of the Roman and Latin legions.

His front he covered with a cloud of skirmishers, by which he masked this alteration of his battle, and with all his native and allied horse, whom he launched to the very ditches and gates of Hasdrubal's camp before the sun had yet risen. The Carthaginian skirmishers, who poured out to meet them, were worsted and driven in with great confusion and slaughter; and Hasdrubal, aroused from his bed by the clamour, rushed out of his tent to behold the plains swarming with the enemy's light troops, and their cavalry wheeling to and fro cutting to pieces the dispersed and scattered bands, whose inferior numbers they had easily overpowered; while the first rays of the rising sun showed him the whole Roman Army in array, advancing in force, as if to the attack of his entrenchments.

Without waiting to let his men breakfast, and scarcely giving them time to arm themselves sufficiently, enraged at finding himself thus insulted in his camp, he at once led out his forces; and arraying them, as on the former days, either that he had not noticed the change in Scipio's formation, or that he did not apprehend its importance, he set his Spaniards in opposition to the Romans on either wings, while his Carthaginians were opposed in the centre to the Spanish allies.

A long interval succeeded before the main battles joined, occupied as on the previous days by fierce and eager skirmishing; which was, however, now far more continuous and better sustained than heretofore, and with nearly equal detriment and success on both sides, either party in turn prevailing and driving in the other, to be again repulsed, until rallied upon the masses of its own infantry.

It would seem that the Carthaginians, for some reason, probably from indecision, and perhaps depressed by the ill success of the past campaigns, did not care to assume the initiative; and it was Scipio's game to defer, as long as possible, the moment of the decisive struggle, in order that the effects of the toil and heat of the day might tell to the utmost on the unfed army of Hasdrubal, which would necessarily wax faint and weary during a long day, under circumstances so untoward.

When the day, however, was far advanced, past noon, Scipio called in his horse and skirmishers, receiving them between the intervals of his maniples, and prepared for the execution of the grand manoeuvre by which he hoped to decide the fate of the day.

To this end he formed three troops of picked horsemen and three *cohorts* of the flower of his light infantry, who had been kept in reserve up to this moment, in front of either of his wings and some little space without them, to the right and left. This done, and the remainder of the horse and *voltigeurs* being held in hand behind his wings, he sent orders to Marcius and Laelius on his extreme left, ordering them to commence the action, and at the same instant extending the light troops, in advance, so as to outflank and overlap the Spaniards, he wheeled up his *legionaries* from line into column, and led at a run, obliquing from the right leftward, full against the Carthaginian left.

The instant when the clang of his trumpets announced that close and deadly onset, his lieutenants on the left performed the same manoeuvre, overflanking the Punic right and obliquing to the right hand, with the deadly volley of strongly-hurled *pila*, followed by the onslaught of the terrible Roman sword.

Meantime, the Spaniards of the centre, merely advanced, and kept moving, sufficiently to preserve their connection with the wings, and admit no gap or break in their order, into which the enemy might drive an entering wedge; but keeping themselves so far retired, as to give the Carthaginian centre, composed of the choice Africans who had never been beaten in a fair field, no occasion to assail them.

These brave men, meanwhile, could not advance or strike a blow; for the forces on either flank, even while they stood stationary, were gradually yielding ground, as overpowered by unequal odds, Romans against barbarians, veterans against new levies, perfectly armed and practised soldiers against tumultuary troops, shepherds and hunters—men full fed against men fasting. Had they advanced, they had exposed their own flanks naked to the Romans, who were already shattering the faint auxiliaries on either reeling wing. Had they attempted to wheel to the relief of their disordered wings, they had left a gap in their mid hues, into which the Spaniards of the Roman centre would have broken like an entered flood.

Ere long, they were compelled, in order to preserve their connection with their wings, borne back by the unequal pressure, to give ground themselves; but they did so, not as men broken or defeated, but orderly, steadily, and at command.

Then at length, as utterly overmatched and beaten, the Spaniards on either flank gave way, the Roman-Spaniards of the centre charged.

All the Punic elephants had become congregated, owing to the circular inward sweep of the Roman wings, in front of the Carthaginian centre, and these huge unwieldy monsters did, as usual, nearly equal mischief to their enemies and their masters. Many were driven back upon the African foot, whom they disordered, and some of whom they trod under foot—many passed through the Spaniards with more or less destruction in their ranks.

The veteran Africans fought, as they always had fought, like men used to conquer; their auxiliaries on either flank had not been beaten without stubborn and gallant resistance, or without inevitable cause, but they were now utterly discomfited and scarcely holding together, when the Roman horse, rested and recruited by repose, swung out to the right and left from the rear of the Roman wings, plunged into their disordered masses, and fleshed their thirsty swords in carnage, avenging and almost equalling that of Cannae.

The *legionaries* of the Roman foot, now victorious on both flanks, and relieved from the necessity of pursuit by the zeal of their own excited cavalry, having no enemy directly in their front, pressed in on the flanks of the Punic centre, which was already struggling against the Hispano-Romans in front, and speedily converted the retreat into a route, the defeat into a complete disaster.

The Carthaginian camp was not far distant, yet it was with difficulty that Hasdrubal's men gained it, and mounted in show of defence on the ramparts. The Romans advanced to assault the works, and it is stated by Livy, that they would have unquestionably carried them and destroyed the whole army of the enemy, had not a tremendous thunder-storm broken out, as is not uncommon among those mountains in the summer heats, and compelled the victors to desist and retire to their own entrenchments, to regain which they had some difficulty, owing to their exhaustion and the fury of the storm.

All that night the Carthaginians laboured incessant among the rain, in spite the thunders, to strengthen their works and defences, expecting that the Romans would surely attempt to storm them on the morrow. But when that morrow came, their auxiliaries and allies were deserting them and passing over to the enemy by thousands at a time, Attas, Prince of the Turdetani, or Sevillans, setting the example of defection, and surrendering two strong walled towns, with their Carthaginian garrisons, to the Romans.

To prevent the spread of this disaffection and the dispersion of his entire forces, Hasdrubal judged it wisest to remove the remnant of his army from the perilous vicinity, and accordingly in the dead of the following night, broke from his position silently, and decamped, leaving his fires burning, and made the best of his way toward the Guadalquiver, seeking to interpose that powerful stream between himself and his pursuers.

This, then, was the famous battle of Elinga, Ilipa or Silpia, as it is variously written by Polybius, Appian, and Livy, which may be regarded as altogether the most remarkable of Scipio's actions, as Cannae was the finest of Hannibal's, the victory being in both cases ascribable to scientific principles and the generalship of the leaders, and scarcely, even in a secondary degree, to the quality of the troops engaged.

It was fought on the principles which are assumed by Napoleon to be the base of all generalship. It was delivered by an army greatly inferior on the whole, yet was fought so that the body numerically inferior was superior, both morally and physically, on the points where it was engaged, and that two-thirds of the defeated force were in fact annihilated before the remainder could be brought into action; and that remainder was necessarily destroyed in the end by the conversion against it of the entire strength of the enemy.

It was in some sort, directly the converse of Cannae;[9] the consequences and termination being identical, though the movements which led to that result were reversed in the mode of fighting, as well as in the circumstances of the engagement.

In both, the defeated army assumed the form of a convex segment of a circle, while the victorious forces overlapped it with a concave exterior semicircle, and finally defeated it by a great general charge of horse and foot on both flanks.

Here, however, the resemblance ends, for at Cannae the attacking army was destroyed, at Ilipa it conquered. At Cannae the defeated army was enveloped in consequence of the forward rush of its own centre into the midst of the enemy, while at Ilipa it was in like manner surrounded, owing to the retirement of the enemy's centre, and the progression of its victorious wings.

It is the very battle which Napoleon intended to fight at Waterloo, and which he would have gained on that celebrated field had he succeeded in forcing back both or either of the British wings, before the arrival of the Prussians on the extreme left toward St. Lambert, and

---

9. *Cannae. Captains of the Old World.*

the grand attack of the Old Guard on the centre; but in that action the steadiness of the British foot prevailed, and the wings, instead of retrograding under the pressure, had actually advanced, so as to envelop the enemy, instead of being themselves enveloped, at the crisis of the day.

In its general effects and influence on the fate of the campaign, and indeed of the war on the Peninsula, Ilipa was to the Carthaginians, what Vittoria was to the French armies in Spain, the virtual cause of their total expulsion from the Peninsula, and of the transfer of the seat of war into their own countries. In both cases, indeed, the struggle was protracted, far more boldly and vigorously by the Gallic than by the Punic leaders, but in neither instance was the issue in truth doubtful or the end beyond the reach of human vision.

It is stated by Appian, whose account of the action differs considerably from that of Polybius, that the loss of the Carthaginian forces amounted to fifteen thousand men, while that of the Romans did not exceed eight hundred.

On the following morning when he discovered that Hasdrubal had decamped, Scipio likewise broke up from his position and pursued in force, and that with such vigour and activity, that if he had followed directly on the line of his retreat he might easily have overtaken his rear. It was, however, judged better to strike directly across the country, irrespective of the Punic line of retreat, so as to interpose between Hasdrubal and the Guadalquiver, and thus prevent his passing that great river, and transferring the scene of operations into the vicinity of Cadiz and the southern seaboard. This being done, and a soldiery and sound measure it was so to do, Hasdrubal was cut off from his resources and forced westward to the Atlantic coast, without the pillars of Hercules.

So soon as he turned in this direction his case was desperate, indeed, and the Roman general gave him no occasion to recruit the strength or spirit of the army, but pressing him home incessantly with the horse and light troops of his lefts well in advance, at length brought him to action with his legions, if that can be called an action which was little more than a massacre, a slaughter not of soldiers but of sheep.

Six thousand men only, and those but half armed, escaped to some bare hills near the coast, which they fortified as best they might, and where they were besieged in form by Silanus, with ten thousand foot and a thousand horse, whom Scipio detached for that purpose, while he returned in person to Tarragona.

In a few days, unable to make any effectual defence of those bare hills without magazines or resources, and both weakened and alarmed by daily defections, Hasdrubal escaped by night to his ships and got off to Cadiz, whence he sent back his squadron to bring off Mago, who joined him soon after in that city, now the last foot of Spanish soil in Carthaginian occupation.

The rest of the forces, abandoned by their leaders, either deserted in a body to the Romans, or breaking up into small bands dispersed themselves among the neighbouring towns, and thenceforth had no existence as an army.

Massinissa, the Numidian leader, hereupon, considering the cause of the Carthaginians hopeless, and foreseeing the ultimate success of the Romans, had a secret interview with Silanus, in which he made overtures to Scipio. These led, in due time, to a firm alliance, and in no small degree, contributed to the Roman victories in Africa, and to the fall of Carthage; and an understanding being effected, the prince returned, with the survivors of his countrymen to his Numidian deserts, never so long as his life endured to swerve from his fidelity to his new allies and masters.

Silanus returned to Tarragona, bringing word to his commander that the war was virtually at an end, and that "no enemy was to be found in the field from the Pyrenees to the Pillars of Hercules:" (*Arnold*) and therefore Scipio, sending his brother Lucius to Rome, with the captives and trophies of his victory, to announce the completion of his work, proceeded himself to Carthagena, there to organise measures for transferring the war into Africa, which henceforth was the darling project of his policy.

Much of what follows in the course of this campaign is nearly unintelligible, Livy's explanation of the occurrences being wholly unsatisfactory, and the conduct of Scipio and his lieutenants inexplicable on any of the known rules or principles of strategy or policy. It is clear that he must have considered the war at an end, and the campaign completed at a blow, when he drew off his entire forces to the north, without, so far as it appears, leaving a garrison in any one of the captured cities, or any force on foot to observe the Carthaginians, who still held the important and powerful sea-port of Cadiz, with a division of land forces and a naval squadron.

How he could have looked upon the work as done, so long as this important stronghold, and convenient base of future operations remained in the hands of an active and enterprising enemy, it is difficult to understand. And, when it is taken into consideration that within a few weeks of his obviously premature withdrawal of his forces beyond the Ebro, he was obliged by a general rising of the Spaniards, excited by the Punic garrisons of the towns now left in his rear, to march back into this very region and to undertake several difficult sieges, besides fighting a pitched battle against the barbarians, it is not easy to avoid coming to the conclusion that he committed a grave military error in not attempting the expulsion of Mago from Cadiz, and so concluding the war by one stunning stroke.

There must, however, have existed, I think, some strong reasons for his not making an effort in this direction, so evident must it have been that Spain could never be considered Roman, or fairly subjugated, while such a port of entrance and base of operations as Cadiz was left to the enemy. How dangerous a system of attack might have been carried on from this place is proved by the fact that, from it, Mago did actually attempt a surprise of Carthagena, while the Roman army was in winter-quarters behind the Ebro; an enterprise which, had it succeeded, would have replaced affairs as at the commencement of the war, and left all the work to be done again.

We must suppose, therefore, that, from the strength of Cadiz—and how strong is its natural position is proved by the heroical siege which it supported against the French Army in 1810—and perhaps from his want of sufficient maritime forces, his squadron having been principally laid up and the men drafted into the legions—he felt his inability to conquer it by storm, and the impossibility of blockading it while the sea was open. Reckoning, also, on the impotence of the Carthaginian Government to aid Mago by reinforcements from home, and the failure of that general to keep the field, he probably calculated that an invasion of Africa would so paralyze the whole policy of Carthage, as to render her possession of this solitary fortress on the Atlantic coast of Spain a matter of little moment.

In view, however, of all that followed, the serious revolt of the Spaniards under Mandonius and Indibilis, the necessity of besieging and storming Illiturgi, Castulo, and Astapa a few weeks later in the season, places in the very heart of the country from which he now withdrew as completely subjugated, the daring attempt of Mago on Carthagena, and his actual invasion of Italy, where he maintained himself until recalled by his countrymen after Scipio had landed in Africa, I cannot but judge this retirement of the Romans to Tarragona as a military error; the gravest, perhaps the only grave one, in all this general's splendid and sound career, and one from the consequences of which his good fortune had as much to do in defending him, as either his judgment or his conduct.

It was at this period of the war, that Scipio undertook an enterprise, which with all its details savours more of romance than of sober history, and which, had it not been justified by its partial success, would have been pronounced rash and indefensible.

Desirous of securing a foothold and an ally on the African continent, Scipio had sent Caius Laelius, so soon as the army returned to Tarragona, on an embassy to Syphax, king of the Massaesyli, the most powerful of the native princes, with the hopes of bringing him over from the Carthaginians to a Roman alliance. Of this, he returned, giving Scipio some hopes, accompanied by an invitation from the prince to the Roman general, to visit him in his own dominions.

Scipio, in consequence, had the audacity to cross the Mediterranean, swarming with Punic cruisers—for in those seas at least the Carthaginian force was superior—with two *quinqueremes* only, the line of battle-ships of that day, and entered the royal port, safely, with a wind so fair and at the same time so strong, that he came into the harbour within a very short period after being first discovered from the shore.

To this circumstance he owed his safety, and Rome, perhaps, her subsequent triumph over her rival; for, by a singular coincidence, Hasdrubal had almost simultaneously crossed over from Cadiz, with seven *triremes*, and was at that time lying in the African harbour.

When the two Roman ships were seen approaching, there was a mustering and embarking, in hot haste, and with a clamorous tumult, of the Carthaginian crews; who overmatched the Romans so greatly that the capture of Scipio was certain, could they have got out to sea, in time to intercept him.

But the fortune of Rome prevailed; the fresh gale bore him into port so rapidly that the Punic galleys had not yet weighed their anchors; and once entered, the law of nations, the respect for a neutral harbour, and, probably, the fear of alienating Syphax, on the part of Hasdrubal, prevented violence.

Of this singular meeting, amid the horrors of such a war, we, alas! know far too little. Whether the crews and soldiery of the hostile fleets mingled, in that moment of transitory peace, in friendly intercourse, exchanging cups and shaking hands, as did the French and English regiments during a lull of battle on the bloody day of Talavera, or whether they held aloof in stern suspicion and resentment, no writer has revealed to us. The rival generals, however, met, we are told, at the royal board of Syphax, and both reclined in amity on the same couch—a pleasing and graceful incident in times and among usages so stormy and so cruel, when no friendly intercourse was deemed possible between individuals of hostile nations; and when the doom of the noblest conquered general was the scourge and the fatal axe.

We are told by Livy, following Polybius, the personal friend and encomiast of Scipio, that this general's manners, singularly combining grace, affability and dignity, produced such an effect on Hasdrubal, that he expressed an opinion, that:

> The Roman was superior in the arts of peace to himself in the deeds of war, and that, such was his fascination in winning the minds of men, he was sure ultimately to succeed with Syphax.

We are also told that on this occasion the Massaesylian king entered into a treaty of alliance with Scipio, who thereupon returned rejoicing, after a stormy passage of four days, to New Carthage. Dr. Arnold shrewdly observes:

> This treaty, however, we may be very sure, was not one of those, which Polybius found preserved in the Capitol.

For Syphax fought, in fact, to the last faithfully for Carthage, and lost his kingdom and his bride by his adherence to her cause. How likely it is, that Hasdrubal should so have expressed himself, may be imagined best, when it is known that he, at this very time, negotiated the marriage of his beautiful daughter, Sophonisba, to the amorous prince, whose fidelity he thus assured to his own countrymen.

Such are the difficulties, to which the historian is subjected by the want of responsible authorities, and the possession only of partial one-sided eulogies, rather than narratives.

Had we a Carthaginian relation of these events, we should hear, probably, how skilfully the wily Africans played with the arrogant and pompous Roman; and how they laughed in their sleeves, at the success of the deceits which they played off upon him.

It is clear, however, that on Scipio's return to Carthagena, how sure soever he might have felt of having closed the war before his departure, and secured the amity of Syphax during his absence, he found affairs in so ill a state, that he was obliged to take the field again in force, and retrace his steps to the scene of his late victories.

Livy's account of these occurrences, wherein he states that the object of this march and counter-march, covering a space of nearly fifteen hundred Roman miles, in and out, was merely to punish the towns of Illiturgi, Castulo, and Astapa, for defection and acts of hostility to the Romans, six years before, is simply an absurdity.

Had it been desired to do that, it would have been done immediately after the defeat of Hasdrubal at Ilipa, when the whole Roman and allied army was on the spot, and the terror of their arms at the highest.

For it must be observed, that Scipio actually marched through Castulo, now Cazlona, and passed the immediate vicinity of Illiturgi, which coincides with Andujar or Baylen, on his way to give battle to the Carthaginians at Ilipa or Elinga, which could not have been far distant from the modern Alcolea; and probably returned by the same route to Tarragona, after his great victory, when probably no resistance would have been offered to his utmost cruelty.

To make this argument more conclusive, we find that there was, at this time, a Punic garrison in Castulo, which though it is stated to have fled thither after the defeat at Ilipa, could scarcely have done so; as at that time the Roman Army was interposed, and as Scipio, on his triumphant return, would never have left it unmolested, had it been then occupied. Probably this garrison was sent from Cadiz by Mago, to reoccupy the country which had been prematurely evacuated; and that a general defection of that half-conquered region was the consequence of the movement, and the cause of Scipio's merciless severity.

If he had erred before, however, in believing his conquest secure, when it was but half gained, he redeemed his error by the rapidity and brilliancy with which he overcame space, conquered the heats of a Spanish summer, and regained his jeoparded acquisitions.

After a desperate defence, and two or three disgraceful repulses of the Roman storming parties, which compelled Scipio to expose his own person in the van, Illiturgi was taken by storm, and mercilessly sacked after the cruel Roman custom. Every living creature, human or brute, without distinction of age or sex, or pity even for helpless infancy, was put to the sword, and the town was reduced to ashes, so that its very site was rendered doubtful.

Castulo, which had successfully resisted Silanus, on the arrival of the commander-in-chief, reeking from the massacres of Illiturgi, surrendered at discretion, but received little mercy, though not dismantled utterly like its neighbouring city. Again Scipio retired northward; but, this time, left behind him Lucius Marcius, with a strong detachment to preserve peace, and receive the other towns of Andalusia to submission, or punish them for contumacy.

How he performed his task, may be judged by the fate of Astapa; the inhabitants of which, preferring death to capture by the Romans, left a body of fifty men with orders to slaughter all their women and children on a huge funeral pyre, built up of all their valuables, in the market place, to fire the city and perish themselves in the flames—orders which were but too faithfully accomplished, while the remainder of the citizens sallied out to sell their lives as dearly as they might, and fell to a man, sword in hand. Such was the terror inspired by the consequences of a Roman victory.

His work thus vigorously prosecuted, Silanus returned to Tarragona; but remained there only a few days, before he was again dispatched to Cadiz with a light division, Laelius accompanying him with a squadron, in order to ascertain if some secret offers to surrender the city, with the Carthaginian general and garrison, which had been made by certain of the Spanish citizens, could be carried into effect.

Slightly to anticipate the course of events, for the preservation of the unity of narrative, it may here be stated, that the plot was discovered by Mago before the arrival of the Romans. He had sent the ringleaders to Carthage under the charge of Adherbal, with a *quinquereme* and a squadron of eight *triremes*, and this force, by accident, encountered Laelius with a similar division of one Roman *quinquereme* and seven *triremes*. An action took place, in which the Punic fine-of-battle-ship was taken by the Roman frigates, while the Roman *quinquereme* sunk two and took a third of the Carthaginian *triremes*, Adherbal scarcely escaping with the remaining five ships to the coast of Africa.

In the meanwhile, Scipio himself had been stricken with one of those aguish Spanish fevers, which proved so much more fatal to the gallant Peninsulars of England than either the bullets or the bayonets of their daring antagonists. He was reduced almost to the doors of death; it was even reported through the land that he was dead.

Then was it seen how much, in Spain, the fortunes of Rome depended on the name of Scipio, and how little the successes of Scipio on the power or name of Rome. History, at this crisis, is worse than mute, mutilated, garbled, and partial, to such a degree, that he who seeks to disentangle its ravelled threads, is bewildered. But the facts, truly stated, though wretchedly interpreted by the Latin writers, speak for themselves, what the eulogists of Scipio cannot speak intelligibly, for the distrust in which we hold them.

The rumour had scarcely gained that Scipio was dead, ere it appeared what was the influence of Scipio and what of Rome. There was no Carthaginian power afoot north-east of the Guadalquiver, yet in the extreme east, between the Ebro and the Pyrenees, the very chiefs, Mandonius and Indibilis, who but two or three years before would have had Scipio for their king, sprang to arms, actuated by the natural wish to exterminate the Romans. Nor was this all. The very Roman legion, which acted as a covering force to keep northern Spain from revolt, and was posted on the Sucro, or Xucar, broke into open mutiny, drove the tribunes from the camps, and gave the command, with the forces and *imperium* of consuls, to two private soldiers, Caius Attius of Umbria, and Caius Albius of the Latin colony of Cales.

From the nationality of these men there is much reason to suppose that this division consisted, not of Romans, but of the Italian and Latin allies—in either event the danger was as imminent, as the occurrence was rare.

But Scipio was neither dead nor sleeping. By a stroke of the deepest dissimulation, not to say treachery, he got possession of the persons of the ringleaders, to the number of thirty-five men, he brought the mutineers, unarmed and at his mercy, into the compass and grasp of steady troops, on whom he could rely, and then having put to death all the chiefs, pardoned the rest, paid them all arrears, for it was on that pretext they had mutinied, and at once led them against the rebellious natives, north of the Ebro.

The action was decisive, though not without severe fighting and heavy loss, no less than twelve hundred of the Romans and allies being slain, and three thousand wounded, (*Livy*). There is nothing, however, in its details worthy of notice. The barbarians were drawn into a deep gorge, whence there was no egress, and there slain, not like sheep, but like wolves at bay. The very completeness of the catastrophe, probably, augmented the loss of the victors. Had there been room of escape for fugitives, they had not stood to their arms so fiercely.

With this, the campaign ended; although, after the Roman troops were in winter-quarters, Mago, having evacuated Cadiz, attempted Carthagena, and was repulsed by its garrison alone. After this disappointment he took possession of Minorca; wintered there in security; thence invaded Liguria in the following spring; made a diversion much more formidable than that of his brother Hasdrubal, and only retired from Italy, after being mortally wounded, on receiving the especial orders of the Senate, to aid in the defence of Africa, against the already too successful arras of Scipio and the now Roman Massinissa.

For, after the defeat of Indibilis, Scipio once more moved southward into the vicinity of Cadiz, for no other purpose than to hold an interview with the Numidian prince; and, having gained him entirely, so powerful was the fascination of his manners and address, arranged with him a private treaty of amity and alliance, and promised him to cross over, as soon as possible, into Africa.

With the departure of Mago and the withdrawal of his African forces from Cadiz, the war in Spain and the Carthaginian rule in that country were indeed ended. The last stronghold of that wonderful family of Barca, after being pillaged, even to the plunder of its temples, by the last of its African lords, was surrendered to Lucius Marcius, and Spain thenceforth became a Roman province.

Incomprehensible as are the causes of the Roman movements during this singular and protracted campaign, the energy and ability with which they were conducted, are above all praise; and, for indefatigable activity and zeal, Scipio is unsurpassed even by the greatest of Roman generals, Julius Caesar. Three times, between the opening of the campaign and the final retirement of the Roman Army into its winter-quarters, did it march and counter-march, over the entire length of the Peninsula, from the Ebro, within a hundred miles of the Pyrenees, to the coasts of the Atlantic Ocean, from Tarragona to Cadiz, a distance of eight hundred Roman miles, six times repeated.

Two general battles of great magnitude were delivered; one army pursued, without a moment's delay, to total ruin; the other completely reduced and pacified. Three strong fortresses were taken by storm; the Carthaginian Capital, Cadiz, was admitted to surrender; a formidable mutiny was quelled with consummate ability. A whole country, not a single enemy left within its borders, rendered submissive to the authority of Rome, and Carthage stripped of her last foreign colony and laid open to the invasion of her unrelenting rival—these were the trophies of Scipio's fifth and most masterly Spanish campaign.

His rewards were the Consulship in the 549th year of Rome, the 205th before the Christian era; Sicily as his province, the war in Africa as his command, the Battle of Zama and the consummation of the second Punic war, as his crowning glory.

Singular, indeed, are the coincidences of this man's career, even to the number of his campaigns, the style of his strategy, his fortunate daring in the assault of fortresses, the scene of his exploits and their termination, with that of the far greater man whose departure, full of years and honours, England is yet deploring—scarcely less striking than those between their mighty antagonists, Hannibal and Napoleon; but of this hereafter. Hannibal's last campaign in Italy had opened, Scipio's first in Africa was on the point of commencing, and the long contest of the rival empires was soon to close with a set duel, as it were, of their two most puissant champions.

At this time, it appears, commenced those jealousies and grudges, which, in spite of his eminent services, embittered all the future life of this great man, drove him into voluntary exile, and ultimately left his ashes in a foreign tomb.

It is not unnatural, that great jealousies should have arisen against the young conqueror, among the older and less successful generals, and among these, Quintius Fabius Maximus was his most constant and inveterate opponent. But it is evident, that Scipio conducted himself with a bold and boastful spirit; insisted on having Africa as his province; spoke of appealing from the Senate to the people, in case of his wishes being disregarded; and, with a touch of that secret superstition, or, as I believe it to have been, daring hypocrisy, founded on a not unjustifiable self-confidence, which has been noticed heretofore, proclaimed himself the predestined conqueror of Hannibal.

In the end, the Senate decreed to one of the Consuls Sicily, with the troops already in that province, consisting of the fugitives from Cannae, and other soldiers exiled to the island, for misconduct during the period of war, with a power to raise a force of volunteers, but not to hold new levies, and permission to cross over into Africa, at his pleasure.

The other was to have Bruttium, and the two *legions*, forming the regular Consular Army, left there by the magistrate whom he superseded.

By a mutual agreement, Scipio received Sicily, with permission to build a fleet of thirty men-of-war, by voluntary contribution of the colonies, and to levy a force of volunteers. With such energy was this accomplished, that twenty *quinqueremes*, or line-of-battle-ships, and ten *quadremes*, the second rates of the day, were launched, fully equipped, manned and armed, within forty-five days from the time the trees were standing in the forest; and, early in the spring, he sailed for his province with seven thousand volunteers, (*Livy* and *Appian*), of horse and foot combined, full of high hopes and confidence of victory

About the same time, in the early spring, Mago, having wintered in Minorca, as has been stated, landed in Liguria with six thousand infantry, (*Appian*), eight hundred horse and seven elephants, and having made himself master of Genoa, speedily drew together such a head of the disaffected Gauls as to cause the Romans considerable disquietude, though not enough, as he had hoped, to divert Scipio from the African expedition.

So far, indeed, was this from being the case, that the first care of that commander on reaching his province, was to send Laelius, who still accompanied him as his lieutenant, with a squadron to the African coast in order to renew his communications with Massinissa. And this he did so effectually, having surprised Hippo Regius, or Bona, within a hundred miles of Carthage, that he returned, after an absence of a few days only, with the strongest encouragement, and promises of the most ample support, laden with the rich spoils of the Barbary plains, then the granary of the world, which he had ravaged far and near.

In the meantime, however, Scipio had determined on a minor, yet highly important enterprise.

The city of Locri, one of the strongest and wealthiest of the Greek towns of lower Italy, had revolted from Rome to the Carthaginians, at the period of Hannibal's greatest successes; but now being weary, it is said, of the cruel Punic sway, or probably foreseeing the approaching ruin of that cause, offered to betray the garrisons of the citadels, of which there were two, one as a seaward defence, the other commanding the town, into the hands of Scipio.

And in consequence, Caius Pleminius, the *propraetor* at Rhegium made himself master of the one, but failed in surprising the other. For several days, the two fortresses remained in the possession, the one of Hamilcar, the other of the Romans, and they fought daily in the streets, until the citizens, uniting themselves with the Romans, shut up the former within his walls, and strictly blockaded him. Hannibal, who was encamped not far off on the River Butrotum, marched down in force to the rescue, and, having sent instructions to his people within the walls to sally and attack the Romans in the town and the citizens at daybreak, appeared unexpectedly, scouring the country with his Numidians, and would have retaken the place, but for the lack of scaling ladders and military engines.

That same night, Scipio crossed over the straits from Messina with his fleet, landed and occupied the town with his legions; and, when the Carthaginians would have renewed the assault at dawn, sallied from all the gates at once, cut to pieces two hundred of Hannibal's advanced parties, and forced him to call off his troops and raise the siege in haste, the Punic garrison escaping by night, having raised an alarm of conflagration, and overtaking their companions by a forced march, more resembling a flight than a retreat.

This was a vigorously conceived, and well-planted blow. By it Scipio recovered to the Romans a wealthy and powerful dependency, struck terror into the disaffected Italians of Magna Graecia, and gained the valuable prestige of having worsted Hannibal himself in the first encounter. Of the troubles which befell in Locri, I take no note; since they, and the cruelties to which they led, rest with Pleminius, not with Scipio; who returned to his own province, after striking this blow, in order to mature his plans for the African expedition.

It is worthy of remark, however, that during this summer, complaints were made of his conduct in Locri and Sicily, so grave as to induce the Senate to send commissioners to investigate the charges. These, on examination, wholly acquitted him, and doubtless on just grounds, since luxury, lasciviousness and tyranny—the things of which he was accused—do not appear to have been of the character of the man; and, on their report, the Senate at once decreed that he had permission to choose what force he should deem good, out of the Sicilian armies, and sail to Carthage on his own judgment.

In obedience he selected the fifth and sixth Roman legions, the defeated veterans of Cannae, whose ranks he supplied with picked men, till they numbered, each, six thousand two hundred foot and three hundred horse; he also chose, says Livy, cavalry and infantry from the allies of the Latin name, equally from the disgraced army of Cannae. For, says Livy, following Polybius, no doubt, he had not the least contempt for that soldiery, knowing that the frightful defeat they had sustained was owing to no cowardice of theirs, and, farther, that they were the oldest and most experienced veterans, and had seen more service, both in the field and in the attack of walled towns, than any other Roman soldiers.

These men had been, in fact, incessantly under arms and in active service for eleven years, during which time, as disgraced soldiers, they were not allowed to set foot on Italian soil, they were not allowed to partake in any noble or grand adventure, and were doubtless burning to retrieve their character by the utmost daring and devotion. On these feelings, no less on their skill and aptitude to arms, Scipio unquestionably relied. In him it was a wise reliance, and worthy of a soldier and a man; and to justify it, it needs only to be said that by them it was not disappointed.

The numbers of the armament, which was embarked in four hundred transports covered by forty line-of-battle ships, with distinguishing ensigns and lanthorns, with provision and water for five and forty days, remain somewhat in doubt. Appian states them at sixteen thousand foot, and sixteen hundred horse. Livy confesses himself unable to come to a decision, since:

> The army is variously described as numbering from twelve thousand two hundred, to thirty-five thousand horse and foot.

Doubtless the truth lay intermediate; and taking into consideration the foregoing statements concerning the army of Cannae, we shall be irresistibly led to the conclusion, that Scipio carried with him a regular consular army, neither more nor less in numbers, though in quality and material probably the best that Rome ever sent out, anterior to the days of Caesar.

Now, a regular consular army consisted of two Roman legions—and two, the fifth and sixth, we are accordingly told that he did carry—and two allied legions of the Latin name—in accordance with which we find that he did select Latin foot and horse. Hence, we shall, I think, hardly err in assuming that there were not only two Latin *legions*, but the identical two Latin *legions*, which served, were defeated and exiled, in conjunction with the fifth and sixth Roman *legions*, and were now permitted with them to retrieve their tarnished reputation. We are expressly told, that the two Roman *legions* consisted each of six thousand two hundred foot, and three hundred horse. The contingent of the Latin legion was equal in infantry to that of the Roman legion, but the force of cavalry was doubled.

We have, therefore, on this base of computation—

Two Roman *legions*—12,400 foot + 600 horse = 13,000 men.
Two Latin *legions*—12,400 foot + 1200 horse = 13,600 men.

Scipio's army, therefore, numbered in all twenty-six thousand six hundred men, of whom only eighteen hundred were horse; so weak habitually were the Romans in this important arm of the service, never with them a favourite, or one in which they excelled.

At daybreak, on the morning after their departure from the port of Lilybaeum, now Marsala, the fleet made Fair Promontory, within a few miles' distance of the port of Carthage; and there, Scipio accepting the name as an omen of good, the fleet cast anchor, and the troops disembarked, and prepared an entrenched camp, without opposition.

Thence, sending his fleet around to Utica, after defeating a reconnoitring party of Carthaginian horse and killing their leader, Hanno, he marched inland, ravaging the country, and took by assault a wealthy African town, in which besides capturing vast booty, he liberated eighteen thousand Roman and Latin slaves, who had pined for years in hopeless captivity in that hated land, the spoil of Hannibal's long ravages in the heart of the Republic.

These, with the booty, he sent back to Sicily by the transports; and then marched inland, in a circuitous direction southward and westward, avoiding Carthage, which he left on his right, she having no force present with which to encounter him in the field. Then, having effected his junction with Massinissa, he sat down before Utica, with his kind forces, while his fleet blockaded it strictly by sea.

Since last the friends had met, the Numidian prince had encountered nothing but disasters. He had succeeded to the crown of his father, Gala, but had been dispossessed of it by Syphax, and the Carthaginians, and was now a fugitive and exile from his kingdom . He brought but two hundred Numidian horse to the Roman camp; but he brought what was of far more worth—his own indefatigable energy and zeal; his deathless hatred of Carthage; his perfect knowledge of the country; his incomparable skill and ardour as a partisan officer, and last, not least, the hearts, if not the arms, of all his countrymen.

Carthage shook to her foundation stone with perturbation and dismay—yet she strained every nerve, and, within forty days after Scipio's trenches were opened against Utica, had collected two mighty armies with which to raise the siege. Hasdrubal arrived the first with thirty thousand foot and three thousand horse, and a few days later, Syphax, with fifty thousand Numidian infantry, and ten thousand of their unrivalled cavalry. Scipio, who had tried every mode already by which to carry Utica, now tranquilly drew off his men, without tumult or loss, and occupying a rocky peninsula connected with the main land by a low sandy neck, fortified it strongly, having his fleet drawn up on the northern or seaward shore, his legions in cantonments on the ridge, and his cavalry on the southern slope, commanding the isthmus. The enemy encamped, separately but not far asunder, hard by, to observe his motions. So closed that autumn, and Scipio's first African campaign.

In the meantime, the consular elections had been held at Rome; and it is worthy of remark, as a proof that the dread of Hannibal and Carthaginian progress was at length dying out, if not extinct, at Rome, that two persons were chosen to be the chief magistrates of the Republic, who were in no sort remarkable as Generals, Cneius Servilius Caepio, and Caius Servilius Germinus.

This was the sixteenth year of the second Punic war, and the 550th year of Rome, equivalent to the 204th before the Christian era. The *Imperium*, or Consular power for Africa, without the rank or title, was given to Scipio, not for the year, as was usual, nor for any limited time, but until the conclusion of the war. And this he was not inclined to procrastinate.

During the whole of the winter season, it appears that he maintained a system of negotiations with Syphax, under, as it were, an understanding of armistice, whether a cessation of hostilities was actually proclaimed or not.

The object of these, might have been, in the first instance, what they appeared to be; a plan to bring over Syphax from the Carthaginian to the Roman party; but it is difficult to understand how Hasdrubal, and the Carthaginian forces, should have tacitly sanctioned proceedings, the avowed intent of which was to deprive them of their last ally.

However this might have been, finding that he made no progress in detaching Syphax from the Punic alliance, Scipio soon resolved on a different line of action; and how far his conduct on this occasion came within the limits acceded to military chiefs, under the term stratagems, it is not easy to resolve.

It cannot be denied that, both on the occasion of the mutiny of his own soldiers on the Xucar, and in the present instance, the character of Scipio is tainted with the suspicion of treachery, to say no more; and in my own opinion, his whole career shows the man not alien from the charge of hypocrisy.[10]

During the whole period of these negotiations, officers were coming and going under flags between the Roman and African headquarters, and in the train and under the protection of these, Scipio

---

10. I am aware that I have been censured by a candid and friendly critic—in the North American Review—for over stringency in my judgments of the characters of the Greek leaders, especially, Miltiades, Themistocles and Alexander, as if I weighed them in the scales of Christian morality, not of heathen virtue. If it be so, I am not aware of it; nor is it in my desire or my plan to do so. I find these men short of the standard which I recognise in Xenophon, and in Epaminondas, leaders in whom I see nothing tortuous. Scipio, in like sort, falls short, to my eyes, as measured beside chiefs, so faulty even as Marcellus or Caesar, much less beside one so noble as Titus Quinctius Flamininus.

organised a regular system of espionage. Veteran soldiers, and shrewd subalterns, in the disguise of camp followers and slaves, made themselves intimately acquainted with all the localities of the camps, all the accidents of their avenues, outlets and defences, all the secrets of their patrols and watch-settings. The African and Carthaginian armies were hutted out on two separate though neighbouring eminences, in temporary buildings, if they may so be termed, of the most inflammable materials—reeds, hurdles, and slight wooden frames covered with palm leaves.

The inflammable nature of the materials suggested the design; and it proved as easy of accomplishment, as of conception.

At the dead of night, the armistice not having been, as it would seem, formally denounced, the Roman forces marched out silently in two divisions. Laelius against the camp of Syphax; Scipio himself against that of Hasdrubal.

Massinissa with his Numidians, and all the horse, was detached earlier, and ambushed on the line of the enemy's retreat.

Then the Numidian huts of Syphax were fired to the windward; the flames ran through these combustibles as over a train of gunpowder; and suspecting nothing less than the presence of an enemy, the terrified inmates rushed out tumultuous and unarmed to extinguish them.

They were driven in, on all sides, by the compact masses of the legionaries; above forty thousand men were roasted alive, in their blazing tenements, trampled under foot by one another in the crowded gateways, slaughtered by the unsparing Roman broadsword. It must have been a very Gehenna upon earth.

Thousands of Arab horses, thousands of camels, dromedaries, hundreds perhaps of elephants, bursting their picket ropes, trampling all under foot in mad stampede, blazing and shrieking into the desert darkness, so many living comets.

Armed men and tender women, helpless babes—for as the Arabs now, the Numidians then had their city in their camp—shrieking in hopeless anguish among the relentless flames. The cheers without of the savage *legionaries*, and the thundering charge of Massinissa's fiery horse on the few wretched fugitives.

Meantime, from the other camp, aroused by the roar of the flames, and the shrieks of their perishing allies, out poured the Carthaginians; unarmed, at first, to wonder, to assist, to tremble—then to rush hastily to arms, to endeavour to form, to be charged home in the darkness, cut down, surrounded, driven back into their quarters, and to find them, too, blazing in a white heat.

Of them, thirty thousand men perished. Of the Numidians, sixty thousand strong, all were destroyed, or so utterly dispersed that they never rallied again to arms, Syphax alone, and a handful of cavalry, excepted.

Never perhaps in all the hideous annals of war, was such a horror.

But for this, shudder as we may, and pity and abhor, we may not reproach Scipio.

Such is the fearful game of war, such the appalling duty of those who play at it—to sink, burn, capture, and destroy.

And this is the game at which, in our Christian nineteenth century, grave senators, gray-headed men with one foot in the grave, would make the nations play, in very wantonness of wild ambition, prating of destiny and progress.

Scipio resumed the siege of Utica, which held out like a Spanish city, like Saguntum, Numantia, glorious Saragossa.

She knew what it was to be taken by a Roman, what it was to surrender to those who never spared.

With considerable spirit and constancy, Carthage resolved to persist; ordered new levies; decreed, once more, to try her fortune in the field.

Scipio could not take Utica, dared not attempt Carthage.

With celerity, which proves their generalship, Syphax and Hasdrubal again took the field, with thirty thousand men; reinforced by four thousand Spaniards, recently raised in Spain, and transported to the seat of war.

The battle which followed was brief, summary, decisive. The Numidians, raw levies and young soldiers, could not stand the Roman horse; the Carthaginians were swept away like chaff before a whirlwind, by the unbridled charge of Massinissa's Arabs. The Spaniards, hopeless of quarter, fought to the last, and were butchered to a man by the legionaries.

The victors were wearied by the slaughter, not by the conflict.

Then was it seen that Carthage was not Rome, but a community of traffickers—not a proud and dauntless aristocracy.

After Cannae, Rome sent abroad two legions into Spain, two more to Sicily.

After the slaughter of "the Great Plains," Carthage recalled Mago from Liguria, Hannibal from Bruttium. Before they could arrive she treated.

She must withdraw from Italy and Gaul; she must surrender all her colonies, all her islands between Africa and Italy, all her war-ships save twenty, she must pay a vast sum of money to defray the expenses of the war.

Hard terms for the haughty mistress of the seas, before whom so late all but the pride of Rome lay prostrate.

Yet she assented. A truce was concluded with Scipio. Ambassadors were sent to Rome.

Meanwhile, Mago's division, recalled from Liguria, arrived on the African coast; himself, mortally wounded in his last action with Quinctilius Varius in the Milanese, died at sea.

Meanwhile, news arrived that Hannibal himself was on the Mediterranean. Then the truce was broken.

History says by the Carthaginians; but history is Roman—is in this case Polybius, the friend and panegyrist of Scipio.

He tells us that the Carthaginians wantonly seized some Roman transports, driven by a storm into the bay of Carthage; refused satisfaction to Scipio's envoys; and endeavoured treacherously to seize those envoys returning to Utica, in violation of their flag.

Hence Scipio was enraged, reasonably and justly; denounced the truce, and renewed the war; but still could not take Utica.

So Polybius.

Dr. Arnold says:

> But it is probable that a Carthaginian narrative of the war in Africa would so represent the matter, that posterity would esteem the behaviour of the Carthaginians, in breaking off the truce when it suited their convenience, as neither more nor less dishonourable than the conduct of Scipio himself, when he set fire to the camps of Syphax and Hasdrubal; and that, although the success was different, yet the treachery in both cases, whatever it may have been, was pretty nearly equal.

By this time Hannibal had landed, and the end was at hand.

He landed at Leptis, now Lebida, a town on the coast, between Cape Bona and Cape Paul, and after refreshing his troops for a few days at Adrumetum, marched directly inland to a place named Zama, five days' journey to the west of Carthage, in the vicinity of which Scipio was devastating the country and capturing the inland towns.

Scipio immediately marched to meet him, having been joined a few days before by Massinissa, with six thousand foot and four thousand of his indomitable and indefatigable horse.

An interview, it appears, took place between the generals on the day before the action; but the details of the conference and the speeches, as related by Polybius and Livy, are manifestly framed to suit Roman tastes, and more particularly to flatter the vanity of the Scipios.

All that we truly know is this, that the conference had no results, and that if an accommodation was proposed, it fell to the ground bootless.

So they met at Zama—the general, who had never lost a battle, and the chief who had conquered all his lieutenants; the general whose glory was Italian, and he whose fame was won in Spain; even as at Waterloo, about two thousand years afterward, and at the close of a similar yet vaster struggle, there met two strangely similar, and similarly pitted champions. And at Zama, as at Waterloo, the brighter and more dazzling genius fell, defeated by the nation, rather than by the man who opposed him.

The child of fortune stood on the threshold of his fate. And his fate was his country's doom.

The forces of the respective armies are not stated, but it is probable that numerically they were nearly equal, if the Romans were not superior, since the Latin historians would assuredly not have held silent, had their forces been inferior.

In quality, however, the Romans were vastly superior. From the first day of the war, the Roman infantry, even their raw, levies, were equal if not superior to the Carthaginian veterans, and, as Dr. Arnold remarks, never had been beaten behind works.

These men were picked veterans of twelve years' service.

And now the superb Numidian cavalry, the arm by which Hannibal had won all his battles, or at least a vast preponderance of it, was on the Roman side.

Hannibal had, it is true, above eighty elephants; but neither at Zama, nor in any other great action, was much effected by their means. They generally injured their own party at least as much as the enemy; and on this occasion Scipio had arranged his forces purposely with a view to frustrating their onset.

In lieu of his ordering the maniples of his three divisions, of *hastati*, *principes*, and *triarii*, in *quincunx*, or like the squares of a chess-board, as was usual, he placed them each in the rear of that before it, leaving long lanes or intervals from the van to the rear; which he filled with light troops in loose order, whose duty it should be to attract the elephants, and draw them harmlessly to the rear, and out of the action.

Caius Laelius was on the left wing with the Roman and Latin horse; Massinissa with his Numidians on the left.

Hannibal had his mercenaries, Ligurians, Celtic Gauls, Balearians and Moors, twelve thousand strong, in his front line—but none now of those hardy, active Spanish foot, in their white linen coats with scarlet hems, whose short stabbing swords had done such deadly work at Cannae—his Carthaginian veterans, like the heroes of the Imperial Guard, he held in reserve, trusting, like his great successor, with them to " strike" the decisive blow, as he had ever done before, and conquer with a thunderstoke.

On his right, he had his Carthaginian *cuirassiers* facing the Italian horse of Laelius; his Numidians he opposed, on his left, to the Numidians of the fierce and headlong Massinissa; but these were outnumbered as two to one, and were perhaps confused and distracted by being opposed to their own countrymen on their own soil, and to a native prince.

The battle began by a charge of the elephants, on the part of Hannibal; but being alarmed by the trumpets and shouting of the Romans, and galled by the skirmishers, some were teased down the intervals of his lines to Scipio's rear, some recoiled to the left and right, and, falling in among their own horse, disordered them. Then Laelius with the Italians charged the *cuirassiers* home; and Massinissa, disdaining to skirmish after the Numidian fashion, broke in like a torrent, with levelled lances on his countrymen.

Both conquered easily; and, on both wings, elephants, *cuirassiers* and Numidians were scattered in wild flight over the sandy plains, and slaughtered for miles in swift and merciless pursuit.

Meantime, the main armies joined, and a conflict ensued, such as perhaps never had occurred during the war. The foreign mercenaries of Carthage were, however, overmatched by the Roman *hastati* and *principes*, and, not being properly supported by the second line of Africans, were at last beaten after a severe struggle. Then, in revenge, they fell on the Africans, and cut them down, while the bloody broadswords of the *legionaries* were fleshed fiercely in their rear.

Hannibal was compelled to make his reserve present their spears, to preserve themselves unbroken, against his own fugitives; and when the broken mob of these reeled out of the action, and dispersed by the wings towards the rear, the Romans found themselves opposed to a new army, the invincibles of Hannibal's Italian conquests; the victors of the Ticinus, of the Trebia, of Thrasymene and Cannae; the men who had never fought but to conquer; to whom battle was pastime, and victory the breath of life.

There was a stern pause—a breathing spell.

Scipio reinforced his lines with the long spears of his *triarii*.

Hannibal brought up his last reserves.

Then, as at Marengo, one battle ended, a second was begun, fiercer, deadlier, decisive, but with a different issue.

The men were matched, as perhaps never wore others; and the fight raged and reeled, hand to hand, foot to foot, cruelly fought with short weapons. Whole ranks went down where they stood, on both sides, with all their wounds in front; and other ranks strode over them, to meet, and fall, and be succeeded in like fashion.

There was no thought of flight or retreat on either side. Romans nor Carthaginians flagged nor wavered. The battle was balanced, until, above the din and clang of blades and brazen bucklers, loud rose the yell of Massinissa's returning Arabs, and the bloody spears of the Numidians and the broadswords of Caius Laelius plunged with fatal execution into the defenceless masses of the Carthaginian rear.

Twenty thousand men were slain in the battle, twenty thousand more were made prisoners. Hannibal, accompanied by a handful of horse, as Arnold well observes:

> With a nobler fortitude than his brother had shewn at the Metaurus, escaped to Hadrumetum. He knew that his country would now need his assistance more than ever; and as he had been in so great a degree the promoter of the war, it ill became him to shrink from bearing his full share of the weight of its disastrous issue.

The Field of Zama ended the Second Punic war; ended almost, indeed, the history of Carthage. That hapless city had no second army, which to risk in the field. Hannibal counselled peace; and peace the conquerors granted, but upon terms which were only not destruction. All their possessions out of Africa must be surrendered; all their war ships except ten; all their elephants must be given up; all their prisoners, all their deserters restored. They must undertake no war out of Africa; nor any in Africa, but with the consent of Rome; their country must be occupied, at their own expense, for three months by the Roman army; and, in conclusion, they must pay the vast sum of ten thousand Euboic talents, or nearly three hundred thousand pounds sterling, as the price of peace.

Hannibal returned to Carthage beaten, but not outgeneraled; and, as he had shown himself his country's greatest soldier in war, he proved himself her best citizen in peace; in both greater than his more fortunate but unequal rival.

Persecuted to death, unworthily, by the great nation with whom he had warred so magnificently, he died, like his mighty follower. Napoleon, miserably and in exile.

Scipio returned to Rome, triumphed, was loaded with honours, and styled the Saviour of his country, Africanus.

Here the glory of his career ends; and here I quit him.

Of his after services against Antiochus I shall not speak; for—though his arms were attended with their usual success—he served only as lieutenant to his brother Asiaticus; and it cannot be determined to whom should attach the greater share of the glory.

Thus far his career was singularly parallel with that of Wellington, as was that of Napoleon with his far greater antagonist—but here the parallelism ends.

Scipio fell into disgrace with his countrymen, partly through their turbulence and party spirit, partly, it would seem, through his own arrogance, and never recovered their favour. He died in voluntary exile at Liternum, and the sad motto on his tomb, *Ingrata patria ne quidem ofsa habebis*, (Ungrateful country, thou shalt not even hold my bones), offers a strange and gloomy contrast to the superb pomp of sorrow with which a nation bore her hero to the grave, when in the noble mausoleum of St. Paul, the conqueror of Trafalgar received the conqueror of Waterloo.

2

Titus Quinctius Flamininus

Of all the truths at which we arrive through a calm and dispassionate study of history, none appears to me more certain than this, that, as regards the career and course of empires, the rise and fall of states, there neither is, nor has been, any such thing as Fortune; that from the beginning of time, to the events born of the present day, every minute particular, every seemingly unimportant incident—or, as men are fond to call it, accident—in the affairs of nations is part and parcel of one grand, universal, all-pervading scheme of divine world-government, projected before the patriarch kings led forth their flocks to feed on pastures yet moist with the waters of the deluge, but not to be fulfilled until time itself shall have an end.

It can hardly, I think, fail to strike the least observant of readers, that unless the civilized world had been for a long period chained together under the stagnant, and in the main, peaceful despotism of the successors of the twelve Caesars, it never would have been prepared to receive that tincture of letters, of humanity, and above all, of Christian faith, with which it became in the end so thoroughly imbued; that in every case, without one exception, it brought over to its own milder cultivation, milder religion, the fiercest and most barbarous of its heathen conquerors.

Not a province of the Western Roman empire but was overrun, devastated, conquered, permanently occupied by hordes of the wildest, crudest, most violent, most ignorant of mankind—Goths, Vandals, Huns, Vikings, and Norsemen, Jutes and Danes, tribes whose very names to this day stand as the types of unlettered force and unsparing outrage. Not a province of that empire, though of its present population not one hundredth part can trace an approximate descent from the original Roman colonists, so vast the influx of the Pagan invaders, but in the lapse of time conquered its conquerors by the arts of peace, and so became the germ of that Christian civilization, that Christian liberty, which—though either, or both, may be temporarily obscured for the moment—we see, in the main, steadily and consistently pervading the Europe and America of the nineteenth century.

That this state of things could have existed, by any reasonable probability at this day, in the event of Darius or Xerxes having overrun and occupied Western Europe, with their oriental hordes—in the event of Carthage having subdued Rome, and filled Italy, Greece, Gaul, Spain, Britain, with her bloody fiend-worship, and her base Semitic trade-spirit—in the event of Mark Antony having won the day at Actium, and broken up the heritage of Rome, like that of Alexander, among a dozen jarring dynasties, instead of leaving it to be centralized into an almost universal empire—in the event of the Saracen having destroyed the *paladins* of Charles Martel at Tours—of the Turks having conquered the Mediterranean at Lepanto, or Continental Europe under the walls of Vienna—few will be found, I think, so hardy as to assert.

Strange, therefore, as it may appear at first sight, the first germs of existing institutions may be said to have been sown on the banks of the Ilissus, the Eurotas, and the Tiber; and the deity, whom the blind superstition of the early Romans venerated as the war-god Quirinus guarding the wave-rocked cradle of Rome's twin founders, was, in truth, the Lord of Hosts, watching over the infancy of that peculiar and appointed people which should make smooth his way before him, and prepare the nations to receive the faith of civil and religious freedom.

For all this wonderful accomplishment of wonderful designs, however, we shall find that the instruments are purely human, although the ends may be divine—that, although the men are never wanting to do His work, when done it must be, it is for the most part, if not always, in blindness, in sin, in wrath, and in the madness of ambition, that they do that work, imagining themselves, vainly, busied about their own miserable ends; and for the doing it they are alone accountable. But not so of the nations, which, having no life hereafter, no individual identity in the world to come, meet their rewards or punishments here, where their virtues or their vices have required them, and thrive or perish as they work toward the completion of His infinite designs.

Nowhere, perhaps, in the whole course of history, is this supervision of the Most High, which even religious men are wont unthinkingly to call Fortune, more clearly visible than in the events of the

Second Punic War.

At home the republic, though undaunted and unequalled of all times in heroism, was weeping tears of blood at every pore, and resisting only with a persistency savouring almost of despair. Abroad it was only by the exercise of sacrifices and self-denial almost superhuman, that she was enabled to maintain her foothold in her provinces of Sicily and Spain.

It seems to us, when we read how Capua, the noblest of her allied cities, opened her gates and made common cause with the enemy, how twelve of the thirty colonies of the Latin name refused their contingents of men and money; how all the north of Italy, then Cisalpine Gaul, from the Var to the Rubicon, was in tumultuous arms against her; how all the proud and magnificent cities of La Puglia and Calabria were leagued with the terrible invader; it seems, I say, as if one superadded call on her resources must have remained unanswered; one more war-trumpet blown by a new enemy must have sounded her death-note.

And there was one moment, when it appeared that this contingency was close at hand. In the year of the city 540, while all the south of Italy was in arms with Hannibal from Capua down to the Gulf of Taranto, and all the north was in that tumultuous state of disorganisation which with Celtic populations is ever the herald of coming insurrection, Sardinia suddenly broke out into open and armed rebellion. Sicily, also, in which Hiero, the fast and faithful friend of Rome, had lately died at a very advanced age, rejected the Roman alliance, and a war of extermination was raging in that beautiful island between the partisans of the two rival powers, and the forces which each could spare from the home conflict to aid its faction.

At this crisis, Philip of Macedon, the descendant of Alexander, and at that time the most powerful of European princes, entered into an alliance, offensive and defensive, with Hannibal, and would in the course of that very summer have crossed the Adriatic, and invaded Italy with some five-and-twenty thousand men, sixteen thousand of whom were the hitherto unconquered phalanx, provided with that arm, in the greatest possible perfection, the want of which had robbed Hannibal of the fruits of all his great pitched battles—I mean an efficient artillery.

In this respect the Greeks were unsurpassed; the Greek engineers were the wonder of the world, as was subsequently shown at the siege of Syracuse; and how great soever the superiority of the Romans to the Carthaginians in this arm of service, it was as nothing to the skill of the Greek artillerists, and the excellence of the Greek machinery.

What this combination might—I should rather say might not—have effected, it were difficult to show; more difficult to show how Rome could have resisted it. For my part, having examined the question in all its lights, I am of opinion that, had this alliance gone into effect, and Philip acted with energy and steadiness of purpose equal to his bravery and ambition, Marcellus never would have taken Syracuse, nor Scipio conquered Spain; but that from both those countries triumphant reinforcements would have poured in to Hannibal, over the Alps, across the straits of Messina, that an Italian Zama would have sealed the doom of Rome, and a Punic ploughshare razed the foundations of the capitol.

But such—it is well for humanity—was not to be the issue of the war. Philip's ambassadors, returning with the treaty signed and ratified by Hannibal, were taken by the Roman squadron off the Calabrian coast, and sent to the city with their papers.

A year elapsed before the treaty could be renewed; and, meantime, the Romans, awakened to a perception of their danger, found means to enkindle the Ætolians and Illyrian pirates against Philip, and in the end to organise a Greek confederation against Macedon, which gave its active and ambitious sovereign plenty of work to do on his own side of the Adriatic. At a later period he found cause to repent that he had ever meditated intervention.

Such strokes of fortune, so historians call them, as that capture of the ambassadors of Philip, which, perhaps, saved Rome—as that strong gale which blew on Christmas Eve on Bantry Bay, dispersing Hoche's armament to the four winds of heaven—such strokes, I say, of fortune, I hold to be the visible agencies and instruments of God's providence, in the government of nations, to the welfare of the world.

From Rome that peril was averted. The arms of Macedon abstained, perforce, from the shores of devastated Italy. The arms of Syracuse, of Spain, were wrested from the hands which would have wielded them in the behalf of Carthage. The arms even of the unbridled Numidians were turned against the masters whom they had served so fatally for Rome. And out of the furnace of that scathing war, the giant form of the chosen republic emerged, without one hair singed, one thread of its vestments injured; and that, like the faithful sons of Israel, by the especial providence of the Almighty.

Years passed, and events hurried toward their consummation. Yet still, though from this date the tide of Hannibal's affairs began to ebb, and that of Rome's to flow with a healthier, prouder current, it was not until twelve more terrible campaigns had been fought out in vain, that the star of the great Carthaginian set in blood at Zama, and the name of Carthage herself, all but one brief spasmodic sound of fury and despair, went out and was forgotten from among the nations.

Then rousing herself, like a galled lioness, Rome went forth to avenge and conquer.

Hitherto she had fought at home for existence, henceforth she fought abroad for dominion; and abroad as at home, until her mission was accomplished and His work done fully to the end, she was invincible, as the fruit of her labours is eternal.

The war, which had been undertaken against Philip by the Romans shortly after his giving them the first offence, had languished from the beginning on both sides, and peace had been concluded between the contending parties some three years before the decisive victory of Zama.

So soon, however, as peace was concluded with Carthage, in the year of the city 552, B. C. 200, true to the latter part at least of her famous motto,

Parcere devictis et debellare superbos,[1]

Rome sought at once a cause of war, whereby to chastise Philip for the comfort given to her enemies in her worst time of need. Nor sought long in vain.

A deputation from the Athenians came seeking succor; the arms of Philip were too near their borders.

War was declared, the Consul Sulpicius landed at Dyrrachium with a regular army, and the campaign commenced by a series of operations in the valley of the River Erigon, in Dassaretia, the object of Philip being to prevent that of the consul to secure his junction with his Dardanian and Ætolian allies. Several sharp skirmishes occurred, in all of which the Macedonians were worsted with loss, and in one instance Philip narrowly escaped being taken prisoner; whereupon he retreated through the mountain-passes, throwing up strong field-works in every available position, but avoiding a general action.

His works all proved useless, being either forced or turned without difficulty by the active and movable legionary tactic of the Romans, against which it became at once evident that so ponderous and un-

---

1. "*To spare the conquered and subdue the proud*,"—the former of which she never did.

wieldy a body as the *phalanx* could not manoeuvre or fight, in broken ground, with a hope of success.

In the end Philip retired at his leisure into his hereditary kingdom, and the consul having stormed and garrisoned the small town of Pelium, on the Macedonian frontier, fell back to Apollonia on the Illyrian sea coast, without accomplishing his object.

Still his campaign had not been useless, for he had snatched the prestige of invariable success from the phalanx, had established the incontestable superiority of the Roman soldiery of all arms to the Greek, and had defeated the Macedonians on every occasion, when they had ventured to await battle.

It is not a little remarkable, and proves clearly the singular adaptability of the Romans to all martial practices, that whereas, scarce twenty years before, we find their cavalry the worst in all respects but personal valour in the known world, and their light troops unable to compete even with the barbarian allies of Hannibal, we now observe them superior in both these arms, owing, as it is distinctly stated by all the writers, to the superior excellence of their weapons, (*Livy*), and equipment, even to the far-famed targeteers and life-guards of Macedonia.

In the following year, Sulpicius was superseded by the new consul, Publius Villius Tappulus, who, taking command of Sulpicius' legions at Apollonia, advanced up the open valley of the Aöus, now Vioza, with the intention of forcing the famous passes, variously known as the Aoi Stenae, or Fauces Antigonenses, and now as the defiles of the Viosa, rather than turning them by way of Dassaretia, as had been done previously by his predecessor. The judgment was sound, the execution naught. For, after marching to within five miles of the western extremity of the defiles, he fortified his camp in the plain, "probably in the valley of the Dryno, [2] above its junction with the Vioza, reconnoitred the position of Philip, who was very strongly posted, in an entrenched camp, at the most difficult point of the pass, a cheval on the river, and occupying both the mountain sides, and there lay perfectly inactive until he was himself relieved by Titus Quinctius Flamininus, his successor in the consular dignity."

This man, of the early Roman leaders, was in many respects one of the most remarkable; in one particular, with the single exception of Caius Julius Caesar, the great Dictator, he stands alone, in honourable contrast to his merciless and cruel countrymen—though quick and

---

2. Col. Leake, *Travels in Northern Greece*, i..

vehement of temper, he was a just man, and both merciful and courteous to conquered enemies. The one blot on his character, to which I shall come hereafter, must be ascribed to the policy of his country, under direct orders from which he was unquestionably acting, not to his own wishes or disposition, to which nothing could be more abhorrent than the duty imposed upon him.

Plutarch informs us that, in his time, "it was easy to judge of his personal appearance," which, unfortunately, he has not described, "from his statue in brass at Rome, inscribed with Greek character, which still stands opposite to the hippodrome, nigh to the great Apollo from Carthage."

As, however, the whole tenor of Plutarch's life is laudatory, and for that gossiping anecdote-monger singularly correct and clear, we may take it as a fact that the nobility of his person was not unequal to that of his character; which I consider the finest recorded of any Roman general or statesman. The author I have already quoted continues:

> He is said to have been of a temperament impulsive and vehement both in his likings and dislikings, but with this distinction, that he was quick to wrath, which quickly passed away, but prompt to kindness which endured to the end. He was very ambitious and very fond of glory, ever anxious to be the actor himself in the best and greatest deeds, and rejoicing in the acquaintance rather of those who needed benefits themselves, than of those who could confer them upon others, esteeming those as material for the promotion of his own virtue, these as rivals of his own glory.

I will add that I can find him guilty of no act—almost alone of his countrymen—of political dishonesty, or of social turpitude. To his country he was a zealous, ardent, and profitable servant; to his friends and associates faithful and true; to his enemies just and clement; and to the provincials, subjected to his dominion, a governor so affable, beneficent and equitable, that when he left their shores they mourned as for a countryman, almost a father of the country.

As a general, he committed no military error; and although his command was limited to little more than two campaigns, they were campaigns of the most important—important not merely to his own country, but to the science of war in general—since they established, beyond a peradventure, the superiority of the tactic and armature of the *legion* to those of the *phalanx*; in other words, of the line to the column tactic.

I give to him this credit, unhesitatingly; for, although Pyrrhus was at last beaten with the *phalanx* in Italy, it was rather by dint of numbers and aid of circumstances than by military skill; and further, it is evident that the great bulk of his armies consisted of targeteers, little different from the *legionaries*, and of Samnites, Tarentines, and other Italian soldiery precisely similar to them, in arms and array.

Again, although Sulpicius had demonstrated the superiority of the individual Roman, to the individual Greek heavy footman; he had not—nor anyone else hitherto—defeated a *phalanx*, unless with a *phalanx*.

When Greeks met Greeks then was the tug of war.

For the rest, the battles of Paullus Æmilius against Perseus, were but the Battles of Flamininus against the father of Perseus, less ably fought, though on the same principles at last successful.

The fact remains, that from the Battle of Cynoscephalae, of which anon, to the end of ancient history, it was an admitted fact, that, unless on a very narrow and perfectly level field, where both its flanks were securely covered, the *phalanx* could not receive battle from the legions with a chance of success; and that as to delivering battle on wide open plains, where rapid manoeuvring and counter-marching could be resorted to, such an idea was preposterous.

Flamininus was educated to arms from his very boyhood, and that in the terrible Italian campaigns of Hannibal; through which he served with such distinction that he had already attained the post of tribune of the soldiers, equal to the modern rank of lieutenant-colonel, under that daring and distinguished leader, Marcus Marcellus, and was on the field when he was slain, rashly periling himself in an affair of outposts near Venusia, in the year of Rome 546, B. C. 208, and in the sixtieth year of his own age.

After the death of his great commander, Flamininus was appointed governor of Tarentum, (*Livy*), in the capacity of quaestor, on its recapture by Fabius Maximus; and there displayed no less ability in the administration of justice than he had previously evinced skill and courage in warfare. Seven years afterward—at the early age of thirty years—he was elected consul; and, although opposed by the veto, (*Livy*), of the tribunes Fulvius and Manlius Curius on the ground that he lacked twelve years of the legitimate age, and that he had never filled the intermediate grades of *aedile* and *praetor*, he was confirmed by the senate, and received Macedonia as his province by lot.

The fact is, that the wars of Hannibal had by this time taught the Romans that an over strict adherence to prescriptive formulae, in times of national peril, is disastrous; and that to meet the ablest adversaries the ablest men must be had, whether all the theoretic requisites to their election had been complied with or not.

Therefore Scipio, the elder Africanus, was sent to Spain with proconsular rank and a consular army, before he was of the just age to fill a *praetorship*.

Therefore Flamininus was elected consul at thirty, although the constitution expressly declared that no one should hold that dignity until he should have fully attained his forty-second year.

Such laws may be, perhaps, generally wise; but the breach of them is always so. Nor does history show any instances, worth remark, of youthful genius elevated by the popular call to early station, and subsequently found unworthy, from the days of Alexander, Scipio, and Flamininus, to those of Pitt and Napoleon.

Nor do I believe that the appointment of the consuls was really, though it was ostensibly, left to the chance of a lot, at least in times of actual war, and national emergency; since we invariably find the best man sent to the place where he was required, which could not always have occurred fortuitously. Doubtless those who superintended the balloting had some method of determining the result, as had the *augurs* and *haruspices* with regard to omens and sacrifices.

So Flamininus was not only elected consul at thirty, but obtained the seat of the great war for his province, and was empowered to pick nine thousand men, horse and foot, out of the Spanish and African veterans, inured to all that was known of warfare in those days by the campaigns of Hannibal and Scipio.

A grand occasion, indeed, and a superb command for an untried commander.

It appeal's that on his entering upon his office, Flamininus was detained some time at Rome, in order to superintend a fast and expiatory sacrifice on account of certain alleged prodigies of evil import; but it is certain that he had understood the consequences of the dilatory operations of his predecessors, and was resolute not to fall into the like error. He sailed from Brundusium for the island of Corcyra, now Corfu, which he occupied with eight thousand foot, and eight hundred horse, much earlier in the season than the preceding consuls had been wont to take the field: and, instantly passing over to the main, in a single line-of-battle ship, hurried onward by forced journeys to the camp, and superseded Villius, in the face of the enemy.

A few days afterwards, his reinforcements coming up, he called a council of war to determine whether a direct attack, or a flank movement through Dassaretia, was to be preferred. The council, of course, determined anything rather than direct action; but Flamininus, perceiving the facilities afforded by the geography of that broken, mountainous, forest-clad region, intersected by deep ravines and impracticable torrents, to the protracting of the war, resolved to take the bolder and more prudent course of trying conclusions, at once, with an enemy whose object it evidently was to act purely on the defensive, and to avoid delivering battle.

Yet, determined as he was, the difficulties of the ground were so great, and so skilfully had Philip availed himself of every defensible point, or coigne of vantage, that many days elapsed before he could decide on the mode of assault.

The River Aöus, now Vioza, an extremely large and powerful river, augmented at every half mile by fierce mountain torrents along the valley of which is the most direct pass into Macedonia proper, at this point breaks its way through a chain of exceedingly abrupt and precipitous, though not very lofty mountains, and forms a gorge of six miles in length, closely resembling that picturesque defile of the Delaware, with which many of my readers are doubtless familiar, known as the Water-Gap.

Forced into a space, two-thirds less than its ordinary breadth, the Aöus has here cut its way through the solid rock, between the mounts Asnaus and Aëropus, now Nemertzika and Trebusin, respectively to the left and right of the defile, which here runs nearly south-eastward. The right-hand mountain, Aëropus or Trebusin, is the loftier of the two, descending in a sheer wall of perpendicular and treeless rock to the brink of the only road, scarped out of the living limestone like a cornice above the torrent, which bathes the base of the opposite hill, leaving no level space between.

Colonel Leake, whose topography of the Grecian battles founded on minute personal inspection, is no less valuable than interesting, says:

> The mountain on the opposite or left bank of the river is the northern extremity of the great ridge of Nemertzika, Asnaus, much lower than that summit, but nearly equal to Trebusin

in height. At the top, it is a bare, perpendicular precipice, but the steep lower slope, unlike that of its opposite neighbour, is clothed with trees quite to the river. Through the opening between them is seen a magnificent variety of naked precipices and hanging woods, inclosing the broad and rapid stream of the insinuating river.—*Travels in Northern Greece*, vol. i

The road, difficult in any event to an army, if defended, is impracticable, (*Plutarch* and *Flamininus*).

In this prodigiously strong pass Philip had taken post, occupying the narrow road with the *phalanx*, and having his main body hutted comfortably among the loose crags of Aëropus, on a conspicuous summit of which was pitched his own royal pavilion, with the banner of Alexander waving over it. The slopes of the opposite hill, Asnaus, was held by Athenagoras, his lieutenant, with the light troops, and all the flanking crags and salient angles of the precipitous hills were mounted with the tremendous military engines, which, though of common use in the defence and attack of the fortresses, had never been brought into field service until now.

Immediately in front of this stern mountain gateway extended a small plain, midway between the Roman camp and the Macedonian lines; and here, after a fruitless parley and attempt at accommodation, from which both parties retired so much exasperated at their mutual pertinacity, that the river, which divided them, alone prevented their personal conflict, the light troops met in action from both armies.

It is scarce to be conceived how, with such obstacles against them, the Romans could have escaped destruction; but it is almost ever the case in mountain warfare that the attacking party is successful.

The gray mists of the early summer morning were still nestling among the crags, and brooding in the deep glades of the hanging woods, when the long, shrill blasts of the Roman trumpets announced the impetuous rush of the light troops; and on they went, headlong and invincible, carrying all before them, and driving in the Macedonian skirmishers like the foam of the Adriatic before the fury of the south-east wind.

There was no dust upsurging from the rocky road to shroud their advance, no smoke-clouds to veil them from the shot of the enemy's artillery. With their bright armour flashing in the sunbeams, as they streamed down the gaps in the mountain summits, and their blood-red banners and tall plumes tossing in the light morning air, on they came, dazzling and unobscured, a fair mark for the deadly missiles, arrows shot off in volleys, vast javelins which no human arm could launch, and mighty stones hurled from the catapults, as if from modern ordnance, which tore their ranks asunder, and levelled whole files to the earth at a blow.

But their extraordinary discipline and admirable armature enabled them to endure the storm; and they made their way through all opposition, until they met the *phalanx*, bristling with its impenetrable pikes, its flanks impregnably protected by the rocks here, by the river there, and its narrow front offering no point assailable. Then they were checked; but, even then, not beaten back, so stubborn was their Roman hardihood, so firm their resolution to be slain, not conquered.

All day long did that deep glen quake and shudder to the dread sounds of the mortal conflict; the thundering crash of the huge stone shot, shivering the trees and shivered on the crags; the hurtling of the terrible *falaricae*; the clash and clang of steel blades and brazen bucklers; the whirlwind of the charging horse; the shouts and shrieks and death-groans; the thrilling trumpets of the legions; the solemn *paeans* of the *phalanx*.

Only when the sun set, and the full, round moon came soaring coldly up above the tree-tops, flooding the bloody stream of the Aöus, and the corpse-encumbered gorge, with silver radiance, did the weary and shattered hosts draw off to their respective camps, from a strife so justly balanced, that none could say which had come off the better, none judge on which side the more or the better men had fallen.

That night, Flamininus sat in his tent alone, anxious, uncertain how to proceed, so terrible had been the loss of life, and so small the ad vantage; when a shepherd was introduced, sent by Charops, the prince of the Ætolians, who should conduct a detachment, by a wild mountain footpath, to a height in the enemy's rear, domineering his whole position.

Four thousand chosen veterans of infantry and three hundred horse, under a tribune of the soldiers, were detailed, instantly, for the service, which would occupy three days.

They should march all night long, such were their orders, for the summer moon was at its full, and the nights light as day and far more pleasant, as being soft with fragrant dews and the cool mountain air. By day, they should halt in some deep, bosky dell or forest glade, to rest and refresh themselves securely. So far as the nature of the ground should admit, the cavalry would lead the way, then halt on the last level. The vantage ground once gained, they should kindle a fire on the summit, but abstain from all active demonstration, till they should perceive the action in the defile at its height. Such were their orders; and in high hope they parted, carrying with them as a guide the shepherd, in chains, as a precaution against treachery, but encouraged by great promises, if faithful.

On the two following days, Flamininus skirmished continually with his light troops against Philip's outposts, relieving his men by divisions, more to divert the attention of the enemy from the stratagem which was in progress, than with any design to harass him; though in both points of view he succeeded admirably; for the superiority of the Roman light infantry soldier to the Greek skirmisher was great indeed, and the Macedonians lost many and good men.

On the third morning, (*Plutarch* and *Livy*), secure that all had gone well so far, by the immovable attitude of the enemy, neither elevated by any unexpected success, nor shaken by any suspicion of his danger, the consul drew up his legionary *cohorts*, in solid column of *maniples*, along the rocky road, before the sun had yet risen, and while the mountain mists still covered the distant peaks with an impenetrable veil.

His light troops, advanced on both flanks, pressed forward along the difficult hillsides, dashing the heavy dew in showers from the dripping underwood, and threatening the camps of Philip and Athenagoras both at once, with loud shouts and a storm of missiles.

Then were renewed the splendour, the obstinacy, and the carnage of the first encounter. Again the Roman *voltigeurs* drove in the enemy's outposts; and beat back the targeteers, who sallied from their works eager for the fray, from post to post, till they came within range of the artillery, when in their turn they began to suffer heavily.

But at this instant the sun arose; the mists melted gradually away from the bare peaks, which now stood forth glittering in the hazy sunshine. With indescribable anxiety the eyes of Flamininus were riveted upon the distant crag, indicated as the decisive point. There was a vapour floating round it dull and indistinct, and browner than the blue mist wreaths—but was it, could it be, the smoke-signal?

For a time all was an agony of doubt and suspense. His officers gathered about the consul; the *legionaries*, seeing their commanders' eyes all turned in one direction, gazed that way also, anxious if ignorant.

Browner the vapour grew and browner; now it soared upward, black as a thunder-cloud, darkening the azure skies, a manifest smoke-signal.

Jove! what a shout arose from the now triumphant cohorts! What a thrilling shriek of the shrill trumpets, answered faintly and remotely, as if from the skies, by another Roman blast, but liker to the scream of the mountain-vulture than to the clangour of pealing brass!—what a clang as of ten thousand *stithies*, when the Spanish blades smote home upon the Macedonian *targes!*

Yet still the men fell fast on both sides, although the Romans won their way, in spite of artillery and pike and sling-shot, at the sword's point; for the Greeks still fought stubbornly, and plied their dreadful engines with deliberate aim at point blank range, unconscious that they were surrounded.

Then came the Latin cheers, and the clang of arms, out of the clouds, rolling down the mountain side, on their flank, in their rear; the rush of charging horse!—In an instant they broke, disbanded, scattered, deserted their defences—all was over.

In the first instance the panic and route of the Macedonians were absolute; and so utterly disheartened and terror-stricken were the men, that, had it been possible to pursue them effectually, the whole army must have laid down its arms or have been cut to pieces.

The ground, (*Livy*), however, was for the most part impracticable to cavalry, and their heavy armature rendered the legions as inefficient in pursuit as formidable in close combat. About two thousand only of the Macedonians fell, more in the battle than in the route; but the whole of the formidable defences, on which they had expended so much time and toil, were carried at a blow, all their superb artillery, their camp, their baggage, rich with the barbaric pomp of the Macedonian royalty, all their camp followers and slaves, remained the prizes of the victors.

Philip, after he had fled five miles from the field, that is to say, so far as to the eastern extremity of the defile he had fruitlessly endeavoured to defend, at length perceiving that he was unpursued, and suspecting the reason, halted on a steep knoll covering the entrance of the pass, and sending out parties along the ridges and through the ravines with which they were familiar, soon collected all his men about his standard save those whom he had left on the field of battle, never to rouse to the trumpet or rally to the banner any more.

Thence he retreated rapidly down the valley of the Aöus, or Vioza, in a south-easterly direction to a place called the camps of Pyrrhus, supposed to be Ostanitza, near the junction of the Voidhomati and Vioza, (*Leake*), where he passed the night; and thence by a prodigious forced march of nearly fifty miles reached Mount Lingon on the following day, where he remained some time in doubt whither to turn his steps, and how to frame his further operations.

Mount Lingon is the eastern and loftiest extremity of a great chain of hills, dividing Macedonia proper from Thessaly on the east and Epirus on the west. It forms a huge, triangular bastion, its northern base overlooking Macedonia, and its apex facing due southward, which is in fact the water-shed between the three great rivers, Aöus or Vioza flowing north-westward into the Adriatic, Penëus or Salamvria flowing eastward into the gulf of Saloniki, and Aracthus or Arta, which has a southerly course into the gulf of the same name, famous in after days for the naval catastrophe of Actium, (*Livy*). The flanks of this ridge are steep, difficult and heavily timbered, but its summits are green with rich, open downs, and watered by perennial springs and fountains, an admirable post of observation, and commanding the descent into all the great plains of Northern Greece.

After mature deliberation, Philip retreated still south-eastward to Tricca, now Trikkala, on the Penëus; and, though with a sore heart, devastated his own country, wasting the fields and burning the cities. Such of the population as were capable of following his marches, with their cattle and movables, he swept along with him; all else was given up as plunder to his soldiers, so that no region could suffer aught more cruel from an invader than did Thessaly at the hands of its legitimate defender. Pherae shut her gates against him, and since he could not spare the time to besiege it, for the Ætolians were coming up with him rapidly, having laid waste all the country around the Sperchias and Macra, and made themselves masters of many strong towns, he made the best of his way back to the frontiers of Macedonia.

In the meantime, the consul, after his victory, followed so hard on the track of his defeated enemy, that on the fourth or fifth day, after reorganising his forces and taking up the pursuit in earnest, he reached Mount Cercetium, some fifty miles in advance of Philip's deserted station on Lingon, where he had given rendezvous to Amynander and his Athamanians, whom he needed as guides for the interior of Thessaly. Thereafter, he stormed Phaloria, received Piera and Metropolis into surrender, and laid siege to Atrax, a strong place, not far from Larissa, on the Penëus, about twenty miles above the celebrated pass of Tempe, in which Philip lay strongly entrenched watching his movements, and not more than forty from the shores of the Ægean.

This small place, however, garrisoned by Macedonians, offered so stubborn a resistance that Flamininus was unable to take it, until the season was waxing so far advanced, that, finding the devastated plains of Thessaly utterly inadequate to the support of his army, and having no harbours on the coast of Acamania or Ætolia in his rear, capable of receiving transports sufficient to supply him, he judged it best to raise the siege, and fall back to winter-quarters in Phocis, on the shores of the gulf of Corinth, leaving the whole of Thessaly ruined, and its principal towns either destroyed by Philip, or occupied by his own garrisons.

During these proceedings of the consul by land, his brother, Lucius Quinctius, who commanded the fleet destined to co-operate in the war, acting in conjunction with Attains and the Rhodian squadron, had made himself master of Eretria, Calchis, and Carystus, the strongholds and principal towns of Euboea, winning enormous booty, and stationed himself at Cenchreae, at the head of the gulf of Eghina, whence he was preparing to lay siege to Corinth, the most opulent and splendid of all the Greek cities, now held by a strong Macedonian garrison, backed by a powerful faction within the walls for Philip.

Marching down into Phocis without opposition, for, except the garrisons of a few scattered towns, there was no force, on this side Macedonia, adverse to the Romans, Flamininus took Phanotea by assault, admitted Ambrysus and Hyampolis to surrender, scaled the walls of Anticyra, entered the gates of Daulis pell-mell with the garrison which had sallied, and laid regular siege to Elatia, which was too strong to be taken by a *coup-de-main*. The capture and sacking of this town was the last military operation of the campaign.

A political event occurred, however, at the close of it, which was even of greater influence in the end, than all the victories of the year, the ratification namely of a treaty of alliance between the powerful Achaean confederacy and the Roman republic, by the consequences of which, joined to the events of the past campaign, all northern Greece from the Isthmus of Corinth to the line formed by the Aöus and Penëus Rivers, and the ridges of Lingon and Cercetium, was united under the eagles of the republic against Philip. Within that region, however, the two splendid cities—Corinth, the siege of which by Attains and Lucius Quinctus had proved unsuccessful, and Argos—still held out for the king, and it was evident that another campaign would be needed for the termination of the war.

Well satisfied with his success, as he had indeed cause to be, for few campaigns on record have more fully and masterly accomplished their end, Flamininus retired into winter quarters in the island of Corfu, while Attains and the *propraetor* Lucius laid up their fleets in the Piraeus, and passed the season of inactivity within the walls of Athens.

During the winter, after the election of the new consuls, Caius Cornelius Cethegus, and Marcus Minutius Rufus, but before it was known whether the conduct of the war would be continued to Flamininus or one of the consuls appointed his successor, a sedition broke out in the town of Opus, and the inhabitants admitted the Romans. The Macedonian garrison, however, still held out, and while Flamininus was preparing to reduce it, a herald arrived from the king, demanding an interview in order to treat of peace. To this the consul, naturally desirous to conclude the war himself, acceded, and a singular interview followed.

A place was appointed on the shore of the gulf of Zituni, near Nicaea, and thither came the Roman general, Amynander king of the Athamanes, Dionysodorus envoy of Attains, Agesimbrotus admiral of the Rhodian fleet, Phaeneas prince of the Ætolians, and with them two Achaeans, Aristaenus and Xenophon. These overland. But Philip came across from Demetrias, now Volo, with one ship of war and five single-banked galleys, and casting anchor as close as might be to the shore, addressed the confederates from the prow of his ship.

Flamininus proposed that he should land, in order that they might converse more at their ease; and, on the king's refusing, inquired who it was of the company whom he feared.

"I fear none but the immortal gods," was the haughty reply; "but I distrust many whom I see around thee, and most of all the Ætolians."

"That," replied the Roman, is a peril common to all who parley with an enemy, that they can place confidence in no one."

" Nay, Titus Quinctius," answered Philip, " but Philip and Phaeneas are not equal inducements to treason; and it is one thing for the Ætolians to find another general, and for the Macedonians to find another king such as I am."

To this argument there was no reply but silence. (*Livy*). Nor, when they came to speak of conditions, could any terms be effected among so many jarring interests; but it was agreed at length that ambassadors should be sent by all the contracting parties to the Senate. A truce was proclaimed for two months, Philip withdrawing, as a security for his good faith, the garrisons from all the towns of Locris and Phocis; while Flamininus, in order to give colour to the proceedings, sent with the ambassadors Amynander king of the Athamanes, Quinctius

Fabius, his wife's nephew, Quinctius Fulvius, and Appius Claudius, all members of his military family.

After a while the delegates returned. The Senate had given no decision. The province and war of Macedonia, when the consuls were about to cast lots, had been continued to Flamininus as *imperator*, the *tribunes* Oppius and Fulvius having strongly represented the impolicy of removing general after general, as fast as each got accustomed to the country and was ready to follow up a first success by a final victory. The argument prevailed, and the option of peace or war was left to the imperator. The Senate was not aweary of the strife, and Flamininus was athirst for glory, not for peace.

No further parley was granted to Philip; and these terms only dictated to him, that he must withdraw his forces from the whole of Greece into his own proper dominions, north of the river Aöus and the Cambunian mountains.

This was of course tantamount to a resumption of hostilities; and both parties, it appears, prepared with equal alacrity and confidence for the final conflict.

The first operation of Philip, who, on finding the necessity of drawing all his resources to a common centre, began to despair of maintaining Corinth, Argos and his Achaean cities, was to deliver them over for safe keeping to Nabis, tyrant of Lacedaemon, on condition that in case of his being successful against the Romans they should be restored to himself, otherwise they should belong to Nabis.

No sooner was that done, however, than the treacherous tyrant, desirous only to retain his new power, made peace with the Ætolians, furnished the Romans with Cretan auxiliaries to act against Philip, and even entered into illusory negotiations for the delivery of Corinth and Argos, than which nothing was farther from his mind, until at least he should have plundered them of all they contained most valuable, and this, with his wife's aid, he lost no time in doing.

These circumstances, however, were but as mere preludes to the great strife which was about to be determined in the broken and uneven country of north-eastern Thessaly, not far from the ground on which Flamininus had closed his last campaign, to the southward of the Penëus, whither both parties were already collecting their powers and drawing to a head.

Almost before the opening of the spring, both leaders were on the alert, and active in preparation; partly by stratagem and the insinuation of a menace, if not its reality, partly by persuasion, Flamininus had the address to bring over the Boeotians, as he had already brought over the Achaeans, to the Roman alliance; and thenceforth, everything in his rear being secure and friendly, he had nothing to do but to look forward and bend up all his energies and powers to the destruction of the enemy before him.

To this end he was well provided; for when his command was continued to him, five thousand infantry, three hundred horse, and three thousand mariners of the Latin allies, were voted him as a reinforcement to his late victorious army.

With these admirable troops, then, he broke up from Elatia, his last conquest, about the vernal equinox, and marching north-westerly by the great road through Thronium and Scarphea, on the gulf of Zituni, arrived at Thermopylae, where, by a pre-concerted plan, he met the Ætolians in council, and three days afterward, encamping at Xynias in Thessaly, received their contingent of six hundred foot and four hundred horse, under Phaeneas their chief magistrate. Moving forward at once with the celerity and decision which mark all his operations, his force was augmented by five hundred Cretans of Gortyna, under Cydas, and three hundred Illyrians of Apollonia, all light infantry skilled with the bow and sling; and a few days afterward he was joined by Amynander with twelve hundred Athamanians, completing the muster of the allies.

Philip meanwhile was labouring under the sore disadvantage which is sure to afflict, and in the end overthrow, all nations which engage in long careers of conquest. Incessant wars, since the days of Alexander, had worn out the manhood of Macedonia. His own wars had consumed the flower of the adults, and those who remained were the sons of mere youths or of octogenarians, begotten while the men of Macedonia were fattening foreign fields with priceless gore.

As, in the last campaigns of Napoleon, Philip's conscriptions of this year included all the youth of sixteen years, while they recalled to the standard all the discharged veterans who had yet power to trail a pike.

So certainly in all ages will the like causes produce the like effects.

Of this material, however, he had constructed a complete *phalanx* of sixteen thousand men, the flower of his kingdom, and the last bulwark of his throne. To these were added two thousand native targeteers, two thousand Thracians and Illyrians, about fifteen hundred mercenaries of all countries, and two thousand horse. With this power he lay at

Dium, now Malathria, on the gulf of Saloniki, awaiting the Romans, by no means despondent, but rather confident of success For although the last campaign had gone against him, as a whole, still the repulse of the Romans from the walls of Atrax by hard fighting, seemed to counterbalance the forcing of the gorges of the Aöus, while it was undeniable that the *phalanx* had fully maintained its ancient renown, and was, for all that had yet been proved, invincible in a pitched battle.

No less secure of victory, flushed with past triumphs, and athirst for future glory, Quinctius pressed on, resolved on the first occasion to deliver battle, his forces being, as nearly ay possible, equal to those of the king, though he had a superiority of about four hundred horse.

On hearing of the Roman advance, Philip broke up from Dium and marched upon Larissa, intending to deliver battle south of the Penëus, with a view probably to the subsequent defence of the defiles of Tempe in case of disaster; while Flamininus having failed in an attempt to surprise the Pthiotic city of Thebes, marched direct upon Pherae, previously ordering his soldiers to cut and carry with them the palisades, of which at any moment to fortify the casual encampment of the night. m. Both leaders, thus aware of the enemy's proximity, yet unaware of his exact position, encamped and fortified their camps, the Roman at about six, the Macedonian at four miles' distance from the town of Pherae.

On the following day, light parties being sent out on both sides to take possession of the heights above the town, which would seem to be the western slopes of Karadagh, formerly Mount Calcodonium—described by Leake as gentle pasture hills, interspersed with groves of oak, but swelling, a little northward on the way to Larissa, into steep, broken hills, topped with bare limestone crags—they came in sight of one another so unexpectedly, that they were mutually amazed, and neither charged the other, but both sent back for orders to headquarters, and were ultimately drawn off without fighting. On the second day, both leaders sent out reconnoitring parties of light-armed infantry with some horse, and these encountered on the hill above the suburbs of Pherae to the northward.

It so happened that Flamininus had ordered two squadrons of Ætolian horse on this duty, wishing to avail himself of their familiarity with the country; and these, overboiling with courage and emulous of the Roman renown, so soon as they discovered the enemy, dared the Italians to the test of superior valour, and charged the Macedonians with such mettle and prowess that they cut them up very severely; after which, having skirmished for a considerable time with no decisive results, they drew off, as if by mutual consent, to their own encampments.

The ground about Pherae, being much encumbered with orchards, groves, and gardens, and cut up by stone walls and thorn hedges, was very unsuitable for a general action, and both leaders, perceiving this, moved early the next morning by different routes, the great ridge of Karadagh intervening between their lines of march, and intercepting all sound or sight, upon Scotussa, a town some ten miles distant in a westerly direction, lying at the base of the hills, and on the verge of the plain.

The Romans marched to the southward, Philip to the northward of the dividing ridge; and, unaware how nearly they were entrenched, both erected their palisades for the night almost within hearing of their countersigns and trumpets.

The third morning, after they had decamped from Pherae, was exceedingly thick and foggy; but in spite of this Philip, who had passed the night on the banks of the Onchestus, persevered in marching upon Scotussa, where he hoped to find ripe corn in the plain for his troops. The darkness, however, increased, and ere long one of those tremendous thunder-storms, for which al the limestone countries of upper Greece are so famous, or rather infamous, burst over his head, with hail, and wild whirling wind-gusts, and forked lightnings, and compelled him to halt at once and intrench himself, at the northern base of the bare, craggy hills, forming the summits of the Calcodonium, known as the Cynoscephalae or dog's heads, though the resemblance does not go far to justify the appellation.

So soon as it cleared a little, though the mist was still so dense that one could scarce see his own hand, he sent out a detachment to occupy the heights of Cynoscephalae. At the same moment Flamininus sent out his troops of horse and a thousand *voltigeurs* from Thetidium, where he lay, to feel for the enemy.

These latter fell suddenly into the ambushed outposts of the Macedonians, neither discovering the others till they were at half spear's length in the gloom. After a momentary pause of amazement, they fell on fiercely, and among the slippery crags, in the dense mist and drizzling rain, the strife reeled blindly to and fro, all striking at once, none parrying, and friend as often injuring friend, as enemy enemy. On both sides, rumour reached the camps, and the Romans being hard pressed and giving way, Flamininus, who was nearest to the scene of action, reinforced his men with two thousand infantry under two *tribunes*, and five hundred Ætolian horse of Archedamus and Eupolemus.[3]

On the arrival of these, the skirmish was exchanged for close combat; and the encouragement given to the Romans, by the prompt succor, doubling their courage, nor that only, but their physical strength, they charged home so vehemently, that they broke the enemy, and drove them to the steep crags; the din of battle receding from the lines of Flamininus, until the cries of his own men, and the shouts of the victorious *legionaries*, aroused and alarmed Philip in his camp.

He, expecting nothing on that day less than an engagement, had sent out his men to forage in the plain; but as he saw how things were going, and as the mist was beginning to melt away before the sunbeams, and the clear blue to show above, he ordered up Heracleides the Gyrtonian, commander of the Thessalian cavalry, and Leon, the Macedonian, master of the horse, and Athenagoras with all the mercenaries save the Thracians, and launched them vigorously against the enemy.

Rallying upon themselves the broken and disordered troops who had preceded them, these in turn laid on with so heavy a hand and so furious an impetus that they bore the Romans back bodily, and drove them over the brink of the heights in consternation and disorder toward their own entrenchments; nor would they have failed to do fearful execution on them, if not utterly to destroy them, but for the devoted gallantry of the handful of Ætolian horse, who charged them time after time; and, when repulsed, rallied and charged again; and so gained that invaluable time, which, as it was in this case, is often victory.

At this moment, seeing that the defeat of his cavalry and light troops was not only serious in itself, but was seriously dispiriting the rest of his army, Flamininus drew out his legions in order of battle, harangued them briefly in words of fire, which kindled every soldier's heart to like passion, and led them straightway into action.

Almost simultaneously, Philip, to whom tidings had been brought that the enemy were utterly disordered and in flight, and who was compelled by the urgency of his officers and the eagerness of his men to give battle, contrary to his own better judgment, which knew the ground to be unfavourable to the *phalanx*, led the right wing of it up

---

3. All the details of this action are from Polybius. *Reliquiae Lib.* xviii.; who is here singularly clear and vivid in his description.

the northern ascent of the heights, directing Nicanor, surnamed the elephant, to bring up the centre and left wing close at his heels. On reaching the summit, which had been left vacant when the Macedonian light troops drove back the Romans, he formed line of battle by the left, and thus gained the ground of vantage.

But while he was yet in the act of forming his right, the mercenaries were upon him, crushed in by the advance of the solid cohorts; for Flamininus had rallied his light troops in the intervals of his maniples, and was carrying all before him with great slaughter, himself leading his left wing, the right and centre being a little retired, with the elephants in front.

Philip thus laboured at once under a double disadvantage, when believing himself the assailant of a disordered foe, he found himself assailed—a perilous thing in warfare—and, secondly, when he was compelled to encounter an enemy in full array of battle, while above one half of his own power was in column of march, and as yet unready to deploy.

Up to this moment, the day had been one of accidents and vicissitudes; but from this moment it was one of the finest generalship and the finest fighting; and in the end the best fighting carried it.

Mindful of the rule never to receive a charge but on a charge, so soon as he saw Flamininus' eagles face to face with him, Philip rallied the retreating horse and mercenaries upon his targeteers, with whom he covered his right flank, and ordered the phalanx to double the depth of its files and prepare to charge.

We have all seen, and all know the effect, of two poor lines of modern infantry bringing their muskets from the shoulder to the charge; the thrill which the sudden clash and clatter, and the quick flashing movement sends to the boldest heart—what then must have been the effect on the spectator, when sixteen serried ranks brought down their huge *sarissse*, twenty-four feet in length, from the port to the level—the rattle of the massive truncheons sloping simultaneously, like a whole field of bearded grain before a sudden blast, the clang of the steel spear heads against the brazen bucklers, and the glimmering flash of seven points protruded in advance of every shield in the front line.

Such was the spectacle which met the eyes of the *legionaries* as they crowned the heights of Cynoscephalae, but no thrill did it send to those stern hearts, but that of ardour and of emulation. Never was such a war-cry heard as burst that day over the rugged hills, for not only did the combatants on both sides, as they rushed to hand and hand encounter, shout with their hearts in their voices, but all who saw it from a distance swelled the tremendous diapason.

The clang might have been heard at a mile's distance, as the pike-points of the *phalanx* smote full upon the bosses of the long legionary shields, and bore back the loose lines by sheer force, orderly still and unbroken; while the Spanish broadswords of the Romans hewed desperately, but in vain, into the twilight forest of the impenetrable *sarissae*.

Stubbornly the Romans fought and long; and when at length broken, they were not beaten; when borne backward foot by foot they still disdained to fly; but fell where they stood and died fighting.

But Flamininus, who had the true eye, the true inspiration of a great general, ever the keenest and the clearest in the most direful turmoil of the headiest fight, had marked, like Wellington at Talavera, a gap in the enemy's array.

Leaving his broken right wing to its fate, he rushed, confident at one glance, of victory, to the head of his centre, and charged, with his elephants in front, by a rapid oblique movement, full upon the left wing of the *phalanx*, as it mounted the heights in marching, rather than in fighting, order. Here, before it could form, almost before it could level its long pikes, it was pierced in a hundred places at once; and, in almost less time than is required to describe it, the fierce Spanish broadswords of the *legionaries*, fleshed in its vitals, had reduced it to a weltering mass of inextricable confusion and almost unheard of carnage.

The Roman left, cheered by the triumph of their comrades, rallied upon themselves and returned to the charge; and simultaneously an unordered movement of a tribune of the soldiers, which should have rendered him immortal, although his name has not survived, decided the victory, as completely as did a like inspiration, on the part of the unrewarded Kellerman, decide that of Marengo.

This nameless tribune—a shame that he should be nameless—when the enemy's left and centre fled, wheeled with a mere handful of men round the rear of Philip's right, and, gaining the very summit from which he had descended, at the moment when the Romans rallied in its face, fell like a thunderbolt on the unguarded rear of its yet unbroken masses.

In any event, a rear or flank attack upon the *phalanx*, so ponderous a column that it could even when unassailed with difficulty form a new face, was perilous; here it was fatal.

The battle was ended as by a thunderclap. Of the Macedonians eight thousand fell in the field, five thousand laid down their arms; their camp was taken, but before the victors entered it, it had been sacked by the Ætolians; their king, not tarrying to burn his papers at Larissa, fled without drawing bridle through Tempe into Macedonia.

Of the Romans seven hundred lay dead in their ranks on the field; so true is Sallust's apothegm, that audacity is as a rampart to the soldier, and flight more perilous than battle.

It was not a battle only that was won, but a war that was ended.

Yet never was a battle won which was so nearly lost, except Marengo; which it in several points resembles.

In the first place, like Marengo, it was in fact not one, but two battles, in which the victors of the first were the vanquished of the second.

In the second place, like Marengo, its last and crowning success was due to an unordered, self-originating, charge of a subordinate officer, with a mere handful of men on the flank or rear of a victorious column.

But in this, unlike Marengo, it was the eagle eye, the prompt decision, and the lightning-like execution of the general in chief, not the shrewd observation of a second in command, that redeemed the half lost battle, and changed the *paeans* of an exulting conqueror into groans of anguish and despair.

With Cynoscephalae, terminates the splendour of Flamininus' military career, but not the splendour of his life.

Philip at once sued for peace, and the general, aware that a war had broken out between Antiochus, King of Syria, and Rome, and dreading Philip's co-operation with him, if driven to despair, at once granted him terms.

He withdrew all his garrisons from Greece; delivered all his fleet, with the exception of ten galleys; paid an indemnification of a thousand talents, for the expenses of the war; gave up his son Demetrius as a hostage, for his faithful observance of the conditions; and, to his credit be it spoken, ever continued true in his allegiance to the Romans.

At first, apprehending trouble from Antiochus, the Senate determined to keep Roman garrisons in the three strongholds of Chalcis, Corinth and Demetrias; but so loud were the complaints of the Greeks in general, of the Ætolians in particular, and so consistent did they appear to Flamininus, that he used the great personal weight and influence he had gained with the people and the Senate, not to obtain personal honours, wealth or distinction, but to procure the complete liberation of Greece, and the withdrawal of every foreign soldier from her confines.

The proudest hour of his life, save one, was when he sat in his *curule* chair, at the Isthmian games, a spectator of the show, and heard the Roman trumpet-blast command attention, and the Roman herald make proclamation—

> The Senate, and the *Imperator*, Titus Quinctius, having subdued King Philip and the Macedonians, give to the Corinthians, Locrians, Phocians, Euboeans, Achaeans, Pthiotians, Magnetians, Thessalians, and Perrhaebians, liberty, immunity from garrisons, immunity from tribute, and the right of self-government, according to their own constitutions.

At first men heard not, or, hearing, believed not, for very joy, that such happiness could be; and they called upon the herald to repeat his proclamation.

Then such a shout arose as rang from sea to sea across the Isthmus. The like of it was never heard before or afterward in Greece. And what has often been said hyperbolically, to lend grandeur to descriptions of the human voice, was then actually seen to happen; (*Plutarch vita Flaminini*), for crows winging their way over the amphitheatre fell into the arena, stunned by the concussion of the air.

As one man, the whole theatre stood up. There was no more talk of the combatants. Everyone spoke of Flamininus, everyone would touch the hand of the champion, the liberator of Greece.

I said the proudest day of his life, save one. For he had one prouder.

Two years longer he tarried among the Greeks, as commissioner to see the treaties carried out; and for a short time he fell into odium with the people he had liberated, for that, when he was warring against Nabis, the cruel tyrant and usurper of Lacedaemon, and might have dethroned him, he made peace, and suffered him to retain his blood-bought dominion. Some were so base as to attribute this to jealousy of Philipoemen. His own statement, and our knowledge of his character bears out that statement, asserts that he could not destroy Nabis, without destroying Sparta, and that in preference to destroying Sparta, he suffered Nabis to go free.

But when he left the shores of Hellas, after interceding twenty times, and mediating successfully between the Greeks and his successors, the Ætolians much desired to make him some great gift, that should prove their great love and veneration. But the known integrity of the man deterred them; for it was notorious that he would receive naught that savoured of a bribe.

At last they bethought them. There were in Greece twelve hundred Roman citizens, who had been captives to Hannibal, and by him sold as slaves. Their sad case had of late been sadly aggravated, as slaves themselves and bondmen, they all saw their countrymen, many their kinsmen, some their brethren or their sons, free, conquerors, and hailed as saviors of the land, to which they were enslaved.

Titus had grieved for them deeply, but he was too poor to ransom them, too just to take them by the strong hand from their lawful owners. So the Ætolians ransomed them at five *minae*, (about twenty pounds sterling), the head; and, as he was on the point of setting sail, brought them down to the wharf in a body, and presented them to him, the gift of liberated Greece. Plutarch says:

A gift worthy of a great man, and a lover of his country.

A gift, say I, which none would have offered but to—what is far greater than a great—a good man. A gift which proves alike the character of the givers, and the receiver. An honour, as few gifts are, to both.

I care not that in Flamininus' triumph those twelve hundred ransomed Romans, of their own free will, walked with shaven heads and white caps, as manumitted slaves, and that the people of Rome had no eyes for the hostage prince, or the barbaric gold, or the strange Macedonian armour—had no eyes for Flamininus himself, but only for the twelve hundred manumitted Romans.

But I do care that the Ætolians knew, from their knowledge of the man, that there was one invaluable gift which it would gladden the heart of the incorruptible of men to receive at their hands, richer than untold gold, inestimable jewels, the priceless liberty of freeborn Romans.

It does not belong to the military career of Flamininus, but it does to the history of his life, that in after days he was sent by the Senate ambassador to Prusias, king of Bithynia, for the purpose of compelling the surrender into their hands of the aged, exiled, down-fallen Hannibal; and that rather than fall into those pitiless hands, which never refrained the scourge and axe from the noblest foeman, the old man had recourse to the—

Cannarum vindex et tanti sanguinis ultor, Annulus.[4]

Nor do I choose to pass it over in silence. Since it is to be remembered that the highest pride of a Roman was to do his duty; and his duty was whatever his country ordered. So that however odious the task imposed, and we know too much of this man's character not to be sure that the embassy to Prusias was odious, a consular of Rome had no choice but to obey Rome's bidding.

There was, moreover, much in the pertinacity with which Hannibal journeyed from barbarous court to barbarous court, in the hope of kindling a fire-brand for Rome's conflagration, even after his own country was prostrate beyond the chance of resurrection, to palliate if not justify the rancour of Romans. The inextinguishable hater has no right to complain if the hatred against himself be inextinguishable.

The last office held by Flamininus, was the censorship—the highest, noblest, purest dignity in the gift of the state; and never—at least in those days—bestowed upon any but the noble and the pure. It was the Corinthian capital to the career of the honoured and honourable Roman magistrate, and such was Titus Quinctius Flamininus.

After this he passes from our sight, and is heard of no more in history.

He was a great general, a great statesman; perhaps of the greatest.

But he was something more than a general, more than a statesman—he was every inch a man.

---

4. The Ring, avenger of Cannae and of so much blood.—*Juvenal, Satire x*. An allusion to the poison, by which he died, and which he was said to keep concealed in a ring.

3

Lucius Æmilius Paullus

Among the ancient Romans, during the elder and brighter days of Rome, more probably than in any other state that ever has existed, was noble birth a requisite to office and command. Save a patrician none could hold a *curule* magistracy or command an army; and by no accident of wealth or splendour of virtue, during her early years, could one rise from the plebeian to the patrician order.

The birth of Æmilius Paullus was of the very noblest, it was said he stood in direct descent from Mamercus, the son of Pythagoras, from his wit and winning ways[1] surnamed Æmilius. This pedigree, together with its explanation, are probably false, as there exists no real reason for any connexion whatever between the Greek Philosopher and Numa Pompilius, whom he is feigned to have instructed.

Yet the legend is by no means without its due weight; for it is clear if his family had not been known to ascend to the highest ascertained antiquity, men would never have sought yet farther to find its origin amid the clouds of fable. That this origin of the Æmilian family was credited by the Romans appears to be confirmed by the fact that he was sent in the year of the city 560, B.C. 194, though he had as yet held no public office, as one of the three commissioners to organise Crotona, the birthplace of his supposed progenitor, into a Roman colony.

His immediate connexions were of the highest. He was the son of that Æmilius Paullus who chose to die on the reeking plain of Cannae rather than survive the shame of his defeat—that Paullus whom the patrician annals of Rome loaded with honour and made the hero of the dreadful day, to the wrong of his unfortunate colleague, who dared to outlive the ruin, that he might save the relics of the army, and did

1. Plut. *Vit. Æm. Paulli. II.* A punning surname not uncommon among the ancients.

not, even in that extremity, "despair of the Republic"—that Paullus, whose name the Roman lyrist, (Q. Horatius Flaccus), has "married to immortal verse," which has transcended its own boasted term of years, and yet lives in the mouths of men, though "the *Pontifex* no longer climbs the Capitolian steps with the mute vestal by his side, and Rome gives law no more to conquered Medes or Persians"

His sister was married to Publius Cornelius Scipio, the vanquisher of Hannibal, and his wife, whom he divorced without giving any cause wherefore, was the daughter of Caius Papirius Matho. By her he had two sons, the eldest of whom was adopted by the celebrated dictator Quintius Fabius Maximus, whose name he subsequently bore, as did his younger brother that of his uncle Publius Cornelius Scipio, both having the suffix Æmilianus, to mark their descent from the Æmilii. The latter of these youths in after days gained great celebrity as the ultimate conqueror and destroyer of Carthage, and as he, like his uncle, received the honorary surname of Africanus, he is often confounded by loose historical readers with his far greater uncle, the victor of the Peninsula and Zama.

With such a birth, such antecedents, such connexions, friends, and name, it is little to be admired that he was early called to the service of the state. It was in the second consulship of his brother-in-law, Scipio, and the thirty-fourth year of his own age, he was appointed commissioner for Crotona; and in his thirty-sixth year he was elected *adile*, in preference, as it is stated by Plutarch, (*Vit. Æmil. Paul.*), to twelve men, all of such worth and distinction that they were afterward raised to the consulship.

In the following year, the 563rd of Rome, B.C. 191, in addition to the protracted struggle which was still carried on in Spain, a war broke out with Antiochus, and being elected Praetor, Paullus received Spain as his province, and proceeded to the command of the veteran army of the *propraetor*, Marcus Fulvius Nobilior, whom he succeeded, with a supplementary force of three thousand infantry and three hundred horse, one-third of whom only were Roman citizens, the remainder being allies of the Latin name.

In this his first campaign, the young soldier had, at least, no marked success, for I can find no mention whatever of the occurrences of his command, Plutarch passing over the events of the two first years in absolute silence, and alluding to his eventual victory as if it had immediately followed his appointment as proconsul. Those books of Polybius which treat of this period are unhappily lost, but from the silence of Livy, who follows him mainly in the narrative of these events, it is evident that he had nothing to commemorate of brilliant conduct, since he was a friend both of the Scipios and of Paullus, and whom he loved, he loved to panegyrise.

If he gained no marked distinction, however, it is equally clear that he incurred no disrepute; since he was re-appointed to his former province of Ulterior Spain, which included all southern Spain, as bounded by a line drawn from New Carthage, Carthagena, north-westward to Salamanca, and thence due west to the mouth of the Durius, or Douro, on the Atlantic coast. This command he held with the rank of proconsul, but with the additional distinction of twelve *lictors*, instead of the usual complement of six, indicating that he held the full consular *imperium*.

His second campaign was positively disastrous, for having moved from his headquarters, probably at Carthagena, into the country of the Bastitani, (*Livy*), corresponding to Jaen, in Andalusia, he was defeated by the Lusitanians, who must have crossed the Sierra Morena and Guadalquivir from their own country, Portugal, with a loss of six thousand men cut to pieces by the revolted Barbarians, who were with difficulty repulsed from an attempt to storm his entrenched camp. After this repulse, he saved the relics of his army only by a retreat of forced marches into the pacified district.

It is to be regretted that the details of this portion of the career of Æmilius Paullus, owing, I presume, to the unwillingness of Polybius to treat of what shed no lustre on his hero, are bald and scanty.

But in spite of his being beaten and forced to retreat with so great loss, it appears that no blame attached to him, since he was still continued in his command; as was rarely indeed the case with a Roman officer who sustained a defeat, especially where his want of success was compensated by no counterbalancing array of past services. None such had Paullus as yet to point, and he must be held fortunate among his fellows, that he was permitted an opportunity of retrieving the disaster, and showing the energy and genius, which, as yet, lay dormant within him.

Perhaps he owed this to his relationship with men who had such claims on the gratitude of the State as Scipio and Fabius Maximus; perhaps he had shown some traits of brilliancy in defeat in bringing off his broken legions, which induced his countrymen to give him yet another trial; perhaps circumstances only favoured him.

The Romans were, at this time, entirely taken up with the war of

Ætolia and Antiochus, which exclusively occupied the public mind. They had immense forces in the field, and all the regular officers of the year were employed in active service. At the very moment when the ill-tidings arrived from Spain, the people were celebrating the triumph of Marcus Acilius Glabrio, the consul of the last and proconsul of the present year, who-had terminated the war in Ætolia, which was now carried into Asia by his successors, over Antiochus, the King of Syria.

It is possible, therefore, that any one of these reasons not sufficing, they were strong enough when taken in combination to secure to him the continuance of a command from which, in less busy times, he might have been summarily recalled. If it were so, it was fortunate for Rome, no less than for her soldiers, since he was soon shown to possess in an eminent degree the military skill and vigour of a great commander, and as such he served his country well.

His province was continued to him, but it seems that he was in no degree reinforced; nor were the men made up to their original complement, for it is directly stated by Livy, that he raised a tumultuary army of new levies, probably of the Roman colonists of his province, which would not have been needed had he still had two *legions*, one Roman and one of the Latin allies, reinforced by a subsidiary division of the two nations, equal to the infantry of a half a *legion*, with the full *legionary* complement of horse.

With this new levied force, however, he delivered battle, and smote the enemy with a great slaughter, killing no less than fifteen thousand, and making prisoner to the number of three thousand three hundred more, besides storming their entrenched camp.

No details of this action are preserved; but Plutarch speaks of two combats in which thirty thousand of the enemy fell, and attributes all the glory to Paullus, saying that the battle was won almost entirely by his strategy; and that the passage of a certain river gave him the certainty of conquering the day.

Two hundred and fifty towns sued for peace and submitted themselves, and the whole population of the province was again reduced to perfect tranquillity and obedience. Whereupon, he reported the war at an end, and throwing up his command before the arrival of any successor, returned to Rome, not richer by one *drachma* than when he left it.

On his arrival in the city the honour of a public thanksgiving to the gods was voted him by the Senate, and he was appointed one of ten commissioners for the regulation of that part of Western Asia which had been won from the arms of Antiochus, by the two Scipios, his kinsmen.

From this time forth we lose sight of him for a period of seven years, during which he does not seem to have been in public life at all, while the notices of his private career are few, jejune, and indeterminate.

He became at an early age—but how early it is not laid down—a member of the College of Augurs, and attained to distinction therein, of which fact we find traces in his warfare against Perseus, in the course of which he showed himself not only to be a man of piety, according to the piety of those dark times, but a man of sound common sense, and in some sort, as things then went, a natural philosopher likewise.

It was during this interval probably, and here Plutarch places it, that he divorced his wife Papiria, for causes known to himself, doubtless, and to her also, but held secret from all the world beside, and exercising the minds of their mutual friends, it would seem, with as much curiosity and interest as if they had been inhabitants of a Western New-York village in the nineteenth century.

One day, it is related to us by the garrulous old Greek chronicler, one of these anxious friends thought it advisable to put Paullus through a course of cross-examination—perhaps he was a brother *augur*, a deacon of the same church. "Is she not chaste?" he inquired. "Is she not handsome? Is she not the mother of your children, that you divorce her?"

"Yes; she is all that," replied Lucius Æmilius, who appears to have had in his composition a certain quantity of grim wit, as Perseus learned in after days to his cost. "But is not this shoe of mine," and he showed a handsome sandal, "well made? is it not new? and yet there is not one of you can tell me in what part it galls my foot"

I imagine they soon ceased asking him such questions. After divorcing Papiria it was that he gave his sons by her to the adoption of Quinctius Fabius Maximus, who had been five times Consul, and more than once Dictator, he having lost his own son, and to Publius Cornelius Scipio, having himself married a second time and having children by his second wife. By Papiria he had two daughters also, one of whom he gave in marriage to the son of Cato, and the other to Ælius Tubero, a man of the highest character and distinction, but so poor, although a Patrician, that his poverty caused remark, yet less remark than the noble equanimity with which he endured it.

He had, it is said, sixteen relations, all Ælii, and they had but one small dwelling-house among them, and one corn-land, which sufficed them all, living around one domestic hearth and altar with their wives and children, among whom was numbered the daughter of Æmilius, who during his lifetime was twice a consul and twice triumphed; for she was not ashamed at the poverty of the man, but greatly admired the virtue which kept him poor.

It is worthy of remark here, that among the Romans, the giving away of children to fathers of adoption, particularly when they were so worthy and noble as in this instance, neither implied any doubt of their legitimacy, nor conferred any disgrace as if they were rejected; but, on the contrary, was esteemed an honour to all parties. In proof of this it may be observed, that in his subsequent grand campaign against Perseus, all these four young men, having the noblest names in the state, formed the military family of Æmilius Paullus, lived in his tent, and served him as his lieutenants, than which no more need be said at present.

In the north-western angle of Italy, lying between the headwaters of the Po, the Maritime Alps, and the Tyrrhenian Sea, lay the nation, or one might rather say the tribes, of the Ligurians; for they were still barbarous, or at the best half civilized; robbers on land and pirates by sea, they deemed it not a reproach but an honour to be esteemed. It was their occupation, their pastime, and their pride.

The bravest they were, and the steadiest of all barbarians in pitched fight. Of a mixed race, between the Gauls and the Spaniards of the coast, they carried on their piracies with perfect daring, even to the pillars of Hercules and the Western Ocean.

With these half savages the Romans were at perpetual feud, for like the children of Ishmael their hands were against every man, and no flag, so that it was a merchantman's, was safe from their fleet corvettes. Yet, though they gave Rome much trouble, forcing her in every few years to send a consular army into their rude, cold, barren, forest-covered country—it is now the garden of Italy, that portion of the kingdom of Sardinia bordering on the lovely gulf of Genoa and embracing that queen of the Mediterranean—still it did not suit her utterly to destroy or subjugate them, for they acted as a kind of outpost or fortification against the Gauls, who were constantly alarming if not invading Italy.

These Ligurians were, moreover, to Rome what her oriental empire is to England, her Algerine colonies to France,-a constant school for the exercise of her soldiery—the education of her generals.

With these hardy and resolute barbarians the Romans had been carrying on a desultory war for several years, the enemy invariably falling back, when too hardly pressed, into defiles among thickets and precipices, where regular troops could not readily follow them; and, as soon as the armies were withdrawn, descending to reoccupy their villages, which the Romans were reluctant to destroy.

Eight years had now elapsed, since Paullus Æmilius defeated the Lusitanians, and ten since his first tenure of office as *Ædile*: he had been a candidate for the Consulship more than once, but always without success, until in the year of Rome 572, 182 before the Christian era, when he was elected together with Cneius Baebius Tamphilus; and, as no foreign war existed requiring the presence of either Consul, abroad or in the provinces, they were both assigned to the conduct of the warfare in Liguria.

During this year, nothing was effected of any moment; but late in the season a rumour arose that the Transalpine Gauls were arming, which, as usual, produced great consternation in Rome; wherefore it was ordered that, while one of the Consuls should return to the city in order to hold the consular *comitia* for the ensuing year, the other should winter at Pisa with the *legions*. It was arranged between the Consuls, that Æmilius should remain with the array, since the brother of Cneius Baebius was a candidate for the consulship; and to this he owed it, that in the ensuing year his authority was continued to him, until the consuls should have held their levies, and should be in readiness to proceed to their provinces.

Early in the season, anxious, as Roman generals invariably were, to effect something which would give him mark before the arrival of his successors, Æmilius broke up from his winter quarters, and, as soon as the spring opened, advanced into the territory of the Ligurian Ingauni, whose principal town, Albium Ingaunorum, still exists, with the title of Albenga, on the western shore of the gulf of Genoa, where the Apennines, at their origin from the Maritime Alps, press down most narrowly upon the sea. Among the lowest spurs of these it would seem he fortified his camp, and thither came ambassadors from the Ligurians, under the pretext of seeking peace, but in reality acting as spies. To these the usual reply was given, that no terms could be listened to, no peace accorded, until they should lay down their arms; whereupon they asked and obtained a treaty of ten days, in order, as they said, to give them time to work the minds of their sparse agricultural population toward peace; and a condition was added, that during the armistice the Roman foragers should not pass beyond the crest of the nearest hills, for fuel or forage, since beyond these lay the cultivated portion of their territories.

By this crafty device, they were enabled to bring together the whole force of their people, who rose in mass, entirely unobserved and unsuspected by the Romans; and to concentrate a vast army close under the rear of these very hills.

Suddenly in the morning, before the armistice had yet expired, the ridges and slopes of the hills were seen to swarm with the countless multitudes of the barbarian host, pouring down the declivities, a torrent of glittering spears, with dissonant music and fierce war cries, to attack the entrenched lines of the Romans. So rapidly impetuous was their descent, and so overwhelming their numbers, that the *legionaries* had neither time to draw out of their works, nor room to form; and, being furiously and incessantly assaulted all day long, it was with great difficulty that they defended their gates, and that rather by passive resistance of bodies against bodies, than by any active operations.

At nightfall, when the enemy drew off, Æmilius sent two horsemen to Pisa, with letters to Cneius Baebius, his late colleague, now proconsul, informing him how treacherously he was beset, and praying him to march to his aid, as speedily as possible, with reinforcements.

It fell out, however, that Baebius had delivered over his army to Marcus Pinarius, the *praetor*, who had sailed for Sardinia; and Marcus Claudius Marcellus, to whom Baebius wrote immediately, commanding in Cisalpine Gaul, next adjoining the Ligurian country, had not a man disposable for his relief, being himself engaged with the Istri, a barbarous people at the head of the gulf of Venice, who were in arms to prevent the settlement of the colony of Aquileia.

Great consternation was excited at Rome, on the arrival of the tidings from Baebius, that Paullus was so strictly blockaded, and that there existed no means of relieving him, from the vicinity. There appeared but one hope of succouring him, and that so tardy as to be at best uncertain—that the consuls should depart at once to the province, with such sudden forces as they could muster. This they were unwilling to do, claiming the right to hold the regular levies, before departing.

The Senate, however, commanded that they should at once pass the gates *paludati*, clad in their war-cloaks, a solemn ceremony, after which they were not permitted to re-enter the city; appoint a day when the soldiers already raised should rendezvous at Pisa; levy all comers; and march forthwith. The *praetors* were instructed to levy two tumultuary *legions* of Roman citizens, and to administer the military oath to all men under fifty years of age; the contingents of the allied cities of the Latin name were ordered out to the number of fifteen thousand foot, and eight hundred horse; and lastly, the naval *decemvirs* were appointed, Caius Matienus and Caius Lucretius, to whom squadrons were assigned; and the former was sent to the coast of Liguria, under orders to co-operate to the utmost with Æmilius and his army.

Never, since the dreadful day of Cannae, had Rome been so vehemently agitated. It was fully expected that the next tidings would be, that the Roman army was entirely cut off; a disgrace not endurable, as inflicted by the hands of undisciplined barbarians, at the very threshold of Italy, and within little more than three hundred miles of Rome itself.

In the meantime, Æmilius sat within his beleaguered works, with difficultly beating off, day after day, the onslaughts of the barbarians, who waxed bolder and more insolent from their impunity, and looking anxiously toward the east for the expected succours.

But none came, nor any reply from Baebius. So that, at length concluding that his messengers must have been cut off by the enemy, and despairing of any relief from without, Æmilius resolved to execute an operation of that excessive daring, which has often been shewn, in desperate positions, to be the truest prudence—to make a sortie *en masse* upon the enemy, and to trust the event to the valour and discipline of his tried soldiery, and to the superiority of their armature and equipment.

A Roman camp was regularly of an oblong square form, with four gates, one in the centre of each side; the *praetorian*, or *questorian*, as it was termed when an officer inferior to a consul was in command, in front; the right principal, and left principal, in the corresponding sides; and the *decuman*, or extraordinary gate, in the rear.

The title extraordinary was attached to this gate, because the defence of it was entrusted to the "*extraordinaries*," or select bodies of picked Roman horse and allied infantry, who acted as the general's bodyguard, and were stationed immediately in the rear of his quarters, between them and the ramparts.

From all these four gates Æmilius had determined to sally simultaneously, and to that end he arranged his dispositions thus:

To the four regular *cohorts* of "*extraordinaries*" he added two others, and placed the whole under the command of Marcus Valerius, his lieutenant, with orders to break cut at the *decuman* gate, at the sounding of the trumpets. At the right principal gate he drew up the first *legion*, with its *hastati* in advance and its *principes* in reserve, under the command of Marcus Servilius and Lucius Sulpicius, *tribunes* of the soldiers.

At the left principal, he stationed Sextus Julius Csesar and Lucius Aurelius Cotta, *tribunes* of the soldiers, with the *principes* of the third *legion* in advance and the *hastati* in reserve. Quintus Fulvius Flaccus, likewise his lieutenant, he put in command of the right wing of the Latin allies at the *quaestorian* gate; leaving two *cohorts* of allies, and all the *triarii* of the two Roman *legions*, to garrison the camp.

This done, he rode round to all the gates and harangued the soldiers, inflaming their spirits, and casting it against them as a reproach, that it was shameful for Romans to be pent up in their defences by a rabble of Ligurian savages. At all points he was answered by cheers and tumultuous shouting, showing him that the hearts of the men were high; and they replied to him, that it was no fault of the soldiers if they were shut up within their gates, for no one had ordered them to sally. Let him order the trumpets sound, and he would soon see what difference there is between Romans and Ligurians.

The Ligurians had two camps on this side the mountains, from which, in the early days of the blockade, they used to issue fully armed and in orderly ranks at daybreak; but after a while, seeing that the Romans never came out against them, blinded with rash insolence, they laid aside all caution, wandering about dispersed, and keeping no sort of order, nor ever taking up arms till they had gorged and drenched themselves with food and wine.

While the barbarians were thus straggling to and fro, anticipating nothing less than an attack, the Roman trumpets sounded the point of war; simultaneously the gates flew open, and with a mighty shout, in which all the garrison left within the ramparts, as well as all the grooms and camp followers, united, outpoured the skirmishers, supported by the solid lines of the legionary foot, the cavalry in the rear of these leading their horses by the bridles.

So sudden and complete was the surprise, that the Ligurians scarcely offered as how of resistance; a straggling and irregular skirmish of scarcely a few minutes' duration followed; and then, those who had held together for a while, broke and fled in all directions, panic-stricken towards their camps. But the Roman horse, mounting on the instant, wheeled round by their own flanks and made a hideous carnage among the fugitives, having execution on them across the whole width of the plain to the base of the spurs, on which their camps were placed, and giving no quarter to any, in revenge for the treacherous breach of the armistice.

It was not long before all, who were not left incapable of flight upon the fatal field, were shut up in their camps, which they made a show of defending. But Æmilius, unsatisfied with his success, was resolved to end the war, on the same day which began it actively, with a crushing *coup de main*; and not even halting his maniples, or giving time that their ardour should cool, and the reaction consequent on fierce excitement begin among them, led them at once to the storm of the inartificial defences, and carried both camps at a blow, with prodigious slaughter.

Above fifteen thousand Ligurians were slain outright, in that day's fighting, (*Livy*); two thousand and five hundred only were made prisoners—a number of enemies put *hors de combat* greater, it is probable, than the whole Roman force engaged that day—since a regular consular army, of two Roman and two Latin *legions*, did not, unless extraordinarily augmented, exceed 20,000 men of all arms; and it is not likely that Æmilius would leave less than two or three thousand for the protection of his camp.

So much more sanguinary in comparison were the battles of old times, when men fought hand to hand, with cut and thrust, their personal animosities kindled, and all the wolfish, gladiatorial rage aroused within them, than those of modern days, in despite the invention of gunpowder, rockets and shells, and all the nominally murderous improvements of recent science in the art of war.

The numerical force of the whole Ligurian host is nowhere stated; but, from the numbers of the slain, it must have been prodigious, since it cannot be supposed that above a third of their whole number was slain, or that a power short of seventy to a hundred thousand undisciplined barbarians, should have sufficed to shut up a Roman consular army, for many successive days, within its defences.

The blow was decisive, and the punishment as effectual as it was well deserved. On the third day after the action, the whole tribe of Ligurian Ingauni surrendered at discretion, and gave hostages for their good behaviour. All the masters and crews of their piratical fleet were arrested and cast into prison; and the fleet itself, consisting of two-

and-thirty galleys, was captured on the coast, by Caius Matienus, the *decemvir*.

Tidings were sent to Rome, by Lucius Aurelius Cotta, and Caius Sulpicius Gallus, announcing that the war was at end, and praying permission for Æmilius to return with his army from the provinces, as there was no more work to do.

Proportionate to the consternation, which had preceded it, was the joy of the people on learning that, instead of losing a consular army, with disgrace and ignominy, they had gained an unparalleled victory, and conquered a nation in a day; and their gratitude to the victor was measured rather by the greatness of their previous fears and the imminence of his danger, than by any extraordinary display of strategetical science or tactical skill in the action itself.

The merit of the exploit lay in the prompt and daring decision to deliver battle, in the vigour and rapidity of the execution, and in the stern energy with which the first success was followed up.

The requests of Æmilius were both granted; the praetors were instructed to disband the city legions, and to remit the levies of the Latin name; and orders were sent to the consuls to discharge at once the tumultuary soldiers and volunteers, who had been raised on the receipt of the first ill tidings.

A thanksgiving of three days' duration, to the shrines of all the gods, was at once voted; and, on his return from his province, the victorious general was honoured with a triumph, in which he displayed five-and-twenty golden crowns, and many chiefs of the Ligurians, captives at his chariot wheels. The spoils taken from the pirates were of small consideration; but the soldiers received three hundred pounds weight of brass coin as their prize money; and the glory of Æmilius was increased by the arrival of Ligurian ambassadors, craving perpetual peace, and promising that their people would never take up arms save as allies, and at the bidding of the Roman people.

Thus creditably terminated the first consulship and second command of this brave man and good soldier; of whom for several years history loses sight entirely, at the end of which period he is only casually named, as appointed their patron by the delegates from farther Spain, (*Livy*), to represent their interests and defend them from the extortions and oppression of their governors. The fact, however, of this selection proves the influence which he exercised over public opinion in Rome; and would lead to a favourable estimate of his integrity and public virtue, since the people who now voluntarily elected him their protector, were the same over whom he gained his first victory, and whom he reduced to the condition of a conquered province.

It is stated by Plutarch that he offered himself after this several times as a candidate for the consulship without success; and that, considering himself neglected by his countrymen, he withdrew entirely from the scenes of public life, and devoted himself to the study of augury, and to the education of his children, not only after the fashion of his country and his ancestors, but also in the letters, arts, and exercises of Greece; himself presiding at their trials of discipline, over the Greek instructors whom he retained about them.

And these were not grammarians, sophists, and rhetoricians only, but sculptors and painters, horse-breakers, huntsmen, and teachers in the mysteries of the chase. So that Æmilius gained the honourable distinction of being the best father, and the fondest of his children, among all the Romans.

But he was not destined to pass the remainder of his days in inactivity, as regards the state, however virtuously spent or well employed might be his time at home. For, whether she might neglect him or no in her days of prosperity and success, when danger came and disgrace seemed imminent, Rome could not afford to forget the good soldier, whom she had never found wanting; and who had once, out of the near menace of dishonour, brought her to glorious triumph.

In the notice, above, of the splendid career of Titus Quinctius Flamininus, it has been shewn how after the close of the Second Punic War, there arose the First Macedonian War, against Philip, out of that monarch's friendship and encouragement rendered to the Carthaginians.

That war was concluded by Flamininus, in two able campaigns, by the Battle of Cynoscephalae, and the proclamation of liberty and self-government to all the states of Greece, at the Isthmian games; and Philip, having made submission, remained at peace with the Romans, until his death in the year 179 before the Christian era, and fifteen after his defeat by the Roman general.

The latter years of his life were marked by consummate wisdom and prudence in the conduct of political affairs, and in the management and development of the resources and powers of his empire; and by facility and rashness, equally conspicuous, in his domestic conduct.

He had taken part honourably and sincerely with the Romans in their Asiatic war against Antiochus, but the ingratitude of the Great

Republic alienated him from them; and it is probable, that his death alone, ascribed to remorse and repentance for the taking off of his rightful heir Demetrius, at the instigation of his elder base-born Perseus, prevented a Second Macedonian War under his guidance against the arms of Rome.

How such a war would have terminated it is now worse than vain to speculate; but when we consider that when the war did commence, three Roman consuls in three several campaigns were completely foiled, their armies several times defeated, and themselves saved from total destruction only through want of energy and courage in their enemy, by the avaricious and imbecile Perseus, we cannot doubt, that under his active, intelligent, and gallant conduct, Rome would have met grave reverse and incurred serious loss of repute before her arms had been crowned with success.

At his death he left his country vastly strengthened in arms, men and resources. He had abandoned all his weak wayside or sea-shore towns, and concentrated his powers inland, in garrisoned cities strong by natural and artificial defences, well armed and victualled, and full of disciplined and athletic men in the prime of life. He left thirty thousand stands of complete armour and arms in his arsenals, eight hundred *medimni* of wheat—which would seem to have been in those days esteemed a considerable provision—though now it would be ludicrously small, when armies are fed from magazines in their rear—and treasure sufficient to maintain ten thousand mercenaries in the field, during a ten years' war in advance of his own frontiers.

With his kingdom, his treasures, his *phalanx*, mercenaries and allies, he bequeathed to Perseus his enmity toward Rome, and the war which he was meditating at the period of his death; but he bequeathed to him no one of those high qualities, which he himself so eminently possessed, and which sometimes, though rarely, we see descending through long lines of illustrious races, as if by hereditary right.

By common consent of all historians, Perseus was treacherous, avaricious, cowardly, and, although free from the vices of his father, addiction to wine and women, was yet more seriously unfitted for success in military projects, which require unbounded liberality, though regulated by sound judgment, through his ignoble love of money, as an end, not as a means, which ultimately proved his ruin.

Which of the two contending parties were to blame in the commencement of the war, it is not now easy to determine, nor is it a matter of much importance. Rome and Macedonia were now antagonists, as inevitably as Rome and Carthage had been such during the preceding conflicts. There was no safety for the Greek States, nominally allies, but in truth provinces of Rome, so long as there remained a strong, ambitions, powerful, warlike and wealthy Greek State on her northern frontier.

Perhaps it is true, as Alison has set forth in one of his philosophic theories, that for a democratic government, or one largely partaking of the democratic spirit, progress is a necessity—that for a nation, once entered on the career of conquest, there can be no safety to the vanquished frontiers, but in advancing them by fresh victories.

However this may be, it is evident, that if Perseus had encroached and committed treacherous aggressions on the allies of Rome, which it is probable he had done, although he denied it, Rome had resolved, aggression or no aggression, to swallow up the Macedonian Empire, and coveted the opportunity of war, which in his state of headstrong dementation Perseus was not slow to afford her.

In the year of Rome 583, B.C. 171, the Second Macedonian war was declared by the Romans, and in the spring of that year the Consul Publius Licinius Crassus was sent to Greece, with Macedonia as his province, carrying with him the first and third Roman *legions*, augmented each to 6,000 infantry, with the usual complements of 300 horse, and two Latin *legions*, besides which he had extraordinary levies of two thousand Ligurians some Cretan archery, and a considerable body of Numidian horse with elephants, which were supplied by a requisition on Massinissa and the Carthaginians.

A considerable space of time was wasted at the commencement of this campaign in conferences, between the Roman commissioners, sent to maintain pacific relations with the states of the Peloponnese, Attica, Boeotia, Acarnania, Illyria, and Epirus, and the king in person. These led to the sending of a Macedonian embassy to Rome, where the commissioners openly boasted that their only object was to gain time, and that they had, in fact, cheated Perseus, having, in spite of the armistice, already taken the initiative, and filled many of the doubtful towns, which, otherwise, Perseus would have seized, with Roman garrisons.

It is remarkable, that the elder and nobler senators, to whom, says Livy, this new philosophy was not agreeable, reclaimed against this breach of national honour and justice, and denied that any gain of territory, empire, or glory, could justify or atone for national disgrace; just as the best and grandest minds of the Senate of the United States have protested against the buccaneering schemes of aggressive and dishonest conquest, which it is the fashion to palliate by a jargon of progress, and of the manifest destiny of the race.

The elder and nobler senators, however, were out-voted at Rome; the eyes of the multitude were dazzled by the glare of false glory; and the success of the ends was permitted to justify the baseness of the means.

The consul landed at Dyrrachium, now Durazzo, on the Gulf of Venice, where he encamped at a place called Nymphea, in the Epirotis. About this time, Perseus broke up the encampment of his army about Pella, the capital and royal residence, marched easterly to the Lacus Begorritis, now Lake Kitrini, in Perrhaebia, and thence southerly to the Tripolis, as it is called, of Azorus, Pythium, and Dolichè, crossing the defiles of the Cambunian mountains into the great plain of upper Thessaly. From the Tripolis he moved southerly to Mylae, on the Titaresius, which he took by storm, and made himself master of the towns of Gyrton, Phalanna, below the junction of the Titaresius and Peneius, or Salamvria, Elateia and Gonnus, two strong places, commanding the important military pass of Tempe, which he fortified with a triple ditch and palisade, and then took post at Sycurium, now Marmariani, a town:

> Situated at the foot of Mount Ossa, on its northern side, looking upon the Thessalian plains in that direction, and backed by Macedonia and Magnesia, abounding in fountains of perennial water, and commodiously placed for collecting corn from the neighbouring territories of Crannon and Pherae.—Leake's *Travels in Northern Greece*.

The consul meantime had marched unopposed through the Epirotis, and entering Athamania had good cause to rejoice that he had met no armed opposition; for the mountain passes were nearly impracticable, and in one especially, at Gomphi, in upper Thessaly, which is supposed to coincide with the defile and singular pillared rocks of Meteora—a hundred men might have arrested his whole force. Thence he advanced, after a halt of a few days, wherewith to recruit his army, to the village of Tripolis Scaea, on the right bank of. the Peneius, about three miles distant from the city of Larissa, and fifteen from Sycurium. At this place he was joined by Eumenes and Attains, kings of Pergamus, with considerable forces of infantry and a few Thessalian horse; and here occurred a slight and indecisive cavalry skirmish, in which fell Cassignatus, the leader of the Gauls of Perseus' army. On the following day Perseus advanced from Sycurium, bringing with him in his wagons water for the troops, the country being arid over which he marched, and as the Romans declined battle, he entrenched a camp at five miles' distance from the enemy.

On the next morning, he advanced as if to attack the camp, and, on the consul sending out his cavalry and light troops, defeated him in a sharp encounter, with the loss of two thousand infantry and two hundred Roman horse, besides six hundred prisoners of the cavalry. This partial success he might have improved into a decisive victory, had he followed the advice of his officers, and led out the *phalanx*; but he was timid, and lost the opportunity which offered not again; Crassus retreating across the river in the night, thus betraying the alarm which he felt, and which would probably have given the victory to a more enterprising enemy, and the king removing to Mopsium.

After this Crassus fell back to a strong position, near Atrax, where he received reinforcements of 1000 Numidian horse, at many foot of the same nation, and two-and-twenty elephants.

After these events Perseus offered peace, which the Romans, with characteristic obstinacy, never treating except when victorious, haughtily declined.

Later in the season, the intermediate portion of the campaign having been consumed by the Romans in the siege of Haliartus, Thebes, and other towns of Boeotia, which had revolted on the news of the victory of Perseus, the consul, who had consumed all the corn in the plains about Crannon, moved down again into the Phalannaea, where, after a fruitless attempt to burn his camp, Perseus surprised and made prisoners of about six hundred foragers, with a thousand loaded wagons. These he sent to the rear, while he pressed the attack in person on eight hundred Romans, under Lucius Pompeius, who had taken post on an abrupt eminence, and were making a desperate resistance.

The king sent orders to the *phalanx* to advance from Mopsium, and tidings were brought to the consul of the state of affairs in the field.

But, the Roman succours coming up the earlier, Perseus was compelled to draw off his men and retreat; and the *phalanx*, having come up tardily and in disorder, met the wagons and prisoners in a precipitous defile, with the river flowing beneath the rocks, near Elateia, now the pass of Vernesi, by which bridge Perseus had crossed the river. There, becoming entangled with these, the Macedonians were compelled to kill the prisoners, and to throw the wagons over the rocks; and, immediately afterwards, being hampered by the influx of the king's retreating cavalry and light troops, found much difficulty in extricating themselves from the gorge which they had inconsiderately entered, nor would have succeeded in doing so, had Licinius Crassus possessed the eye and intelligence of a general or the spirit of a soldier.

It was an ill-fought campaign, discreditable to both parties, for although the Romans were worsted in the main, and lost repute as the greater losers, either party exposed itself to total defeat, and owed its security to no conduct or courage of its own, but to the imbecility and over-caution of the adverse leader.

This indecisive affair finished the first campaign of the Persic war, for the king leaving a strong garrison in Gonni for the defence of the pass of Tempe, retired into Macedonia proper, and the consul went into winter quarters at Larissa, dispersing his command among the towns of the Thessaliotis for the convenience of subsisting them.

In the following year Aulus Hostilius Mancinus, the successor of Crassus, had no better fortune than his predecessor; for he was nearly surprised by Perseus, and made prisoner, during his passage through Epirus to join his army in the Thessaliotis; and afterwards was beaten by that king, and found himself ultimately unable to make his way into Macedonia, either by force through Elimea, or secretly through Thessaly.

Unable to cope with their enemy in the field, the Roman leaders betook themselves to cruel persecution, and the most savage plunderings of their allies, and such Greek cities as were so unhappy as to fall into their hands.

The golden days of Rome were now at an end, valour and conduct were no longer the stepping stones to rank and power; but wealth, however gotten, lent a golden key to its possessor whereby to unlock the gates of office, and lust, avarice, corruption, cruelty, instead of continence, frugality, integrity, and courage, became, except in two rare instances, the characteristics of the Roman magistrate—name, whilom, so majestical and mighty.

In the year 585 of Rome, 169 of Rome, and the third of the Persic war, Marcius Philippus was elected consul for the second time, a brave, energetic, active man, but above sixty years of age, and of a corpulent and bulky habit, which seriously interfered with his services in the field.

Landing at Ambracia early in the spring the consul moved at once into Thessaly, where he was met by Hostilius with the army, which he gave up to him in the vicinity of Palaepharsalia, when he resolved immediately on marching, without delay, into Macedonia, though it was not easy to determine by which road he should advance; some recommending the route by Pythium, others that across the Cambunian mountains, and yet others that by the lake of Ascuris, now Ezero, over the towering forest ridges of Olympus.

Having reached the Perrhaebian *tripolitis*, he fortified an entrenched camp between Azorus and Dolichè, and there learned that Perseus had detached Asclepiodotus, with ten thousand light troops, to guard the pass of Volustana, now Servia, in the Cambunian mountains, which commanded the passage of the Haliacmon, now the Injekhara, or Vistritza; that he had sent Hippias, with twelve thousand Macedonians, to keep the castle of Lapathus, above Lake Ascuris, on the crest of Olympus; and lay himself at Dium, a fine and well fortified city to the north-eastward, situate at the eastern foot of Olympus, between that mountain and the sea, and occupying the whole breadth of the defile, which is but a mile in width, the half of which space is covered by the impassable morasses at the mouth of the River Baphyrus, while all the remainder, with the exception of a small level, which might have been easily closed by a ditch and palisade, is blocked up by the Temple of Jupiter and town of Dium.

The Gorges of Tempe, with the strong fortresses of Gonnus and Condylum were occupied in force by the soldiers of the king, and all ingress into Macedonia appeared absolutely barred against the Romans.

Marcius, however, resolved to force the passes of Olympus, by Octolophus, and sent forward his son Claudius in advance, with 4,000 men, following him in person with the whole army. So steep and perilous was the way, so abrupt the declivities of the broken ravines, and so difficult the pathless pine forests of Callipeuce, through which they had to force their passage, that in two days they made but fifteen miles; and in the middle of the third day, at the end of seven miles, found themselves in the presence of Hippias and the Macedonians.

Marcius being informed by express of the enemy's whereabout, advanced at speed and occupied a height above the lake of Ascuris, commanding a view of the whole of the sea-coast from Herachia to Phila, which height has been identified with that of Rhapsani, above Lake Ezero, by that able and indefatigable investigator. Colonel Leake, whose personal observations on the geography of Ancient Greece, have done more to elucidate the history of the Greek wars than those of any other commentator. This agreeable writer, abridging from Livy, who himself copied the narrative of Polybius, an eye-witness accompanying the consul in his march, in his quality as an Achaean envoy says:

> After a day's repose the consul led his forces against Hippias, and both on that day and the following there was a continued combat, but of the light troops only, the nature of the ground not admitting of any more serious conflict. The fame and power of Rome were, at this moment, in the utmost peril; but the consul, fully sensible of his hazardous situation, judged that it would be more dangerous to retreat than to advance, and Perseus, fortunately, having made no attempt to support or relieve the fatigued troops of Hippias, the consul left Popillius with a sufficient force to observe them, and began a descent to the maritime plain, in which, at the end of four days of extreme labour, he pitched his tent between Libethrium and Heracleia, (nearly midway from the defiles of the Peneius, or Salamvria, at Tempe, and the strong pass at Dium).

So formidable were the labours and perils of the descent, that the elephants were only got over it by means of platforms resembling bridges, upon which they were induced to advance, when the supports were gradually cut away in succession, and the monstrous beasts were compelled to slide on their rumps down the frightful declivities; many of the infantry rolled in their heavy panoply down the slopes, where it was too steep to walk securely; and the cavalry, painfully leading their horses by the bridles, were yet in worse plight than the footmen.

Livy admits that, had the Macedonians been led by one of their ancient hero kings, the consul must have been inevitably destroyed; but Perseus, when he knew that the Romans were checked and brought to a stand in the mountains, when he could even hear the battle-cries and the clang of arms from the pine-clad mountain ridges, and mark the wavering of the battle by the increasing or diminished clangour, sent no succours to his gallant lieutenant, much less rushed himself into the conflict, in which he surely must have prevailed; but kept ranging up and down the coast, from Dium to Heracleia, in utter indecision, if not in base personal terror, until he learned suddenly, while in the act of taking a bath, that the consul had descended from the mountains, and was encamped on the sea-shore. Colonel Leake continues:

> Even here had he not been opposed to an enemy who was under the influence of that dementation, which is the surest prognostic of falling power, his position was still little less than desperate, as he was surrounded on every side by strong passes in the hand of superior forces, and without the means of obtaining sufficient supplies for his army by sea.

But Perseus crying out that he was conquered without a battle, plundered the town of Dium of its golden statues, that they should not fall into the hands of the Romans, sent two of his friends, one to Pella and the other to Parthus, with orders to throw all the royal treasures into the sea—both these men he caused afterwards to be murdered, so great was his mortification at his own disgraceful terror—and recalling all his garrisons from Volustana and Tempe, he fled, by forced marches, to Pydna, and thence into the interior of Macedonia.

The remainder of the campaign was passed by the Romans in opening up their communications by the various defiles, in reducing the garrisoned towns of Perseus, and pacifying the whole of Perrhaebia and the Thessaliotis, but no foothold was gained in Macedonia proper, nor did the war seem any nearer to a successful termination, than on the day when it was declared.

So ended the third year of the Persic, or second Macedonian war. For the next year Lucius Æmilius Paullus and Caius Licinius Crassus were elected consuls, the former for the second time, in the fourteenth year after his first tenure of that office; and to him, with great confidence in his abilities and high hopes of a prosperous result, the Roman people committed the conduct of the Macedonian war.

It is stated by Plutarch, that, when the inclinations of the people began evidently to concentrate upon himself, as upon the one man suited to carry this war, which had so long languished, to a creditable termination, Æmilius evinced considerable reluctance to become a candidate; and that, when he did so, after much solicitation, he stated publicly that, on his first election he had sought office at the hands of his people for his own pleasure, but that on this second occasion he had been sought of them to be their general at a time of need, and therefore, owed them no gratitude, but, on the contrary, was owed by them obedience, yeoman service, and all that an intelligent and unquestioning spirit of discipline could render.

In this life of Æmilius Paullus, old Plutarch appears to better effect than usual; his gossip is, for once, much to the point, and appears characteristic of the man, and, what is more, he seems to have studied his authorities carefully, and at times differed from them, instead of setting down every loose assertion as a matter of fact. The fact of his differing is valuable, as showing a desire to elicit the truth from conflicting statements, if otherwise valueless, as it is in my opinion, where he differ from Polybius, himself a veteran soldier, and a spectator of a portion at least of the events which he narrated as an eye-witness, though unhappily his narrative is lost to us, unless in so far as it is preserved by Livy, who has here followed closely in his footsteps.

Supposing now that the old chronicler has, as is wont, leaned a little to the marvellous, and to the magnification of his hero, we cannot yet fail to perceive that there was something unusual in the manner of Paullus' nomination at this juncture, from the account of Livy, who disagrees with Plutarch as to the direct appointment of that officer to the Macedonian war, stating that he obtained it, as usual, by allotment. Since it is clear that he demanded, as a preliminary, even to his making a report on the condition of the war, that commissioners should be sent into Macedonia, who should strictly scrutinize the state of the Roman Army, as to discipline, present force, temper, and the position which it now occupied, who should report on the disposition of the allies, and of the various Greek States, and on the preparations, available resources, and real strength of Perseus.

We find no demand of this nature previously made on the Senate by any Roman commander, and its being made in this instance, and immediately conceded, goes far to prove these facts, first, that war had now come to be considered as a regular science, and to be managed in all its operations scientifically, not at haphazard, according to the chances of the occasion, the temper of the moment, and the mere courage of the leaders and the men. Secondly, that this war, although in no wise affecting the integrity or safety, much less the existence of Rome in a national point of view, was regarded as a matter of the first importance, and to be dealt with now, after the delays and disappointments of three successive campaigns, successive generals, powerfully, scientifically, and conclusively. Thirdly, that the man now selected for its conduct was fully acceptable to the people, and implicitly trusted by them, inasmuch as powers and facilities were unhesitatingly accorded to him, which had, probably, never been asked for at any previous date.

When these commissioners returned, they made their report to the Senate to the following effect, (*Livy*), that the Roman army had advanced in Macedonia with far greater loss than advantage; that Perseus held all Pieria, which he had occupied in force; that the two armies lay face to face, the River Euipeus only intervening; that the king was indisposed to deliver battle, and that the consul had not the means to compel him. That the Macedonians had thirty thousand men under arms, while Appius Claudius had not a sufficient number to maintain, effectively, even a defensive war, and was, moreover, in want of corn for his men. That many of the allies of the fleet had been lost by various diseases, and that many more, those from Sicily in particular, had deserted and gone home, as having received neither pay nor clothing. To this they added, that no faith could be reposed on Eumenes, whose fleet went and came as wind and tide bore it, without reason or pretext. They reported, however, that the good faith of Attalus was eminently proved, and this, it would appear, was the only word of satisfactory import that they brought back from the seat of war.

Meanwhile Perseus was said to be gathering immense subsidiary forces of Gauls and Illyrians—as he might in very deed have done, had not his base avarice and absurd self-confidence, amounting to actual dementation, led him to break his pledges, and alienate these most necessary friends—and his fleets were riding the Levantine seas in triumph, bringing in rich convoys of grain for his army, comforting his own friends, making new maritime alliances, and striking terror to the hearts of those who favoured Rome, in all directions. So soon as the commissioners had delivered their report, Æmilius laid the question of the conduct of the war before the Senate, and it was then seen of what importance to the State this protracted conflict was regarded, and how fully were appreciated the talents and energy of the new general; for preparations were made to place him at the head of armies far more considerable than had been sent abroad since the fall of Hannibal, and to carry out all the details of the project on the finest scale.

In the first place, they ordered a levy to be made of seven thousand Roman foot and two hundred horse, with the same force of infantry and double the number of cavalry of the Latin allies—these as a reinforcement to the two Roman legions already forming the consular army of Macedonia, which were to be augmented to the extraordinary rate of six thousand infantry and three hundred horse in each—and yet, in addition to these, a levy was ordered in his behalf of six hundred Gallic cavalry. It is impossible, therefore, that the actual force, in command of which Lucius Æmilius Paullus took the field in person, could have fallen short of twenty-seven thousand eight hundred men, of whom nineteen thousand eight hundred were Roman citizens, and eighteen hundred horse.

If, however, it is to be understood—and I do not perceive how it can be understood otherwise, for such was the invariable practice of consular armies—that the two Roman legions already in Macedonia were accompanied—as we know to have been the case in the instance of Licinius Crassus, in the first campaign of this very war—by two Latin legions of equal infantry force, with their cavalry contingents doubled, the whole number of swords and *pila* in the army of Æmilius Paullus, would amount to forty-one thousand men, of whom three thousand were horse.

And this I conclude, by all analogy, to have been his command, which was rendered yet more available by the permission accorded to him, of choosing from the whole number of tribunes of the soldiers, then in the state—a rank corresponding as nearly as possible to that of our lieutenant-colonels—such men as he should himself prefer to command the *legionaries*.

An advantage which will not be held trivial by any men who are experienced in military affairs, and who know how much the morale of an army is affected by the quality of its officers, and how surely even inferior troops, if well led, will prevail over better men if officered by persons in whom they have not confidence.

Besides this consular army under his own guidance, a powerful diversion was to be made in his favour by Lucius Anicius, a second extraordinary *praetor*, who was detailed to support him, in addition to Octavius, who commanded the fleet, with two full legions, and a supplementary body of ten thousand infantry and eight hundred cavalry of the allies, besides five thousand more allies from the naval colonies to man his squadron. The whole of this expedition, which was to move against Gentius and the Illyrians along the eastern shores of the Adriatic, and on the western frontier of Macedonia, so as to prevent auxiliaries joining Perseus from that quarter, amounted to twenty-two thousand regular infantry and cavalry, and five thousand marines. The fleet of the Praetor Octavius was manned by at least ten thousand men of the naval colonies; and the whole power set in motion against Macedonia this year, under the consul and the two *praetors*, did certainly not fall short of seventy-eight thousand men of all arms, without taking into account the irregulars, and local or foreign auxiliaries, who were attached to them.

Of these, we know that in the preceding campaigns, there were Numidian horse and foot to the number of about five thousand, with twenty-two elephants, not to mention Cretan and Thessalian light troops, and although these auxiliaries are not especially mentioned as present in the campaign of the Enipeus and the Battle of Pydna, it is little likely that they were withdrawn when they were most needed.

In short, it seems that in every possible respect, whether we look to the numbers, the physique, and the equipment of the soldiery, or the morale of the officers, Rome had rarely, if ever, sent out an armament superior to this, which, it appears, Senate and people had both predetermined should finish the war and the campaign together, and with the two the kingdom of Perseus, and the dynasty of Philip and Alexander.

On the last day of March the consuls celebrated the solemn Latin festival in the Capitol, with an unusual attendance of citizens and provincials, Livy says:

> All men presaging with almost certain hope, that there would be a summary conclusion of the Macedonian war, and a speedy return of the consul in magnificent triumph.

On his return to his own house, from the Capitol, after this splendid show, Plutarch tells us—and the anecdote is not without its interest, as characteristic both of the time and of the man, who, it will be remembered, was famous, as an augur—Æmilius met his little daughter, Tertia, in the vestibule, crying bitterly.

Taking up the child and kissing her, he inquired what ailed her, that she wept, when she replied, among her tears, "Do you not know then, father, that our little Perseus is dead?"

Perseus was a little pet dog of the children. Whereunto the consul, "With good fortune have you spoken, and I accept the omen."

When we come to his exorcisms of the moon labouring in eclipse, an eclipse which he had himself foreseen, and of which, by his permission, Sulpicius Gallus had premonished the soldiery, we shall have occasion to look farther into the superstition, or political sagacity, which led a man, superior both in knowledge and strength of mind to his cotemporaries, to condescend to mummeries so childish to our modern eyes.

It was at this period, in the teeth of forces such as I have enumerated, and on the point of being confronted by a general, in that day, of unrivalled activity, that Perseus, by an inconceivable fatuity, and with an avarice so miserable as to excite pity, if its absurdity did not awaken ridicule and scorn, thought proper to dismiss auxiliaries, which might well, as Livy admits, have changed the whole fortune of the war, and would, beyond a doubt, have indefinitely protracted it, whom he thus converted into overt enemies—as Plutarch ironically observes:

> And that too being not a Lydian, nor descended from Phoenicians, but one affecting to aim at the valour and virtue of Philip and Alexander by right of descent, who had overcome all obstacles, by holding that great events were to be acquired by money, not money by events.

For shortly before the embarkation of Æmilius, the Bastarnae, a Gallic or Celtic tribe of Sarmatia, corresponding to Hungary and Poland, had sent him mercenary troops, to the number of ten thousand horse, and an equal number of foot soldiers, trained to fight either as infantry or cavalry, mingling and keeping pace with the squadrons, and mounting the horses of those who fell in action.

These men had no use of agriculture, or commerce, nor even of pastoral life, studying and practising one art alone, that of arms and war, by which they had their living, They were tall and strong of person, admirable for their skill in exercise, daring and superb in their contempt for wounds or death. In them the Macedonians placed the highest hopes, believing that the Romans would not brook their onset. They had stipulated to receive ten *aurei* [2] for every horseman, five for every footman, a thousand for their leader, and had advanced to Desudaba, a town in Moedica, corresponding to part of the modern province of Rumelia, on the northern portion of Poeonia, in Thrace.

Desudaba is shown by Colonel Leake to have stood on the site of the modern Rumanovo, 22.5-42°, and to effect his junction with these bold and hardy auxiliaries, Perseus marched half his army from the Enipeus, where he was guarding the passes of Olympus into Macedonia proper, to Almana, on the Upper Axius, or Vardhari, whence he sent Antigonus to the Barbarian camp to invite the Bastarnae to advance to Bylazora, now Veleza, a town situate in the passes from the Dardanice, into Macedonia, and to depute their chiefs to meet him at Almana, where he promised them supplies for their route, and costly presents for their chiefs. The Bastarnae, would not, however, stir without receiving their pay, which Perseus, in his insane avarice, shrank

---

2. Plutarch. *Vit. Æm, Paul.* 12. The *aureus*—was £0 16 6, or $3 51.

from bestowing; and, after some miserable chaffering, in the course of which the king affected to require but five thousand instead of twenty thousand auxiliaries, finding that he was no more inclined to pay that smaller body than the whole force, they withdrew in vehement indignation to the Danube, devastating all the country through which they passed.

The sum demanded was a large one, doubtless, amounting to nearly a quarter of a million sterling, but Livy, following Polybius, a cotemporary and most competent judge of such matters, asserts roundly that by his dismissal of these men, he sealed the fate of the war, and of his empire, and his life, he says:

> For had this power been led into Thessaly against the Romans, through the passes of Perrhaebia, while the king sat still on the Euipeus, it could not only have devastated all the rich Thessalian plain, from which the enemy subsisted their forces, but could have even stormed the towns which the Romans could not have succoured, being forced to make head against Perseus on the river. So that, in fact, the cause of Rome would have been ruined for that campaign at least, since they could neither have held their ground after the loss of Thessaly, which alone, supported them, nor could have forced the passes into Macedonia, the Bastarnae being in force on their left flank and in their rear.

With similar idiocy—for it seems, in fact, nothing less—and even with greater treachery and baseness, he deceived Gentius, the king of the Illyrians, lost the advantages of his alliance, and ultimately abandoned him to the mercy of the Romans.

He had, it seems, promised Gentius three hundred *talents*,[3] though he actually paid him but ten, and having succeeded in inducing him to commit himself against the Romans, by the seizure of their delegates, he fancied him sufficiently involved, refused to make good his promise, and shortly afterward, when the Praetor Amicius took the field against him, suffered his country to be overrun, his capital stormed, and himself, with all his family, made a prisoner, without striking a blow, or even moving a man to effect a diversion in his behalf.

Such fatuity is inconceivable, for a single glance at the map of Macedonia, immediately to the northward of the modern kingdom of Greece, shows conclusively that had Gentius, with his Illyrians,

---

3. The *talent* of Agza was £404 14s. 2d., or $1759 22.

risen along the eastern shores of the Gulf of Venice, barring all Illyria, Orestis, and the Epirotis, as they might easily have done, while the warlike Bastarnae, pouring down through the passes of Paeonia, and the rugged defiles of the Cambunian mountains, occupied all the intermediate country, and the rich plains of Thessaly, Perrhabia, and the Histiaeotis, the Romans would have been shut up and surrounded between the difficult defiles of the Enipeus and Tempe, the ridges of Olympus and the Thermaic gulf, with the whole of Northern Greece in arms against them in their flank, and in their rear, rendering their retreat to Italy, or their relief by the advance of reinforcements utterly impossible.

But for the fatuity or dementation of the last of the Macedonian kings, it is difficult to conceive, how all the *talents*, energy and vigour of Æmilius, all the discipline and gallantry of his subordinates and soldiers could have saved him from a repetition of the catastrophe of the Caudine forks, or his army from unconditional surrender or total destruction.

It appears from the narrative of Livy, and from the recorded oration of the consul at his triumph, that he left Rome on the first of April, immediately after the celebration of the Latin Games, sailed from Brundusium, in Calabria, at sunrise, crossed the Straits of Otranto, and occupied Corcyra, now Corfu, with his whole fleet at three o'clock in the afternoon of the same day. Thence he proceeded, making a circuit, the reasons for which are wholly inexplicable, five days journey, in a direction removing him at every mile from the seat of the war, to Delphi, where he performed sacrifices of lustration for himself, his army, and his fleet, and hence again five days journey to the camp of the consul, Philippus, whom he succeeded, on the southern bank of the River Euipeus, between the heights of Olympus on his left and the sea.

His course lay through the sublime and romantic defiles of the Peneius, celebrated through all time as the vale of Tempe—though the word vale is most inapplicable to the scenery of the pass, since it is an abrupt gorge, barely affording space for the noble river and the narrow track between sublime precipitous limestone crags, which is thus vividly described by the graphic pen of the illustrious traveller whom I have so often quoted.

> In this space the opening between Ossa and Olympus is, in some points, less than one hundred yards, comprehending, in

fact, no more than the breadth of a road in addition to that of the river, which is here much compressed within its ordinary breadth in the plains, and not more than fifty yards across. On the northern bank there are places, in which it seems impossible that a road could ever have existed, so that the communication was probably maintained anciently, as it is now, by two bridges, or by ferries. It is evident, at least, from the marks of wheels, and the Latin inscription, that the *via militaris*, or main route, was in the present track.

In some parts of the pass there is sufficient space for little grassy levels, and even in the narrowest places the river's bank is overshadowed by large plane trees, throwing out their roots into the stream. In the meadows, when the ground admits it, are copses of evergreens, in which Apollo's own daphne is mixed with the wild olive, the *arbutus*, the *agnus castus*, the *paliurus*, and the *lentisk*, festooned in many places with wild grapes and other climbers. The limestone cliffs rise with equal abruptness on either side, but their white and bare sides are beautifully relieved by patches of dwarf oak, *velanidhies*, and a variety of the common shrubs of Greece, while occasional openings afford a glimpse of some of the nearer heights of the two mountains clothed with large oaks and firs; in other places, where both sides of the ravine are equally precipitous, a small portion of the zenith only is visible.—Leake's *Travels in Northern Greec*e, iii.

It was through this beautiful but difficult mountain pass, which had been opened at the close of the last campaign by Spurius Lucretius, lieutenant of the Consul Marcius, that Paullus now marched up his reinforcements to join the army, which lay in its entrenchments facing the enemy, and separated from him only by the deep and precipitous bed of the river Enipeus, now known as the Litókhoro, having a Turkish village of the same name on its right bank, not far, probably, from the site of the Roman camp.

Colonel Leake says this torrent, for such it is more properly termed than a river, containing little water in summer, but full of quicksands and whirlpools in the time of wintry rains:

Has its origin in the highest part of the mountain, (Olympus), and here issues between perpendicular rocks, five or six hundred feet in height. The opening presents a magnificent view of the summit of Elimbo, the snowy tops and bare precipices of which form a beautiful contrast with the rich woody heights on either side of the great chasm above Litókhoro. From the village and opening, the ground falls on both sides of the river in a long uneven slope to the sea-side, terminating to the south at the river of Platamona, (the ancient Apilas), and to the north, extending to the plain of Katerina. The torrent flows from Litókhoro in a wide bed, between precipitous banks, which gradually diminish in height to the sea. On the opposite side of the gulf are seen Saloniki, (the ancient Thessalonica), Cape Karaburnu, (the Ænean promontory), Mount Kortiatzi, and a range of mountains, which appear to form a continued range from the latter summit, as far as the extreme cape of Pallene. It is reckoned four hours from hence to the Monastery of St. Dionysius, which is situated just below the summit of Olympus, not far from the head of the great ravine of Litókhoro.

Bearing this description in mind, the reader will easily follow the thread of events that ensued, understanding that the seacoast trends nearly north and south from the mouth of the Peneius, or Salamvria, to Pydna, the scene of the ensuing action; the sea lying to the eastward, and the huge masses of Olympus thrusting themselves forward, like a huge pastion protruding from the continuous range of the Cambunian mountains, and with them barring the whole southern frontier of Macedonia.

Through this barrier there are but three passes. The first is this, of the Enipeus and Dium, by the seashore; which, from its origin at the Apilas or Platamona, to its descent into the beautiful plain of Katerina, beyond the Turkish village of Andreotissa, is about fifteen British statute miles in length; and nowhere exceeds two and a half miles, or twenty *stadia*, in width. Of this pass the Enipeus, or Litókhoro, is the first great line of defence; and the strong town of Dium, standing at its narrowest point, where the space between the sea and the precipitous shoulder of Olympus is narrowed one half by the impassable swamps of the River Baphyrus, is its key.

About eighteen or twenty miles inland, from the mouth of the Enipeus, and due northwest from it, lies the second pass of Petra, having the castle of Pythium, as an outpost, some five miles in its front. This pass is said by Polybius, who was familiar with the country, to be ten *stades*, or about a mile and a quarter in height, and, crossing the neck which connects Olympus proper to Mount Pierus, of the Cambunian chain, gives access to the plain of Katerina, in the rear of Dium, so that by it the first pass and its defences can be turned to the left.

Again, due west of the pass of Petra, at the distance of twenty miles, as the crow flies, lies the third pass of Volustana, now Servia, over the ridge of the Cambunian chain, giving access to the chasm of the Haliacmon, now the Vistritza, and thence by the lake Begorritis and the valley of the Lydias, or Karasmak, to the interior of Macedonia, and the royal residence of Pella.

By this last pass it was, that Perseus himself had come down from his metropolis at the commencement of the war; and, in the opening of the last campaign, he had garrisoned it so strongly with ten thousand targeteers, under Asclepiodotus, that the consul, Marcius, did not choose to attack it, but, Tempe being occupied at that time by Perseus, forced his way through the mountains by Lake Ascuris, now Ezero, to the position in front of the stern barrier of the Enipeus, which the army now occupied.

The pass of Volustana was still so formidably protected that the Romans do not appear to have even contemplated attacking it, this year; but when Perseus heard of the approach of Paullus Æmilius, he sent five thousand Macedonians, under Histiaeus, Theogenes, and Medon, to secure Pythium, and the pass of Petra; while he lay himself on the Enipeus, which he had strongly fortified with castles, palisades, and fieldworks abundantly provided with artillery, an arm in which the Macedonian kings were extremely powerful.

At Thessalonica lay Athenagoras, his father's best general, and Eumenes, with two thousand targeteers as a garrison; but on the approach of Octavius with the fleet, which accompanied the advance of Paullus, becoming alarmed for the safety of the coasts, he despatched Androcles with reinforcements, ordering him to prepare an entrenched camp in front of the docks and arsenals; and sent Antigonus with a thousand horse to the Ænean promontory, Cape Karaburnu, to protect the rustic population from any attempted descents.

Having taken this strong defensive position, it was the plan of Perseus to risk nothing, to deliver no battle except in defence of his works, which he believed impregnable, and so to wear out the enemy, until the war should perish of exhaustion.

The plan of the campaign was indisputably well blocked out; and the Roman commander's position was anything but favourable, either, for offence or defence. To force his way forward seemed impossible; to subsist his army from the rear by the dangerous pass of Tempe was both difficult and insecure; and to depend entirely on his naval squadron for supplies, was a last resort, rather than an intention of the campaign.

Indeed, it is difficult to conceive how even the talents of Æmilius could have extricated himself and his army from total ruin, had Perseus, according to his first design, brought down the Bastarnae through all the north-western passes from Olympus to the Haliacmon, thrown them upon his left flank and rear by the *tripolitus* of Perrhaebia, and occupied the defiles of the Peneius, while Gentius and his Illyrians should have poured down through the Epirotis and Dassaretia, and taken possession of the whole of the Histiaeotis and Pelasgiotis in his rear.

From this peril, however, the Romans were relieved by the deplorable avarice and imbecility of the king, who converted the Bastarnae into open enemies by his parsimony, and through a wretched breach of faith allowed Gentius to be overpowered and made captive, with all his family, within the walls of his own capital.

Failing even these auxiliaries, as they need not to have failed, it is not easy to see how the consul could have extricated himself, had the garrison of the pass at Petra been in sufficient strength, and sufficiently wary for its defence.

It would seem, that the most obvious plan, for a general having a fleet at his command, would have been either to embark his whole army, and change the scene of operations, by relanding at the mouths of the Axius and Lydias—Karasmak and Vardhari—thus interposing himself between the king and his capital, treasuries and resources, and establishing himself in the heart of Macedonia proper; or at least to send round a strong division by sea to land anywhere along the shores of the plain of Katerina, to the north of Dium; which would have produced the same effect as the forcing of the pass of Petra, and thus turning, with much less danger, one would think, and less risk of failure, the position of the king on the Enipeus. So obvious, indeed, does the first method appear, and so masterly a stroke would it have been, that I conclude there must have existed some cause which we cannot now discover, rendering it impossible; perhaps the insufficiency of the squadron for the transport of so large a force; since so patent a method of striking at pleasure where he would, could hardly have escaped so clear-sighted and cool-headed a soldier as Paullus.

It is probable, also, that some other obstacle existed to the transmission of a smaller body of men, such as that with which. Scipio did actually turn the position of Dium, by sea, to the plains of Katerina; which obstacle might be discovered in the nature of the coasts by personal investigation, and it is to be regretted Colonel Leake did not extend his researches to this point of the question, owing, probably, to his not having considered it in this fight.

When Paullus first arrived at his position between the Apilas, or rivulet of Platamona, and the Enipeus, the former being entirely dry, with the exception of a little which lay in a few stagnant pools near the shore, his army suffered considerably from the want of water; until suspecting the existence of secret subterranean channels from the absence of visible streams, and the greenness of the mountain slopes to his left, he caused wells to be sunk along the base of the mountains, and soon obtained a copious supply of pure and limpid water, which both recruited his men, and raised his own credit with the soldiery.

This done, he proceeded to introduce several changes into the service, the necessity of which would seem to indicate rather a relaxed state of discipline on his arrival. The first of these was to institute a system of transmitting orders, for all manoeuvres, silently and without tumult through the ranks; which was effected by instructing the *tribune* of the soldiers to pass the word to the centurion of the first *cohort* of the *legion*, and he to the centurion of the second, and so on throughout, whether the order was to be transmitted from the van to the rear, or *vice versa*. It is singular enough, if such be the case, that so simple a system should have occurred to no leader of so martial a nation as the Romans, before Paullus; and that all orders should have been given by shouting, a mode so liable to be misunderstood, or to be adopted by unauthorized persons; but the fact can scarcely be doubted, since Polybius, from whom Livy borrows his narrative, was a contemporary, and himself a military man of considerable standing, who would, therefore, be most unlikely to make such a blunder.

In the second place, he ordered the sentinels to stand on guard in future without either shield or pike, since they were not on duty to fight, but to watch; and he had observed that when they became weary, the men would lean on their *pila*, and, propping their chins on the edges of their long bucklers, go deliberately to sleep; while the glitter of their arms showed the enemy very clearly where they were posted, and how to avoid them. In like manner, he caused the outposts, the men of which had before his time been kept on duty in complete armour, with their horses bridled, from sunrise to sunset, during the arid summer-heats, which in Greece are insupportable, to be relieved every six hours, so that they should be fresh at all times to encounter a sudden assault.

When these orders had been promulgated and regarded by the troops with approbation, he harangued the men, telling them, that in a well regulated army it was for one general only, either by himself, or with the aid of such council as he should elect, to consult and provide what should be done. That those officers or men who were not of the councils, had no opinions to deliver either secretly or aloud. That soldiers had but three duties to look to—that their bodies should be in the best condition for strength and agility; that their arms should be in the nicest order; and their food constantly cooked in anticipation of sudden orders. That for all other things they must trust to the care of the immortal gods and their own commander. That in armies where the soldiers debated, and the general was swayed to and fro by the babble of the vulgar crowd, no good was to be looked for. That he would himself perform the duties of a commander, in giving them the occasion for conducting themselves as they should in action. That they should take no care for the future, but when the signal should sound for battle, then strive to do their duty.

The consequence of these orders and alterations was an incredible improvement in the discipline, physical condition, and morale of the array. The men were indefatigable and constant in exercising their bodies, in burnishing and sharpening their armour and weapons, in practising under arms, fencing and hurling the javelin; so that every one felt assured that whenever the enemy would give them an opportunity to deliver battle, that army would close the war by a glorious victory, or die in the cause of honour.

In the meantime, the consul reconnoitred the chasm of the Enipeus at all points, where he might cross it to attack to the enemy; but the solution was not easy, for the river bed itself lay in the bottom of a vast gorge or trough, with precipitous walls of limestone rock on both sides above three hundred yards in height, with but few accessible paths down the clefts, and those steep and dangerous; the breadth of the bottom of this strange chasm, which in the winter sent down a wild roaring torrent to the sea, filling the gorge from side to side, was a thousand paces, rough, and broken with great boulders and deep-cut water-courses, through which flowed deviously a swift, but scanty stream. The farther side was fortified with towers and bastions on all the crags and salient points, and with breastworks and palisades closing all the rifts and passes of the rocks, and bristling with catapults, and mighty crossbows, and all the terrible artillery of the day.

Nor if the consul was on the alert, was Perseus less energetic or awake. Seeing that Paullus was intent to pass, he moved his camp nearer to the chasm, and as often as he saw the head of a Roman column moving, with its blood-red banners flashing above the glittering *pila*, some corresponding movement, on his side, showed that the Roman's intention was anticipated, and that there could be no passage had across the Enipeus, without the severest fighting, in the teeth of obstacles which seemed even to the Roman *legionaries* insurmountable.

Thus for some days lay the two armies face to face, on the alert indeed, but as yet inactive, and never, says Livy, did two so considerable hosts lie so close encamped, in such tranquillity and repose.

In the meantime, news arrived which increased the spirit of the Romans in no less degree than it depressed the morale of the Macedonian army, that Gentius had been utterly conquered in Illyria by the *praetor* Anicius, and with his entire family, and state, and people, had surrendered to the Roman Republic; and shortly after this the hostages of the Illyrians were brought into the Roman camp, by which the circumstances became known throughout the country, although the king had taken all the means in his power to prevent the dissemination of the news. A few days afterwards, the Rhodian ambassadors arrived at headquarters, with the same threats which had excited so much indignation at Rome among the senators; that they would make common cause, namely, with Perseus, unless the Romans would grant him peace. If the civil assemblies in Rome had been indignant, much more furious were the members of the military council; and some would have had the envoys driven headlong out of the camps, without an answer; but the consul decided that they should remain a fortnight, at the end of which time he would give them their answer.

This done, as if, of set purpose, to show the Rhodians how small weight Rome attached to their protest or their attempts at pacification, he held a council of war as to the best method of operating against the enemy.

Some, and especially the veterans of the old school, were for forcing the passage of the Enipeus at all hazards; for they insisted, that the Macedonians would not stand an assault of the Romans *en masse*, but would desert their works, as they had done much stronger places, during the past campaign, at the first onslaught.

Others would have Octavius sent with the squadron sent against Thessalonica, thinking by such a diversion to compel Perseus to withdraw a portion of his forces from the chasm of the Enipeus, which they insisted was impregnable, no less from the nature of the ground, than from the superiority of the enemy in artillery and missiles.

To neither of these counsels, however, did Æmilius lend his ear; but, dismissing the council, without himself expressing an opinion, he caused to be summoned to his presence two traders of Perrhaebia, men whose good faith and acquaintance with the country were both well known to him, Caenus and Menophilus by name, from whom he secretly enquired, what, and how easy of access were the passes of Perrhaebia.

They replying, that the road over the pass of Petra was of no peculiar difficulty, if undefended, but that it was now formidably occupied by the king's troops, he at once decided to turn the right of Perseus by that pass; believing it certain, that it could be carried, and the enemy thrown down from the heights, by an unforeseen night attack; in which the Macedonians would lose the advantage of their superiority in the use of missiles and archery, and the success of the Roman soldier at close quarters, with his favourite weapon, the stabbing sword, might be regarded as certain.

Having determined, then, on this line of operation, he entrusted the conduct of the enterprise to Publius Cornelius Scipio Nasica, and to his own son, Fabius Maximus, as his second in command. There is a slight discrepancy in the accounts of this affair, as given by Polybius and Plutarch, the latter of whom professes to narrate what occurred, on the authority of Scipio himself in a letter to a certain barbarian king; the latter stating the detached force to have consisted of three thousand Italians, meaning, probably, Romans, and five thousand Latin allies of the left wing, while Livy, on the faith of Polybius, rates the whole force at five thousand only.

In order to conceal his intentions, Paullus sent orders to Octavius, who lay with the fleet at Heracleia, some eight miles in his rear, close to the mouth of the Peneius and the commencement of the pass of Tempe, to have food cooked enough to supply a thousand men with ten days' rations; and, giving out that he was about to attempt an expedition against some place on the coast, instructed Scipio to march to the naval station, as if with a view to embarkation. This done, he was directed by a long detour of above sixty miles through the defiles of Tempe, and thence by way of Phalanna, now Karajoli, in the gorges of Mount Titarus, Oloosson, and Pythium, on the south-western declivity of Olympus, to force the pass of Petra, and descend into the plain of Pieria, near the town of Hatera, now Katerina, in the rear of the king's position.

This march was calculated to occupy three days, and the departure of the detachment was so timed, that it should arrive at Petra in the dead of night, and assail the enemy before they should be conscious of its approach.

On the following morning at day-break, in order to divert the king's attention from what was in progress on his rear, the consul attacked the outposts of the Macedonians, who were stationed in the bottom of the great trough, through which flowed the torrent Enipeus, with his light infantry, the extreme ruggedness of the banks and the precipitous cliffs of six hundred feet descent, preventing the heavy infantry from joining in the action. A series of fierce skirmishes took place through the whole length of the chasm, every thicket of dwarf oaks and arbutus, every knoll and gully being occupied, on this side or on that, by the archers, javelineers, and slingers, and resolutely contested, with more loss of life, than prospect of advantage.

In the use of missiles the Macedonians and their barbarian allies were vastly superior; they had, moreover, recently introduced a new weapon, which is described as a wooden shaft, of about twelve inches, provided with three wooden projections, resembling the feathers of an arrow, and armed with a steel head of six inches. This was driven from a sling, consisting of two cords of unequal length, with fearful velocity, and penetrating the stoutest armour, inflicted ghastly wounds, and did terrible execution.

On the one side, Perseus, full of confidence in the impregnable strength of his position, in his strong works, and his admirable skirmishers, looked down from his castles on the height; on the other side, the consul, with his *legions*, observed from the ramparts of his camp, the reeling of the doubtful fray, well pleased, we may be certain, as hour after hour passed by of the long Grecian summer day, and still the king showed no sign of consciousness that an enemy was already on his flank, and would soon be in his rear.

From the first paling of the east, till the noonday sun was blazing in the zenith, the chasm of the Enipeus rocked and rang to the din of the Roman trumpets, prolonged by a thousand echoes, to the war-cries of the barbarous auxiliaries, to the hurtling of the close-shot missiles, and once and again to the clash and clatter of close combat, when the Romans joined hand to hand.

On both sides the men fell fast, the scanty waters of the summer dried river were crimsoned with blood and half choked with carnage. So long as they were at shot of arrow and javelin distance, the Romans suffered the most; but whenever the ground allowed them to close, the superiority of that admirable infantry became apparent, and the *legionary* soldier approved himself both steadier and stronger than the shield-bearing Macedonian or the bucklered Ligurian.

Still the loss of Æmilius was the heavier; and as he had no interest in pressing matters beyond the mere creating a diversion, he caused the trumpets to sound the recall at noon, and had the satisfaction of seeing Perseus set his watches for the night, and reoccupy his position, apparently satisfied with the day's result, and unconcerned as to the future.

On the following day, the same scene was enacted, saving this only, that the minds of the men being excited and their animosities enkindled by the preceding conflict; they fought more desperately and with greater individual prowess than before. The Romans, resolute to maintain their old renown, came on so dauntless, through the storm of desolating missiles, with the sword, that the light troops of Perseus could hold no head against them, but fell back step by step, first slowly, then in confusion, then almost in total route, until they were rallied at last, and made a new stand under the cover of their works.

Then the great engines, and all the formidable artillery of the Macedonians opened upon the *velites* of Æmilius. The huge *falaricae* and massive stones tore their way through and through them, striking down even the rear ranks, as they pressed on to assault the works; but still they kept the ground which they had won, though under terrific loss, nor did they waver in the least, or cease from the conflict, until they were called off by signal at a somewhat later hour than on the preceding day.

Again Perseus returned in perfect security to his quarters, and the consul betook himself to his camp, anxious indeed, but full of sanguine hope that his manoeuvre was, by this time, beyond the risk of failure.

On this night, in effect, Scipio Nasica reached the town of Pythium in the first hours of darkness, and, enveloping the place with a cordon of posts and sentries, so that no tidings should be conveyed to the Macedonian garrison in the pass of Petra, gave his men several hours of rest to recruit them from the fatigues of their long and toilsome march, and to prepare them for the last and most formidable ascent, and the storm of the heights.

And here occurs a second discrepancy between the narrations of Plutarch and Polybius; in which we shall have little difficulty in adopting the relation of the latter, as most agreeable both to probability and the state of affairs at the time, besides that he was a contemporary, and almost an eye-witness, of the events which he describes.

It is stated by Plutarch that Perseus was informed by a Cretan deserter of the arrival of Scipio's detachment, which he makes to have accomplished the whole march in a single day, and then, nor till then, sent an opposing force of ten thousand mercenaries and three thousand Macedonians, under Milo, to defend the pass of Petra; who, he says, were beaten after a severe engagement, in which Scipio fought hand to hand with a Thracian, whom he slew, the Macedonian leader flying dishonourably in his shirt.

Polybius, an old and accomplished soldier, relates the sequence of events as above stated in the text, merely adding that the Macedonians were surprised in their sleep, and cut to pieces or driven down the heights, in an affair of a few minutes duration. A single glance at the map will show the extent of the march of Scipio, round two-thirds of the whole circumference of the pile of Olympus; a distance established by the personal observation of Colonel Leake, as exceeding sixty miles, over extremely difficult ground, and agreeing perfectly with the time assigned to the march by Livy, following Polybius, as occupying a portion of three days. Plutarch was ignorant of the ground, and wrote, credulously, from hearsay, and partially on the authority of a young soldier, proud of the exploits of his first campaign.

Again, apart from the direct assertion of Polybius, that the pass of Petra was guarded from the opening of the campaign by a Macedonian garrison in force, it is evident that it must have been so guarded; for we know that Perseus was aware of its existence, since he had protected it efficiently in the two previous campaigns; and had, by its occupation in that immediately preceding, compelled the Consul Marcius to force his way across the central mountain itself, between the defiles of Tempe and the highland gorge in question. Furthermore, had Scipio reached Pythium, only five miles distant from Petra, before any garrison was placed at the latter place, or any tidings of his march had reached the king, no force could possibly have arrived at the spot from the Macedonian headquarters, on the Enipeus, at least twenty miles distant on the shortest possible line, in time to contest it.

Lastly, Perseus did not receive the intelligence that Scipio was in his rear until the morning of the third day had fully broken; for he still lay in his quarters observing the consul, who was manoeuvring in his front as if he desired to pass the chasm of the Enipeus, by his own right, lower down toward the sea, where the gorge was wider and less precipitous.

For the rest, the variance is trifling. Even in a sudden surprise and night attack, even where the affair is but of a few minutes duration, and the surprised party is totally routed, there is always more or less sharp and tumultuous fighting, the men springing to their arms on which they were sleeping, and each striking, as Harry Wynd struck, for his own hand, and to secure his own safety, if not his party's victory. It is, therefore, as probable that Scipio should have killed a Thracian with his own hand, in the chances of a darkling skirmish, as it is natural that, in the elation of a maiden victory, he should have dwelt upon the circumstances and slightly magnified them, in describing the events by a gossiping letter to his friend.

That Milo escaped in his shirt is a corroboration of the fact that he was aroused from his bed to imminent battle; since if he had once been armed, he would neither have had the leisure nor the desire to strip, preparatory to a flight down the craggy declivities of Olympus.

On the morning, therefore, of the third day after his countermarch from the Enipeus to Heracleia, Scipio had done his work fully and well. He was in absolute possession of the heights commanding an easy descent into the plains of Pieria, directly in the rear of the king, and having thus admirably executed the plan of the consul in turning the enemy's left, would, in a few hours time, have cut off his retreat to the northward into Macedonia, and so compelled him to fight, hemmed in between inaccessible mountain heights on one side, and two armies and a hostile fleet on the others.

From this predicament he extricated himself only by a rapid retreat, which he commenced without a moment's delay, so soon as the tidings were brought to him, whether by a Cretan deserter from the Romans, or by a fugitive of his own men, and prosecuted with such celerity that he reached a convenient battle-ground in front of the fortified town of Pydna before noon, without any serious molestation from Æmilius, whose movements were necessarily slow and cautious, until he had passed the great ravine.

Colonel Leake, whom I have already so often quoted, travelling over precisely the same road by which Perseus retreated with Æmilius at his heels, found that it occupied him one hour and twenty-five minutes, of ordinary Turkish travel, which he elsewhere rates at about two and three-quarter English miles to the hour, to reach Malathria, the site of the ancient city of Dium; the strong place which Perseus had clung to so long, and was now forced to abandon without striking a blow, in consequence of the skilful march by which Scipio had turned his right. Thence one hour and twenty minutes more brought him to "abroad, rapid stream, full of fish, small in the dry season but after the rains wide, full of quicksands, and dangerous to pass." At the end of thirty minutes further he entered Katerina, beyond the channel of a broad *charadra*, or dry torrent, which, as it would seem, coincides with the ancient Hatera, on the southern edge of the beautiful Pierian plain.

This fair tract of mingled corn land and rich woods he crossed in one hour more to the villages of great and little Ayan, immediately beyond which the heights commence, still cultivated, and adorned by two antique *tumuli* on the right hand slope toward the sea, which he regards as fixing the locality either of the actual field of battle, or of the site of the royal city, Pydna.

The distance and the structure of the land both accurately correspond with Livy's narrative; the former being from twelve to fourteen miles, while the latter exactly coincides with the events of the battle; for there is in front of Ay an a plain, affording room for the manoeuvres of the *phalanx*, traversed by a small river of two branches, and bordered by heights such as would give convenient retreat and shelter to light infantry, precisely as described by Livy, Strabo, and Plutarch; whereas the whole country northward, so far as Methone, now Elefthero-khori, in the midst of which Kitro—where some persons have placed Pydna—is situated, "affords no sufficient plain, but consists, with the exception of a few level spaces on the seashore, entirely of the last falls of a mountain, which Plutarch names Olocrus."

Immediately on discovering the retreat of Perseus, the consul extricated himself from the chasm of the Enipeus with as much speed as was consistent with good order; and pursuing him through Dium, between the swampy lagoon of the Baphyrus and the inaccessible crags of Olympus—a strong place and capable of long defence, but now completely turned and rendered untenable by Scipio's detachment, which was already in its rear—effected his junction with his lieutenants in the Pierian plain, into which they had descended so soon as they had won the pass of Petra. There can be little doubt that this movement was effected down the valley of the strong stream, which Leake crossed in an hour and twenty minutes after leaving Malathria, on the ancient site of Dium; since that stream, "which receives most of the waters from the northern end of Olympus, as well as those which descend from the southern extremity of its continuation, the Pierian ridge," has its source close to the summit, in the very pass of Petra. Thence, hurrying across the beautiful Pierian plain, here ten miles in breadth from the sea to the hills, and about six or seven miles in length, he came to the banks of the little river with its two branches, called by the countrymen Æson and Leucus, in the rear of which, and in front of the strong town of Pydna, the powerful and splendid army of Perseus, formidable in numbers, excellent in discipline, admirable and glorious in armature, was advantageously posted, ready to deliver battle.

This distance, which Colonel Leake actually traversed in about four hours and a half with the miserable Turkish post horses, the consul accomplished by mid-day, having broken up from his former camp at daybreak, which is very early during the summer soltice in Greece, and having his forces already under arms and in the field, when the king evacuated his lines and began his retreat.

This, although it would be considered a remarkable feat of marching, has often been equalled in modern days, and is certainly by no means an astonishing or impossible forced march for a Roman Army, inured as it always was, beyond any that the world has since witnessed, to fatigues, hardships, and muscular exertion.

It was on the 21st of June, 168 B. C, as rendered positively certain by the eclipse which occurred the same night, (*Livy*), and not on the 3rd of September, as erroneously stated by Livy, that Æmilius had at length the satisfaction of seeing that enemy who, during three campaigns, had completely baffled as many Roman consuls, and whom, a few short hours before, he had himself scarcely hoped to draw into the field, now forced to offer battle; and that in a situation where he had no works or artificial defences, no natural strength of ground on which to rely; whence farther retreat was impossible; and where it must now be determined only by the respective skill of the leaders, and discipline and valour of the soldiers, which had the better cause.

But the heat was excessive; the fatigue of marching in heavy armour, which reflected and redoubled every sunbeam, through the dust and glare of noon, had been intolerable; water was scarce along the line of march, and the men were suffering sensibly from thirst, the worst of pests to an army on the eve of battle.

Yet so high was the ardour of the men and so eagerly did they clamour to be led on the instant against the enemy, that Æmilius did not deem it prudent to damp their spirits by an open refusal, though he had no thought of assailing such a body as the famous Macedonian *phalanx* on ground of its own choosing, with men exhausted by the heat and thirst of a mid-summer forced march; he had recourse, therefore, to a stratagem by which he kept his own men satisfied, and the king in doubt as to his future movements.

To this end, while the officers were arraying and forming the men, he hurried the *tribunes* of the soldiers and urged them to accelerate their motions, so that there was much rapid marching and countermarching under the blazing sun; while he himself rode to and fro, animating the men by harangues and exhortation, as if he were about to lead them to immediate action. At first, the men cheered lustily, and demanded to be led without delay to the attack, but before their formation was completed, the heat waxing greater and greater as the day advanced, their visages became less animated, their voices lost their cheery tones, and ere long many were seen, though still keeping their ranks, to rest upon their spears, or prop their weary bodies on their long shields.

So soon as he perceived that this state of things was apparent, he openly commanded the *centurions* of the first *cohorts* to measure and stake out the face of a retrenched camp, and to station the baggage, whereupon the soldiers openly expressed their satisfaction that they were not called upon to fight under heat so intolerable; for they had already become sensible of what, in their first eagerness to engage, they had overlooked, their own lassitude and languor.

All his lieutenants and all the leaders of allies, among these Attains of Pergamus, were about the general's person, and all had approved his intention to attack without delay, for even to these he had not yet opened his true mind. When they perceived his altered disposition, all the rest held their peace, none disapproving, except Scipio Nasica. He presuming perhaps a little on his recent services, took on himself to admonish the consul of the danger of allowing the enemy to escape, which he would surely do by night, when he would have the power to wear him out among the fastnesses of Macedonia, and to elude all his efforts to bring him to battle, as he had those of all former commanders.

Æmilius, though he might well have been offended at such freedom, even from so distinguished a youth, contented himself with replying good-naturedly:

I also once held, O Nasica, the opinions which you now hold, and you will one day hold such as I do now. In many chances of war I have learned when to deliver and when to refuse, battle. Now when we are in array it is no time to teach you wherefore it is best to abstain today. Seek that on another day. Now rest content with the authority of a veteran general.

To this of course, there was no reply, and so soon as the camp was traced and the baggage stationed, Paullus drew off the *triarii*, who were, as usual, in the reserve; then the *principes* of the second line, the *hastati* who were in the front rank remaining under arms to check any movement of the enemy, should he venture to attack. Lastly he retired the *hastati*, century by century, countermarching to the rear from the right, while the light troops and the cavalry still kept face to the Macedonians, nor did he withdraw these until the front of the camp was perfectly fortified, and the ditch completed all around it.

Perseus, although willing to have accepted battle, was well content to defer it until the morrow, his soldiery being cheered by the idea that the Romans had declined battle, and drew off on his side to his quarters, under the walls of Pydna.

So soon as the camp was fortified, Caius Sulpicius Gallus, who had been *praetor* in the preceding year, a man of sufficient science and astronomical skill—vast science for those days!—to calculate eclipses, by the consul's permission, harangued a general convocation of the soldiers, telling them that the moon would be obscured from the second to the fourth hour of the coming night—that is to say, from about half-past nine to eleven o'clock, modern time[4]—and that this would occur from purely natural causes, the moon being in fact obscured by the shadow of the earth. Wherefore none should be alarmed, nor deem it a prodigy, since it was by no means more remarkable than that the new moon should increase and the old decrease, both phenomena being attributable to the same cause.

At the hour which he had specified the moon began to be obscured, but the soldiers in consequence of the words of Gallus were not alarmed, only they admired what they deemed the superhuman

---

4. The division of the day and night, each into twelve equal hours, was as yet unknown. The natural day from sunrise to sunset, and the night *vice versa*, were yet in use; and, of course, the hours varied in length. At the summer solstice the day began at 4h. 27m. and ended at 7h. 33m. The night began at 7h. 34m. and ended at 3h. 33m. The twelve hours of the day consisted each of 1h. 15m. 30s.: of the night of 44m. 30s.

wisdom of the man. Æmilius, however, who, as we have seen, was a great augur and accurate observer of the old ceremonies, although his liberal mind and clear intelligence led him to permit the explanation of Gallus, whether that he did not himself accept it, but clung to the old belief, or that he deemed it wise to humour the superstitions and amuse the minds of the soldiery, caused them, according to the ritual, to observe the period of obscuration with the clangour of brazen utensils and the kindling of bonfires and beacons, until the moonlight should return.

At all events, the Romans were not dismayed, but, on the contrary, when the full disc reappeared in all her glory at the exact moment predicted by their tribune, were filled with great joy and certain expectation of victory. In the camp of the Macedonians, on the other hand, all was consternation and dismay, and the rumour went secretly abroad that the phantom of Perseus had been seen in the eclipse, and that his fall was portended by the prodigy.

On the morrow, the consul sacrificed and sought a favourable omen from the entrails of the victims, but until the twenty-first ox was slain, and it was already the third hour, 6h. 58m., a.m., the signs were unpropitious; then at length it was announced that acting on the defensive the Romans should have the day.

Even then, however, the consul shewed no eagerness for action, but called a council of war and explained the reasons of his inactivity on the preceding day, and his plans for the future.

Neither party, indeed, seemed greatly to desire instant action, and preferred waiting an occasion of advantage to making a direct attack. It was not likely, in fact, that the king, after omitting to commence the battle when the *legionaries* were weary and exhausted, the day before, and their line of battle but imperfectly formed, should venture to assail them now in their works, Æmilius, according to Livy, had neither wood nor forage in his camp, and had sent out parties to collect both, Therefore he was willing to abide his time.

About the ninth hour, however, 2h. 31m. p.m., a circumstance occurred, whether by accident, or, as some authors say, by the design of Æmilius, desirous to deliver battle agreeably to the conditions prescribed by the *augurs*, of acting on the defensive, which soon brought on a general action.

The little river, from which both armies watered, lay nearer to the enemy's camp that that of the Romans, and out-posts were stationed on either bank to protect the watering parties. On the side of Æmilius were two *cohorts*, the Marrucinian and Pelignian, and two troops of Sammite horse, under the command of Marcus Sergius Silus, and in addition to these, immediately in front of the hues, a stationary guard, under Caius Cluvius, consisting of the Firman, Vestine, and Cremonense *cohorts*, and the Placentine and Æsernine troops—all these of the Italian allies.

On the enemy's bank was an advanced guard of eight hundred Thracians; but between these parties all was quiet, and until nearly three o'clock of the afternoon there seemed no prospect of any active operations.

At length, while both the outposts were standing tranquilly on guard, a baggage horse escaped from the hands of the Roman grooms, who were tending the animals, and dashed into the river, not above knee-deep at that time and season

Three of the soldiers having dashed into the water in pursuit, speedily brought it back, though it had been captured by two Thracians, who were leading it across the channel toward their own bank; and one of these was slain.

A few of the Thracian advanced guard, irritated at seeing their countryman cut down before their eyes, crossed over the stream to avenge his death; more straggled over, one by one, and in the end the whole detachment passed to the Roman side, and closely engaged the outpost.

In aid of these the advanced guard of the camp poured down, and in a few minutes the action became so close and determined, that the *legionaries* flew to arms, with such ardour and alacrity, clashing their weapons, and demanding to be led down to battle, that Æmilius, called from his tent by the tumult, and seeing that the conditions of the *haruspices* were accomplished, since the enemy had advanced to the attack, did not judge it expedient to restrain any farther the fierce spirit of the soldiery.

He led them forth, therefore, from the camp, without delay, and proceeded to form them, as usual, on the southern verge of the little plain beyond which the low broken hills rose in the direction of the walls of Pydna, in sunny slopes with shadowy hollows intervening, beautifully checkered with cornfields and luxuriant woodlands. In the bottom, on either side the little river, the ground was open and unencumbered, covered with short greensward, sloping down eastwardly to the shore, where it is bordered by a narrow strip of yellow sand, on which break in small sparkling ripples the tideless waves of the blue Ægean.

No lovelier landscape is to be seen in the lovely land of Hellas; no more convenient field for the shock of armies, and on it was speedily to be decided the fate of that mighty Macedonian Empire, which had endured now nearly five centuries since its first rise to power under the reign of Philip the First, surnamed of Macedon, the conqueror of "that dishonest victory at Chaeroneia, fatal to liberty, which had subdued all Asia by the uninterrupted victories of Alexander, and become the mistress of one half the world, and which was now to fall, as if reluctant to adorn the hands of the first driveller and dastard who had disgraced her glorious dynasty."

Before advancing, however, he directed Scipio Nasica to ride out and report how things were going with the combatants already engaged, and what was the aspect of the camp of Perseus; while he himself, after reviewing his line of battle, rode through the ranks from century to century, encouraging the men, and calling upon them, since the battle was of their own seeking, so to carry it out that the end might cast no disgrace on the commencement.

In the meantime Scipio returned upon the gallop, announcing that the whole army of Perseus was arrayed and in motion, and that the *phalanx* itself was formed and at hand.

Then was to be seen a sight splendid almost beyond conception or example; a mighty army, full of puissant youths; disciplined to the perfection of the improved Greek tactic, introduced and completed at Chaeroneia, the Granicus, Issus, and Arbela; and resplendent with all that barbaric pomp, and semi-oriental luxury, the first of which had ever been effected by the Macedonian kings, and the second rendered indigenous since the days of Alexander.

In the advance were the Thracians, (*Livy*), tall and robust of form, keen-eyed and stern of feature, their left arms covered with great round shields, wondrously white and polished. They wore black scarfs floating over both shoulders, and brandished in their right hands huge pikes of enormous weight, with long swordlike heads. After the Thracians came the mercenary *auxiliars*, among whom the Paeonians, diversely clad, and armed after the fashion of their divers nations.

To these succeeded that picked and splendid corps of the Macedonians proper, the royal body-guard, known as the **phalanx** of Leucaspides, men equally eminent for their strength and valour, the elite of the nation, gleaming in gilded armour and conspicuous for their crimson cassocks. These held the centre as their post of right, and were followed close by the remainder of the *phalanx*, who formed the right wing in line of battle, and were called Chalcaspides, from their burnished shields of brass. In addition to these two *phalanxes*, which formed the great strength of the Macedonian armies, there were yet other Macedonians carrying round *targes* and *sarissae*, like the soldiers of the *phalanx*, but in other respects more lightly accoutred, who in action were divided on the two wings, but were now conspicuously and hardily advanced before the whole.

The whole plain seemed on fire with the blaze of their armour, as they rose into the sunlight emerging from the channel of the stream, and the neighbouring hills re-echoed their shouts, as they cheered each other emulously to the fray.

With such daring and alacrity did this magnificent soldiery advance, and so rapid was their step, that the first men slain fell within two hundred paces of the Roman lines.

To reconnoitre their advance, Æmilius rode out in person, and as he saw that splendid column wheel up into hue of battle by the right, all the Macedonians, both of the *phalanx* and the targeteers, bringing down their shields and bucklers from their left shoulders, and sloping their long *sarissse* to the charge, like a field of levelled grain, at once, at a single word and a single motion, he was stricken at the moment not with wonder only, but with awe, as looking upon the most terrible spectacle which he ever beheld; and of this he was wont to discourse often and openly in after days.

At the time, however, he dissembled his anxiety beneath a gay and cheerful countenance, and a front of confidence, inspecting the array of his legions, unarmed either of casque or corslet, as if regarding the affair of little moment.

Plutarch quoting Polybius says:

But the King of the Macedonians, ere the battle was well began, rode away terror-stricken to the city, under the pretext of sacrificing to Hercules, who receives not dastardly sacrifice from dastards, nor grants unlawful boons. For it is unlawful that he who shoots not should hit the mark; that he who stands not should conquer; that he who is wholly fruitless should prevail; or he who is utterly a coward, prosper.

But the god was present to the prayers of Æmilius Paullus, for he prayed for strength in the battle, and to conquer victory with the spear, and fighting himself, called upon the god to be his ally.

In the meantime, the Peligni were closely engaged with the Macedonian targeteers; and, their missiles exhausted, having only short swords to oppose to the terrible sixteen foot *sarissae*, they were unable to break into their closely compacted order. Whereupon Salius, their chief, snatching their banner from the ensign-bearer, cast it into the middle ranks of the enemies. Thereupon a deadly struggle ensued, the Peligni straining every nerve to recover, and the targeteers to retain the colours; the former hewing and hacking with their sword-blades at the long pikes of the Macedonians, striving to dash them aside with the bosses of their bucklers, or even to wrest them from their grasp with their bare hands; the latter charging their spears with right and left, and rushing forward with such blind and headlong fury, as to drive their points through shield and breastplate, and even to hurl the men over their heads, transfixed from side to side.

The Peligni having their front ranks thus utterly destroyed, and many in the rear of these wounded and cut to pieces, began to retire slowly, as men completely overpowered, although not yet utterly in flight, toward the mountain on their left, called Olocrus by the natives.

At this time, it appeared to Æmilius that all was lost; and, seeing his troops giving way at one point manifestly, and at all others hesitating, or at best advancing feebly and timidly against the iron hedge of spears, which the unbroken *phalanx* presented, as it swept on in accurate array over the corpse-encumbered plain, he gave way to his wrath and indignation, and rent his general's cassock, in the extremity of his ire. But, whether disordered by their success at some points, which caused sections of the front to outstrip the others, or by the inequalities of the ground, which prevented them all from keeping accurately dressed along a line of such extraordinary length, they were, ere long, necessarily dissevered, intervals of greater or less magnitude beginning to show themselves in the face of their late compact array.

Even in the imminent danger of defeat, when to a less acute and cool observer all must need have appeared desperate, the marking glance of Æmilius Paullus detected, in an instant, the fatal gap in the array of Perseus, as did that of Wellington the no less fatal break in Marmont's columns at Talavera; and his quick decision suddenly laying hold of the weak point—which is, by the way, the radical and inseparable defect of the *phalanx*—he at once resumed the offensive at all points, and in an incredibly short time, by the combined effect of address, audacity, and good fortune, converted what was already all but a defeat into an unexampled victory.

Resolving that it must be his aim to break up that one great inexpugnable battalion into fragments, and to reduce the single general action into a number of independent encounters, wherein the peculiar tactic and favourite weapons of the Romans must secure the defeat of the enemy, he called all his staff and lieutenants about him, and instructed them to direct all their efforts to the penetration of every gap or interval, great or small, in the front of the *phalanx*, and for that end to lead a succession of wedge-like attacks against all the disordered or weakened places, which they might detect in the face of the line. When he had issued these orders, and seen that they were passed through all his army, he took command in person of one of the Roman legions, and led it himself into action, plunging into the interval between the targeteers, who had pressed forward too far in pursuit of the defeated Peligni, and the Chalcaspides, who formed the enemy's right. Lucius Albinus, himself a consular, carried the second Roman *legion* gallantly into the Leucaspides, or royal lifeguard, of the centre, and held them nobly at bay; while the elephants and the Latin allies were launched against the left of Perseus, which was still engaged in action on the river.

At this point, the first advantage was gained by the Romans; for although the elephants were, as usual, a name only, without utility, the allies of the Latin name followed up their attack by so bold a charge on the Thracians of the left, that these soon broke and turned to flight. The onset of the second legion next broke the Leucaspides, of the centre.

Livy says:

> Nor, was there any more evident cause for this victory, than this—that the number of independent attacks on various points along the front of the *phalanx*, the power of which is immense and the array inexpugnable, so long as it preserves its compact order, bristling with levelled pikes, first caused it to bend and waver to and fro, and then broke it into pieces.
> For, if it is once, compelled to wheel in sections, it becomes immediately disordered by the act of bringing about its ponderous and unwieldly spears; and, if assaulted on the flanks or in the rear, its destruction is certain.
> Thus it was, that the Romans charging by alternate *pelotons*, and retiring the intermediate *cohorts*, shook their formation

and ultimately penetrated the *phalanx* at many points; whereas, if they had joined battle equally along the whole front, they would have blindly impaled themselves upon the pikes, and have gone down like the Peligni, unable to endure the concentrated weight of the Macedonic onset.

At the same time, the charge of the consul himself, who, though above sixty years of age, fought hand to hand in the van like a boy, performing at once the duties of a general and a private soldier, pierced the Chalcaspides on Perseus' right in fifty places; so that the whole army was soon weltering like a huge stranded monster unable to make any adequate resistance to its innumerable foes, who pierced and hewed it to pieces, front, flanks, and rear, at the same moment.

For when the *legionaries* had once got within the points of the tremendous *sarissse*, the Macedonians, though they fought stubbornly, in knots or singly, to the last, could make no impression on the long stout bucklers of the Roman soldiers with their feeble daggers, even as their own light targets, could offer no resistance to the sweeping blows and impetuous thrusts of the Latin broadsword.

At length such as could escape from the tumult, casting away their arms, rushed into the sea, and stretching suppliant arms toward the mariners of Octavius' squadron, which was within hail of the shore, implored their lives, and begged for quarter.

These miserable men, as they saw the pinnaces of the fleet put out and row toward them, fancying that their mission was to save, swam on to meet them, but found too late that there was no mercy to be hoped at the hands of Romans. They were ruthlessly butchered, almost to a man, unable to resist or escape; for the waves were less deaf to their entreaties than the soldiers of the fleet; and the few who made their way back, by dint of strong swimming, to the shore were, if it be possible, more barbarously entreated than their comrades; for, as they emerged from the surf, the elephants, compelled by their drivers, seized them with their trunks and dashed them to pieces against the ground, or trampled them into the sand under their colossal feet.

Never was so complete a victory, so horrible a carnage. Of the Macedonians twenty thousand were killed outright, in the action; six thousand, who had found refuge in Pydna, were made prisoners; and about five thousand others were captured during the flight.

Of the victors, there fell not above a hundred; and these mostly Pelignians, who were stricken down in the first onslaught; and a few more only were wounded.

The battle lasted only from the ninth hour, about half-past two o'clock modern time, to the tenth, or a little before four, so rapid was the destruction, when the *phalanx* was once disordered; and, had it commenced at an earlier hour, few, if any, of the Macedonians would have escaped; for the closing in of evening, and their ignorance of the country prevented the pursuit from being urged by the Romans with their usual activity.

The engagement lay entirely between the infantry of the two armies; for the dastard Perseus fled, as we have seen, at the first onset, with all the splendid squadrons of the sacred horse, which, had they charged the *legions* home, while the Peligni were in confusion, and the *phalanx* was advancing in full career unbroken, might well have decided the fortune of the day; and would, at least, when victory had declared against them, have covered the retreat of the *phalanx*, and put a stop to the hideous slaughter.

The Roman cavalry, it seems, was never brought into action until the affair was over; when they assisted in cutting up the remnants of the *phalanx*, which, by its desperate and sustained resistance, nobly supported its time-honoured renown, and enabled the targeteers of the right wing, and Cotys, with his Odrysian horse, to get off unmolested.

Perseus, who had galloped off with all his horse and his regal train, by the military road into the Pierian wood, turned aside from the direct way with a mere handful of men at night-fall, the remainder of his cavalry dispersing themselves among the various cities, with the exception of a few, who arrived at Pella before him.

In the dead of night, worn out, desperate, and deserted by nearly all his friends, he reached the royal residence, and there such of his people as had escaped the carnage refused to join him, so much did they dread his tyranny and the cruelty of his disposition, now exaggerated beyond all endurance by the consciousness of his misconduct in the action, and the utter ruin, which was its consequence, Euctus only and Eudoeus, with the royal children, were ready to receive him; and both of these servitors, it is said, he slew with his own dagger, for having presumed to address and counsel him with more freedom of speech than he deemed consistent even with his fallen fortunes.

After this, Evander, the Cretan, Neo, the Boeotian, and Archidamus, the Ætolian, alone adhered to him, with whom and the Cretan mercenaries, five hundred in number, who remained faithful to him, from no favour or affection—but simply on account of the gold he carried with him, he set forth from Pella in the fourth watch of the night, which commenced, at this season of the year, at about half-past two, a.m., and pursued his way northward, to the Axius, or Vardhari; earnestly desiring to cross it before day, as he seems to have flattered himself that it would put a stop to the pursuit of the Romans.

Thence he made the best of his way to Amphipolis, and thereafter to Galepsus, over against the island of Thasos at the head of the Ægean sea; where having recovered somewhat from his immediate terror, and relapsed into his wonted disease of avarice, he mourned bitterly with tears over the loss of some gold plate which had belonged to Alexander the Great, and had been lost or plundered by the Cretans in their flight; and besought a loan of his friends with abject entreaties. Having succeeded in obtaining from some of these the sum of, thirty talents, which ultimately fell into the hands of the Romans, he took ship for the island of Samothrace, and there threw himself into sanctuary in the Temple of Castor and Pollux, the Dyoscyri.

In the meantime the Roman Army, which had pursued the flying Macedonians for nearly fifteen miles with such slaughter that, when they crossed the river Leucus on the following day, it still flowed red with the blood of the slain, returned late in the evening to the camp on the Enipeus. And as the leaders returned, one by one, the camp followers met them with loud shouts of joy, carrying torches in their hands, and escorted them in triumph to their tents, which were blazing with illumination and decorated with ivy boughs and bay wreaths from Olympus.

But while all others were intoxicated with the joy of triumph, great affliction and sorrow fell upon the consul, for the younger of his two sons, whom he loved the most, and of whom he anticipated the highest things, was missing.

He was a youth of the noblest spirit and promise, and had been observed on that day, though little more than a boy in years, conducting himself with the utmost credit, and fighting more like a veteran than a tyro.

When the news went abroad among the soldiers that he was missing, they leaped up from their suppers, and, seizing firebrands, rushed to and fro tumultuously, and in consternation, some to the pavilion of Æmilius, and yet more to the spot where the dead laid heaped the thickest, without the palisade. And all was confusion throughout the camp, and the plain was alive with moving lights, and voices of men, shouting Scipio! Scipio! for he was greatly admired, and beloved of the army beyond any other officer.

Very late, however, when he was already despaired of, he returned from the pursuit with two or three companions, who had followed it the farthest, reeking with the blood of the enemy; for he had been carried away, like a young hound of noble blood, by the unmixed love of the chase and rapture of battle.

This is he, who won in after times the title of the Second Africanus, the conqueror of Numantia and destroyer of Carthage, by far the greatest Roman of his day, and foremost both in prowess and renown. Him, then, the soldiery received with mighty acclamations, and conducted in triumph to the consul, who, Fate and Fortune deferring for a while the stern retribution they were about, ere long, to exact for his present glory, was permitted to enjoy the pleasure of the day, unmixed with anything of sorrow or regret.

On the day following the battle, having given the spoils of the slain to the infantry of his army, and permitted his cavalry to plunder the neighbouring country, provided they should not absent themselves from the camp above two nights, the Consul sent his son Quintus Fabius Maximus, Lucius Lentulus, and Quintus Metellus, to Rome, with despatches and tidings of the victory, and thereafter marching leisurely along the sea-shore, fixed his camp at Pydna, where he received the surrender of Hippias, Medon and Pantauchus, the principal friends of the king, who came to his headquarters for the purpose of giving up themselves, with the cities of Beraea, Thessalonica, and Pella, to his discretion.

Within two days, nearly the whole of Macedonia had surrendered unconditionally; for the people, though of a most loyal nature, and singularly attached to their kings, had suffered so much that they could endure no more in their behalf, and had, moreover, lost all confidence in Perseus himself, and were disgusted alike with his parsimony, his imbecility, and his want of courage.

Advancing from Pydna, whence, ignorant of the king's flight, he had sent Scipio with an advanced guard of horse and foot to Amphipolis, with instructions to devastate all Sintice, or the interior of Thrace, toward the Haemus mountains, and to make head against any farther movements of Perseus, he reached Pella in two days' march, where he tarried several days, receiving embassies of congratulation from all parts of the country, but above all from Thessaly. Thence, hearing of the king's flight to Samothrace, he marched in four days to Amphipolis, where the whole population came out to receive and hail him, not as subjects deprived of a good and just king, but as men liberated from the servitude of an impotent and imbecile tyrant; to such a degree of abasement had declined the royal house of Philip and Alexander.

It is said that, while offering sacrifice in Amphipolis, fire descended manifest from heaven, and consumed the victim on the altar, an omen so sublime and noble, that the repute of Æmilius stood as high for sanctity and favour with the gods, as his renown in war and military glory. Nevertheless, he made no stay, nor slept upon his late won laurels; but, hurrying in pursuit of Perseus, and anxious to visit and overawe all the regions which had of late been under that king's control, he carried his arms across the Strymon, into the Odomantice, and established his quarters at Sirae.

Within a few days the fleet of the praetor Octavius arrived at Samothrace; and, after a vain attempt to escape on shipboard, in which he was frustrated by the treachery of his confidant, Oroandes, the unhappy monarch surrendered himself, with his eldest son, Philip, his other children having previously fallen into the power of the Romans, at discretion. He was immediately conducted on shipboard, and conveyed, together with his children and the treasure to which he had postponed his honour, his empire, and—as it appeared, in the end—his life, in the praetor's ship to Amphipolis.

From that port, tidings were immediately forwarded to the consul at his headquarters, informing him of the capture or Perseus and the absolute termination of the war, which, regarding it in the light of a second victory, he celebrated by magnificent sacrifices, while he sent Quintus Ælius Tubero, his son-in-law, and one of his principal lieutenants, to escort the fallen monarch to his presence.

It is to the credit of Æmilius Paullus, that, being the officer of a nation especially cruel to its conquered enemies, and in an age when mercy, much less courtesy, to captives was unknown, he treated Perseus with unusual tenderness and consideration, inviting him to his own table, and holding him in free ward, under the charge of Quintus Ælius, until such time as the will of the senate should be ascertained concerning him.

With this event the military career of Lucius Æmilius Paullus, as, in fact, the history of Macedonia, as an independent nation, closes.

The former, though he was continued for another year in his command, in order to complete the subjugation and pacification of Macedonia, Illyria, and their dependencies, being already above sixty years of age, and satisfied as well with the glory he had acquired, as with the fatigues, the perils, and the fierce excitement of the dread game of war, never again held, or sought, any military command.

During the ensuing year he reduced many of the smaller dependencies, and punished several of the more contumacious allies of Perseus, and reduced Macedonia, which was divided into four several departments, between which no intercourse of commerce, or right of intermarriage was permitted, to the condition of a Roman province. This was effected, however, so skilfully, as it was the wont of the Roman government to do, that the people, instead of regarding the loss of their liberties and national independence as a hardship, were led to esteem it a deliverance from the autocracy of their native princes.

Reorganised into republics; permitted to legislate, and execute their own laws, for themselves; released from all tribute or taxation, except for their own local purposes; and deprived of no privilege except that of working the gold and silver mines, which became state property of Rome, they were, indeed, subject to no hardship or exaction, but exempt from many evils which they had experienced before. They were, indeed—except for that abstract wrong, the deprivation of distinct and independent nationality, which is, in truth, only a wrong exactly proportioned to the degree in which the principle of liberty is valued and understood by any people—it is probable, physically, in a better condition, under the protection of the all powerful republic, than under the capricious tyranny of their natural rulers.

The last act of Æmilius Paullus is one to be regretted. It is in no wise to his honour, though it originated not with himself, but was enjoined on him by the direct mandate of the senate, which he could scarcely have avoided without incurring the charge of treason.

Seventy towns of Epirus were treacherously occupied, under peaceful and friendly pretexts, and during the period of an undenounced armistice; when they were cruelly and insatiably plundered, and no less than one hundred and fifty thousand of their miserable inhabitants sold into hopeless and perpetual slavery.

Of so dark actions, in those days, were even the greatest, and, as they held themselves, most magnanimous of nations capable; and so little were the commonest and most obvious laws of national morality and justice understood or regarded.

On his return to Rome, Æmilius was, for some time, denied the honour of a triumph, owing to the factiousness of his own army, which had been disappointed in the amount of spoils divided among them, and to the insolent seditiousness of some of the tribunes of the people.

But his deserts were too conspicuous, his ability too apparent, and the services rendered to the state too glorious to be overlooked; and it was not to the Senate only, or to the aristocratic party, of which he was one of the oldest and most prominent personages, but to the generally consentient voice of the people, indignant at the wrong done to their ablest general, that he owed the enforcement of his rights.

The envy and malevolence of his enemies thus overcome, Paullus Æmilius triumphed for three successive days—on the 28th, 29th and 30th of December, B.C. 167, with unusual glory and magnificence; the greatest monarch of the most glorious and renowned empire of the known world being led, with all his family, a sad procession, at his chariot wheels, followed by such a pomp of military arms and ensigns, such a luxury of statues, pictures, tapestry, and plate of gold and silver, such a treasure in coin and bullion as had never before, in the palmiest days of Rome, ascended the sacred way to the eternal capitol.

Perseus, it is said, appealed to the consul's clemency to spare him the humiliation of being haled a captive, through the shouting populace, at the wheels of his triumphal car.

But it was not in the nature of a Roman to comprehend such a plea, or to feel compassion for one who had filled so splendid a place, next to the immortal gods, yet could brook to endure such an abasement, or meanly deprecate that disgrace which he could so readily, and, according to the notions of the time, so nobly, have avoided by a self-inflicted death.

For such a prayer he could feel no pity; for such a suitor entertain no feeling but contempt, mingled, perhaps, with a sort of sense of personal injury, in that a king, whom he had conquered, should lack the courage or the pride to die, at least, a man.

The stern old soldier replied, therefore, only by a short sardonic laugh.

> That, which he asks of me, has been in his own power, and in his own hands, from the beginning, and is so yet. Let him see to that.

But when the triumph was concluded, and Perseus was thrown into that horrible dungeon, the Tullianum, he made interest in his behalf, and procured him to be removed to Alba Fusentia, where he was held in durance, at least, in a clean and commodious prison-house, until death put an end to his woes; whether by heartbreak, as some say, and slow natural decline, or, as others assert, by deprivation of sleep, through the cruelty of his guards, whom it irked to stand, day by day, and night by night, on duty so dull and distasteful.

It is little probable, that, had he insisted with the Senate, Æmilius could have obtained better terms for his vanquished enemy; so little was it the practice, or in accordance with the ideas of the day, to spare a captive leader, who usually, after adorning the triumph of the conqueror, was led to the block, and mercilessly scourged before beheading, as if he had been the vilest malefactor.

This honour is due, especially and alone to Lucius Æmilius Paullus, that he is the first and only instance on record of a Roman general, who sought and obtained a remission of the death penalty for the victim of a Roman triumph.

The cruelty and the crime were in the age, the people, and the system. The mercy and the grace were in the man. To the man, then, be the honour.

The family of Perseus became speedily extinct, all save one son, who earned a contemned existence, as a scribe and lawyer's drudge, in the town of Alba, where his father died. If he left issue they were unknown, and low as the fortunes into which had declined the mighty house of Alexander.

Nor was Æmilius himself not an example of that instability of human things, and uncertainty of human happiness, which the ancients were wont to ascribe to the retributive or compensative action of divine justice, if not to the direct envy which the gods themselves were believed to entertain for mortal glory.

Of four sons, the two eldest, Quintus Fabius Maximus, and Publius Cornelius Scipio, each surnamed Æmilianus to indicate the house from which he sprang, had been given by their rather in adoption to two of the noblest families in Rome. Two only, yet boys, but of rare promise, remained at home to bear the name and sustain the honours of the proud Æmilii.

Of these, the elder, in his fourteenth year, died on the fifth day before his father's triumph; the second, in his twelfth year, on the third day after it, leaving the house vacant of heirs male, and the race at an end after the present generation.

In the following noble and touching speech, which is given nearly identically by both Plutarch and Polybius, and which may be therefore regarded as, in the main, authentic, so striking an epitome is contained of the events of the campaign, as well as so true a delineation of a Roman general's feelings in a moment so blended with pride and exultation, sorrow and disappointment, that I cannot, I think, do better, than lay it entire before my readers, he said:

> Although, I believe that you are not ignorant, Romans, how fortunately I have administered the affairs of the Republic, and how, within these few days, two thunderbolts have struck my house, since on one day my triumph, and on another the funerals of my two sons have passed, as spectacles, before your eyes; yet, I would pray you, permit me to compare, in such spirit as I ought to bear, my own private fortunes with the state felicity, in which you bear a part. On leaving Italy, my fleet set sail at sunrise; at three in the afternoon of the same day, I held Corcyra with my whole squadron. On the fifth day, thereafter, I performed sacrifices of lustration at Delphi, in my own behalf, and in that of my army.
>
> Thence, on the fifth day I reached the camp; and, having received the command, and made some alterations in the defective discipline which stood greatly in the way of success, seeing that the enemy's defences were inexpugnable, and that the king could not be forced to deliver battle, I turned him by the pass of Petra, compelled him to fight, and conquered him in a pitched battle. I reduced all Macedonia to the dominion of the Roman people; and that war, which through a period of four years, four consuls, my predecessors, had so conducted, as to leave it always to their successors in worse condition than they themselves received it, I brought to a close in fifteen days.
>
> Of other successes, as it were, a superabundance followed. All the dependencies of Macedonia surrendered; the royal treasures fell into my hands; the king and his children, as if the gods themselves had given them up, surrendered from the Asylum of Samothrace. So great, indeed, was my good fortune, that I began to suspect its excess. I began to dread the perils of the sea, during the transportation of the royal treasures, and my victorious army, homeward. When all arrived in Italy, secure, with favourable winds, and I had nothing more for which to pray, I hoped, that, since from the height of prosperity the tide is wont to ebb, the change of fortunes might befall my family, not the Republic.

And I now trust that the public fortune is retrieved from reverse by the peculiar calamity of my own house, whose triumph, as if in very scorn of human chances, has been interrupted by the death of my two sons. And when I and Perseus are set up as two examples, the noblest, of the fate of mortals, he who, himself a captive, has seen his children led before him captives, yet possesses them alive. I, who triumphed over him, ascended in my chariot to the capitol from the death-bed of one son, returned from it to find the other expiring his last breath.

Nor from so fair a race of children is there one left to bear the name of Lucius Æmilius Paullus For the Cornelian and the Fabian House have two, granted to them in adoption, out of so numerous a progeny of sons. In the house of Paullus, beside himself, there is no survivor. But under this calamity of my own family, your happiness and the prosperity of the republic are my consolation.

With this noble and patriotic speech concludes the public career of this good man and admirable soldier, unless we add thereto his election to the censorship, in the year of the city 550, B.C. 164; the most dignified and almost sacred office to which a Roman magistrate could aspire, but one which conferred honour on the holder, as an evidence of his integrity and purity of life, rather than influence or power.

He lived four years after his elevation to this dignity, and died, universally regretted by his countrymen, as one of the most able, honest, and virtuous citizens of the commonwealth, at a time when the commonwealth itself was degenerating into baseness and corruption.

At his decease, his sons, though adopted into other families, honoured his memory with funeral games; and it is worthy of remark, that on this occasion was first presented to a Roman audience, the Adelphi, the last comedy of the poet Terence.

So passes from our sight Lucius Æmilius Paullus, of whom it may be said with truth, that he left behind him but one soldier, and that his own son, who could compare with him in ability or success; that he was a pure man in an impure age; and that while his virtues and nobility of soul were emphatically his own, the crimes with which he has been unreasonably and unjustly charged by a modern historian, (*Schmitz. Hist. Rom.*), of repute, were those of his country, which he served, as it was his duty, with unquestioning fidelity.

4

Caius Marius of Arpinum

Quid illo cive tulisset
Natura in terris, quid Roma beatius unquam,
Si circumducto captivorum agmine, et omni
Bellorum pompâ, animam exhalasset opimam
Cum de Teutonico vellet desceudere curru.
       Juvenal, Sat X.

  Concerning this very remarkable man, notorious equally for his virtues and his vices, both of which were extraordinary and superlative, Plutarch observes that, in common with Quintus Sertorius, the rebel partisan of Spain, and Lucius Mummius, the conqueror of Corinth, we know him by no third name; but he fails to indicate the nature of the name which is wanting, or the cause—identical in the instances cited—of its absence.

  Every Roman of established family, whether patrician or plebeian, had three names. The first, or *praenomen*, corresponding to our Christian name, was peculiar to the individual, and was given to boys either on their attaining the age of puberty, at fourteen, or on assuming the *toga virilis* at sixteen years—the *nomen* was that of the house, as Cornelius, Fabius, Æmilius, and the like, almost invariably terminating in *ius*, or *eius*—the last occasionally contracted into *oeus*—and indicating the common origin and clanship of many families—the *cognomen*, which stood the third, was that of the family, had almost any termination, and often alluded to some individual peculiarity, whether of person, character, temperament, or profession, in the first founder, such as Strabo, the squint-eyed; Asper, the harsh-tempered; Cursor, the swift of foot; Bubulcus, the herdsman and many others, which descended to posterity apart from any personal application.

A fourth name, or *agnomen*, was occasionally added, but always as a personal distinction commemorative of some great deed, some state service, or some foreign conquest, as Africanus and Asiaticus, severally applied to three Scipios, Numidicus to Metellus, and Achaicus to Lucius Mummius, named above, as the conqueror of Corinth. This fourth name, however, in all cases died with the first owner, and in no respect affected his heirs or family.

In the case of adoption of any member of one house into a family of another house, yet another modification of the fourth, and in some cases a fifth name was brought into existence, the person adopted receiving in lieu of his own *praenomen*, *nomen*, and *cognomen*, those of his adoptive father, with suffix of his own clan name, its termination altered from *ius* into *ianus*. For example, the second son of Lucius Æmilius Paullus was adopted by Publius Cornelius Scipio, the conqueror of Hannibal and victor of Zama, thence called Africanus. The youth adopted was thereafter known as Publius Cornelius Scipio, from his adopted father, Æmilianus from his natural father's house, and afterward Africanus also, not that he inherited the *agnomen* of his adopted father, but that he himself won the same honorary title, as the destroyer of Carthage.

To a person, therefore, intimately acquainted with the history of Rome, the names of any man are as clearly distinctive of his genealogy, of the circumstances of his life, and of his rank and honours in the state, as are the armorial bearings of a noble Norman to the eyes of one skilled in heraldry.

All Romans of respectable origin, as I have above stated, bore three names, for even the *plebeians* had houses, some of them exceedingly ancient, and so distinguished of old as to have become in some sort, although plebeian, noble.

The absence of the *nomen* proper, or clan name, indicated, therefore, not a *plebeian* only, but a *plebeian* without connections or antecedents—one of the lowest class, and, so far as birth and hereditary position are to be regarded, the most ignoble.

Marius was born at Arpinum, a small Latin town originally belonging to the Volsci, taken by the Samnites, retaken by the Romans, and ultimately raised to the dignity of a municipal town, when its citizens were enrolled in the Cornelian tribe.

The possession of the *municipium* did not of itself render all the citizens of any place citizens of Rome, in the fullest sense of the word. One class of these boroughs retained the perfect administration of their own local affairs, their own legislative and executive magistracies; their natives sharing many privileges of Roman citizens, but not possessing the power of voting at Rome, and remaining ineligible to office.

A second class was completely incorporated with the Roman State, and possessed every right of the Roman citizen, but as such, being esteemed part and parcel of Rome itself, lost the internal administration of their own affairs, which were directed either by *quatuorviri*, elected by the popular voice, or by a single prefect, appointed by the city *praetor*, sent annually from Rome. Yet a third class, their inhabitants being Roman citizens in the largest sense, retained their own magistracies, and their own internal government.

Of these three classes Arpinum stood in the second order, being governed by a single prefect, and having become in all respects a part of Rome, of which her citizens were citizens likewise; and of Arpinum, Marius was a citizen, of *plebeian* rank, serving in the equestrian centuries; the latter circumstance at this period of Roman history, involving merely military distinction, and probably indicating the possession of more or less property, but having no relation whatever with social distinction or civil privileges.

At this period of Roman history, senatorial rank had long ceased to be a condition of birth or a patrician privilege, having become a consequence of the tenure of certain magisterial offices, the candidates for which depended for election on the popular vote of Rome, and might aspire from any condition or order of the state.

Citizens only of Rome itself, or of such *praefectural* boroughs as held the full Roman *franchise*, were eligible to such offices as conferred senatorial rank; but citizens of all the boroughs, *praefectures*, and colonies, which had not the right of suffrage, or magisterial eligibility, at Rome, when they had held senatorial magistracies in their native towns, were so far at least Roman citizens, as to be eligible, as we should say *ad eundem*, to the parallel dignities in the state.

The last named condition does not apply to Caius Marius, who had never served Arpinum in any capacity, for Arpinum had no separate national existence; but was himself as a perfect citizen, though of the very lowest class, eligible by the people to any, even the highest, dignity, in regular official gradation.

I have dwelt somewhat at length on these particulars, not that they have any material bearing on the military or political progress of this celebrated demagogue, but that, in my opinion, they have everything to do with the formation of his character, with the creation of his political principles, with his undying hatred to the aristocracy, whether as to individuals, or as to a collective body, and with the atrocities, into which he was led by his insatiable ambition, and almost insane hatred of the nobles.

It has been clearly shown by Niebuhr and Arnold, that, since the passage of the Hortensian laws, the Roman constitution was as equally founded on justly balanced rights, and well considered interests of all classes in the State, as is perhaps possible in any form of human government.

An equal power was possessed by the higher and lower legislative bodies; the higher, or *senatus*, being chosen by the lower, much after the manner of the English House of Commons; the lower being the whole body of the Roman people, voting in their primary assemblies.

Neither to be a senator, nor to hold any dignity in the republic, was it necessary to have patrician birth, or noble ancestors. The noble houses held no longer any distinctive privileges, any hereditary rights, save perhaps some few connected with religious or superstitious office—which could offer, if any, but temporary resistance to the popular will, whether for good or evil—and in fact had no political advantages over the most lowly born of their fellow citizens, beyond that influence attaching to wealth, education, or descent from famous names and a truly noble race, which ever has had, ever will have, and needs must have its weight, under whatever form of government, from the aristocratic rule of the great Persian dynast, to the pure and unmixed democracy of the fierce Athenian mob.

> It is certain that the senate retained high and independent powers of its own, which were no less sovereign than those possessed by the assembly of the tribes; and in practice, each of these two bodies kept up for a hundred and fifty years a healthy and vigorous life in itself, without interfering with the functions of the other. Mutual good sense and good feeling, and the continual moderating influence of the college of the *tribunes*, whose peculiar position, as having a *veto* on the proceedings both of the senate and the people, disposed them to regulate the action of each, prevented any serious collision, and gave to the Roman constitution that mixed character, partly aristocratic and partly popular, which Polybius recognised, and so

greatly admired. And thus the event seems to have given the highest sanction to the wisdom of the Hortensian laws; nor can we regard them as mischievous or revolutionary, when we find that, from the time of their enactment, the internal dissensions of the Romans were at an end for a hundred and fifty years, and that during this period the several parts of the constitution were all active. It was a calm not produced by the extinction of either of the contending forces, but by their perfect union.— Arnold *Hist. Rome*, vol. ii.

These were, indeed, the palmy days of the Roman constitution. United among themselves, self-respecting and respecting each other, all orders of the state were equitably and happily governors and governed. All alike respected the laws, which all alike had a share in enacting; all alike obeyed the magistrates, which all alike had a share in creating.

The rights, social, political, hereditary, territorial, of all parties were respected by all, because the privileges of no one class interfered with the rights of any other. And the interests of none were obnoxious, because none had interests incompatible with the public good.

Such had been the state of things at home, since a period shortly preceding the invasion of Italy by Pyrrhus the Epirot, in the year of Rome 474, B. C. 282. And abroad, so far as her allies and Italian subordinates of the Latin name are concerned, the conduct of the Republic in the main must have been just and beneficent, and the advantages derived by the Italian states from her must have been at least equal to those which she obtained from them; since of thirty colonies not one had swerved from its fealty, much less joined the enemy, or made common cause with Carthage, even after the disastrous and all but fatal carnage of Thrasymene and Cannae, when Rome, shattered to her very centre, reeled like a foundering vessel, as on the point to sink; and when on them, the faithful partners of her adverse fortunes, fell the brunt of Hannibal's cruel devastation, and above a moiety of the losses of that protracted and, as to them it must needs have appeared, almost unavailing war, rested on them alone.

So do not persecuted dependencies in behalf of persecuting governments.

They fought for Rome, because they felt themselves in almost all points Romans, aspired to become so altogether, and deemed it, justly, to be the best of all things for a people, at that day, to have a portion, together with her fortunes, whether good or evil, in the powers, the privileges, and the name of Romans.

It is idle, therefore, to talk henceforth in Roman history of the oppression of the patrician houses; for they had long lost all powers to oppress, whether as patrons their clients, as creditors their debtors, or as the legislative and indirectly executive power of the state, the plebeians as a body.

The whole case was now altered; and, in the dissensions which followed, the patrician houses and the patrician members of the senate were acting strictly, in the main, as the conservative party of the state, and the maintainers of law and order against the ultra democrats, and the wicked and unscrupulous demagogues who led them, by flattering their worst qualities, and ministering to their basest passions.

It was not at that time in Rome the question whether the general will of the people should be carried out or frustrated —for the laws, the magistracy, the judiciary, were all of the most ultra popular creation; and there were no human means of counteracting the people's will, when it was once proved to be the general will, in the mode, under the forms, and in accordance with the laws, prescribed and framed by none others than the people themselves.

But the question urged, and the right claimed by the ultra democratic party then, precisely as they are those by the ultra progressionists at this day, were simply these—that the primary popular will, or the will of what might be claimed by any party, without proof, to be a vast majority, should at once become law, overriding and annihilating on the instant all existing statutes, all vested rights, all constitutional obstacles, all solemnly sanctioned treaties; in a word, all opposition, human or divine.

This the patrician party set themselves seriously to oppose; and it is probable, nay! it is almost certain, having a due regard to the analogies of human nature, that such a party, under such circumstances, agitated moreover by apprehensions of constantly decreasing privileges on their own part, and constantly growing encroachments on the side of their adversaries, should resist, with injudicious and intemperate warmth and obstinacy, reforms in themselves harmless or even salutary, only because they emanated from a party of whom they believed, not without some show of reason, that no good could come.

Irritated by such opposition, which they, naturally perhaps, knowing it to be fruitless, regarded as factious, the *plebeian* party, or democratic party rather, for the unity and cohesion of the old parties of the state had been long ago broken up and abolished, was easily stimulated by its leaders into acts of violence, in illegally carrying measures into effect, which might just as easily have been righteously enacted by the due operation and under the sanction of existing laws; and, thereafter, into rapacity, iniquity, and outrageous wrong, in striving to overturn all existing institutions, that no man should have any rule which to follow, or government to obey, beyond his own arbitrary and absolute will.

I am far, therefore, from intending to say that patrician supporters, whether in or out of the Senate, did no wrong themselves towards others, either in resisting innovations when in the minority, or in redressing abuses and punishing injuries, when unexpectedly and casually reinstated in the majority.

The proscriptions, the atrocities, the usurpations of Sylla and the aristocrats were no less infamous, nor a whit more pardonable; than those of Marius and the democrats; because they were second in point of time, or consequences of prior excesses.

In point of policy they were yet more ill-considered, as more fatal, since they diverted the general indignation from the primary aggressors, to themselves, who should have been the redressers, not the bloody and barbarous avengers of by-gone wrong.

Moderation, mercy, and justice, punishment sternly and impartially exacted of the guilty, some voluntary concession of harmless privileges claimed, some graceful reform of trivial grievances still existing, when the aristocrats regained their authority, would certainly have completely reinstated them in power; and, in all reasonable probability, would have preserved inviolate and incorrupt that admirable Roman constitution of the sixth century, which, before the commencement of the seventh, was convulsed and destroyed by hideous anarchy, and buried in the cold obstruction of a centralised despotism within a hundred years from the first attack upon it by the great soldier and dishonest citizen of whom I am now to treat.

I do, however, unhesitatingly assert that on the accession of Marius to his first *curule* office, his party had no political grievances whatever whereof to complain; nor their antagonists any political privileges whatever injurious to the public weal.

Had there existed any such things, legal redress and legal reforms were easy and certain; for the populace, as an unity, had the moiety of the legislative, and the appointment of the whole senatorial, executive, and judicial powers of the state.

Social wrongs there were doubtless; as there ever have been, and probably must be, in all human societies, so long as wealth shall have power to corrupt, and men be found so weak as to be corrupted. Social wrongs can, however, be restrained, if not extirpated, by legal control; and the poor, who complain of the corruptions practised by the wealthy, would do well to remember that they are themselves partners in the guilt; that to take, is no less a sin against the republic than to offer, a bribe; and that unlimited wealth would be powerless to buy, if poverty would not be sold.

To cling to hereditary pride when hereditary privilege has passed away, to value personal distinction, antiquity of birth and splendour of descent the more, as the power and prerogative, which once attached to them, diminish and depart, is the innocent, the impuissant, but the inherent, sin of decayed aristocracies.

Never is the disinherited noble so jealous of his titular distinction, of his ancestral name and hereditary renown, as when, save these, he has nothing left of which to be jealous. Never is he so contemptuous toward the upstart, the new man, the nameless tenant of time-honoured dignities, as when he has most cause to envy him.

As the *ancienne noblesse* of the *Faubourg St. Germain*, in the days of the Burgher King, or the intrusive emperor, so were the old patrician houses, in the times of Caius Marius.

Such powerless and unreal scorn might extort a smile of compassion from the good and great; a sarcastic sneer from the cynic, a bitter jest from the stoic; but in the ruthless bosom of the "stung plebeian," the man of but two names, it aroused a bitterness of hellish hatred almost inconceivable, a thirst for vengeance, to be slaked only in torrents of pure and noble blood.

To the student of Roman history, it is a matter of the deepest regret that at the very period when authentic and contemporaneous narration may be said to have fairly commenced, and when events unparalleled in magnitude and interest were taking place, both in the circumstances of the foreign world—against which, liberated by the fall of Carthage from all danger to her own security, the great Republic had now turned her arms with a fixed purpose of universal conquest—and in the polity of the state itself, wherein changes the most important were in progress, he is met by a fatal *hiatus* in history itself, and has nothing on which to rely beyond an abridged epitome, a few scattered fragments, and some bald gossip of garrulous old Plutarch, who, for a while, must be held perhaps the best extant guide.

Of all the mighty enterprises and great achievements of the sublimely bad *plebeian*, which raised him to such a pre-eminence of glory, that the grand Roman Satirist, (*Juvenal. Sat.* X), could conceive nothing within the range of nature comparable to his beatitude on the day of his Teutonic triumph, we have scarcely any details, beyond a mere enumeration of his battles, his victories, his glories, and his crimes; if we except the elegant relation of his Jugurthine campaigns by the classic hand of Sallust; while of his yet more glorious and scarce less cruel rival.

Triumphant Sylla, he whose chariots rolled,
On Fortune's wheel.

. . . . nearly the same obscurity conceals the brightest exploits. Their wars, defensive and offensive, set by their success an indelible mark on the pages of Rome's military annals, as did their political strife and personal hatred on those of her constitutional history; but of the means by which each or either attained his extraordinary ends, we are reduced, unfortunately, to judge principally from results, all precise information being lost concerning the principles and arts of their warfare, and even concerning the particulars of their greatest actions.

It is probable that Caius Marius was born in or about the 597th year of the Republic, and the 157th before the Christian era, of unknown parents, and in the lowest class of society. He is described by Velleius Paterculus, as a grim-featured, unkempt man, pure in private life, but rugged and uncivilized to excess; and Plutarch states of him, having seen his marble statue at Ravenna, in Gaul, that his aspect was harsh and morose, and that having, from his early childhood, applied himself to arts of strength and manhood, and to the acquisition of military, rather than civil, knowledge, he was violent of nature and unable to control or moderate his passions. He never condescended to learn Greek letters, or to use the tongue, holding it absurd and disgraceful to study the language of a people who were enslaved to their pupils. And could he have been induced to sacrifice to the Greek Muses and Graces, the Greek chronicler, Plutarch, says:

> He would not have put so disgraceful a coping-stone of savage ignorance and brute cruelty, to his deeds of war and statesmanship.

He was first employed under Publius Cornelius Scipio Æmilianus, son of Lucius Æmilius Paullus, the conqueror of Perseus, at the celebrated Siege of Numantia, in Spain, where it is not a little singular that he was brought into association with the young Jugurtha, who was at that time serving the Romans in command of large bodies of Numidian cavalry, the contingent of his uncle Micipsa, who is said to have been actuated in employing him in such duty by a desire of ridding himself, by some of the chances of war, of one in whom he foresaw a dangerous and ambitious rival of his own sons for the crown of Numida.

Be this as it may, under the auspices of the distinguished commander who destroyed Carthage, both these young men learned and practised, side by side, those arts of war and principles of strategy, which they were, at a future period, destined to put into application one against the other. But they, for the moment, contended only in diligence of study, patience of hardship, resolution to endure and audacity to do, who should in after days maintain a darker contest; which should deserve the most infamous repute, as most vindictive, sanguinary, ruthless, and unrelenting of butchers and usurpers.

With the exception of courage, and a sort of cold integrity which cannot fail to remind one of the vaunted incorruptibility of Carlisle's favourite monster, Robespierre, Marius appears to have possessed no one redeeming quality or characteristic, no one liberal taste or gentle feeling.

He was a great leader and an unconquerable hater, and no more. Jugurtha had not even the poor palliation of integrity of life; he was in all respects a thorough and untamed barbarian, with all his vices and few of his virtues.

It may be that their early intercourse had something to do with the similarity of their savage tempers, and brutal careers,—however different their fortunes. While they were comrades, it is certain that both highly distinguished themselves, so that Scipio was induced to bring them prominently forward, noticing them in his dispatches, employing them in hazardous expeditions, where they might win a name, and often honouring them with invitations to his table.

On one of these occasions, it is said, that, when his officers were drinking around the general and striving to gain his favour by adulation, someone asked Scipio, where, after his career of glory should be ended, the Romans might hope to find such another general and consul as himself; to which Scipio replied, laying his hand playfully on the shoulder of Marius, who reclined the next to him on the same couch. The narrator adds:

Perhaps here so quick were they both, the latter to display his greatness, while yet but a youth, the former to prognosticate vast ends from such beginnings.

For some time after the conclusion of the Spanish war, Marius appeal's to have led a retired civilian life, for it is not until the year 635 of Rome, or 119 B. C, that we find him occupying the place of tribune of the people, during the consulship of Lucius Caecilius Metellus, surnamed Dalmaticus for his conquests in that country, and Lucius Aurelius Cotta, the former of whom was his fast friend, and in some considerable degree brought about his election, while the latter found in him a vigorous and unscrupulous political antagonist.

In this office, he conducted himself with all the stern and self-sufficient firmness and courage which his whole after career so clearly proved him to possess, but exhibited as yet no symptoms of the inordinate ambition and savage temper which became his chief characteristics.

His first measure was an act, *lex Maria de Suffragiis*, relating to the police arrangements of the election, by which to prevent the polling of the votes of those who were neither citizens nor electors. The law was wise and salutary, but a party of nobles, with Aurelius Cotta, the consul, at their head, endeavouring fraudulently to defeat it, by withholding the authority of the Senate, Marius, in his quality of tribune, threatened to commit the consul, and subsequently Lucius Metellus, the *princeps Senatûs*, to prison, should they not allow a reconsideration of the matter, and its reference to the people with the senatorial sanction.

This counsel fortunately prevailed; the bill passed into a law, and Marius gained great popularity for the resolution and bravery with which he had maintained the right against aristocratical aggression. Before he vacated his office, however, he had equal occasion to prove himself no more liable to plebeian than to noble intimidation. One of his colleagues, having moved a distribution of grain from the public granaries, either gratuitous or at a rate far below the market prices, among the indigent citizens—a common expedient of the factious Roman demagogue to carry mob popularity at the expense of the common weal, and against all sound principles of public economy—Marius resisted the pernicious innovation with so much power and such indomitable will, that he gained his object; and showed himself hitherto, although a member of the popular party, no blind partisan of a faction, but a man willing and capable to compel the administration of equal justice in the state.

After passing through this necessary step of tribuneship, it would appear that Caius Marius failed in his efforts to obtain the office either of *plebeian* or *curule Œdile*, for both which he sued and was defeated in a single day, owing to the uncompromising harshness and arrogance of his demeanour. (*Plutarch, Vit. Caii Mar.*),

Sometime afterward, becoming candidate for the *praetorship*, he obtained it, though not without great difficulty, owing to, the strenuous opposition of the nobles, and to some suspicion of bribery, which would seem not to have been without some show of foundation, since Cassius Sabaco, a senator of his faction and his familiar associate, was degraded from the senate by the Censors, owing to his alleged privity in the corruption. In his *praetorship*, he appears to have performed nothing of moment: and, after the expiration of that office having obtained by lot, the *pro-praetorship* of farther Spain, he is said there to have suppressed the predatory habits of the native tribes, among whom, as in the Celtic races generally, robbery of cattle, on a large scale, and the prosecution of deadly feuds and frays were deemed in no wise discreditable, if not decidedly the reverse. Thus far this singular man does not appear to have done much, either in military or civil life, worthy of mark, and what little he had done rather of negative than positive merit.

The greatest testimony as yet in his favour, even as a man of action, is the reported favourable opinion of Scipio, under whom, however, he could only have served in a very subordinate rank; and indeed even this evidence is in some degree discredited by the fact that fifteen years elapsed between his supposed exploits at Numantia, and his attainment of the secondary office of Tribune of the Commons.

In this, although he unquestionably showed himself a person of courage and steadfastness and an upright citizen, he as clearly failed to produce any extraordinary impression even on his own party, which were rapidly gaining the ascendant in the state, since they did not rally about him, or put him forward successfully as their candidate for the higher, much less the highest dignities; and it is distinctly stated that he was desirous on his return from Spain of applying for the consulship, but did not venture to become a candidate.

Still it may not be doubted that he had shown signal marks of capacity in some sort; for, though he possessed no wealth, which had gradually become there—as it is unhappily becoming with us—the easiest key to popular consideration; nor marked political influence; nor the charm of affability; nor any social grace of public or private life, he continued to rise in public opinion, and espoused a lady of the haughty patrician family, who claimed to trace their pedigree to Iulus or Ascanius, son of Æneas, the Trojan colonist of Italy, and founder of Alba Longa, whence the royal race of Rome. This lady was the aunt of the afterward famous Caius Julius Caesar the final subverter of the Republic, which after him, had, in fact, but for a few years, even a nominal existence. So near have we approached the end.

At this period in the history of Rome we find, on careful observation, that almost everything that was good in the constitution, and in its divisions and parties, had already been changed, altered, or destroyed.

It was no longer a strife between the old *populus* or privileged *burgher* class, and the proletarian *plebs* possessed of few rights and ineligible to any dignities. It was no longer a struggle between the senate and the old houses, and the people at large, these for the retention of oppressive prerogatives, and those for the extension of rightful privileges. It was no longer even the legitimate social struggle for lawful dignity, by lawful election, between the haughty exclusionists of the old senatorial and sacerdotal houses, and the ardent and ambitious representatives of newly-risen famihes.

The old aristocracy had ceased to exist. The old *populus* had no privileges. The old *plebs* no oppressions. The senatorial dignity, and thence the very highest offices were attainable by the meanest citizen, were in the gift of the general assembly, of which every Roman citizen was a member, and an equal voter.

But wealth had invaded the Roman republic, like an entering ocean tide of corruption. A new class had sprung up in the state, unknown of old, the *equites*, or, as we persist most absurdly in translating the word, knights.

This class, which was originally composed merely of the wealthier order of citizens, who were compelled to serve in the legions, of the old form, on horseback, at their own expense, as privates, without privilege or prerogative, had long since fallen into abeyance. After the withdrawal of Hannibal from Italy, the Roman citizen never served on horseback; and the cavalry was supplied by the Italian colonies, the allies of the Latin name, and yet more largely by mercenaries, Numidians, Thracians, Gauls, Illyrians, and the like. Perfectly clear is this, from the fact that, in his Gallic conquests, Julius Caesar finding the want of Roman horse on whom he could rely, drafted a portion of his *legionary* foot, and mounted them as tumultuary cavalry for the time of need.

This class, as it now existed, had no more connection with horses, or horse-service, than had their predecessors with those chivalrous duties and that high honorary rank, which is naturally connected with the English word, knight, so strangely misapplied to this Roman order by modern historians.

In the year 123 B. C, or of the City 631, by the Sempronian laws of Gracchus, a new *ordo equestris* was created, (*Anthon's Class. Dic., Article Sempronia*), by which all persons possessing the rank of *eques*, from the having a horse assigned to them at the public expense, or from holding sufficient income to entitle them to that distinction, as liable to serve on horse at their own expense, were exempted from cavalry service, but required to perform the duty of *judices*, something intermediate— to state it briefly—between jurors and our justices of peace.

For a time, this name of *eques* did not carry with it anything worth having; and, within a few years, the judicial powers of the *equites* being abolished by the Aurelian Laws of Sylla, not even a shadow of state power. But, to come strictly to the point, from the day when they ceased to be cavalry privates, they were to the end money-holders, money-buyers, money-lenders, government-contract-brokers, farmers of public revenues, and so masters of Rome.

They possessed no position in the state, except that which their wealth gave them. They were not, and could not be, senators, except by popular election to senatorial offices. They were vastly rich—deedly despised, both by men who had done great deeds themselves, and who could point to great deeds of old, done by their ancestors, and utterly scorned and hated by the new men, builders up of their own nobility and names by their own exploits, though nameless and without ancestry. Even the nobles might associate with these latter, notwithstanding their want of ancestry and images, as if worthy of their own merits to have possessed both. Neither the nobles nor the populace would tolerate men, who, owning nothing but money, claimed to be superior by that alone, to families, or individuals of noble ancestry, distinguished service and undoubted merit.

The nobles scorned them for their arrogant assumption and pretentious ostentation, as perhaps they envied them for the wealth, from which these arose, coupled to their lack of honours either transmitted or acquired. The people hated them for their high-swollen abundance, their utter uselessness as men, and their insolent pride, more offensive than that of the nobles. Therefore, the *equites* compelled, in some sort, to form a class of their own, determined to become the dominant class through the only means which they possessed, and in the end effected their object. Wealthy, ignoble, lazy, gaining money by money, holding all things—as money dealers ever do—even to themselves, venal, they laboured to reduce everything to their own standard, by rendering all things from the highest office to the lowest vote venal likewise, and in doing this also they succeeded.

From that period money ruled Rome; and all distinction of political parties, according to the distinctions of birth, high name, virtue, "vigour of bone, desert in service," or social position, was obliterated. Henceforth all was a gigantic scramble for the tenure of office—office to be purchased by wealth, and to be rendered productive of wealth, the only end for which to purchase it.

Henceforth, all distinction ends between *Patrician* and *Plebeian*. All true distinction even between Aristocrat and Democrat. The aristocrats, of this latter day, or the men of noble families and ancient principles, strove in council, or in arms, for the maintenance of the Old Republic. The democrats struggled for the abolition of all orders, all privileges, all property—the *plebeian* democrats, from pure hatred to nobility, and from an honest but ignorant desire to promote the interests of their class—the democratic nobles for anarchy, out of which to create despotism. The *plebeian* democrats, as the Gracchi, Flaccus, Saturninus, Glaucia, Saufeius, Sulpicius, Marius, Cinna perished more by the results of their own extravagant excesses and atrocities, than by the efforts of their enemies.

The true republicans, styled by their enemies aristocrats, fell everywhere by the sword of war, of massacre, of private assassination—fell with Cicero at Liternum, with Pompey at Pharsalia, and were extinguished with the last of their order, Cassius and Brutus, at Philippi.

The vicious nobles calling themselves democrats, using the wealth of the capitalists, and the blood and bone of the deluded populace, killed the republic, made the empire and ruled the world. But the world at length became aweary of them and their rule; and after centuries of frozen despotism, thawed at times only by deluges of virtuous blood, their empire, child of wealth and corruption, itself became venal, and fell by the very elements from which it sprang.

From the year 123 before the Christian Era, capital governed Home. From that year, venal and infamous, she tottered to her fall;

and with but a few momentary efforts, brilliant but brief, at recuperation, declined hourly thenceforth to the abyss in which were soon to be entombed her liberty and glory.

This digression is needful, because to the reader of my sketches a brief synopsis must be given, in order to his comprehending the changes in the condition of the state and in the character of the times, and the effect produced by them on the character, principles and natures of men; so that individuals and actions should be in the natural order and rule of one century, which would have been impossible, even as exceptions and monstrosities, in that preceding it.

So that within one century from that splendid and unrivalled act of self-devotion, by which the whole body of the Roman Aristocracy surrendered its entire property to the last pound of silver, to the exigencies of the state, or that scarce inferior act of magnanimity, by which it would not descend to rebuke the ten delinquent colonies—when Hannibal was thundering at the very gates—the same Republic should have produced in quick succession, a Saturninus, Marius, Sylla, Cethegus, Catiline, Caesar. Nor perhaps may this sketch fail altogether to attract the attention of men of modern times to the gradually growing influence of capital, not only over personal integrity, personal honour, and personal independence, but even over the national faith, justice, honour, and uncompromising nationality of countries.

This preamble, I trust not tedious, leads to the condition of public affairs, when Marius was again called to command for Rome, and to the reasons, not more of his being called to office, than of his subsequent career.

Shortly before the commencement of the Jugurthine war, Micipsa, the son and successor of Massinissa, the old ally of the Romans and sole monarch of all the sea-coast of Africa, westward so far as the River Molochath or Mulucha, which divided his dominions from those of the king of Morocco, and inland so far as the country of the Tuaricks and the Great Desert, died, bequeathing his kingdom between his sons, Adherbal and Hiempsal, and his nephew Jugurtha, who was son of his base-born brother Mastanabal. Jugurtha, however, who was evidently the favourite of his people, the best horseman, hunter, warrior of his tribe, who had been known often to slay the lion, hand to hand, in personal conflict, who had won eulogies and honour even from the warlike Romans, who was in all his actions, all his characteristics a genuine son of the desert, not content with a portion of the kingdom to which he felt that his capacity, if not his birth entitled him, aspired to the mastery of the whole.

His brother kinglings, (*Sallust vit. Jug*), *reguli*, as the Romans termed them, must have been distasteful to their people, who dreaded, and with justice, the interference of the encroaching Italians, who never withdrew their foot from a spot of earth whereon they had once set it, whether as friend, ally, mediator or avenger. And to this encroaching people Adherbal and Hiempsal paid, it would seem, assiduous court, associating with the Roman alien traders of the coast-cities, aping Roman manners and usages in their courts, deferring in all things to the officers of the Roman province, and in a word, submitting to the proud republic as their masters.

M. Michelet, the celebrated historian of the Roman Republic, endeavours strenuously to prove that Jugurtha has been improperly stigmatized as an usurper, and that such a title applies more justly to his unhappy kindred colleagues, he says:

> Those who consider him such, ought first to have ascertained whether a law of inheritance existed in the deserts of Numidia. The barbarians generally chose for a king the most worthy member of a family. The Numidians thought that the will of a deceased person could not overbalance the rights of a nation.— *Rome Rep.*

All very eloquent and good, if it were in the least true. But it is not. For in the first place no barbaric nations of the Eastern races, have ever had, or claimed to have, elective chiefs, but have at all times been governed by hereditary princes of the ruling family—since whatever deviations have occurred from the true hereditary line of succession arose from the intrigues of the court and harem, or the practice of kindred assassination, at once the reproach and bane of polygamous barbarian despotisms, and by no means from the popular voice.

In the second place, facts prove that the kingdom of Numidia was hereditary in the heir male of the royal line. For Massinissa, the first Numidian king with whom the Romans seem to have come into personal contact, succeeded his father Gula on the throne, and was in his turn succeeded by his own eldest son Micipsa, without the smallest tumult or even opposition from the people. He dying bequeathed his kingdom to his sons and his base-blooded nephew, who owed his preservation from the secret knife to which he would probably have been doomed, as a dangerous rival and competitor of his cousins, to his own prowess displayed at Numantia, and to his known intimacy with many of the Roman magistrates and nobles; perhaps, in some degree to his personal astuteness and popularity with his people, rendering it difficult to take him off in secret.

True it is that the faith of his countrymen, and the inveterate obstinacy of their adherence to him, unto the very last, through all extremities of fortune, after he had assumed the undivided sovereignty, sufficiently indicate him the choice and favourite of his countrymen, while it goes far to prove the falsity of the terms fickle, fight, and inconstant, as applied by their enemies to the Numidians, who never to the end, even when he had become suspicious, sudden and sanguinary, swerved from their fealty to the king, whom if they had not elected to the crown, they assuredly elected to follow.

I note this merely to correct an error. Jugurtha was assuredly an usurper in every sense of the. word, as he was also deeply imbued in the guilt of kindred bloodshed. But usurpation, in oriental despotisms, is not regarded as a crime, but rather as an evidence of courage, capacity and conduct in the usurper. And among brothers born of the slaves of the harem, there is so little of intercourse, affection, or even usage of kindred, that fratricide is to this day a thing of hourly occurrence, generally regarded with no abhorrence, but looked upon rather as a strong measure of policy, excusable on the plea of stronger necessity.

Therefore, though I cannot assume, with M. Michelet, either that Jugurtha was not an usurper, or that he regarded himself as the lawful king and punished his unfortunate cousins with death, and torture before death, as themselves usurpers; neither can I regard the crimes and kindred assassinations of this wild, indomitable man, as they would be regarded, if the work even of a civilized Greek or Roman, much more of a man of the present time and dispensation.

Be this, however, as it may, scarce had the princes separated after their first conference, before Jugurtha succeeded, by debauching the followers of Hiempsal, in having him murdered by his emissaries, in his own lodgings in the town of Thirmida, within his own dominions. His head was carried to Jugurtha, who at once throwing off the mask invaded the territories of Adherbal. These were the richest and most populous regions of Africa, the mercantile half Romanized cities, and the wealthy agricultural districts of the coast. Adherbal, therefore, had the more adherents, but the other had the better men and soldiers of the desert.

Adherbal sent envoys to Rome, but prepared armed resistance, was conquered and fled into the Roman province of Carthage, leaving his rival the undisputed sovereign of all Numidia.

Jugurtha sent envoys also, with much gold, for he knew the Roman aristocracy of the day, and with orders to make the most profuse largesses, wherever friends might be gained among the influential nobles, or votes purchased in the Senate; and so perfectly did they play their part, that ere long they reported to their master, that he might safely leave his cause to the decision of the Republic.

The event proved the justice of their judgment. Both parties pleaded their causes; and, when the envoys had withdrawn, after an earnest debate, in which all those to whom justice and right were dearer than wealth, and with them Æmilius Scaurus, one of the most influential senators of the day, spoke and voted for assisting Adherbal and punishing Jugurtha. Jugurtha's bribes prevailed over what little yet remained of Rome's honour.

It was decreed that the kingdom of the late monarch Micipsa should be equally divided between the kindred disputants by ten commissioners, the principal personage of whom was Lucius Opimius, a man of consular dignity, who on account of his sanguinary suppression of the faction headed by Caius Gracchus and Fulvius Flaccus, was the most powerful person in Rome with the aristocracy.

Him Jugurtha, though he esteemed him as an enemy, yet received with such high consideration, and with so adroit a mixture of flattery, and gifts, which he could not decline as bribes, and promises, that he brought him over to his party. Others, a majority, of the commissioners, he gained over by the same means, but with less caution. A powerless minority preferred good report to gold.

In the end, the usurper gained what he desired, the western country of Algeria, larger in extent, richer in men, adjoining the frontiers of Morocco, including all the northern spurs of the Atlas chain, and the desert of Angad, the country of the Kabyles and Berbers, to this day the most terrible of the Mediterranean tribes of Africa—while to the share of Adherbal fell the eastern division, adjoining the Roman province, well cultivated, abounding in marts of trade and well built commercial cities, its coasts full of secure harbours, its fields productive and stocked with cattle, the commercial, agricultural, Italianised Africa of the coast—for the effeminate, unwarlike, peace-loving sovereign, undoubtedly the preferable region.

Still he was by no means contented; for who has heard at any time that the greed of ambition is satiable by ministering to its appetite. On the contrary, having won the stake for which he played almost against his own expectation, and confirmed by the event in his estimate of

Homers absolute venality, he even overrated the influence of gold, on her magistrates, and seemed to imagine that there was no audacity of crime for which the highest bidder could not purchase impunity. Consequently no sooner had the commissioners of the Republic returned to Italy, than he once more armed and invaded the territory of his cousin, who, first sending deputies to beseech the speedy aid of Rome, took the field unwillingly against his able and unscrupulous opponent.

The two armies met at nightfall, near the sea shore, not far from the city of Cirta, now Constantina, which cost the French so much time and toil and blood in the outset of their Algerian conquest, and, as the day was too far advanced for immediate action, encamped on the ground they occupied, in sight each of the other's outposts. But when the night was well nigh spent, before the skies had begun to glimmer with grey, Jugurtha surprised the camp, and either cut down or utterly dispersed the troops of Adherbal, before they had shaken off the heaviness of sleep, so that they never again rallied. Adherbal himself escaped with a handful of horse to Cirta, so quickly pursued that, had it not been for the multitude of Roman citizens and Italian traders within the fortress, who manned the walls and beat off the Numidians, the war between the two kings would have been begun and ended in the same day. Nothing frustrated by this repulse, however, he laid close siege to the place, hoping to anticipate the arrival of the Roman deputies, who, he well knew, would be dispatched so soon as the news of his proceedings should reach the city.

The envoys arrived, before he had succeeded in his object, with instructions to see both the kings and to order them on pain of the high displeasure of the Roman people to lay down their arms and submit their differences to the Senate. To Adherbal, who was closely blockaded in his walls, they were allowed no access. From Jugurtha they obtained no satisfaction, but only vague expressions of his respect for the Senate, indefinite charges of treachery against his cousin, and promises to send an embassy with full power to treat on all matters to the city. And no sooner did he believe them to have left Africa than he again pressed the siege, and straitened the blockade of the fortress, in itself almost impregnable.

Reduced to the last extremity, and knowing his garrison to be almost devoid of provisions, Adherbal with great difficulty procured two persons, who should make their way through the lines and convey letters to Rome; which in fact arrived there safely, were read before a crowded Senate, and created so much excitement and indignation that it was no easy matter for the bribed *fautors* and partisans of the Numidian to prevent the immediate declaration of war, and despatch of an army to the aid of his injured kinsman.

They prevailed, however, and in lieu of an army, the *regum ultima* ratio, three arbiters were again despatched, but now men of weight, dignity and force, with Scaurus at their head, who made such speed to reach the seat of action that they landed in Utica, on the third day after their leaving Rome, and summoned Jugurtha to repair forthwith into the province to justify his proceedings.

Not daring, as yet, openly to defy the Senate, yet resolute not to give up his favourite project, he made one desperate attempt to storm the place, which failing, he proceeded with a small bodyguard to the province, and held several conferences with Scaurus and the envoys, wherein he was threatened with the instant vengeance of Rome in case of his continuing to beleaguer Cirta, even for another day.

Undeterred and immovable, however, in his secret purpose he equivocated and played fast and loose, until, after wasting much time and effecting nothing, this second embassy returned to Rome, leaving Jugurtha ample opportunity to complete his designs. One point he had gained already of no small weight, for during their protracted conferences, he won over Scaurus by his extraordinary donations, who having been, when most of his party were already corrupted, the keenest impugner and prosecutor of the king, was henceforth his closest confederate and counsellor in all his secret schemes.

It was not long ere the news of the failure of this second embassy reached Cirta; and at once the Italian and Roman citizens of the garrison, not dreaming that the barbarian could possibly dare so much against the majesty of the Roman people as to harm their persons, compelled Adherbal to surrender, on promise that his life should be spared. And he, having no other choice, though there was nothing on which he set less reliance than the faith of his kinsman, surrendered, only to be put to death, with every refinement of cruelty, by protracted tortures. Nor did his advisers fare better, for no sooner were the gates opened, than every adult capable of bearing arms, Numidian or Roman trader indiscriminately, was slaughtered by the soldiers of the desert, and the place given up to sack and pillage.

Of all Jugurtha's actions, this is to me the strangest and most inscrutable, since his end was sufficiently gained by the simple destruction of his rival, nor can any reason be imagined why he should have needlessly provoked the farther indignation of the proud and fierce Republic, by the wanton torture of their client, and the violation of the sacred character of Roman citizen. The apology of M. Michelet for this act, as if "he considered the anti-national candidate an usurper," cannot, as I have above demonstrated, be admitted. Nor is it shown by anything which has up to this time appeared in history, that Adherbal, whose adherents fought in his behalf faithfully if feebly, was regarded as the anti-national candidate. Still less is it proved, as that celebrated historian asserts, that "his hatred led him to confound Rome with Adherbal," since it is perfectly evident that he still confided in his ability to bribe the magistrates and purchase the friendship of Rome.

It must have been, either a deed of mere frenzy, such as a barbarian impotent to command his passions might commit during a passing gust of fury, soon to be repented, or a deep laid stroke of policy, whereby to render all his nation as guilty as himself of Roman blood, so as to have them desperate of pardon to the end, in case his plans should fail for buying bodily the whole corrupt republic—and to me the latter seems the more probable supposition, in view of the character and subtle genius of the man.

This last outrage was the drop which overflowed the cup of popular indignation, nor could the friends of the usurper prevent the dismissal of Jugurtha's embassy unheard, or the despatch of a consular army under Calpurnius Bestia, by way of Sicily into Numidia.

This occurred in the year of Rome 643, B. C. 111, which is the date at which commenced the Jugurthine war, terminated only after five years' hard fighting, to the lasting disgrace of Rome's officers and armies, by the great soldier who is the subject of the present memoir. It is remarkable that, almost simultaneously, with the commencement of the contest between the African princes, which led to this his first war, the Teutons and Cimbri, who furnished him his greatest triumph, appeared on the northern threshold of Italy, and came in contact with the Romans on the reverse of the Carnian Alps. But of this hereafter.

On his arrival in Numidia, Bestia commenced his operations with some vigour, took a considerable number of captives and a few towns, when Jugurtha proposed to treat—with Jugurtha to treat was to seek occasion for corrupting his enemy, and by aid of Scaurus, one of the consul's legates, he easily succeeded in the present instance. His bribes were immense, and a treaty was concluded, for the eyes of the public, by which Jugurtha surrendered himself, with his army, elephants and treasures a prisoner at discretion—but apart from this, and overruling it, was a secret compact guaranteed by the consul, whereby liberty, life and the sovereignty of Numidia were secured to the usurper. Thirty elephants, vast numbers of horses and cattle, and a small quantity of money was given up, for the sake of form, an armistice was proclaimed, and Bestia returned to Rome to hold the consular elections.

But this last act of infamy was too barefaced, and the plebeian indignation waxed so furious, that the Senate were overawed and dare not resist the clamour for inquiry raised by the whole popular party and enforced by the impetuous eloquence of the *tribune* Memmius. Jugurtha was cited to appear at Rome, as a witness to the corruptions which had been practised in Africa, under a written pledge and safe conduct from the Senate, and, what he valued yet more highly, the plighted faith of Longinus Cassius, who was sent to summon him.

Not the least strange or romantic incident in this man's strange and romantic career, is that, steeped to the lips as he was in blood of Romans, he had yet the effrontery, and the confidence in his ability, to carry all before him by corruption, to obey the citation, and actually appeared in the city, which no man had ever so defied and outraged, in the garb indeed and with the demeanour of a suppliant, but with the heart of a triumphant king. Immediately on his arrival he secured the advocacy of the shameless tribune Caius Boebius, and fearlessly appeared in the Senate, which sat with open doors, that all the people who thronged the vestibule and every approach to the temple, might hear the proceedings.

But when Memmius opened the case and produced Jugurtha as his witness, Caius Boebius interposed his sacred tribunitial veto, ordered the king to hold his peace, and, in spite of the clamours and fury of the indignant multitude, by dint of dauntless impudence finally put an end to the proceedings. Shortly afterward, while Jugurtha was yet detained in Rome, there appeared yet a new claimant of the throne, in the person of one Massiva, son of Gulussa, a younger but legitimate son of Massinissa; and his proceedings appeared so dangerous to the usurper that he procured his assassination, even within the walls of Rome by the intermediacy of his confidant Bomilcar. So recklessly and openly was this crime committed, that the agent was detected, and, his master procuring him the sureties of fifty Roman citizens, to whom he bound himself to make good their losses, instantly absconded to Africa.

The agency of Jugurtha was not to be doubted, but his privity to the crime could not be proved, and his safe conduct covered him. Ordered to depart from Italy within a given time, he turned back, after he had passed the gates, and gazed on the city long in silence. "A city to be bought," he said, "if she might find a buyer."

He entered that city once again, when five years had passed, to die; but three centuries had elapsed before his words were proved prophetic, when Rome was actually for sale to the highest bidder, and found a buyer in Didius Julianus.

The year 110, B.C., was far advanced before the consul Spurius Albinus, who succeeded Bestia, arrived with reinforcements to the army in Numidia; and by his customary artifices, offers to treat, promises to surrender, and probably by bribes also, Jugurtha contrived to protract matters without the drawing of a sword, until the time came round when the consul must return to preside at the Comitia. During his absence, which was prolonged by the dissensions of the tribunes in the city, taking advantage of the inconsiderate rashness of his lieutenant, Aulus Albinus, who thought to win the honour of concluding the war at a blow, the desert warrior drew him into an ambuscade, forced him to surrender at discretion, passed his army under the yoke—a disgrace which had not befallen a Roman army since the catastrophe, above two centuries before, in the Caudine forks—and compelled him to evacuate Numidia within ten days.

The grief and rage in Rome, on the receipt of these tidings, is more easily imagined than described. The armistice concluded with Marius was denounced, Aulus Albinus was utterly disgraced and ruined, and Quintus Caecilius Metellus, a noble of the highest character for integrity and capacity, who was elected consul with Silanus, received Numidia, with the Jugurthine war, for his province.

In the year of the city 645, B. C. 109, with strong reinforcements and Caius Marius as his lieutenant, this able soldier landed in Numidia, and, for the first time since its commencement, the war was prosecuted with ability and vigor. After some months well spent in reorganising and redisciplining the army, the physique and morale of which were entirely broken, Metellus took the field, wasting the country far and wide, with fire and sword, and keeping himself continually on his guard. When Jugurtha attempted tricks and treasons, he frustrated him at his own weapons, tampered with his envoys, and offered them such a price for the delivery of their master, dead or alive, that the wily Numidian found himself, for once, outdone in treason, and desisted.

A few days afterward, having garrisoned Vaga, a large inland town, the Numidian having ambushed him on his line of march near the River Muthul, he fought a pitched battle at great disadvantage, but by his own masterly dispositions and the able support of his lieutenant Marius, defeated the enemy with loss, and totally dispersed his army. Thereafter he proceeded through the interior, devastating the open fields, burning the cities, putting all the adult males to the sword, while Jugurtha, indefatigable and indomitable as Abd el Kader, or Hyder Ali, those greatest masters in desultory equestrian warfare, hung on their flanks, interrupted their communications, threatened them at all points, invisible but ever near, realizing the boast of the tyrant of the Carnatic to his English assailants, "that they should not know his whereabout once in a month, but that he would hear of theirs at every drum-beat."—Alison, *Hist. Europe.*

At length, weary of this delusory and unsatisfactory warfare, the consul resolved to bring the war to a close by the reduction of all the enemy's cities, and therefore laid siege to Zama, the largest and richest town of Numidia, and principal treasury of the king. He pressed the assault strenuously and fiercely, resolute to win it by escalade, sap or storm, when suddenly Jugurtha, coming up unforeseen, fell on the Roman camps, while the legions were attacking the place, and all but carried them, and so desperate and so persistent was his attack, that night, rather than the prowess of the Romans, closed the affair of the day; and foiled, rather than repulsed, the indomitable prince drew off his almost victorious squadrons, only to encamp close by the lines of the Romans, and to recommence the battle on the following morning, with the like near hope of victory, and failure of entire success.

The battle lasted all day long, with fluctuating fortunes, the Romans assaulting the city on one side, while they resisted from without the furious and sustained charges of the king, who poured his horse and foot on them, pell-mell, with constancy never before displayed by Numidians in array of battle. As before, night alone terminated the indecisive conflict. Neither army was victorious in the action, neither was worsted; but with Jugurtha, clearly remained the honour, as did in fact the success, of the day; for his object was the relief of Zama, and that object he gained.

Metellus drew off his army, weakened and dispirited, from the trenches, and finding that his able and active antagonist would fight him only desultorily, with his horse, after his own fashion, or on ground and at times of his own choosing, and moreover, that the season was drawing to a close, dispersed his army into winter quarters, in the towns which had been won from the king. Thereafter, since arms had availed him little, he had recourse to intrigue and corruption; and these weapons served him better than the more legitimate means of warfare.

By tampering with Bomilcar, Jugurtha's agent in the murder of Massiva, and operating now on his apprehensions, now on his cupidity, by promises of indemnity at the close of the war, and the offer of vast sums for the betrayal of his lord and king, dead or alive, into the hands of the Romans, he induced the miscreant to undertake the office of infamy.

He, having influence on Jugurtha's mind, as his chief counsellor and most trusted friend, by instilling into it suspicions as to the faith of the army, the fealty of his people, and the loyalty of his personal attendants, worked him at length to treat for peace with the consul.

For Metellus, the overture was all sufficient. Summoning, to a council of war, all of senatorial rank from winter quarters, he gave audience to the king's envoys, and rendered them this answer, that if the king desired peace of the Romans, he must first give them proof of his sincerity. By this transparent fraud, the barbarian, less wily than the honest Roman, was induced to surrender all his elephants, horses, arms, and two hundred thousand pounds' weight of silver; which it is absurd to suppose he would have done, unless upon conditions; and then, when it was understood that he was incapable of further resistance, he was commanded to come in and surrender himself at discretion.

The same base deception, atrocious breach of national integrity and honour, of which Scipio, the organ of the Roman aristocracy, had been guilty toward Carthage, was here attempted.

But like Carthage, cheated, disarmed, betrayed, defenceless, the desert-born refused to resign his liberty, resolute to deserve, if he might not gain, success.

So the Senate decreed a thanksgiving to the gods, and continued Metellus as proconsul, in command of the Numidian war and province.

About this time, Marius, whose fierce ambition and bitter hatred of the nobles grew daily—the former stimulated, probably, by the growth of his renown, the latter irritated by the scornful deportment of his chief, Metellus—was in execution of his official duties at Utica, where he fell in with a certain diviner of future events; who so strenuously assured him that he should succeed in his next enterprise, be it what it might, that he, understanding his canvass for the consulship to be intended, determined to offer himself a candidate.

It appears that this strangely constituted man, deaf, as he showed himself, in latter times, to any sentiment of humanity or mercy, to any reverence for aught natural or divine, was yet abjectly superstitious, relying implicitly on the tricks and juggleries of necromantic and *haruspical* diviners, and in his later days, carrying about with him a Syrian, or perhaps Jewish, witch or sorceress, named Martha, to whose guidance he in a great measure committed his actions.

By the promises of this person, by the inflammatory and seditious instigation of the trading *equites* and revenue-farmers of Utica, who finding their lucrative operations injured by the existing war, were desirous to terminate it at all hazards—above all, perhaps, by a sneering reply of Metellus to his request for leave of absence, in order to canvass for the first magistracy of the Republic, he was inflamed to such a degree of confidence, that he resigned his commission as legate to the consul, and repaired to Rome, after a treacherous attempt to procure Jugurtha's surrender or slaughter at the hands of one Gauda, aided by Nabdalsa and Bomilcar.

This Gauda, urged by hopes of succeeding to Jugurtha's throne, as well as the knights and base traffickers of the province, and the turbulent and disaffected of the soldiery, was induced to write most urgently to his friends and partisans in Rome, in flagrant censure of Metellus and his conduct during the war, and to assert roundly that with half the army, now on foot, Marius would bring the war to a glorious close in a single campaign, which had languished four years under Metellus and his predecessors.

At the same time the town of Vaga, which had been garrisoned by Metellus in the previous year, revolted, and put its garrison and all the Italian residents to the sword, not without suspicion of treachery on the part of the Latin governor, Titus Turpilius Silanus, who only escaped the daggers of the Numidians, to die under the rods and axes of the Roman *lictors*.

This occurrence added, for the moment, to the outcry against the aristocracy; and the rabble, having gained a temporary ascendancy over the nobles, who were utterly depressed and downcast by the passage of the Manilian law, Marius, by the basest and most flagitious appeals to the prejudices, the violences, and the fury of the mob, secured his election and the province, to which he aspired.

In the meantime, during his absence from the seat of war, Metellus had pressed matters to the utmost. He had made himself master of Vaga, by a stratagem, through which he led the inhabitants to mistake his forces for those of the king; when he charged them home, entered the gates pell-mell with the fugitives, and punished their defection, as was usual with the Romans, when victorious, by a wholesale massacre.

The conspiracy of Bomilcar and Nabdalsa had been discovered by Jugurtha, in the interim, and the guilty dealt withal, as their guilt merited; but, from that day forth, Jugurtha's fall was dated. From that day forth, he placed no trust in man; he slept not over two nights in one place, nor often one, without a change of bed and chamber. He wore secret armour, he scarce dared eat, or drink, for fear of secret poison. His mind, like the iron soul of the great English Protector, broke down before the never-absent menace of private assassination. And now, once more, finding that his own arms were turned against himself, and that he was yet more inferior to the Romans in perfidy and murder, than in the balanced field of battle, he tried the chances of an openly delivered conflict; fought well and long; but, after half winning the day, as he had ever done, where he fought in person, was beaten by the superior constancy and steadiness of the *legions*.

Many of his horses and arms, most of his standards were taken; but he lost few men; for the Numidians never involved themselves so deeply but that they could easily retreat; and then, the knowledge of the ground and their natural agility saved them. Thence he fled to Thala, one of his royal cities, his principal treasury, the seat of his *harem* and the abode of the kingly children, situate in the midst of difficult and dreadful deserts, infested by wild beasts and deadly serpents, and at fifty miles' distance from the nearest water.

Here, at length, he thought himself secure; for he never deemed it possible that a Roman army, with its ponderous infantry, its baggage and its artillery, could traverse such a waste as intervened; never doubted that, if they should attempt it, fatigue and thirst would do the work of the sword. Metellus, however, by pressing all the cattle of the country into service, and loading them with water vessels, seized from all dwellings, far and near, brought his men to the walls in safety; when rain fell in such abundance, at an unusual season of the year, which both parties attributed to supernatural influences or to the destiny of Rome, as to render their farther operations easy.

Jugurtha escaped from the walls, by night, with his children and treasures, and thenceforth led a nomad life, never halting in one place for above a single day and night, lodging in the black tents of his tribe, and hoping to frustrate treason by rapidity of movement. He, who had been faithful to no man, had not looked, it would seem, to find all men unfaithful. It was the certain termination, but not for that the less bitter, of his false career. Forty days after he had fled, the citizens of Thala held out manfully; but, when Metellus had completed his lines of circumvallation, when he had raised a bank, on which to bring up his engines against their walls, and was on the point of storming the place, the Roman deserters, who were the strength of the defence, destroyed all the valuables, and consumed themselves with the royal treasures, in voluntary conflagration. The city suffered the extremities of sword and fire, and Roman clemency spared no living thing, human nor brute, of the devoted fortress.

After the capture and destruction of this place, having no longer any army or fortified town, which he could hope to defend, Jugurtha retired into the country of the Gaetulians—a race of men entirely savage and ignorant of the very name of the Romans—corresponding to the modern regions of Belad el Jerid, and Beni Mezzah, south of the Atlas chains, and extending over all the oases of the Great Desert, even to the land of the true negroes.

These Gaetulians, it is probable, differed little, if at all, from the Nomadic Tuaricks, and perhaps some of the Berbers, who occupy the deserts and slopes of the Atlas, to the present day, from time almost immemorial; and of these, by degrees he collected vast hordes; reduced them into something like the form, if not the discipline, of an army; and, having induced Bocchus, king of Mauritania, one of whose daughters was in the number of his wives, to make common cause with him, advanced once again to try his fortune with the sword.

It is remarkable that in all these campaigns, these victories and sieges, the Romans had penetrated but a short distance from the borders of their own province, Zama being actually within its confines, and neither Cirta, nor Thala, the last boasted victory of Metellus, being above three degrees distant from Carthage itself; whence to the river Mulucha, or Molochath, the frontier between Numidia and Mauritania, it was certainly not less than eight hundred miles. And even now, at the close of the fourth campaign, it was still on Cirta, in which Metellus had his quarters, his military chest, his prisoners and his booty, that Jugurtha made his present demonstration, in conjunction with his late allies.

Metellus was, however, aware, when the confederate kings marched up to his fortified camp, that Marius was the consul of the year, and of the province; and that, by gaining a victory, he should gain glory not for himself but for his deadliest enemy, whose election had already wrung bitter curses from his tongue, and bitterer tears from his eyes, albeit unused to weep. He therefore gave them no opportunity of fighting, much less offered them battle, but had recourse to protracted negotiations, endeavouring to detach Bocchus from the alliance, but taking no steps to bring the war to a close.

He was now, in his turn, deprived of his command, which he handed over to Marius; who had returned more arrogant and insolent than ever, as one who had succeeded and gained his point by dint of that very insolence, by flattering the passions of the mob, by inveighing against the culture and accomplishments of the nobles, and by glorying in his own sordid and brutal ignorance. He brought with him as his legate, Aulus Manlius and new levies, something greater than he was entitled to raise by the decree which he had obtained. But in raising these levies, he had been guilty of a breach of the constitution, a treacherous, calculated crime, which in truth more than one cause, perhaps than all others united, tended to overthrow the republic.

Up to this period, from the earliest ages, it had been only the citizens of the first five, property-taxed classes, who had the privilege of serving in the legions—these were all householders, men of family, with lands, trades, professions, children, hereditary rights and interests in the state, and the strongest inducements to maintain the commonwealth, rather than support any individual chief against it. Contrary to law, Marius raised his reinforcements entirely from the proletarians, penniless, houseless, reckless vagabonds, to whom the camp became the country, and the will of their commander the orders of the state.

Up to this period, there is scarce an instance of a Roman army mutinying against its general, however cruel or obnoxious—not one of a Roman army abetting its officer in treason to the state. While the *legions* were composed of the best citizens in the state, who looked forward to a return to home, opulence, respect, domestic joys and civic honours, such an event was impossible. From the day when Marius levied the *proletarian* class into the *legions*, treason to the state, and fidelity to the individual chief, became the rule with Roman armies; and Julius Caesar only consummated the treason, when he introduced barbarian *cohorts* under the desecrated eagles.

These desperate and hard-handed men, however, inured to bear all hardships, and to mock at all dangers, were the stuff whereof to make soldiers, if not patriots; and Marius was of the metal to lead such; and he did so, if brutally, bravely and victoriously. So soon as Publius Rutilius had surrendered the army into his hands, for Metellus shunned the aspect of Marius, unable to endure the sight of things, which he could not even bear to hear recited, Marius took the field, and displayed sagacity and resources no less extraordinary, than his indefatigable industry and vigour, in anticipating every movement, in foreseeing every march, in detecting every ambush, of the kings.

He beat them many times in skirmishes, swooping down on them on their forays, when driving booty from the lands of his allies; and, at last, defeated Jugurtha in a pitched battle, totally routing and disorganising his army, in the plains nigh Cirta. But it needed not his discernment to perceive that to beat an enemy in pitched battles, who lost nothing but a few arms and standards, whose troops dispersed, like *radii* from a centre, rendering pursuit and carnage impossible, and rallied again in two or three days, at a hundred miles' distance, as effectually as before, was to do nothing toward terminating the war.

To take and hold all the towns, to occupy the whole face of the country, until such time as the indomitable chief should be captured or slain—this was the only plan that offered ought of success, and to this he applied himself, with the stern vigour which ensures fortunate results. If Metellus had taken Thala with great difficulty and great glory, he must take Cafsa, in all respects a more arduous and perilous undertaking. For if Thala lay far in the bosom of arid solitudes, Cafsa, was situate a hundred miles deeper in the desert; and, whereas the former city had many living springs around it, when the burning sands, in the midst of which it stood, were passed, the latter had but one, within the walls, by which the inhabitants were supplied; so that a besieging army must depend solely on the water skins it brought with it, and either take the place by a *coup de main*, or fail utterly, and probably perish in retreating. But Marius was equal to the emergency.

Without suffering a hint to transpire of the drift of his expedition, he marched suddenly with an abundance of sheep and cattle, which were slaughtered daily for the men, and their hides instantly converted into water skins. On the sixth day of their march, when they arrived at the last river they should see, he halted all day; saw that every skin was filled; abandoned all his baggage; loaded both men and beasts with the precious water; and marched all night, halting before daybreak in a hollow dell among hills, where his force was entirely concealed. He did the same on the second day; and before dawn on the third, reached a spot among the sand-hills, within two miles of the city-gates, whence he could observe all, himself unobserved. As soon as it was daylight, suspecting nothing less than the vicinity of an enemy, the inhabitants issued from the walls and scattered over the country, intent on their daily business.

Then instantly from his ambush, Marius launched all his cavalry and light troops, who speedily beset the gates, shutting out the better part of the defenders, while he followed leisurely in person with the *legions*, keeping his men well in hand, and suffering none to leave the ranks for plunder. Surprised and bereft of half their forces by the suddenness of the attack, the wretched inhabitants had nothing but to surrender at discretion, and bitterly had they cause to rue it.

For with a fiendish cruelty, characteristic of the man, no less than of the nation, justified by the tyrants' plea, necessity, the city was burnt to the ground, every adult inhabitant was put to the sword, all the rest, old and young, male and female, were sold into slavery, and everything they had possessed was divided as prey among the soldiers. Sallust says:

> This atrocious deed, contrary to the rules of war, was not committed through wickedness or avarice on the part of the consul, but because the place was important to Jugurtha, difficult of access to us, the inhabitants fickle, having once broken their faith, incapable of constraint either by fear or kindness.

Napoleon's plea, to the letter, for the cold-blooded massacre of the four thousand Albanians and Arnaouts at Jaffa:

> We are in the desert; we cannot keep them prisoners and feed them; they have broken parole before; if we spare them, we shall but have to conquer them again.—*Alison I.*

So he shot them all. Not from cruelty or thirst of blood, but from *necessity*, the palliative and apology of more cruelty and crime, than called down heavenly vengeance upon the cities of the plain.

After this barbarous, and to his own men, all but bloodless victory, Marius attacked, one by one, all the fortified towns of the district. A few resisted, and were stormed; the most were deserted by their panic stricken garrisons, terrified by the fate of Cafsa. But to surrender availed the wretched inhabitants no more than to resist; in either case alike their dwellings were given up to the torch, their persons, wherever found or captured, to the sword.

At this stage of the war, Marius had penetrated farther into the country than any Roman leader at any previous date, having now advanced the eagles so far as to the neighbourhood of the River Mulucha or Molochath, which was the frontier between the dominions of Jugurtha and Bocchus the Mauritanian. In the midst of these arid and burning solitudes, constituting what is now known as the desert of Angad, there stood a precipitous isolated rock, on which had been erected a fortified burgh and citadel, reputed impregnable, which contained the last royal hoards of treasure, and was itself the last stronghold of the unhappy king.

To this place, not without incurring the charge of inconsiderate rashness and vain ambition, Marius laid siege; and so strong were the natural defences of the place, and so desperately were they maintained, that, having failed in repeated attacks, and lost many of his best men, to the serious damage of his credit, he was on the eve of abandoning the undertaking, when one of those accidents, which so often change the whole aspect of events in warfare, converted his perilous position into a glorious triumph.

A straggler from one of the auxiliary Ligurian *cohorts*, who had passed round to the rear of the rocky mount, on the front of which the fortress stood, in search of water, having discovered many snails, in those days esteemed a delicate article of food, crawling among the mossy crags, began to gather them; and so, as he found them more and more numerous as he proceeded, began to climb higher and higher in pursuit of them, until he had arrived at such an elevation above the plain, that he conceived an idea of turning his ascent to something of greater advantage than mere snail gathering. So he persisted, unobserved, until he had attained a point, whence he could almost look down into the castle, which, deeming attack impossible from that quarter, had no sentinels or outposts, but had all its garrison on the alert upon the ramparts toward Marius' camp and the scene of action.

A vast evergreen oak, it seems, grew out of the crevices of the rocks, and shooting upward, toward the light, overhung the plateau of the citadel, and afforded a ladder to the active mountaineer, by which he reached a station whence he could see and study all the defences of the place, and facilities of his own position. Having observed all that he might, he descended, "not rashly as he had mounted, but trying and examining all the passes," (*Sallust*), and went straightway to Marius, to whom he described all that he had seen, suggested an attack, or diversion in that quarter, and volunteered to lead a detachment for the purpose. Marius, who when he received these tidings, knew not what method to adopt, whereby to avoid the disgrace of a fruitless siege and inglorious retreat, eagerly caught at the opportunity thus afforded him.

He sent persons, on whom he could depend, to test the truth of the Ligurian's tale; and these reporting that some one had recently ascended the rocks, he detached five trumpeters, with four chosen centurions as a support, all under the command of the Ligurian, with orders to mount as silently as possible until they should have reached the commanding position, and thence, when the front attack should be at its height, to sound the charge at the highest pitch of their instruments and voices, and make a violent demonstration on the rear.

The men were equipped in regard both to agility and silence, with leathern bucklers and head-pieces which would neither clang nor glitter, and were barefooted, to climb the better over the slippery moss and dripping rocks, than in the heavy clouted shoes, which were the ordinary wear of the Roman soldier.

The plan succeeded from point to point, the ascent was made successfully in spite of all the difficulties, and when Marius, aware of their good fortune, was cheering his men to the closest and most desperate attack, exposing his own person and omitting nothing which might tend to success, this trifling forlorn hope entered the empty citadel, the whole garrison of which had flocked to the lower battlements, and sounded their war notes, as if already masters of the place. A sudden panic fell on the defenders, and the spirit of the Romans rising in proportion as that of the Numidians declined, the place was carried by escalade, the gates were forced, and all within the walls were given up to plunder, indiscriminate massacre and havoc.

Sallust says:

> Thus corrected by chance the temerity of Marius received glory instead of censure.

But this sentence is too sweeping; for of all other mortal matters, war is the most dependent upon chances. If all strong hill forts were to be held by leaders as impregnable, because generally so reported, no places would be attacked or taken. The chance of turning an enemy, by the flank or rear, is one of the most probable accidents of mountain warfare; and the chance of so carrying this strong place was, in all likelihood, one of the reasons which induced Marius to assault it, though the peculiar path by which it was eventually won was discovered only by the curiosity of a straggling forager of the camp. The fact, that the fortress was commanded by a loftier position, proves that it was not impregnable, and therefore decides the point that Marius was not to blame in laying siege to it.

If there be any censure just, it is probably this, that he had not earlier caused the position to be fully reconnoitred in the rear, before making real attacks in front; but on this point at this distance of time, it is impossible to decide; and it is most evident, that, while the personal accessibility of Marius to information from the lowest and least regarded source, can scarcely be too highly praised as a fine characteristic of a great captain, his celerity in adopting, vigour in prosecuting, and perfect success in carrying out the project, prove him a general of great versatility and quickness of genius.

At this period of the war, Marius' *quaestor* Lucius Sylla, who had been left at Rome to complete the levies of the Latin and allied cavalry, arrived at the camp with a great body of horse. This man, destined hereafter to become the great rival and deadly enemy of the general, under whom he now commenced his career of arms, had led, it would appear, up to this time a life of luxury and dissipation, varied only by application to letters, in which he was a distinguished proficient, equally conversant with the languages and literature of Italy and Greece, and had not entered conspicuously into the arena of politics. He was a member of one of the noblest and grandest of the great patrician houses, the famous *gens Cornelia,* which had already produced so many good and eminent citizens, and was hereafter to give birth to several of the most odious yet illustrious monsters.

Of this family had come Cossus, the slayer of Lar Tolumnius, and, after Romulus, the first who bore the *spolia opima* to the Capitol; of it no less than twelve distinguished Scipios, all of whom had deserved well of their country in the field or in the forum; and of it were to come a Lentulus, a Cinna, a Catiline, a Dolabella, in addition to the great man now entering upon the stage of history. He was a man of profound learning, mighty spirit, vast ambition, sedulous in his attention to business, though addicted too much to pleasure, eloquent, crafty, versatile, excellent in dissimulation, easy of access to his friends, lavish of largesses, equal in capacity to his fortune, which was so wonderfully great and constant, that men doubted whether he were more able or more fortunate in his achievements.

That one with such nobility of birth, refinement of tastes, and literary acquirement should be utterly antagonistic, to a rude, low-born, brutal-mannered person of ignoble habits, ignorant, and glorying in his ignorance, is not surprising; and though in this war he did good service to his chief, in it likewise, arose the first hostile controversies, which soon grew up into deathless hatred, and racked Rome to its entrails with intestine brawls and battles. Jugurtha had at this time lost all his places of strength, most of his treasures, many of his best men, not a few slain by his own suspicious fury, and had no hope of protracting even a defensive war, without the aid of foreign alliance and resources.

To this end he solicited his father-in-law, Bocchus, to assist him with a Mauritanian army, and ultimately prevailed on him; but not until he had promised to resign to him a third part of his dominions, should the Romans be driven from Africa, or the war concluded with his territories undivided.

Marius, who at this period had no enemy in the field, and who probably regarded the war as virtually at an end, withdrew his forces from the desert regions, which he had conquered with so much difficulty, and which probably afforded no facilities for wintering an army, toward his headquarters at Cirta, where he proposed to go into winter quarters. He was on the march for that place, when the combined armies of the two kings were upon him, before he had so much as a suspicion of their proximity, and engaged him so suddenly and with such vehemence, when there was scarcely an hour of daylight remaining, that the *legions* had neither the time to secure their baggage, nor to form order of battle.

Assailed at once on all points by Moorish and Gaetulian horse, who charged them home, not in regular line, but in a multiplicity of troops and squadrons, now striking here, now there, cutting the *legionaries* down and spearing them in front, in flank, in rear, the Romans were unable to preserve their formation; but yet fought with such steadiness and valour, the veterans and new soldiers being so united in the maniples as to give firmness and solidity to the whole, that they succeeded in forming a number of squares, or circles, as chance threw them together, and in protecting themselves and repulsing the enemy until nightfall.

Never yet had Marius been so hard bestead, or so nearly defeated, as on this occasion; and it was only by his own exertion and his exhibition of great personal qualities, that he prevented the defeat and disorganisation of the forces. As the night closed in, so far from discontinuing their attacks, the barbarians, confident of success, pressed the more closely on the legions; until at length, having by exposure of his own person, by fighting hand to hand with the enemy, and rallying them by exhortation, example, remonstrance, and in short every available effort, the consul reduced his troops to something resembling discipline and order, and beating off the cavalry of the kings with a great final effort, marched with his foot at double quick time to a hill, which he had observed in the vicinity; and there posted them, as best he might in the darkness, for night had now fallen thick and starless, to bivouac on their arms, without food or fires, in the midst of the enemy.

His cavalry, under Sylla, he detached to a short distance, where, on an inferior knoll or hillock, there was a large and perennial spring of water, with precise instructions that they should kindle no fires, nor show any lights whatsoever, in order as far as possible to conceal their position from the enemy, who sat down in the low grounds all around the hills, and passed the night after the barbarian fashion, revelling, shouting, singing and exulting about their watch-fires, as if they were victorious; for so seldom had they fought the Romans without incurring total rout, that to have held their ground was to them sufficient cause for triumph.

Marius had in pursuance of his plan forbidden the trumpets of the *legions* or the clarions of the horse to sound, as was usual, the watches of the night, or the relief of the guards; but when toward dawn he observed, as he had expected, that the Numidian watch-fires had burnt down, that the barbaric din had died away, and that, worn out with the fatigues of the past day and the riot of the night, the enemy had dropped into the lethargy of exhausted drunkenness, he ordered all the instruments to sound the charge at once, and broke down, from both hills together, fully prepared for action, on the half-awakened and panic-stricken hordes of the desert.

There was no stand, no resistance, no, not for a minute's space. At first they stood at gaze, paralyzed and lost in consternation, then fled in utter rout. In that action more of the enemy were slain than Jugurtha had lost in all his previous battles, for the unwonted panic of the men, and the heavy sleep from which they were but half aroused, prevented them of their usual activity in flight. No defeat could well be more thorough and decisive; yet Marius, as he persisted on retiring to his head quarters, relaxed no precaution, more than if his enemy had been in full vigour, (*Sallust*), of operation. He marched as if in presence of a hostile army, in a hollow square with his baggage and camp followers in the centre, Sylla's cavalry on his right, and Aulus Manlius with the archery and slingers on his left. He fortified his camp nightly, stationed strong outposts of the *legionary cohorts* before the praetorian gate, caused a portion of the auxiliary horse to patrol all the environs, while he held another body in reserve, at all times under arms, within the ramparts.

It was well that he did so, for on the fourth day after his former defeat, when the Romans were already in the vicinity of Cirta, the videttes came in at once from all quarters, announcing the presence of the enemy in each several direction, for the indefatigable Numidian had once more rallied his tumultuary squadrons, and detailing them into four divisions, was prepared to attack at once on all points.

Uncertain, accordingly, whence he should be assailed, Marius made no present change in his dispositions, but prepared to deliver battle in the same order in which he marched, as being equally fortified on all hands. So soon as the enemy appeared in the van, Sylla halted the main body of his horse on the right to cover that wing, while he himself and others of his officers at the head of single troops, each very closely arrayed, charged the enemy's cavalry and kept them at a distance, while the general made head with the *legions* against Jugurtha's impetuous onslaught on the van.

In the meantime, Bocchus came up in the Roman rear with his Mauritanian foot, led by his son Volux, who had not been present in the last action, and fell on boldly, making considerable impression by this unexpected diversion. News of this being speedily brought to Jugurtha, by some of his wild horsemen, who were wheeling like hawks everywhere about the flanks of the column, he galloped off unobserved, with a handful of men to the rear, on which he made an attack so fiery and impetuous, shouting in Latin to the *legions* that they were fighting to no end, since he had slain Marius with his own hand, and showing his sword reeking with blood from hilt to point—for he had fought very valiantly, and slain a Roman *legionary*—that they wavered, and becoming dispirited, while the barbarians waxed bolder and more strenuous in the charge, could scarcely be restrained from flight.

At the critical moment, however, when all was on the hazard of the die, Sylla, who by his sustained and incessant charge of alternate, or unconnected, squadrons, had cleared both wings from the tumultuary clouds of Numidian horse, wheeled rapidly to the rear and charged the Moors of Bocchus in the flank with such energy and vigour that the whole body turned, as a single man, and betook themselves to precipitate flight. Marius, meantime, relieved from the presence of Jugurtha and the pressure of his indomitable desert cavalry, restored the battle in front and converted what had been almost a disaster into a complete victory. Jugurtha himself, while exerting himself most heroically to perfect his half-conquered success, was hemmed in by Sylla's troopers, saw all his best men cut down to right and left around him, and at last, with his armour hacked from his body, dripping with his own and his enemies' blood, got off alone through a storm of cuts and thrusts all directed at his own person.

Better for him had he there fallen. The rout was complete, the carnage horrible; and for the first time in his extraordinary career, he left the field, without having designated a rallying point, or made arrangements for the reorganisation of the army, or the levying of a new one. He had, in fact, fought his last battle, expended his last resource, brought forward and lost his last reserve, exhausted his last ally.

On the fifth day after the action, ambassadors came from Bocchus to the Roman winter-quarters in Cirta, requesting Marius to send his most confidential assistants, with whom he might treat for accommodation; and Sylla being sent in connection with Aulus Manlius, negotiations were set on foot with the wily and perfidious Mauritanian, which terminated in his treacherous surrender of his suppliant and kinsman into the hands of the common enemy.

It must not be supposed, that this conclusion was reached at one interview, or as the fruit of a single conference. A second delegation reached Marius, while, after placing the main army in winter quarters, he was engaged in besieging a royal fortress, garrisoned wholly by Roman deserters, which he speedily destroyed. These delegates, it seems, on their way had fallen into the hands of Gaetulian robbers, and having been plundered and stripped by them, had escaped to Sylla, who received them with hospitality so profuse, and largesses so ample, that he recommended himself in the highest degree to the barbarian king. Shortly afterward three of the Moors proceeded to Rome, in company with the quaestor, Cneius Octavius Rufus, who was on his return after bringing pay for the army in Africa, and who should introduce them to the presence and favourable notice of the Senate.

While this embassy was in Rome, obsecrating the commiseration, and seeking the friendship, of the Senate, which they ultimately obtained, Bocchus again wrote to the Roman general, requesting him to send Sylla to confer with him, by whose decision there were hopes that all matters in controversy might be brought to a final determination. Marius understanding that the surrender of Jugurtha was implied under this wary circumlocution, despatched his able young subordinate, with an escort of Latin cavalry, Balearic slingers, auxiliary bowmen, and the Pelignian *cohort* equipped in light infantry order, for the convenience of rapid marching. After considerable suspicions of treachery on the part of the Mauritanian king and his son Volux, who accompanied Sylla with a sort of guard of honour, and who once appeared on the point of betraying his guest to a division of Jugurtha's cavalry, the *quaestor* at length arrived at the royal seat of Bocchus. For a long time the treacherous barbarian doubted, fluctuated, whether of the two he should betray, cajoled, flattered, promised without performing; but at last, awed by the intrepid and immovable firmness of the young Roman, he determined against his countryman, his son-in-law, his brother king; murdered his familiar friends and counsellors, and surrendered himself, loaded with fetters, into the hands of the *quaestor*.

This glory Sylla rated so high, that, to his last hour, he used as his signet ring a gem engraved with the representation of himself receiving the captive king, and so earned the immitigable and immortal hatred of the unforgiving man, who considered it an attempt to rob him of the fame which was his right, of terminating at length, a war which had defied, for six whole years, the utmost powers of Rome, and bringing into subjection and slavery an enemy than whom, save Hannibal, the republic had never known one more dangerous or desperate, and who had debauched, defeated, deceived, or exhausted three successive Consuls and their armies, and yielded only after six consecutive campaigns, when not an inch of territory was left to him, nor a single fighting man on whom he could rely.

Thus, with great and merited honour to Marius, was this long and harassing war terminated in the year of the city 648, and 106 B.C., when the successful general was no longer consul, but commander, with consular powers, until its conclusion. Unimportant, so far as danger to the existence, or to the constitutional or territorial integrity of Rome, the Jugurthine war had been a severe and galling thorn in her side, from its commencement; it had seriously shaken the prestige of invincibility which had so long clung to the arms of Rome; it had demonstrated the infamy of many of her senators, the imbecility of some of her generals, the undisciplined and mutinous spirit of more than one of her armies; and it had sorely aggrieved her haughty pride, that a petty chieftain of wild desert horse should have held her armies at bay, and subjected them to disgraces which they had never endured from the gigantic strength of Carthage, the unequalled science of Hannibal.

Great, therefore, was the rejoicing when it was known at Rome, that the war was concluded, as by a thunder-stroke, and that he who had so long eluded the vengeance and mocked the majesty of Rome, was now but a chained culprit, awaiting her not questionable mercy.

The next year Marius was detained in Africa to regulate the affairs of the province, to sub-divide the territory of Jugurtha between Bocchus, Hiempsal, and Iarbas, the two latter, princes of the family of Massinissa, and to establish a regular and lasting peace, still with the office of proconsul; and while he was thus engaged, the consul of the year, Cneius Manlius Maximus, with Quintus Servilius Caepio, his predecessor, now proconsul, underwent an overwhelming defeat on the banks of the Rhone, losing no less than 80,000 men in the action, at the hands of the Teutonic and Cimbric hordes, whose first appearance, on the frontiers of the commonwealth, has been noticed as coincident with the election of Quintus Metellus to the consulship.

The terror inspired by the approach of these most formidable barbarians brought about the second election of Marius to the consulship, as the only man capable of preserving the republic in such a crisis; and he was accordingly recalled to Italy, with his army, to take the triumph which had been long decreed to him, and to make preparation for the ensuing campaign.

Marius triumphed, therefore, with unusual glory and magnificence; for the rabble were rejoiced at the splendid achievements of their plebeian favourite, which they regarded in the light of a victory of their own over the hated nobles, and greeted him and his troops, men chiefly of the same ignoble stamp, with extraordinary congratulation.

The victor brought into the treasury, at this triumph, no less than thirty thousand and seventy ounces of gold, and fifty thousand seven hundred and fifty ounces of silver, besides a large sum of coined money. It is singularly characteristic of the arrogant and overbearing temper of the man, that in this moment of his first triumphant exaltation, it was his first thought to turn his own glory to the humiliation and confusion of the senate and patricians, to whom nothing could assuage his rancorous hatred; for, contrary to all precedent, all usage or decorum, he entered the senate in his triumphal robes, the palmated tunic, the purple *toga*, the sceptre and the crown of bays, as a victorious monarch, not as the civic magistrate of a republic. He gained nothing, however, but lost by this act of insult and bravado; for so general and openly demonstrated was the rebuke which it excited, that he was compelled, by a sense of his error, to withdraw on the spot, and exchange the offensive garb for *habiliments* more befitting the presence and the place.

It is no less characteristic of the people and the time, that at the very hour when the victorious general was offering sacrifice to Jupiter Optimus Maximus, in the capitol, the captive king, stripped of his royal robes and his jewelled ear rings torn violently from his bleeding ears by the brutal haste of the executioners, was plunged naked and alive into the horrible and filthy dungeon of the Tullianum, wherein, at a later day, Catiline and his brother traitors were to expiate their guilt by the hangman's noose.

Still in his extremity the pride of the desert-born deserted him not; and, as he was cast into the foul and foetid cavern in which he was destined to perish by starvation, he looked around him with a grim smile of defiance—"Ye Gods! your hot baths in Rome are mighty cold," (*Plutarch vit. Mar.*), and then died, like the wolf, in silence.

Such was the doom wreaked by Rome on all her vanquished foes, the best and greatest, as the vilest and most degraded. The murderer of Hiempsal, the ruthless torturer of Adherbal, the exterminator of his kinsman's and benefactor's race, we cannot pity or excuse. But we must remember that the slaughter of all kindred rivals to the crown has been the immemorial law, and fratricide, from the remotest period to this day, the constant practice of the barbarous courts of Southern and Oriental Africa and Asia; that the crimes of Jugurtha were rather those of his country and of his caste than of himself, as individual. His patriotism, his enduring valour, his indefatigable resource, and his indomitable energy were his true crimes against Rome, and dearly he abided them.

His faithlessness, as alleged by the Roman, was evidently but the usual stratagem and device of the savage, as employed against the civilized man. Had it been far more real, Rome was debarred from the use of the plea by reason of her invariable treachery to all with whom she treated, not least to himself, whom she captured only in the end, by a kinsman's treason.

To sum him in a word, he was a thorough savage, with all his energies and instincts. His vices have come down to us, doubtless, exaggerated by the report of his enemies; his virtues, if he had any, beyond courage, have escaped their record. If he was in any degree comparable, however, to his conqueror Marius in cruelty, in treachery, in any form of monstrous sin, he may be declared, as by the Roman formula, *Jure Caesus*.

And here a few words may not be out of place, considering the singular and formidable hordes of barbarians, with whom, to its great peril, the Roman Republic was now, for the second time, brought into contact, and from whom Marius was destined to win his greatest renown, and that glory which constituted him in the opinion of the noble Roman satyrist, the happiest and most blest of all things that had their origin of earth. These were the tribes known by the Greeks, indiscriminately, as **Κιμμεριοι** and **Κελται,** and by the Latins as Cimbri and Galli, which, though in fact distinct tribes, had yet so considerable an affinity, both in language and customs, that a common origin, and in fact an absolute identity, was attributed by the ancient historians to all the hordes which successively poured down from the north and east upon the southern and western countries of Europe.

It appears that the first entrance of the Cimmerians, as they were termed so long as they inhabited, what has always been regarded as their original soil, of which they were held indigenous, the lands along the Black Sea, from the Danube to the Don and Volga, dates[1] from about the year 631 before the Christian aera; when they are said to have been forced westward by an incursion of the Scythians, themselves propelled by a similar irruption of the Massagetae, from the Steppes of Upper Asia. From this period history is silent as to their exact course, but it is clear from ethnographical investigations, that they migrated slowly, by annual journeys, to the north-westward, leaving numerous colonies as they passed along, which constantly cast out inferior emigrations, until they were echelonned, as it were, along all the affluents of the Danube, and that great river itself, from the Euxine to the Rhine and Elbe, and to the peninsula of Jutland, and perhaps even northward yet to Finland and the shores of the Arctic Ocean.

Celts or Gael the Cimmerians, Cymri or Kymri, certainly were not; but it is no less certain, that among the Celtic Gael who had from time long antecedent to all authentic history, occupied all the vast territory extending westward from the Appenines, the Alps and the Rhine to the Atlantic Ocean, including all Tuscany, Lombardy, France, Holland, Belgium, Portugal, and Spain, not omitting the British Is-

---

1. Amedee Thierry. *Hist. Gaul.* Vol. I. Introduc.

lands, they found many tribes, particularly the Belgic race of France, and the Bretons of southern England and Wales, with whom they acknowledged community of tongue and blood, and with whom they at once fraternized.

Diodorus Siculus states positively that they were Cimmerians, afterwards called Cimbri, who, under the name of Gauls, took Rome, and reduced it to ashes in the 364th year of the city, and the 389th before the Christian era; who again, a hundred years later, broke down into northern Greece, marched against Delphi and were utterly defeated and dispersed by the Greek *hoplitae*; and who yet again, after ravaging Thrace and Macedonia, passed the Hellespont, entered Asia Minor, and established themselves there under the name of Galatae, or Galatians, which is merely the Greek form of the word *Gaël*, and probably merely a various form of the closely allied sound Keltae. This is, nevertheless, in some degree doubtful, for it would appear from unmistakeable evidences of language, and other points to be noticed hereafter, that, on the second Cimbric invasion, of which I have now to treat, it was with a portion only of the tribes who had settled in Italy or Gaul at the period of the first irruption, that the Cimbri had a community of tongue, and made community of cause.

How this may be soever, the strongest division or horde of Cimbri which had remained north of the Rhine, were suddenly driven from their lands in Jutland, and around the Baltic,[2] as some aver, by a violent earthquake, followed by a fearful inundation of the sea, which was raised from its bed,[3] and swallowed up large tracts of the low country; or as others assert, by their own restless spirit and praedatory habits.[4] Uniting themselves thereupon with the Teutonic races of the vicinity, they rushed to arms, resolved on a general emigration *en masse*, and carrying with them in their *wains* and chariots, all their wealth, all the aged, the women and the children, poured down a more destructive deluge even than that of the sea which had dispossessed them, upon the rich and civilized districts of the south.

The Cimbri were led by their chiefs, Boiorix and Caesorix, as their names are given to us Latinised, and the Teutons by Teutobochus their king, a man of gigantic frame, and of such extraordinary agility, that it was a common feat for him to vault over four, and even six horses abreast, as is occasionally done in modern circuses, by aid

---
2. Appian. Bell. Illyr.
3. Claudian. Bell. Get. 638. Amedee Thierry *Hist. Gaul.* Part 11. Chap. 2.
4. Strabo, Lib. VII., chap. ii.

of spring boards and scenic apparatus. The horde consisted of at least three hundred thousand fighting men on its departure from the Baltic; but as it constantly rallied upon itself the scattered tribes of kindred or assimilated origin through which its route lay, in spite of its losses in war, it was constantly increasing in numbers, and waxing like a mountain torrent swollen by innumerable affluents, at every league, vaster in volume, fiercer in impetuosity, and more formidable to whatever stood in the way of its tide.

Leaving the Baltic, they at first turned their course south-easterly, ascending the course of the Elbe and Oder, until they reached the elevated plateau occupied by the great Cercinian forest, lying between the Erzgeber, Sudetic, Carpathian, and Schwartzwald chains, which had been constantly held, since the first barbaric irruption, by the Boii, a Cimbric tribe, whose name, Bogh or Beog in the vernacular Kymric, signifies the Terrible. This kindred race, proving the correctness of their nomenclature, resisted the approach of their northern compatriots with such vigour, and offered so strenuous an opposition to their transit through their territory, that the great horde passed on directly southward, leaving the Boii to the left, crossed the Danube, wasted all Noricum and Vindelicia with fire and sword, exterminating all before them, and laid siege to the capital Norica, now St. Leonards, a town situate on the northern descent of the Carnian Alps, in close contact with the frontiers of the Republic.

In the year of the city 641, B. C. 113, the consul Cneius Papirius Carbo received Illyria as his province, and the charge to watch the movements of the Cimbri, as his duty. But he, having warned them to avoid the Roman Territory, and respect a city which was protected by the Republic, and having received a pacific reply with a declaimer of any intent to settle in Noricum, and a voluntary offer to withdraw their forces, fell into the common error of undervaluing his enemy, and attacked them treacherously and at unawares, having deceived them by peaceful professions.

For once, treason met its reward, and Papirius was disgracefully defeated, with the loss of forty thousand men, as it is said, and would have lost all his army but for a violent tempest, which favoured his retreat. Still, notwithstanding their success, they shunned entering the proper territories of Rome, but skirting the Carnian and Rhoetian Alps, devastated Illyria with the utmost barbarity, laying all waste from the Adriatic to the Danube, and from the Alps to the mountains of Thrace and Macedonia, where they still encountered the outposts of the Romans, and still shrunk from the encounter. In the third year they entered Switzerland, following the valley of the upper Rhine; and at the sight of the vast train of wagons loaded with booty, the tribes of the Helvetians, always a restless, warlike people, inclined to Nomadic expeditions, the Tigurini or canton of Zurich, the Toygenoe, or men of Zug, and the Ambrones, a Cimbric race who had been formerly expelled from the plains of the Po by the Etruscans, rose in arms, unanimously, and swelled the tide of havoc and extermination; these last alone were thirty thousand strong in warriors bearing shield.

Hence turning the northern extremity of the Jura, the augmented horde rushed into Gaul, which it entered in the country of the Belgae, themselves a Cimbric race of the first epoch of migration, speaking a similar, if not identical language. These armed to resist the irruption, but conferences followed, and the two nations fraternized; the Belgae giving up to their visitors a fortress, reputed impregnable, in the country of the Aduatici, not far from the present city of Tongres, where they left all their enormous booty with a garrison of 6000 men, and the great horde agreeing to respect the Belgic country, and passing onward into central Gaul, which was mercilessly devastated from the Marne and Rhone, (*Amedee Thierry*), westward to the Atlantic, and southward to the Mediterranean sea and the Pyrenean frontiers of Spain.

This work of almost unprecedented rapine and carnage, occupied another year, and in the fourth year after their defeat of Carbo, in the consulship of Metellus and Silanus, B. C. 109, they turned their arms toward the Roman province, but still dared not enter it, daunted by the invincible prestige of the Roman name, but sent deputies to Silanus, who had Gaul for his province, requesting the Republic to assign them lands in fief, for which they offered to do them perpetual man-service in war. Silanus, however, replied haughtily, that "the Republic had neither lands to give them nor service to require of them," (*Florus III.*), crossed the Rhone, and was utterly discomfited with the loss of his whole army.

In the following year the Gaelic and Celtic population having risen, and successfully maintained the defensive line of the Rhone and the Cevennes, until the arrival of fresh *legions*, the hordes divided themselves into two bodies, the Tigurini, under Divico, their king, making a northward sweep, in order to enter the province by the bridge of Geneva and fords of the Upper Rhine; the Cimbri, Teutones, and the remainder of the Switzers, persisting on the southern line of operations. In this year, Marius' first consulship, his colleague Lucius Cassius Longinus, who had Marcus Æmilius Scaurus for his lieutenant, was opposed to these formidable barbarians, and being compelled to divide his forces in order to make head against their double movement, shared the fate of his predecessors.

Being anticipated in his movement through Switzerland, to seize the passes of the Jura, Cassius was cut to pieces, with his lieutenant Piso, and all his bravest *legionaries* within view of the ramparts of Geneva, (*Livy* and *Bell*), the remainder of his army surrendering, and being passed under the yoke; while Scaurus, with no better fortune, delivered battle in the south, lost his whole force, and remained himself in the hands of the enemy.

And now emboldened by their own successes, and totally despising the terrors of the Roman name, which they had held so powerful, until they found its defence so weak, the barbarians determined to pass the Alps, and try the strength of this vaunted foe at close quarters.

It was debated in the Cimbric councils, whether Italy should be ravaged only to extremity, or whether the whole race of Romans should be utterly destroyed, the city peopled by the Teutons and Cimbri, and the Kymric substituted for the Latin tongue, (*Quinctilian*). And the latter course they had already decreed and sworn to take, (*Pluto*), when their prisoner Scaurus was introduced in fetters for examination, and by the constancy of his replies, though it cost him his own life by the dagger of the infuriated Boiorix, preserved his country from the influx of the savage hordes, mad with lust of conquest, and flushed with gore.

Once more they turned aside before the stern rampart of the Alps, and applied themselves thoroughly to subjugate the Narbonese, or Roman province, part of the population of which, the Tectosages and the people of Thoulouse, being of kindred race, deserted the Roman Republic, threw the garrison of Thoulouse into chains, and joined the barbarians.

But meantime a breathing space was gained, the consul Quintus Servilius Coepio, B. C. 107, came out with strong reinforcements, reoccupied the province, gained possession of Thoulouse by a stratagem, plundered that city, with the Gaulish temple of Belenus and the sacred lake, (*Strabo*), of their accumulated treasures, some say to the amount of 110,000 pounds weight of gold, and 1,500,000 pounds weight of silver, (*Justin*)—the most of which he seems to have converted to his own use,—and terminated the campaign without any action or feat of arms against the enemy, who, it would appear, had again moved to the westward. In B. C. 106, Coepio was in his turn superseded by Cneius Manlius Maximus, but continued to act, as his lieutenant, at the head of his own army, serving as a separate division, yet with such jealousy and hostility toward his colleague, as could not but be injurious, and was nearly fatal to the Republic.

An insult offered by this rash and corrupt man to some deputies of the Cimbri, wrought these excitable savages to such a pitch of fury, that they solemnly swore, with hideous rites, war to the utmost, without quarter, and devoted all the captives and the plunder to the immortal gods. The onset of the savages was appalling; their charge, especially that of the Ambrones, was irresistible. The Roman camps were both forced, almost simultaneously. Eighty thousand Roman soldiers, and forty thousand slaves and camp followers fell by the sword's edge. All the rest, save ten men, (*Paulus Orosius* and *Thierry*)), who escaped with Coepio and Sertorius, fell into the hands of the barbarians, and in conformity with their vow, were instantly hung on the nearest trees. All the arms, armour, and baggage were broken to atoms; all the gold, all the valuables, the very horses of the army were cast into the abysses of the turbid Rhone.

Since the fatal day of Cannae, no such disaster had befallen the Roman *legions*; no such ignominy had fallen on her arms; no such panic stricken the hearts of the people. There was but one sentiment now, in any heart or on any tongue; there was but one man capable to save the Republic. But had not the fortune of Rome once more stood her, almost supernaturally, in stead, even Marius might have come too late, and the Alps and Appenines, and the Po itself, might have yielded the keys of Italy to the exterminators, or ere he could come, hot-footed from Numidian deserts to his country's rescue.

But fortune or fate, be it which it may, befriended her; from the blood-stained shores of the Rhone the barbaric hordes ebbed westward, for the moment, desolating all the Mediterranean shores of Gaul, and poured themselves in a torrent, through the southern passes of the Pyrenees, into the smiling plains of Spain, which they destined to like outrage.

Thus was gained time, of all things the most precious in war; and with it the means, the spirit, and the man, competent to meet and conquer the crisis.

Contrary to law, which forbade any man to be elected consul, except present on the Campus Martins, or any to hold that office twice in succession, Marius was chosen consul for the second time, while absent in Numidia, closing up the last business connected with the Jugurthine war; and the people, whose favourite he was, rejoiced to have their turn in violating the forms of the constitution, in behalf of one of themselves.

For the noble Scipio, they said, had been as illegally elected by the nobility, when under age, and absent in Spain, and that, not to save Rome but to destroy Carthage; and wherefore should not a greater than Scipio, their own great Plebeian, be elected by the people, not to ruin an enemy, but to preserve the Republic, which he alone was capable to do. He was chosen, therefore, as I have said, almost unanimously. with Caius Flaccius Fimbria as his colleague, and being recalled to Rome, with his army, triumphed on the day when he entered on his office, the 1st of January, 106 B.C., in the year of Rome 652, as is recorded above, in order to preserve the continuity of the tale of the Jugurthine war, of which this triumph is the actual and appropriate termination.

Immediately on the opening of the season, Marius proceeded by sea to Marseilles, with his own legions, the Plebeian troops whom he had at first introduced to the honours of military service, whom he had formed to suffering, toil, and blood, in the terrible desert marches, desperate battles, and wild sieges of the Numidian war, who had shared with him the glories of his triumph, and were prepared to follow him to the world's end, through either fortune.

Rallying upon these, the relics of the old consular and praetorian armies of Gaul, he now proceeded to exercise them, not only in marches and counter-marches, in castrametation and all things connected with actual warfare, but in works of engineering and internal improvement the most prodigious. The mouths of the Rhone, it appears, a turbid, feculent river, sweeping, down its current, volumes of alluvial soil, had become so completely obstructed with bars and mud-banks, that the roadstead and embouchure were inaccessible to vessels of burthen, an inconvenience which Marius, whose forces depended for their supplies on their navy, was determined to obviate. Partly on this account, partly adopting the pretext, in order, by constant labour and strenuous occupation, to keep his soldiers out of the reach of idleness, luxury, relaxation, and mutiny, he made them construct a vast navigable canal, from the river above Arelate, or Arles, to the sea, which afforded not only ingress to the largest vessels, but a valuable and permanent line of defence.

For many years this great work, which was known as the Fossae Marianae, became the real entrance of the river, and a maritime and commercial channel of the highest importance; a city of the same name sprung up at its seaward mouth, the memory of which still survives in the small marine village of Foz, (*Thierry*), and the revenue arising from the entrance and clearance duties was of great advantage to Marseilles.

So severe were the toils undergone by the troops, that half in better jest, half in angry earnest, the *legionaries* called themselves the "Marian, (*Plutarch*), mules;" and it was a common saying that his unrelenting severity, his inflexibility in punishment, his violence of temper, harsh voice, and unsmiling countenance, rendered him as formidable to his own men as to the enemy. Doubtless, the rigorous enforcement of strictest discipline, doubtless, severe and frequent punishment was necessary to cohibit the turbulent natures and daring insolence of the classes upon whom the character of *legionary* had now descended,— and so it was, in fact, proved; for it is distinctly stated, that the delay and dispersion of the barbarians into Spain was doubly serviceable to Marius, as he not only gained the time necessary to indurate the bodies of the men by athletic exertions, but to bring their minds to like tone and robustness by discipline and practice, and to teach them to know and understand his own nature. And in the end they did so; for he had qualities which endeared him to the soldiers, in spite of his sternness and cruelty, rigid abstemiousness, perfect integrity, unbending impartiality,—and for these they came to love him, and to say that his appalling mien and savage voice were fearful to the enemy indeed, but to his countrymen a safeguard and defence.

Thus passed, in inactivity, as regards actual warfare, but far otherwise as regarded the physique and morale of the *legions*, the second consulship of Marius. But still it was known that, although absent, the barbarous enemy were not far aloof; and yet again, contrary to form, but it cannot justly be said contrary to the interests of the state, Marius was elected in his absence, for the third time, chief magistrate of Rome. In truth, the very fact, that the chief magistrates of Rome, for the time, were necessarily her generals also, shows that the rule, however excellent in peace, against the continuance of office in the same hands, would obviously work ill in time of war, when the conduct of long, tedious hostilities must be entrusted to one, and he the best and ablest soldier, in order to ensure any reasonable hope of success.

And, indeed, whenever such emergencies had existed, these laws and formulae had long been practically void. During the Second Punic War, the law was suspended, prohibiting the successive re-election of consuls, in the cases of Marcus Claudius Marcellus, Quintus Fabius Maximus, and Quintus Fulvius Flaccus, the first two of whom held that dignity five times, and the third four times in succession, merely on account of their eminent superiority as generals. At the same time, on the first occasion, when it became necessary to select an absent general, in order to avoid removing him from the seat of war, that rule was violated also; as, doubtless, it would have been in the cases above mentioned, had any of those officers been actively engaged abroad, at the period of holding the consular comitia.

In this year, 103 B.C., Lucius Aurelius Orestes was the colleague of the great Plebeian; but again, the season passed idly and without alarm, the Cimbric and Teutonic hordes being still occupied, either in ravaging the already twice ravaged shores of southern France, or in endeavouring, bootlessly, to penetrate the interior fastnesses of Spain, whence they were at length expelled by the Celtiberians. When the time for holding the elections at length arrived, Orestes, his colleague, having died in office, Marius seeing that no enemy was at hand, left his army in charge of Manius Acyllius, and proceeded to hold the *comitia*.

And here he was guilty of a despicable and scandalous piece of demagoguism, with the aid of one of his most infamous and unscrupulous tools, the *tribune* Lucius Saturninus; for, when this creature nominated him consul, the fourth time, he affected to decline, through modesty, the proffered honour, and afterward angrily and absolutely to refuse it, until Saturninus charged him with treason to his country, in that he would excuse himself from his duty in leading her armies in such imminent peril of the Republic. Then, pretending to yield reluctantly, a farce so barefaced that it failed to deceive anyone, he accepted the candidateship, and found himself once more general and chief-magistrate, with his own veteran legions at his orders, and Quintus Lutatius Catulus, a man of noble birth, sterling integrity and virtues that commanded even the favour of the mob, as his colleague.

In the spring, as soon as the weather favoured military operations, the Cimbri, refluent from the rocks of central Spain, and the cognate Celtic tribes which held them, and on which they had failed to produce any effect, rushed back into central Gaul, where they rallied on themselves the Teutons, the Ambrones, and the Tigurini, who had tarried behind, not crossing the Pyrenees, and the Tectosages, who were still partially in arms, notwithstanding their defeat and the capture of their king, Copillius, by Sylla, in the last campaign. Thus augmented rage, and the avarice of plunder, and the lust of conquest—perhaps in some sort necessity, for Italy alone, of all Western Europe, had thus far escaped devastation, and was alone perhaps now capable of supporting their greedy myriads—determined them to bring their quarrel with Rome to instant issue, and to assault her, hand to hand, within her boasted ramparts of the Alps.

To this end, they again divided their multitudes, and while the Cimbri, guided by the Tigurini of Zurich, left France as they had entered it, by turning the northern extremity of the Jura into Switzerland, passed thence by the Tyrol into Noricum, or Austria, and prepared to assault the Rhaetian or Carnian Alps to the north of Upper Italy, not far from the place where they first came into contact with the legions under Carbo.

Meanwhile the Teutons, led by their terrible king, Teutobochus, and accompanied by the Ambrones, who seem to have been held as the warlike flower of the hordes, rushed toward the mouths of the Rhone, boasting themselves that they would sweep the Roman *legions* like dust, out of the province, and join their comrades by the passes of the Maritime Alps, in the plains of the Po, wherein they had appointed their rendezvous.

But there lay an unexpected lion in their path,—the grim African veteran, confident of his own resources and the spirit of his soldiery, and snuffing the approaching slaughter on the wind. In the first instance he had taken post at the confluence of the Isere and Rhone,[5] awaiting the approach of the enemy; but so soon as he discovered that the Ambrones were pouring down the river by its left bank, he also retrograded by the right toward the sea, and taking a strong-height in the vicinity of Aries, where the two roads, one through the passes of the Maritime Alps, the other by the Ligurian coast, between the mountains and the sea, diverge toward Italy, fortified it securely, and stationing himself firmly, resolved to maintain the strictest defensive, until such time as he should find occasion to deal them a decisive and overwhelming blow. They did not cause him to tarry long before they made their appearance:

> Infinite in numbers, terrible in aspect and armature, unlike to any other race of men in their hideous cries and howlings.—
> *Plutarch.*

---

5. Paulus Oros. V. 16. *apud* Amedee Thierry.

With all their battle cars and cavalry they drew out in the plain, calling on the Romans to come out and fight them, like men; and when Marius prohibited the eager *legionaries*, even from skirmishing with them, or casting darts from the ramparts, reviling them with scornful and insulting ribaldry and obscene gestures, until the hearts of the soldiers burned with indignation, and they complained bitterly of Marius, that he led them not forth to do battle, as became men and Romans.

But not for this did Marius alter his plan of operations, not even when a gigantic Teuton chief strode up to the gate and challenged him to single combat. At the insult he laughed grimly, bidding the barbarian go hang himself, if he were tired of living, [6] and, when he insisted, sending out a gladiator to do battle with him, as his equal in arms. During this time, however, his men became accustomed to the wild appearance, strange tongue, and frightful gesticulations of these formidable savages, and at length began to regard that as ridiculous which had at first filled them with awe and consternation.

Finding, at length, that the Romans could not by any device be drawn out of their stronghold, the Teutons assaulted the lines three days in succession, omitting no efforts to storm them, and fighting with the desperation of wild beasts rather than the courage of men. In every attack, however, they were bloodily repulsed, and the *legionaries* soon became as well used to their mode of fighting as to their shouts and gestures, and in the end regarded them alike, as of small moment.

Still the crafty veteran persisted, encouraging his men by the favourable divinations of the *seeress* Martha, and making himself acquainted with the most secret councils of the enemy, by means of a young officer, Sertorius, who understood the Celtic tongue, and often, wearing the Celtic garb, mingled with the Teutons and Ambrons about their watch-fires, and rendered his leader the master of their private designs, himself unsuspected. (*Plutarch*).

Hopeless, in the end, either of storming the works, or of inducing the consul to deliver battle, they became restless and weary of delay, and took the unmilitary and headlong course of rushing onward heedlessly, leaving this formidable power unregarded in their rear. Then might the infinity of their numbers be in some sort approximated; for as they filed along beneath the Roman ramparts, with their warriors and cavalry, their women and children, their baggage *wains*, their cattle and their beasts of burthen, six whole days were consumed by the

---

6. *Frontin Stratagem*, IV., 7. *ap.* Am. Thierry.

passage of this living torrent, in one continuous unintermitted flow. And ever, as they rolled along, they howled and reviled the Romans, asking them "What news shall we carry of you to your wives? for we shall see them speedily," (*Plutarch*).

So soon as the hordes had all passed by, Marius broke up from his stationary encampment, and followed them by slow marches, not pressing so closely on their rear, as to bring on an engagement, nor falling so far behind as to allow them to gain a clear march in advance, but always encamping within a short distance of them, and ever in strong natural positions, which he farther strengthened by artificial defences, so as to set surprise at defiance.

Ere long the combined multitudes arrived at the well-known watering place of Aquae Sextiae, now Aix, in Provence, where the pleasantness of the situation, the beauty of the scenery and the delicious thermal waters, which everywhere welled up from the ground, had caused a small town, with public baths, and all the luxuries of the day, to grow up. Thither, during the summer, it was the fashion for all the magistracy, aristocracy and wealth of the province to resort, as much for luxury and pleasure, as for the medical properties of the waters.

And here, having plundered the place, which offered no resistance, of all the valuables it contained, especially wine and provisions, the barbarians had crossed the little river Coenus, now the Arc, with their wagons and baggage, and established themselves in two camps, the Ambrons in one, close to the banks of the rivulet, and not far from the walls of the town; the Teutons in another, more remote, and nigher to the acclivity of the mountains.

Here also, speedily came Marius, and according to his wont, at once seized and occupied a strong hill between the town and the enemy's camps, commanding the whole valley. Favourable, however, as was the position in many respects, it had this defect, that it entirely lacked water, which was only to be had from the stream close to the quarters of the Ambrons.

It is said that the site was purposely chosen by Marius, who had now resolved to deliver battle, and desired to bring on the conflict apparently by accident, and at the same time to add to the valour of his soldiers the strong incitement of necessity.

But when the men grumbled and complained of thirst, Marius laughed at them, and pointing to the river, told them there was water enough, but it must be bought by blood. They then clamoured for instant battle, but still their immovable leader replied only, "First fortify the camp."

At this time the barbarians, already gorged with food and wine, and languid after their recent baths, were lying here and there in groups, revelling in the warmth, and overcome with the unwonted luxury, and some were yet delighting themselves in the sparkling and tepid waters. In the meanwhile the *legionaries* being hard at work, pitching their palisade and raising the *vallum*, the slaves and camp-followers rushed down to the stream to procure water, carrying beside their water-vessels, axes and cleavers, and some of them pikes and swords, and coming suddenly on the barbarians basking half asleep in the sun, put them to the sword without mercy.

At the cries of these, the enemy drew together, especially the fiercest and bravest of their tribe, the Ambrons, who, thirty thousand strong, had the greater share in the defeat and butchery of the Romans, under Manlius and Coepio. And these, though their bodies were oppressed with food, and their spirits excited and dissolved by the unmixed wine, advanced not in disarray, but clashing their arms and leaping in harmonious time, shouting at once their own national name, "*Ambra! Ambra!*" whether as exhorting one another, or as proclaiming their own race boastfully, to terrify the enemy.

Then Marius restrained his men no longer; and it so happened that some *cohorts* of the Ligurian auxiliaries were the first men in the plain, and these, strangely enough, though ignorant of the fact, and now wholly amalgamated with the people among whom they dwelt, descendants of an Ambron or Umbrian tribe, which had been banished centuries before by the Etruscans, from the plains of the Po, and had lest all recollection of their origin, except the national name and war-cry, *Ambra!* And when these heard the clamour of the barbarians, whether astounded or in defiance, they too set up the same wild cry, (*Plutarch*), and both parties shouting at the pitch of their voices in savage rivalry, and endeavouring each to outdo the other, the neighbouring mountains redoubled the din, and the valley of the Coenus was filled with the uproar, before the adversaries had even come to blows.

The passage of the river, it would seem, shook and disordered the formation of the Ambrons, who dashed into it recklessly, at sight of the *cohorts*, and before they could reform their order, the Ligurians were upon them, with a fierce charge, sword in hand. But the *legions* came to the succour of the Ligurians, and pouring down from the upper ground, to advantage, on the Ambrons, forced them back, bodily, by sheer force, into the channel, where rashly blended, and striking indiscriminately at friend and foe, they were slaughtered with prodigious carnage, and the rivulet was so heaped with carcasses and defiled with gore, that the conquerors had as much blood as water whereof to drink.[7]

Improving his victory to the utmost, Marius instantly passed the river, and drove them, with tremendous slaughter, to their encampment, fortified by a square of ponderous wagons. There, however, the pursuit was arrested by the desperation of the women, who rushed out, armed with axes and broad swords, cleaving down, in their blind rage, equally the pursuers and the pursued, fighting even more fiercely than their husbands, and suffering wounds and death in scornful silence and unmoved constancy.

As night fell, the consul drew off his *legions*, repassed the river, and took post, as before, upon the hill from which he had descended, but which he had been prevented from fortifying by the encounter, brought on, as I understand it, by accident; since it is not consistent with the known skill and caution of a leader so sage and circumspect as Marius, to have left the ordering of his battle intentionally to hazard; and it is perfectly consistent with the character of Roman historians to invent plausible reasons or excuses for any action of their heroes which they cannot themselves account for, and which they imagine to require apology.

That night was one of unmingled horror; for the barbarians bewailed their losses and bemoaned their dead, not with weeping and groans, like human beings, but with appalling howls and roarings, like wild beasts, to which their nature seemed to be in some sort assimilated. And a gloomy superstitious horror brooded over the gory plain, and the Romans, though victorious, were awe-stricken, and Marius himself was ill at ease, knowing that his camp was unfortified, and expecting at every hour an onslaught from the barbarians. But they came not either on that night or on the following day, but occupied the time in preparing their arms and making dispositions for battle.

After it was dark, Marius detached one of his staff, Claudius Marcellus, with three thousand soldiers, to gain the rear of the savages by a wide detour, to place himself in ambush close behind their lines, which were drawn up immediately in front of the first spurs of the mountains, covered with hanging woods, and full of deep ravines, heavily shaded with thickets of oak. The remainder of his forces, having caused them to breakfast heartily, and arm themselves before dawn,

---

7. *Floras, lib.* III. Chap. iii. *apud* Am. Thierry, *ut supra.*

he marched out of his entrenchments, as soon as it was light, and arranged them on the brow of the hill, while he launched his cavalry into the plain, to insult the camp of the barbarians.

Enraged at this sight, and beholding the *legionaries* arrayed without the palisades, the Teutons armed in haste, and rushed out to chastise the horse, who retired, skirmishing before them in troops and squadrons, faster and faster as they neared their comrades, until they had thrown the enemy into the disorder consequent on a rash and ill-conducted pursuit. Then, wheeling diverse, they gained the flanks of their own army, and drew up in perfect order, just as the hordes came roaring and bellowing and clashing their huge cutting broad-swords against the steep acclivities of the knoll, up which they swarmed liker to ravenous wolves, than to men and soldiers.

But Marius commanded his men by no means to charge, but to stand firm and receive them with the tremendous volley of their ponderous *pila*, hurled from above with double violence, and then to meet them steadily, in serried order, with linked shields, as they came staggering up the slippery ascent, breathless, and with no sure foothold, on the points of their two-edged Spanish swords. Nor was he not the first to enforce his precepts by his own example, for he was inferior to none of his army in personal vigor or athletic hardihood of body, while in fierce courage he surpassed the boldest.

On this day he showed himself not only an admirable leader, but a soldier unrivalled in the use of his own weapons. His orders were obeyed, and his example followed, with perfect success; after a long and deadly conflict, in which the whole front ranks fought hand to hand in a series of mortal single combats, foot by foot the Teutons were forced bodily back, fighting like incarnate fiends, every blow and thrust falling upon them from above, with fatal execution, until they were thrust down in increasing disorder, to the level ground at the base of the hill. With the repulse of the barbarians, simultaneously the Romans advanced, descending from the ridge which they had so stubbornly maintained, in a single ordered line.

The Teutons naturally became more and more disorganised by their descent from the broken ground into the valley of the Coenus; and their confusion was still augmented by the charges of the Latin horse from the flanks, and the steady forward pressure of the unbroken *legions*. They fought from morn until long past noon, and Marius himself avowed that he saw none of their backs, until at last they were borne backward across the river by sheer dint of fighting and bodily pressure, nearly to their own encampment, when with the stern, short blast of the Roman trumpets, and the wild Roman cheer, Claudius Marcellus rose from his ambush and charged them at full speed in the rear. That ended the battle; the barbarians broke, disbanded, dispersed. The most of them were slaughtered on the ground by the soldiers; those who escaped the first carnage, were hunted up by the natives of the country, and knocked on the head, wherever they were overtaken, as if they had been mad dogs.

According to the best accounts, one hundred thousand men were slain in the action and the subsequent pursuit. The wide plains to the eastward of Aix were literally fattened by the blood and corruption of the slaughtered and unburied carcasses. The name of Campi Putridi, still preserved in its modern title of *Pourrieres*, speaks volumes, and tells more by the untutored eloquence of oral tradition than all the pictured pages of history.

The camps being stormed, and all the wealth of the hordes, accumulated from the plunder of half Europe, falling to the lot of the soldiers, they voluntarily bestowed the whole on their leader; and he, either not to be outdone in generosity, or from genuine superstition, to which, it is clear, he was not inaccessible; or yet again, from some now inexplicable policy, devoted the whole to the gods, and in solemn pomp of crimson sacrificial robes, was about to kindle it with the torch, as the grandest of holocausts, when fleet riders were seen in the distance, urging their horses to the utmost.

The sacrifice was suspended; the couriers arrived on the spur, and hailed the general, "for the fifth time, consul."

Among the clash of arms, and the shower of laurel crowns and garlands, which fell about him like rain, the sacrifice was accomplished; a pyramid of earth was raised on the "Putrid Plains," and until the close of the fifteenth century a monument stood there, representing Marius upborne on a buckler, as *imperator*, by his soldiers. A shrine was raised on the spot to Victory; the site of which was still held consecrated, until Christianity itself was abolished in the first French revolution, as the church of St. Victoria, and is to this hour commemorated in the name *Deloubre*, of the nearest hamlet, from the old Latin word *Delubrum*.

But while he was yet in the full appreciation and enjoyment of his victory, news reached him from his colleague, Quintus Lutatius Catulus, that the second storm had burst on the north-eastern frontier of Italy.

The Cimbric division of the hordes having made the necessary detour, had come down the valley of the Etsach, by Bolzano, Trent, and Roveredo, and leaving the men of Zurich as a defensive rear-guard on the crest of the Alps, had descended in force into the plains of the Transpadane country.

Catulus, who had posted himself on the Italian slope of the Alps, fell back before the deluge, and took post on the right bank of the Adige, keeping his army in some degree *a cheval* on that river, which was there crossed by a wooden bridge, fortified by a strong *tête du pont*, on the left bank, well fortified and strongly garrisoned; and here he thought to make his stand.

But the Cimbri came down the Alps, rushing down the steep glassy slopes, seated on their shields, as if on sledges, careering, unobstructed, over all obstacles of precipice, ravine or *crevasse*, and organised themselves in the vast plains, in such force as to set all opposition at defiance.

Not caring to attack the Romans in their lines, or to force the passage of the bridge, they performed works which sufficiently attest the vastness of their numbers, and prove that the exaggerations—as they are termed—of the old historians, are but the simple truth. They rolled such masses of earth, rock, and timber, into the channel of the Adige, that instead of crossing the river in their front, they threw it into a false channel in the rear, and so passed dry-shod through its empty bed.

Thus turned in his position, and finding that his soldiers were on the point of deserting him, Catulus made a virtue of necessity, ordered a retreat, which he could not prevent, crossed the Po, and took post where best he might, rather, it would seem, with a view to keep his force together, than to cover Rome.

That these formidable hordes had no real object in view, either as regards settlement or permanent conquest, now becomes perfectly evident; since, instead of marching direct to Rome, which was wholly undefended, even by the dispirited and demoralised troops of Catulus, they dispersed themselves over the rich alluvial delta of the Po, and the teeming plains of the Brenta, revelling in the unusual delights of bread, cooked flesh, and abundant wine, until they became, as it was said, *effete*, luxurious, and lazy.

Marius, in the meantime, on receipt of the news, set his army instantly in motion; it is not stated by what route, but it is rendered evident, by the course of events, that it must have been by the road which leads direct from Aix, across the Maritime Alps, by the Col di

Tende, or by the pass of la Traversette, under the Monte Viso, into the valley of the upper Po, and thence by Turin, toward Milan, whither, leaving Rome totally uncovered, Catulus moved to meet his puissant reinforcement, and this done, took ship himself for Rome, in order to consult the senate and arrange the plan of the subsequent campaign. It was expected, at this period, that he would take his triumph for his great recent victory over the Teutons, but he declined it for the present, in consequence of the absence of his army, which was entitled to share in the honours of ceremonial, and which was yet on the route to join Catulus.

In the meantime, he joined his colleague in person, and did all in his power to keep up the courage of his dismayed soldiery, until such time as his own victorious veterans came up from the Rhone, when he at once repassed the Po, and prepared to deliver battle in the Transpadane country, for the purpose of preserving Lower Italy intact.

What could have induced the barbarians to turn again to the westward, and go in search of the consular armies, when they might have marched direct upon Rome, leaving the *legions* two hundred miles to their right, cannot be easily accounted for, unless it be, that still ignorant, as it would seem they were, of the defeat and annihilation of their allies, the Teutons and Ambrons, they made this counter-march towards the Maritime Alps, in the hope of joining them on their descent from the mountain passes, or on their entrance by the sea-shore of Liguria.

Again, when they perceived that the Romans were prepared for them, they hesitated to attack, and demanded lands from the Republic, whereon they might themselves settle, and a farther apportionment of territory for their brothers, the Teutons.

But Marius laughed them to scorn and made reply, "Let be your brothers the Teutons, for they have lands enough, and will have for evermore, which they have received from us already." But the savage emissaries, understanding the irony and disbelieving the fact, reviled him bitterly, and threatened the Romans with present punishment, at the hands of the Cimbri, and future vengeance from the Teutons so soon as they should arrive.

"They have arrived already," replied the consul, ordering Teutobochus and the Teuton prisoners to be led forth, "and it is but fitting that you should salute your brethren, as you will not see them again in a long time."

On hearing this, full of grief and rage, the deputies returned to the Cimbric hordes, while Marius quietly prepared his army for the encounter; and it is said, that on this occasion he made a change in the form of the *pila*, the ponderous heads of which were ordinarily secured to the massive shafts by two stout iron rivets. The lower of these Marius now caused to be removed, and its place supplied by a weak wooden pin, which would break so soon as the weapon had transfixed the great bull-hide buckler of the Cimbri, so that the shaft would bend at an angle with the head, and hang down to the ground, embarrassing the soldier, and forcing him to abandon his cover, and fight unprotected.

When all was now fully prepared, Boiorix galloped up to the fortifications of the camp, and challenged Marius to name time and place when the Romans and Cimbri might fight it out, and decide who should possess the country—to which Marius replied, that it was not the wont of the Romans to consult the choice of their enemies as to the mode of giving battle; but that, nevertheless, desiring to oblige the Cimbri, he would, in this case, meet their challenge. He, therefore, named the third day from that time, for the combat, and the Raudian plains, the name of which is probably preserved in the name Rho, of a small village a few miles to the eastward of Vercellae, now Borgo di Vercelli, between the Tesino and the Sesia, some thirty miles to the east of Milan, as the place of encounter, the ground being suitable for the operations of the Roman cavalry, and sufficiently extensive to accommodate so large a concourse.

Here he took post on the appointed morning, on the eastern side of the plains, so that the fierce rays of the blazing Italian sun should be full in the eyes of the enemy; and that a violent east wind, which was blowing from the backs of the Romans, and raising whirlwinds of dust which literally obscured the heavens, should also fight against them.

Marius commanded thirty-two thousand men, Sylla leading the cavalry of the whole, and Catulus twenty thousand three hundred—the latter occupying the centre with his combined force, while the legions of Marius were divided into two bodies, stationed on the wings; for he had so arranged it, thinking that the battle would be decided by flank attacks, and that he should so secure to himself the honour of the day.

In spite of the disadvantages under which they laboured, the hordes advanced undaunted to the attack, their infantry were arrayed in an immense solid square, the ranks and files being composed of equal numbers of men, and extending, according to Plutarch, thirty *stadia*, or nearly four miles, in each direction. This, however, must be a palpable exaggeration, for the highest number attributed to them by Livy, whose reckoning is the largest, is but two hundred thousand killed and prisoners, none having escaped the carnage; and it is evident that so many men in close order would not occupy anything approaching to that space of ground. For the square root of two hundred and two thousand five hundred, being four hundred and fifty, that is a sufficiently near approximation to the numbers of rank and file, which would compose a solid square of two hundred thousand men.

The marching space allowed to each soldier, according to Polybius, himself a soldier and tactician, was six feet square in open order, and one yard square when serried in the *synaspismus*, or order of linked shields. So that the utmost space which could be covered by a solid square of two hundred thousand men, will not exceed nine hundred yards square in open, or four hundred and fifty, in serried order. But it is stated, (*Plutarch*), that by a strange and incomprehensible precaution, the first ranks of the Cimbri were attached, man to man, by great iron chains, rivetted to their girdles, whether to render their order more solid, or to take from the soldiers any hope of escaping by flight. This would, of course, indicate the closest possible array of battle, and the lesser square as the utmost extent of their body.

Thierry understands the passage as meaning that the camp, wagons, plunder, and non-combatants, together with the infantry, occupied a square of thirty *stadia*, but Plutarch's words will not bear this construction, for he says:

> The Cimbric infantry advanced tranquilly from out their defences, making their depth equal to their front; for each side of their array had thirty *stadia* of length.

The whole passage must therefore be set down to mere inconsiderate and reckless Latin exaggeration, which it is useless to attempt to explain or modify, since it unquestionably had its origin in a deliberate intention to deceive, for the purpose of magnifying the prowess of the Romans.

The cavalry of the Cimbri, fifteen thousand strong, was not the least formidable portion of their army. They were splendidly equipped, and made a glorious show, with helmets fashioned to imitate the heads of terrible wild beasts with jaws open, as if to devour, and wide-expanded wings above all for crests, with glittering corselets of steel, and resplendent white bucklers. Their javelins were doubly-pointed, having a head at either extremity, and when they came to close quarters they used great, heavy, cutting broad-swords.

These terrible troopers were the first to commence the attack, not by a direct charge to the front, but by a wide sweep to the sword hand, with the intention to turn the Roman left, and fall on their unguarded flank. And the Roman generals perceived and understood the feint, but were unable to restrain their men, one of whom crying out, that the enemy were flying, the whole body rushed forward in pursuit. At the same time, the infantry of the barbarians came on, surging and tossing like a huge entering sea, and Marius washing his hands and vowing a whole *hecatomb* to the gods if they might conquer, and Catulus likewise beseeching them to sanctify to him the fortunes of that day, the soothsayers pronounced the omens favourable, and the conqueror of the Teutons, shouting aloud that the victory was to him, led his men to the charge.

Thereupon a strange thing fell out; for the dust hung suspended in such dense volumes over the whole plain, that the motions of both armies were totally obscured, (*Plutarch*), and that Marius, with his entire division, passed without the enemy's lines, encountering no one, and, marching forward into the plain, missed them completely, and wandered about in the darkness, utterly at fault and ignorant what to do; so that the main brunt and surge of the barbarians broke down upon Catulus, to whose division Sylla was annexed, with his cavalry, and that the victory and the glory were to them. Of the manoeuvres or accidents of the day, nothing is known but that the conflict was long and bloodily contested, hand to hand.

The heat and the sunshine fought for the Romans, and the Cimbri, used to cold regions, and the almost Arctic cold of their vast and gloomy forests, were utterly unable to endure the sultriness of an Italian summer; for the conflict occurred on the third day previous to the calends of August, that is to say, according to the Roman mode of reckoning, on the thirtieth of July, or the very hottest and most intolerable portion of the year. Smothered with whirlwinds of dust, driven directly into their eyes and nostrils, and blinded by the glare of the sun, when it blazed out in occasional glimpses, redoubled by the repercussion [8] of its beams from the brazen armour, the savages fell on with little vigour, out of breath, reeking with perspiration, and instead of covering their bodies from the enemy's blows with their bucklers, sheltering their faces with them from the unendurable fierceness of

---
8. *Floras, liber III.* Chap. III. *apud* Thierry.

the morning and noonday light.

The darkness also befriended the Italians, for while it prevented them from seeing to their dismay the innumerable ranks of the Cimbri, it likewise hindered those from availing themselves of their numbers; while their want of discipline and the immobility of their huge unwieldy masses, embarrassed, moreover, by the very means which they had adopted to ensure their steadiness, rendered them singularly liable to the disconnected and desultory charges of an active, flexible, and easily handled enemy, such as the *legions*, who eventually pierced the hordes at all points, and slaughtered them ruthlessly, giving no quarter to men, who chained together by ranks, when once disordered, could neither wheel nor fight to advantage, much less fly.

When at last the Cimbri were driven back to their wagons and fortifications, the women standing on the defences, in black robes, with dishevelled hair, cut down the fugitives with axe and claymore, slaying their brothers, husbands and fathers, as mercilessly as the Roman enemy. Then having vainly [9] offered to the consuls to surrender, on condition that their honour should be spared, and that they should be allowed to devote themselves to perpetual chastity as servants of the Vestal virgins, they took the last and sternest resolution. Slaughtering their children, dashing their brains out against the naves of the wheels, or casting them to be trampled to death under the hoofs of the beasts of burthen, not one of them survived the destruction of their horde, which was to them their home, their country, and their all, on this side of eternity.

One of them was found suspended from the top tilt of her wagon, with her twin children hanging from her ankles; others, for want of trees, hung themselves by halters to the horns and legs of their oxen, and then goaded them to their speed, and were trampled under their impetuous hoofs. All perished, nor was one reserved to be dragged at the chariot wheels of the cruel conqueror, or to minister to the brutal pleasures of the savage soldiery. Of the men, from one hundred to one hundred and forty thousand fell on the field or were slaughtered in the pursuit; sixty thousand, less happy, were taken prisoners, sold as slaves to the cruellest and basest servitude, or kept for the bloody sport of the gladiatorial arena.

Even after the conclusion of this awful catastrophe, when the Romans attempted to penetrate into this scene of carnage and horror, they were yet assailed by a fresh enemy, the fierce and faithful dogs of

---
9. *Paul Oros. lib. V. c.* 16. *Floras ut supra.*

the horde, which defended the encampment and the dead bodies of their masters, with such desperate fidelity, that no entrance could be had until they were exterminated by flights of arrows, the men not choosing to encounter their fangs at close quarters.

The rear guard of the Tigurini, who had been posted on the height of the Alps, hearing of the general ruin, fell back into Noricum, which they wasted far and wide, and thence retreated into Switzerland, where they remained tranquil until a fresh frenzy for emigration drove them again, a half century later, into Gaul, where they perished, with most of their nation, by the sword of Julius Caesar.

Thus ended the career of the second and last of those barbarous Celtic hordes, which swept the whole southern continent of Europe, from east to west, devastating, destroying, with fire and sword, like a very scourge of God—leaving no track of their progress but ruin and ashes, no monument but solitude and devastation—hordes, which founded no nation, erected no institution, bequeathed no discovery, left no heritage to posterity of art, of intellect, of improvement, of progress, of humanity; which have planted only in the lands where they tarried longest, ignorance, barbarism, superstition, all the passions, with few of the virtues, of the original savage, flagrant and vital to the present day.

Unlike the Goths and Vandals, they never assimilated themselves to the more cultured races among whom they settled; never adopted one of their refinements, never built up a single edifice of liberty, of law, of literature, of science; never erected anything in lieu of what they pulled down, whether cities, institutions or principles; but having been sent, as it were on a mission of extermination, would, on their own total extermination, were such a result at this day possible, be remembered, only by the records of the ruin they have wrought, and the traditions of their rash and reckless valour, which seems to have been their nearest approximation to a virtue.

Therefore, what was supposed to be the extermination of the race so immitigably hostile, and it must be added, so terrible to the Romans, was rewarded in Marius with great and extraordinary honours. After the news reached Rome of the destruction of the enemy, the citizens made libations, (*Valer*), to his name, as never had been done but to the immortal gods; the very magnates, who had always hitherto opposed him as an ignoble person admitted to the highest honours of the state, now acknowledged him the saviour, (*Livy*), of his country; and the whole state, with one consent, adjudged to him the honour, unjustly as it would appear, of triumphing alone for both victories, to the exclusion of his colleague. This, however, he refused to accept, (*Plutarch*), whether that he wished to affect a moderation which he did not possess, or, what is much more probable, since there was nothing of moderation, and very little of affectation, in the character of Marius, that he dreaded the opposition of the soldiers, who might prevent him from triumphing at all, should he defraud his colleague of his share of glory.

The pomp was a grand one, and purely martial. There were no ingots of uncoined gold and silver; no urns and vases of money; no pictures, no statues, no luxury of conquered monarchs, only the huge and battered arms of the enemy, attesting the puissance of the warriors and the obstinacy of their resistance; only the men themselves, mighty of bone and sinew, grim-visaged, fierce and sallow; only their king, Teutobochus, fettered like his companions in defeat, and so tall in stature, that he towered above the trophies of his conqueror.

From that day forth, Marius set no bounds to the insolent arrogance of his demeanour, to the extravagance of his ambition. He adopted as his device, and wore ever carved on his buckler, the face of a Celt making grimaces, with his tongue thrust out.[10] He pretended to equality with Bacchus, the conqueror of India; and is said, henceforth, to have drunk only out of a two-handled Carchesium, which had been used, as tradition went, by that demi-god himself, during his career on earth, though it is not so clearly indicated by what means it came into the hands of the great plebeian consul.

At this period, he stood unquestionably the first Roman citizen, the first Roman general of his day, perhaps, in all respects, the most considerable and greatest man of the world in that age. Hitherto he had done everything for his country, nothing against it. He had conquered every enemy he had encountered; he had saved, beyond doubt, the republic from the greatest peril that had threatened it since the days of Hannibal; and if he had proved himself a bitter and rancorous hater of a large class of his countrymen, and as an individual, a man of brutal temper and all surpassing arrogance, he had done nothing hitherto contrary to his duties as a man, a soldier, or a Roman.

From this time forth he did nothing well, nothing honourably, nothing generously, nothing victoriously, whether as a man, a general, on a citizen. Empty ambition for place, deadly detestation of the senate, and an insane lust after noble blood, became from this time his

---

10. Cicero de Oratore, *lib*. II. 266. Quinctilian VI. 3. *apud* Amedee Thierry,

only ruling passion, his only spring of action—

Exilium et Career Minturnarumque paludes,
Et meudicatus victa Carthagine panis,
Hinc causas habuere.

With his Teutonic and Cimbric triumph, the military career of Marius is in fact finished, for although he bore arms again throughout the social war of Italy, he achieved nothing of consideration; and though a Roman general, acted continually as if he desired the success of the Italian confederacy, to which he actually belonged by birth, and with whose cause he in fact identified himself at a later period. But a brief sketch of his after career is necessary to a full comprehension of his character, and to the easier appreciation of the history and circumstances of his successors.

Although he had been already five times consul, with great glory, and had now nothing to gain by a prolongation of office, he procured his election for the sixth time, by having recourse to bribery, to flattery of the mob, to the most abject pandering to prejudice, and to every dirtiest and most dishonourable trick of the demagogue. Elected to his sixth consulship, in the year of Rome 654, B. C. 100, which year is also famous for the birth of Caesar, so nearly have we now arrived to the dissolution of the republic, he leagued himself to the factious tribune Saturninus, the *praetor* Glaucia, and the *quaestor* Saufeius, who for the space of nearly a year, positively governed the state, after their assassination of Nonius Sufenas, overpowering the senate and magistracy by the terror of the violence and daggers of a rabble of desperate ruffians, the refuse of the disbanded soldiery whom Marius had infamously and illegally mustered into the *legions*, and who were now ready to follow any leader, whether for or against the state, who should give them plunder and blood.

By dint of this terror they succeeded in passing many atrocious laws, subversive of all rights of property, of all constitutional principles, and giving all powers, legislative, judicial and executive, to the primary and tumultuary meetings of the city rabble, held in the streets and public places, under no sanction of law or guarantee of order.

By this means, not without recourse to personal violence, Marius procured the banishment of his detested enemy, that most virtuous and respectable citizen Quintus Metellus Numidicus, and would have proceeded, by aid of his factious tools, to what extremities it cannot be said; for having armed their hands and excited their minds to contempt of all right and reason, he was now so little able to restrain them, that in his despite they rushed headlong into their own ruin.

At the subsequent elections, the three confederates of the consul, Saturninus, Glaucia, and Saufeius caused one of the candidates for the consulship, who seemed likely to prevail over Glaucia in the canvass, Caius Memmius, to be murdered on the ground, while the tribes were in the act of voting. Alarmed themselves at the consequences of this outrage, and of the fierce indignation which it occasioned among all classes, the conspirators armed their adherents, seized the capitol, and openly defying the Republic, had instant recourse to arms.

The senate now assembled, and taking courage from the emergency, invested the consuls with dictatorial power by charging them "to see that the Republic took no harm," while the *equites*, the nobility, and all the citizens of rank, respectability and station, took arms and flocked to the standard of the Republic.

Marius was fain to vacillate and spare the offenders, but the rebellion was so flagrant, the crime so palpable, and the general feeling of the city so strong, that he dared not resist the commands of the senate. The capitol was invested in form, and held out for several days, until the water-pipes were cut, when it surrendered at discretion; and the conspirators, whom Marius still desired to favour, were confined in the hall of the senate, until the consuls should receive farther orders. But the citizens, who were yet in arms, seeing the palpable intention to discharge these firebrands and assassins without trial, much less punishment, broke into the place, put them all to the sword, and by that terrible blow restored the constitution, the authority of the senate and magistracy, and the true freedom of the state. Two consuls were elected of the conservative party, Metellus was recalled from banishment, and Marius, finding himself too weak to overthrow, as yet, the government of Rome, retired, for a while, into private life—happy both for himself and his country had he emerged from it no more, for his return to the helm of state was a return only to defeat, disgrace and death.

Unable to endure a meeting with Metellus, he took ship for Asia Minor and Galatia, under pretext of sacrificing to the "mighty mother" of the gods, but in reality with a view to force Mithridates into a war with Rome, by his intrigues and insults, in the expectation that he should therein find employment and occasion for fresh triumphs. For the time, however, he was disappointed, and returning to Rome, took a house close to the forum, which was frequented by crowds of his turbulent adherents. At this time, occurred his first open rupture with his great rival, arising from the presentation by Bocchus the Mauritanian, of twenty golden statues to the temple of Victory, on the Capitoline, among which was a group representing the delivery of Jugurtha, fettered, into the hands of Sylla. This trophy Marius would have pulled down as an unjust attribution of his own honours to another, while Sylla as eagerly insisting on its preservation, the civil wars would even then have commenced, had not the differences of the two enemies been temporarily composed by the Marsic league against Rome, and the breaking out of the devastating wars of the Italian confederacy.

This war, arising from the refusal by the senate of the just demands of the Italian allies, particularly the Marsi, Peligni, Vestini, Marcini, Picentes, Ferentanae, Hirpini, Pompeiani, Venusini, Apuli, Lucani, and Samnites, to be admitted to the privilege of citizenship of Rome, which they had supported and defended with their valour, their blood, and their treasure, during the most critic and perilous portion of her career, broke out in the year of the city 663, B. C. 91, and continued for three years to rage throughout Italy with terrible fury, and to the lamentable desolation of the country. Above three hundred thousand men were slain in this internal conflict; many flourishing towns which had escaped the ravages of both Pyrrhus and Hannibal, were reduced to piles of ashes, and Rome herself survived only through the fidelity of the cities of the Latin name, which had long enjoyed a modified franchise, and which, as in the second Punic War, remained true to the fortunes of the Commonwealth.

Of this war, little is known, as there exists in history, at this present moment, a singular hiatus. All the most distinguished Roman officers were employed, including Pompeius Strabo, the father of him who was afterward known as Pompey the Great—Coepio, Messala, Lucius Julius Caesar, Sylla, Marius, and Perpenna,—the two latter of Italian origin, though in the Roman service. On the side of the confederates were men of nearly equal merit and capacity—Pompedius Silo, Pontius Telesinus. Judacilius, Ventidius, and Vettius Cato.

Of the Roman leaders Pompeius Strabo, Lucius Caesar and Sylla alone obtained either credit or success. Marius and Perpenna would neither give battle, nor follow up advantages when they fell in their way; and so evidently was the former temporizing, if not conspiring with the enemy, in the hopes of their ultimate success, that he was forced to resign his command on the plea of nervousness, but in truth because lie perceived that he was distrusted and suspected by the people, and falling into discredit through the successes of his enemy, Sylla, as contrasted with his own inactivity.

After a while the war languished, either party feeling its inability to conquer, and was ultimately composed by the gradual admission of the inhabitants of the Italian cities to the desired *franchise*. Those who had not taken arms at all being first admitted, then those who had desisted from weariness, and lastly, all who should lay down their arms within a certain time.

The contest terminated, though in truth there had been no victory in the case, by the triumph of Pompeius Strabo for the storming of Asculum, and the election of Lucius Cornelius Sylla, henceforth surnamed Felix, the Fortunate, to the consulship and conduct of the Mithridatic War, in the year of the city 666, B.C. 88, in acknowledgment of his exploits, nor only in this Marsic or Social war, but on every occasion when he had held an independent command.

The next question was how to dispose of the new Italian citizens, who out-numbered in individual voters all the Roman citizens of the old thirty-five tribes; and who, had they been merged in them, would have constituted a majority in each tribe, and consequently carried the whole assembly, swamped the old Roman vote, and actually governed Rome.

They were formed into eight new tribes, which, voting last in the assembly, after the old tribes had delivered their voice, had little influence or effect in the state,—an arrangement as unjust to the new citizens, as the other would have been to the old *burghers*, which was one of the main causes of the bloodshed, dissensions, horrible anarchy and cold, centralized despotism, which soon succeeded.

At this moment one Sulpicius, a tribune of the people, and the counterpart, in character and villainy, of Saturninus, Glaucia, and Saufeius, revived the former conflicts between the popular and senatorial parties, as before, at the secret instigation and with the connivance of Caius Marius, and as before by means of a rabble of three thousand armed gladiators, whom he called his anti-senate, and by whom he over-awed the state, and virtually governed it. In the course of his proceedings a violent sedition arose, in which Pompeius, son of the present consul and son-in-law of Sylla, was openly butchered in the street, and Sylla himself escaped murder only by flying to his army of six *legions*, which were lying in Campania, awaiting the arrival of their general, to set out for Greece, to which they were ordered.

So soon as Sylla had left the city, Marius began to play his part openly, in concert with Sulpicius, and procured the revocation of Sylla's appointment to the Mithridatic War, and his own appointment in his lieu, by one of those tumultuous and illegal street-conventions which arrogated to themselves, and too often obtained the power, if not the right, of superseding the regular laws and appointments of the senate and magistracy, according to the forms of the constitution.

Officers were sent off at once to take the army out of the hands of Sylla and his subordinates, and hold it until Marius should arrive; but these men were at once slain in a tumult of the soldiery, and Sylla marched at once with his six *legions* upon Rome, with the declared purpose of liberating the senate and the state from what was in truth the dominion of a lawless, rebellious, and usurping faction, and of restoring the authority of the proper magistrates, without the desire of personal aggrandizement. Entering the gates partly by force, partly by stratagem, he cleared the streets, not without some sharp fighting and the conflagration of some parts of the city, of the partisans of Marius, restored the power of the senate, whom he instantly convened to deliberate on the state of affairs and procured the passage of a law declaring Marius and twelve of his principal adherents, enemies of the state, as men who had violated the laws of the Republic, seduced slaves to desert their masters and to take arms against them, and of having himself warred against Rome in its very streets.

Of these desperate and dangerous men, the abominable wretch Sulpicius—whose place in history is beside Saturninus, Glaucia, Saufeius, villains of smaller parts though not less atrocity, than Catiline, Marius himself, and their competitors in infamy, in modern ages, Fouché, Marat and Robespierre—was dragged from his hiding-place amid the marshes of Minturnae, and put to death summarily as a traitor, his head being exposed in the forum on one of the public rostra.

Marius, more fortunate, obtained a vessel at Ostia, and set sail for Sicily or Africa, but being forced into Circeii by stress of weather, fled for concealment to the same marshes of Minturnae, near the mouth of the Liris, now the Garigliano, where he buried himself to the chin in the obscure and fetid mire, which failing to seclude him from his pursuers, he was captured and cast into prison at Minturnae. Here he was ordered for execution; but by the connivance of the magistrates of that Italian town, who did not choose to sacrifice the countryman and friend of their nation, he was suffered to make his escape, and even furnished with a ship, which conveyed him first to the coast of Sicily, whence he was driven by the officers of the republic, and thereafter to Africa and Carthage, where occurred the romantic incident of the great outlawed hero being found seated, desolate and alone, on a fallen pillar's base amid the desolation of Rome's prostrate rival, which has given a theme to so many painters and poets.

The story may here be mentioned, how a Cimbric slave and gladiator was sent into the dungeon of Minturnae, with orders to despatch the mighty exile, and how he recoiled from the terrific aspect and appalling voice of the grim septuagenarian; and how, on the brief, stern question in those awful accents—"Man, darest thou slay Caius Marius!" he rushed headlong from the prison, leaving the gates unfastened, and cast down his bloodless sword before the magistrates, crying, "I cannot kill this man."

The legend, however, is a mere fiction, framed by the partisans of Marius, partly to exaggerate the awe and mystery, which still surround his name, partly to exculpate the magistracy of Minturnae of their treason to Rome, in suffering so great a criminal to escape their justice.

After his arrival at Carthage, and his repulse thence by the *praetor* Sextilius, he concealed himself in bye-places and islands on the wild Numidian shore, the scene of his early triumphs, until he was recalled by his late colleague and partner in guilt, Cinna, to complete the horrors of his atrocious career, by a death no less horrible than his life had been hideous and detestable.

No sooner had Sylla departed with his troops against Mithridates, whose progress in Pontus, Lesser Asia, the islands of the Archipelago and the mainland of Greece itself, was very formidable, and who had recently caused to be massacred in a single day, every Roman citizen, without distinction of age or sex; in his dominions, than Cinna, who had solemnly sworn fealty to the republic and fidelity to the constitution, as Sylla had reconstituted it, on the old time-honoured model, broke his troth and resuscitated the ancient riots, favouring the claim of the new citizens, whose cause henceforth became identical with that of the old demagogues, the factious *tribunes*, and their rabble of incendiaries and assassins.

Being defeated in his object, and forced to leave the city by his colleague Octavius and the aristocratic party, he withdrew into the fields, levied one army, brought over two more, recalled Marius and the exiles, and once more declared war on the commonwealth.

Marius returned, the Italians joined him to a man; the armies of all the generals, who should have opposed him, composed of *legions* of *enfranchised* slaves, aliens, proletarians, and all the off-scourings of the great corrupt city, whose camp was their country, and their most lavish leader the chief-magistrate of the republic, deserted their generals and united themselves to the rebellion. Rome, besieged and closely invested, being pressed by hunger and having no hope of relief, surrendered, and at the head of a Roman army, Marius and Cinna entered the gates of Rome as a captured city, devoted to all extremity of havoc, rape, and butchery.

Marius, with a loathsome affectation of humility, refused to wear any garb but mourning, having his face besmirched, his coarse gray hair disordered, and his raiment in tatters, as if an exile and a suppliant, until the senate should reverse his attainder, and restore his freedom of the city. They did so, and he entered, and the very stones of the *via sacra* cried, "Woe!" as he marched in triumphant.

He was surrounded by a body-guard of liberated slaves, whom he named *Bardiaei*, who, at his slightest nod or gesture, or his failing to return the salute of the passers by, cut them down ruthlessly. By his direct orders, every member of Sylla's, party who could be found, was indiscriminately slaughtered, not that they were his enemies, either personal or political, but only that they were nobles by birth, true to their order, and conservators of the Roman constitution.

For live consecutive days this hideous slaughter lasted; the maddened multitude joining the slaves and massacring, at hazard, all that were reported noble, virtuous, friends of their country, above all, rich, until disgusted and sickened at the carnage and the gore, which literally flooded the kennels, Cinna and Sertorius, Marius' own friends and colleagues, brought in regular troops, put all the *Bardiaei* to the sword, and restored tranquillity, if not peace, law, or order.

Among the victims of those hideous days, similar only to the Parisian Saturnalia of the accursed directory, fell of the noblest men of Rome, Cneius Octavius, the consul, Marcus Antonius, the orator, C. Julius Caesar, Quintus Lutatius Catulus, reputed the most virtuous man of his day, and Marius' own colleague in the battle with the Cimbri, and Lucius Cornelius Merula, the chief-priest of Jupiter, who bled himself to death, to escape ignoble butchery, in the capitol, and sprinkled the sacred things with his illustrious gore.

In the year of Rome 658, 86 B.C., despising all the forms of polity, and desirous to the last to exhibit his contempt of Rome, and his detestation of the nobles, disdaining to be re-elected, Marius proclaimed himself, in the seventy-second year of his age, for the seventh time consul.

A few days afterward, to the great joy of his citizens and the great good of liberty and humanity, the monster, whilom styled the saviour of his country, died universally feared, and yet more detested.

His death was equal to his life in horror, for he died literally fury-hunted by his guilty and blood-drunken conscience; he could not sleep by night, so hideous were the terrors of his dreams; he dreaded alike the darkness and the light; and ever there seemed to ring in his ears the strange verse of a well-known poet—

"Δειναὶ γαρ κοῖται καὶ ἀποιχομένοιο λέοντος."

"*Dreadful is the lair, even of the dying lion*"

And thus, to avoid the agonies of his own mind, he took to frantic orgies and incessant drunkenness, and so, having been notorious from his youth, upward, for frugality and temperance, expired a madman and a drunkard, exclaiming that the very cup he craved mantled with human gore.

His character may be summed up in half a dozen words; it is nearly the most detestable in history; would be so altogether, had not his kindred spirits, the French Jacobins, outdone him in all excesses of atrocity and guilt.

As a general, there is nothing known of him, which is not admirable, as a man, nothing that is not detestable.

There was no feature of generosity, no caprice of magnanimity, no casual whim of humanity, in his hard, stern, ruthless spirit.

Even his ambition had nothing in it grand or ennobling. He coveted power, indeed, and won it; but it was at last only the power to kill. His hatreds were as insensate as they were savage. The nobles had never wronged him, unless a single sneer of Metellus be a wrong expiable only in blood; on the contrary, in common with all classes, after his defeat of the Teutons and Cimbri, had joined in loading him with honours, and hailed him *pater patriae*.

To speak of him as a statesman, a politician, even a reformer, is idle; for in all his seven consulships he advocated no principle, introduced no considerable measure, carried out, nor even attempted any reform. Like the parrot cry of the elder Cato, "*Delenda est Carthago*," his sole maxim was destruction to the nobles. He destroyed them, and with them his own fame, and the freedom of his country. Had there been no Marius, there could have been no Caesar; and the sentence of Velleius Paterculus, that, in regard of his conquest of the Teutons and Cimbri, Rome had no cause to repent having produced a Marius, is but the unmeaning peroration of a rhetorician.

His early services were utterly effaced by the infamy of his last days, and he expired in the act of subverting the constitution of his country, of destroying all her legitimate and capable defenders, and of delivering the once free and noble commonwealth to the icy chains of a silent, centralized autocracy, the most abhorred by men, and by the gods abandoned.

6.

Lucius Cornelius Sylla, Felix

Triumphant Sylla! Thou who didst subdue
Thy country's foes, ere thou wouldst pause to feel
The wrath of thine own wrongs, or reap the due
Of hoarded vengeance, till thine eagles flew
O'er prostrate Asia. Thou who with thy frown
Annihilated senates. Roman, too,
With all thy vices, for thou didst lay down,
With an atoning smile, a more than mortal crown—
The dictatorial wreath.

This great and fortunate soldier was of birth no less noble and exalted than his rival and enemy, whose career we have just traced to its close, was low born and ignoble. Of the grand Cornelian family—which had given to the Roman Republic so many of its best and greatest citizens, which was thereafter to produce so many of its direst fire-brands—from which had sprung Cossus, who slew with his own hand Lar Tolamnius, and bore to the capitol, second to Romulus only, the *spolia opima*—from which had sprung twelve noble Scipios, among whom the conquerors of Hannibal and Antiochus—from which, beside himself, the all-victorious, sprang Cinna, Dolabella, Lentulus, Cethegus, the parricides of Rome and mates of the arch-traitor Catiline—he was as mighty and consistent a champion of his order, as was Marius its unvarying and uncompromising foe.

He was born in Rome in the year of the city 617, B.C. 139, in the consulship of Marcus Æmilius Lepidus, and Caius Hostilius Mancinus, of poor, though patrician parents, about seventeen years later than Caius Marius, to whom he was in every respect the natural opposite, no less than the self-constituted opponent. In daring valour, strategic skill, and unrelenting temper alone, did they bear, each to the other, some resemblance. But the mere physical brute courage of the *plebeian* of Arpinum could as little compare with the astute considerate valour of the proud Roman Patrician, as could the boorish ignorance, of which he was so disreputably proud and boastful, compare with the refined and graceful scholarship, the fine literary taste, and polished eloquence of his rival.

As the one was morose, churlish, rugged of bearing, harsh of temper, abstinent of wine and women, averse to all social pleasure, so was the other affable, courtly in demeanour, jovial in his humour, lavish in his largesses, luxurious in his life, and fond of gay and riotous society. So that it was afterward remarked that the vengeance of the Patrician wore an aspect far more terrible and loathly than that of the ruthless *plebeian*; for that the latter derived his cruelty from the impulses of a savage and morbid temper, while the former, of an easy disposition, sentenced with a smile on his lips, and signed his death warrants among his wine cups.

He does not appear, naturally, to have been a man of violence, or of that hot and heady ambition, to which some of his later acts have been attributed, but to have been rather driven by succeeding circumstances to the greatness, which he in the end attained, than to have been spurred to it by any resolution to command fortune and conquer place.

At all periods of his life indolence, luxury, and the true Italian's appetite for the *dolce far niente*, seriously combated his mounting energies, and clogged the soaring wing of his aspiring genius; and to the end, his strangely mingled love of the highest mental refinements; and the lowest sensual indulgences, strove for the mastery with his lust of victory and thirst of vengeance. His very abdication of the power, to reach which he had waded to the knees through blood, was dictated as much by his desire for luxurious literary leisure, his love for the green woods and deep pastures of his estates at Cuma, for solitary wanderings by the ever-sounding shore, and for the wild excitement of the chase, as by his weariness of government, his contempt for those he governed.

In person he was tall, well built, and athletic, but his countenance was strange and unprepossessing in the extreme; for his light blue eyes had a terrible pale glare, which was exaggerated by a *scorbutic* ruddy efflorescence overspreading one half of his features; so that his face was compared by the buffoons of Athens, when he was besieging that city, to a mulberry sprinkled with meal. The first step of Sylla toward advancement was one by no means reputable, nor such as should grace the entrance of a youth of aristocratic birth into the world; for originally poor in pecuniary fortune, he became moderately rich by means of a legacy bequeathed to him by a woman of evil fame, with whom he had held most intimate connexions, and who died deeply enamoured of him. To this was added the legacy of his mother-in-law, who loved him as her own son, and from whom he inherited her entire possessions, which rendered him if not rich, at least, entirely independent of the world's frowns or caresses.

For a considerable time, it would appear that he remained content with what he had, leading an indolent, licentious, literary life, and living with associates, and in a manner clearly discreditable to a man of his origin and ancestry. It was not until the year of Rome 647, 107 B.C, in the first consulship of Caius Marius, and the fifth campaign of the Jugurthine War, that he made his appearance on the political theatre of Rome; when, being elected *quaestor* in the thirty-second year of his age, he was sent into Numidia, in command of the Italian cavalry, and that of the allies of the Latin name, which had not been levied and arrayed early enough in the campaign to accompany the consul on his departure for his province. He arrived in Africa, and brought up the cavalry contingents to the camp of Marius, at the time when having taken Cafsa by storm, he was beleaguing the hill fort near the Mulucha, which he took only with so much difficulty, by following the suggestion of the Ligurian snail-catcher, as it is above recorded.

Here, though previously a *tyro*, and utterly unacquainted with military matters, he soon became the ablest and most energetic cavalry officer in the service, and so much beloved by the soldiery, that no one could vie with him in popularity, or the observance with which he was treated. Generous to the extreme and lavish in his liberality, he gave largely, lent yet more profusely, never required back his money at the hands of anyone, seemed ever anxious that all should be in his debt he owing nought to any, jested and sported with the men, marched among them when on the route, watched by their bale-fires in the dark night watches, never suffered anyone to outshine him when anything was to be devised or done; above all, never cavilled at the consul, nor spoke ill of the absent, be it who it might, and by these means speedily rendered himself incredibly dear both to Marius and the army.

Shortly afterward, in two sharp actions fought by the kings of

Mauritania and Numidia united, he rendered the most signal services at the head of his cavalry, and contributed in the greatest degree to the defeat of the enemy, whose horse he severely handled and dispersed by a sustained series of charges, by alternate squadrons, after which he dashed his mounted masses against the unguarded flank of the Moorish infantry, until then victorious, and put them utterly to flight.

A little later in the season, when the consul, after having placed his troops in winter quarters, had set forth to attack one of Jugurtha's isolated strongholds, leaving Sylla in command, with *propraetorial* dignity, an embassy sent by Bocchus of Mauritania, to treat with Marius, fell into the hands of Gaetulian robbers, the Tuarick Arabs, it is like, or the wandering hordes of the Beni Mezzah, on the skirts of the great desert; and having with difficulty escaped with their lives only, stripped of everything, by the sons of Ishmael, whose hand was then, as now, literally against every man, received protection and the most bountiful hospitality from the hands of the young horse-officer, who farther instructed them how they should approach the commander-in-chief, and by what means they might hope to gain his ear.

By this politic conduct of Sylla, and by the graceful manner, doubling the favour conferred, with which he treated the proud and sensitive barbarians, the Romans gained much in the estimation of the Mauritanians, and an interchange of mutual good offices led to such feelings on the part of Bocchus, that, when he began to repent him of his alliance with Jugurtha and his falling fortunes, and to bethink him of sacrificing that unhappy prince to his mortal enemies, he personally requested that Sylla might be the officer entrusted with the negotiations, and there is much reason for believing that it is to his calm, considerate, politic, yet resolute spirit, that the success of those which ensued, may be in great part ascribed.

Having been sent into Morocco, with an escort of cavalry, bowmen, and a *cohort* of Pelignian foot armed, in light infantry fashion, with slender javelins, round bucklers, and short swords, he made his way resolutely to the royal residence, under circumstances in the highest degree dangerous, and calculated to awaken the distrust and suspicions of the Romans.

On the fifth day of his march, he encountered Volux, the son of Bocchus, at the head of about a thousand horse, who, according to their usage, came, scattering themselves in small bands and squadrons over all the open country, so as to convey the idea that they were in much larger numbers than indeed they were, and to cause the Romans to reform their ranks and prepare for immediate action. On a nearer approach, however, this cause of apprehension vanished, and it was speedily ascertained that the company, which had called forth this alarm, was but intended as a guard of honour and mark of courtesy to his guest, by the despot of Mauritania.

On the third day after this meeting, graver causes of suspicion appeared; and from the relation of the circumstances it cannot well be doubted that treason was intended, and that, if not positively determined, the surrender to Jugurtha of the Roman envoys was seriously meditated by the Moor. The camp was already pitched and fortified, and the sun was already setting when Volux came suddenly into Sylla's quarters, downcast of countenance, confused of speech, and seemingly bewildered by terror, informing him that he had just learned, from his advanced videttes, the presence of Jugurtha at the head of a considerable power, who, doubtless, intended to cut off the expedition. In this emergency he urgently counselled Sylla to break up his camp at once, and retreat by night, as far as possible on his homeward route, of course abandoning the purpose for which he had come so far into the desert.

This Sylla indignantly refused to do, expressing his perfect confidence in the courage of his own men, and in his ability to resist any attacks which could be made on him by the cowardly squadrons of a thrice beaten foe, and swore that at all risks he would penetrate to the palace of the king, or leave his bones to bleach on those burning sands, rather than turn his back, he a Roman, to a horde of skulking savages. Nevertheless, he resolved to move by night, and, so soon as his soldiery had cooked and supped, decamped silently, leaving his watch-fires burning with sufficient fuel to keep them alive until morning. Throughout the live-long night they marched wearily, through the deep sands, in gloom and doubt, if not dismay; and, in the gray of the early dawn, while the soldiers, harassed and worn out with this double march, were for a second time measuring and fortifying a camp which they were not destined to occupy, Moorish horsemen came tearing in, with bloody spurs and coursers in a lather, exclaiming that Jugurtha was scarce two miles distant, and advancing in array of battle.

Sylla himself, no less than his escort, was now satisfied of the treachery of Volux and the guard of honour; but, though he made all his dispositions and harangued his troops as if for immediate action, he would not listen for a moment to those who would have had him take instant vengeance on the prince; but, calling him aside, and invoking the Almighty Jove to be a witness to him of the villainy and treason of Bocchus, ordered him to be gone from the Roman camp, which held no place for traitors. Thereupon, Volux shedding tears and protesting his good faith and that of his father, with all possible asseverations, offered either to send his Mauritanians forward in advance, or to leave them behind altogether, and to proceed alone, with Sylla and his escort, as a hostage for their safety, through the middle of the hordes of Jugurtha, to whose activity and subtlety in obtaining information of his route, he attributed all that had occurred.

This offer, as the best thing to be done under the circumstances, was' accepted; and, at the head of his slender but dauntless escort, observing everything while seeming to observe nothing, and constantly on his guard, though to all appearance careless and perfectly at his ease, the proud impassive Roman rode along, side by side with his tawny conductor, chatting and laughing gaily, through the whole length of Jugurtha's large and loose array, the wild Numidians handling their weapons, and bending their dark brows around the little band, which yet they dared not assail, so terrible was the report of their prowess.

Doubtless, his fate, and that of his company was determined; and, had he taken any other course than that which he adopted on the moment, he would have been sacrificed to the treacherous jealousy of his host and the unconcealed malignity of the yet unconquered usurper. But his firm resolution and the suddenness of his action took Jugurtha by surprise, and frustrated his design. A few days farther and he reached the royal abode of Bocchus, whether at Mequinez, Fez, or Teza does not appear, where he was received with high consideration by the king, with whom he had many interviews, both private and official, before the business which he had at heart was brought to a termination.

That Bocchus doubted long whether of the two, the Roman or the Numidian, he should betray to the other; that he was many times inclined to favour his kinsman, his countryman and his brother king, against the insolent and aggressive invader, whom he hated, only less than he feared him; and that he was determined only in the end, by his apprehension of the invincible power and invariable forward movement of Rome, never checked or delayed, but still sweeping onward, cold, certain, inexorable as fate itself, we are informed by all the contemporaneous authorities; and, were we not so informed, we might assume it as a fact, for it is in the nature of man and the immutable order of things that it should be so.

But the firm, proud, self-confident, unswerving, ever-tranquil, but ever aggressive spirit of the great aristocratical republic was admirably represented and reproduced in the cool, self-sufficient, daring and arrogant temper of its youthful envoy; the versatility of whose witty, jovial, licentious, easy humour, cold withal, and hard and penetrating as steel "of the icebrook's temper," polished and pliant, yet entrenchant and unforgiving, naturally made the deepest impression on the impulsive and impetuous, yet infirm and unstable, temperament of the Barbarian, and rendered him but a toy in the hands of the shrewd, resolute, worldly-wise Italian.

After much consultation and many interviews, Bocchus first declared that he would offer no obstacle to the Romans in terminating the war with Jugurtha, in any way that should suit their pleasure; that he would not suffer that prince to pass the Mulucha, inward into his own dominions, nor himself cross it outward to his assistance. But shortly afterward, on Sylla's suggestion and persuasion, backed by the promises of vast gifts from the Senate, and the concession of half the territories of Numidia, he agreed, if possible, to make himself master of Jugurtha's person and deliver him up to the Romans.

Prospects of a peace with Rome, by the mediation of Mauritania, were held out to the Numidian, and after much vacillation, many misgivings, many suspicions, effaced, reconceived, and again overcome, the arch deceiver was deceived to his rum, and agreed to an interview with Sylla, in the presence of his father-in-law, who should act as mediator and arbiter between them.

Until the very evening previous to the interview, the Moor had not finally made up his mind. At a late hour of the night he held a privy meeting of his cabinet councillors, and after some debate, without disclosing anything of his own mind, again dismissed them, and remained long in secret deliberation with himself. Toward morning he caused Sylla to be summoned to him, and thenceforth, his purpose being at length resolved, he vacillated no longer.

On the morrow, it being announced that the prince was at hand, Bocchus proceeded, in company with the Roman *quaestor*, and a few courtiers and friends, to meet his kinsman, as if to do him honour, and with these ascended an isolated mound or hillock, in full view of his own troopers, who were close at hand and well instructed what to do; whither came Jugurtha also, with a few personal attendants, all unarmed, as it had been provided in the articles regulating the method of the interview.

Scarcely had he ascended the side of the mount, and appeared in the group on the summit, when persons, who had been placed in ambush near, rushed in on all sides, cut to pieces all the followers of the unhappy prince, seized him, and loading him with fetters delivered him into Roman durance, soon to experience at the hands of the republic the usual fate of all who resisted the force of Roman authority, and were reduced to taste of Roman mercy.

It is not, perhaps, strange that Sylla should have so much valued and prided himself on this occurrence—since men are not apt to underrate, but rather to over estimate, their early services and successes—as to wear on his signet ring a representation of the surrender into his hands of this formidable and detested captive. It was unquestionably an important service which he had rendered to the state; and it no less certain, that to him and his coolness and courage the merit of the capture is to be attributed.

But it is passing strange that the Mauritanian, whose part, in the transaction was merely venal infamy, kindred treason, and breach of hospitality unpardonable even in the robber of the desert, should have been willing to perpetuate the memory of his own baseness in a group, which he presented among thirty others, of golden statues, to the temple of Victory on the Capitoline, representing himself as seated on his chair of state delivering his son-in-law, loaded with chains, to the Roman *quaestor*.

This signet ring kindled the secret rage of Marius against his gallant subaltern, for he regarded it as an attempt to supplant him in his rightful claim to the honour of terminating the Jugurthine war, forgetful that he was himself liable to the same accusation from his predecessor and former commander, Metellus; and that Sylla, as an active member and partisan of the aristocratic faction, might actually be grimly and sarcastically laughing at his reclamations, as if he had avenged the wrong done to his brother noble, by him who now complained of the like wrong.

The statues of Bocchus, however, at a somewhat later period, cast the animating spark into the smouldering fuel, and, on the instant, into intense and furious life started the long-concealed, but not dormant, hatred.

Nothing prevented that hatred from kindling half the world into open discord, except the outbreaking, at that very period of the Marsic or Social war, in which both the parties were called to serve Rome in arms, and in which they both found new cause for jealousies, disgusts and rivalries, which increased their native animosity, and involved the commonwealth itself in their deadly struggle for supremacy.

In the meantime, notwithstanding his lurking envy and detestation of his *quaestor*, Marius still respected his talents so highly and regarded him so excellent and energetic an officer, that he employed him in his Teutonic and Cimbric campaigns, during his second, third, fourth and fifth consulships; and was justified, by the high distinction of his services, and his entire suppression of all personal likings and dislikings, for the confidence which he placed in him. In the third of these campaigns, the Tectosages, Gauls of the neighbourhood of Tolosa, in the Roman province, having risen in rebellion and united their arms to those of the Teutons, were left behind by their allies during their wild expedition to the Pyrenees; and Marius, who was in command, and on the watch for the return of the most formidable hordes by the passages of the Rhone, entrusted the management of this independent war to Sylla, now serving as his *legatus*, who conquered the barbarians in several sharp encounters, killed many[1] of their bravest chiefs and took their king [2] Copillus.

In the great battle with the Cimbri, on the Raudian plains, Sylla was attached, with the cavalry division to the army of Catalus, on which fell the greater share of the hard fighting. But owing to the extreme heat and the clouds of dust, which obscured the whole field of battle, it was almost impossible even for the immediate actors to see what was passing, and consequently very little is known as to the actual occurrences of that tremendous day, beyond the mere fact of its being won by the Romans.

In the year of Rome 651, B. C. 93, fourteen years having elapsed since he held the office of *quaestor* under Marius, Sylla again offered himself as a candidate for office, but not in the regular succession of place, which was required by the forms of office; for, whereas he ought to have first served as *Ædile*, he aspired at once to the office of *Praetor*.

In this instance, however, his ambition was disappointed, not that the people were offended at his grasping at the higher office, contrary to the routine; but that, from his intimacy and supposed correspondence with the king of Mauritania, an idea prevailed that he possessed unusual facilities for procuring strange and terrible wild beasts from the interior of Africa, and that the spectacles, which it would be his

---

1. *Velleius Patercul*, II. 17—*apud Am. Thierry*
2. *Plut. vit. Sylla IV.*

duty to exhibit in the quality of *Ædile*, would be of extraordinary rarity and splendour. Perceiving, therefore, that he was frustrated of his wishes, he now caused it to be given out, that, in case of his election the following year as *Praestor*, he would exhibit the same shows, which would have been expected of him in the inferior capacity; and the people, who were already beginning to be actuated in their choice of candidates by the sordid desire, attributed to them at a later day by the great Satirist, for *panem et circenses*, gratuitous bread and the spectacles of the circus, at once preferred him to the post he coveted. The price, which he paid for this public favour, amounted to no less than the exhibition at one time of one hundred male lions in the amphitheatre, which were baited to death by Mauritanian hunters, for the gratification of the degraded and blood-thirsty populace.

During the year of his *praetorship*, nothing occurred of sufficient moment to give any exercise to his talents, or to afford him any opportunity for engrossing glory. But, in the following year, he was sent into Asia, on a diplomatic, rather than military, mission, to reinstate Ariobarzanes and Pyloemenes, in their respective kingdoms of Cappadocia and Paphlagonia, of which they had been severally dispossessed by Mithridates, and Nicomedes king of Bithynia.

This duty he early performed, without any considerable Italian force; for, raising a large body of Cappadocians, he defeated and cut to pieces a number of Armenians, who attempted to resist him, and driving Gordius from his kingdom established Ariobarzanes in his place. Shortly after this cheaply gained success, while he yet tarried on the banks of the Euphrates, he received a visit from Orobazus, the *embassador* of the king of Parthia, who had never before had any intercourse with the Romans, and who was, perhaps, hardly aware of their national existence, much less of their gigantic and overshadowing power.

And this Sylla ascribes to himself as a singular piece of good fortune, that he was the first Roman officer to whom came an embassy from this wealthy, arrogant, and remote barbaric kingdom, demanding to be admitted, according to the comity of nations, to terms of amity and alliance with the great commonwealth of Italy. Nor did he fail to take advantage of the circumstance for the assertion of his own dignity, and the maintenance of the supremacy of Rome; for, having caused three *curule* chairs to be set for himself, the monarch whom he had restored, and the envoy of the great Parthian king, he placed himself in the central seat, which was the highest of the three, and, sitting there, transacted his affairs, as if in the presence of subordinates and inferiors.

This arrogant act of assumption, which was praised or reprobated in Rome, according as it was attributed to personal insolence and pride, or to the proper maintenance of the glories of the Roman name, is said to have cost the unfortunate Orobazus his life; his fierce barbarian master, prouder even than the proud Roman, causing him to be put to death, as his reward for submitting humbly to an affront, which was considered to carry something of degradation, even to the regal tiara of the great Parthian despot. It was on his return from this mission, that the contest, to which allusion has been made above, broke out between himself and Marius in regard to the golden statues in the Capitol, which the latter would have pulled down as derogatory to his renown, and was brought to a close only by the dreadful war which kindled all Italy, like a sudden and devastating conflagration—which came near to destroying utterly that wonderful and time-honoured fabric of Roman power and constitution—which seemed to have survived the successive assaults and imminent conquests of Gauls, of Greeks, of Carthaginians, Teutons and Cimbri, only to be driven to the very jaws of destruction by its own allies and confederates, in an unjust and parricidal conflict.

It is reported that, at the time of his interview with Orobazus the Parthian, a learned Chaldee, a soothsayer by profession, and a shrewd judge beside and scrutinizer of the thoughts, hearts, and characters of men, after long and earnestly examining the countenance, deportment, and movements of the *propraetor*, declared confidently that he had that in him whereof to make the greatest of all living men, and that, for his own part, he marvelled only that he did not at once assume the place which it was equally his right and his destiny to fill.

However this may be, whether as to the truth of the relation, or to the effect produced on the mind of Sylla by the prediction, it is certain that from this period he began to aspire, and to ascend rapidly to the highest stations in the gift of the Republic.

In the year of Rome 664, B. C. 90, Lucius Julius Caesar and Publius Rutilius Lupus being consuls, the Marsic, or Social war, broke out furiously; all the Italian states of the middle and lower peninsula taking arms simultaneously, with the avowed determination of utterly annihilating the power and abolishing the very name of Rome, while they would build up at Corfinium a new metropolis, which should be the capital of all Italy consolidated, and the seat of imperial dominion for all freemen of Italian birth.

In the first conflict Lucius Caesar was defeated by Vettius Cato with the loss of two thousand men, near to the city of Æsernia, in which he was immediately invested; while his colleague Lupus was yet more disastrously beaten by the Marsi, remaining himself with three thousand of his soldiery dead on the field of battle. In the following year Cneius Pompeius Strabo and Porcius Cato, were elected consuls, the former of whom beat the Marsi in a pitched battle with great loss, and afterward stormed Asculum, where the troubles had first commenced, and where the Romans had undergone the worst outrages; the second consul falling gallantly in the attack of the Marsic entrenchments.

In this war the Romans had, on more than one occasion, seven independent armies in the field together, under as celebrated leaders as ever set *battalia* in array; such as Pompeius Strabo, father of Pompey the Great, Caepio, Marius, Metellus, Dolabella, Perpenna, Sylla, and Messala; more than three hundred thousand Italians perished, cut off in the flower of their age and prime of utility to their country, in this lamentable civil strife; more cities were taken, burned, razed to the ground, so that their very sites became doubtful, than by Pyrrhus and Hannibal together; yet little is known of the details of the war, and yet less of the conduct and merits of the generals.

Marius, it is known, wholly failed to distinguish himself, chiefly, perhaps, from disaffection to the cause, and from a secret leaning to the side of the confederates, whom he would not have been sorry to see victorious over the haughty and hostile aristocracy of Rome, being himself of Italian, not Roman, blood; and possibly hoping, in case of their success, to become himself the head of the new confederacy. Before the conclusion of the war he resigned his command on the plea of nervousness—a singular complaint for one who, a few years afterward, waded chin deep in civic and kindred gore, shrunk from no unheard of atrocity, and proved himself a monster of cruelty, to be rivalled only by his fellow-fiends of an after age, the French Marat and Robespierre.

When the contest closed and the Italians were admitted to the city tribes, he identified himself with their cause, and perished as we have seen in the attempt with their aid to subvert the constitution, annihilate the liberties, and destroy all the legitimate defenders of the country, under whose banners he had won his glorious laurels, and whose highest magistracies he had filled oftener, if not more splendidly, than any other man who had lived, or should live thereafter, to the end of

Roman time.

Sylla's career was more fortunate as well as more glorious, both in regard to his civic principles and his military skill; and to him, with Strabo, the conqueror of Asculum, is ascribed the principal credit for bringing to a close this cruel and unnatural strife, and restoring at least a temporary tranquillity to the land. As his reward, on the cessation of hostilities, he was raised in the year of Rome 666, 98 B. C, to the office of consul, in the nineteenth year after his first service in the Jugurthine war under Marius, and the forty-ninth of his age, being seven years later than the legitimate period when he might have been constitutionally preferred to that exalted position. Macedonia, with the war against Mithridates, whose gigantic strides towards universal dominion now principally excited the apprehensions of Rome, and rendered it necessary to her safety that he should be summarily checked in his career of Oriental conquest, was allotted to him as his province.

No doubt, in the commencement of the war with Mithridates, as generally was the case with Roman hostilities, the Republic was in the wrong; as this great struggle arose from the unjust interference of the Commonwealth in the internal affairs of Asia Minor, and its deposition from the throne of Cappadocia, of Ariarathes, the son of Mithridates, whom he had raised to the dignity of king of that country, on the failure of the direct line of Cappadocian kings, who were of a cognate race to his own, bearing the hereditary title of Ariarathes, from a period prior to the conquests of Alexander the Great.

Who was the rightful successor and nearest heir to that ancient barbaric throne, cannot now be readily ascertained; nor does it in truth greatly matter to the reader of history. Barbarous oriental dynasties have never at any time maintained direct hereditary successions; foreign conquests, domestic usurpations, and kindred murders, being of occurrence so frequent, that they often outnumber the instances of direct transmission of royal authority. At all events, whether Ariarathes the son of Mithridates, Ariobarzanes the Cappadocian pretender, who was supported by the Romans, or some other person descended more closely from the extinct dynasty, had the legal right to succeed, it is perfectly clear that the Romans had no plea of right whatever, nor any pretext for interference in a country so remote as Cappadocia, and so widely severed from all their interests and connexions.

Against Ariarathes, then, they stirred up Nicomedes, king of Bithynia, and raised three armies of the weak and unwarlike Asiatics, under the Roman generals, Lucius Cassius, and Oppius, with orders to dethrone Ariarathes, and drive him from his kingdom. But the fortune and skill of Mithridates prevailed; Nicomedes was conquered in a pitched battle, and his forces were so completely routed and dispersed, that the war was terminated by that one defeat. The native armies under the Romans offered no resistance worthy of the name, and Mithridates, advancing steadily westward, was everywhere hailed as a deliverer by the Greek cities, both of Asia Minor and Europe, so bitterly did they detest the heavy yoke, which, under the name of liberty and self-government, the Commonwealth had imposed upon them.

Up to this time Mithridates had in no respect overstepped the limits of national self-defence, violated the laws of war, or in any way aggressed upon the Romans. But, at this period, having made himself master of all the Greek Asiatic isles and cities, he committed an atrocious crime and no less flagrant political error, by issuing a circular to all his prefects, satraps, and military or naval officers, that, on the thirtieth day thereafter, every free-born Roman or Italian citizen, man, woman, or child, should be put to the sword, and thrown into the fields unburied. To all slaves, who should murder their masters, freedom was proclaimed; to all debtors, slaughtering their creditors, half the vacant estates were decreed as a reward; to all who should assist or shelter a living Roman, or bury an Italian corpse, death was the penalty. In one day, vast numbers of Romans and Italians, principally of the quality of *equites*, the publicans, revenue-farmers, extortioners and oppressors of the people, perished under circumstances of aggravated cruelty and insult.

The number of persons slain is variously stated by Dr. Schmitz at 80,000, and M. Michelet at 100,000 souls; but I can find no verification of these numbers in Appian, Plutarch, Livy, or other authorities which they quote, and am inclined to hold with Mr. Ferguson, in his Roman Republic, that "the number of persons who perished in this massacre, if ever known, is nowhere mentioned." (Livy Epit. 78. *quidquid civium Romanorum in Asia fuit, uno die trucidatum est.*)

There is no doubt, however, that the massacre did occur, with unusual instances of barbarity; that it comprehended all the Italians, (*Appian bell. Mithridat*), naturalised in the country; and—which is proved by the universality and completeness of the carnage—that it is attributable no less to the prevalent hatred of Rome, than to the orders of the despot. Thereafter Mithridates took possession of Cos, and most other islands of the Archipelago, Rhodes only fortifying her harbours and closing her cities against him, and giving shelter to all the Italian fugitives who escaped from the main; then sailing to Egypt he made himself master of Alexander the heir to the throne, and plundered the royal treasuries of Cleopatra of much bullion, many works of art, statues and precious gems, and much feminine apparel, with which he returned triumphantly to Pontus.

Shortly after these occurrences, in the year of Rome 666—B.C. 88—Archelaus, the king's general, having taken possession of Delos and other places which revolted from Athens, and slain about two thousand men, principally Romans, made himself master of the Piraeus; collected all the treasures, brought from Delphi, in the Acropolis; and constituting Aristion, an Athenian, tyrant of Athens, slew all the Romanising Greeks in the city, reduced the whole of Boeotia to subjection, and gained an immensely strong foothold in Upper Greece. Meanwhile the gigantic army of Mithridates, consisting, it is said, of a hundred and twenty thousand men, with a gorgeous array of splendidly caparisoned cavalry, vast bodies of archery and skirmishers, and a train of scythe-winged chariots, wherewith to sweep the plains, was collecting in the wide champaigns of Thessaly and Macedonia, where the nature of the country especially favoured equestrian operations, and presented a power, with which no Roman force in Greece had a chance of coping.

It was exactly at this moment, when Roman citizens had been slaughtered in the most savage and unprecedented manner, when one Roman general, Oppius, had been publicly mocked as he was carried a prisoner through all the towns of Asia Minor; and another, Manius Aquilius, had been killed by pouring molten gold down his throat, when Cornelius Sylla the consul had been ordered to take command of six legions lying in Campania, the only disposable force in Italy, and proceed to Greece in order to defend it against this formidable foe, that Marius and his infamous tool the tribune Sulpicius, filled the streets of Rome with sedition and anarchy, and finally brought, for the first time since the entrance of the Gauls, hostile armies to do battle within the very walls of Rome.

Young Pompeius, the son of the present consul, and son-in-law of Sylla, was murdered in the market-place by the gladiators of Sulpicius; all order was at an end, and Marius, with his friend, held absolute rule in the city, annulling the decrees of the Senate by irregular and unconstitutional street assemblies of the mob, and exercising perfect sovereignty over the city and state. Their first move was to abrogate the command of Sylla in the Mithridatic war, to which he had been formally and legally appointed by the Senate, and to nominate Marius in his place.

This whilom hero and idol of the people, was now a feeble, obese, old man of seventy, who had already resigned his command in one war, on the plea of nervousness and infirmity; who had of late given himself up entirely to avaricious money-hoarding, and foul debauchery in his beautiful mansion at Misenum; and who, now since the Mithridatic war had broken out, promising opportunities for gratifying his taste for rapine and his lust for fame, had been making himself the laughing stock of the people, by exercising himself in arms and practising athletic arts in the Campus Martins, with his bloated body, hoary head, blood-shot eyes, and attenuated and effete limbs, unable to support the weight of a buckler, among the youth of Home.

Sylla was already with his army, on the point of embarking, when this atrocious act of injustice and violence was committed; but when the officers came to the camp with instructions to receive the command at his hands in the name of Marius, the soldiers rose in tumult, stoned the commissioners to death, and called on Sylla to lead them to Rome, in order to restore the authority of the Senate, and reinstate the magistrates in their constitutional power.

Now it is not denied or disputed that Sylla and Pompeius Rufus were the true and authorized magistrates of the state, that the city and state were completely in the hands of a violent, unscrupulous and lawless faction, and that the Senate, under instant fear of their lives, dared not resist the usurpers, nor had it in their power to command the consuls, as it was their duty to do in similar emergencies, "to see that the Republic took no harm."

The absence of such instructions renders the subsequent conduct of Sylla, whatever might have been his intentions, no less lawless than that of his rival; and it is greatly to his reproach that it must be recorded, that he was the first one who marched a Roman army, under the ensigns and bearing the arms of the commonwealth, against the walls of Rome. Whatever his private provocations and resentments, as an officer of the republic he had no justification for turning against any portion of the citizens the weapons entrusted to him by all for the defence of all, unless under the most positive and unquestionable orders of the proper authorities; and whatever might seem to him the emergency of the times and the peril to the state, as a portion only of the executive, endowed with neither legislative nor judicial powers, he had no right to construe the wishes, or anticipate the commands of the Senate.

For this breach of law and order he must be justly held responsible, although his great moderation and abstinence from any effort at self-aggrandisement, would seem to show that thus far, at least, he had simply the reconstitution of the state at heart, and had no personal ends or aims to gratify. Nor is his conduct to be the less regretted, because it is by one, professing to be a zealous friend and conservator of the constitution, that this fundamental principle thereof was violated, that no officer should enter the walls of Rome while he held the military *imperium*, or was even in command of an army, much more at its head.

From this unhappy day this clause fell into absolute disuse, or was at least so habitually violated, by every military chief who chose to esteem himself or his faction wronged, or who was ambitious of honours or powers greater than he possessed, that from this date, to the downfall of the Republic, Rome, more frequently than not, was under direct military occupation.

It was Marius, who in the first instance, designedly and traitorously, so altered the constitution of Roman armies that the soldiers in fact ceased to be citizens, and could be used by their leaders, on whom alone they depended, against the state; but it must be admitted that Sylla is the first who did so use a Roman army; and to him the guilt of that first example and of all the horrors that ensued, must be ascribed by impartial history.

When it was known that Sylla, stung by his wrongs, was in full march on Rome, at the head of six *legions* devoted to his will, not Marius, Sulpicius, and their infamous adherents, but the Senate itself and all the best citizens were appalled and shocked; those at their present peril, these at the awful precedent, and the terrible uses to which it might be perverted.

A deputation was sent out by the senators to meet the army and arrest its progress by representations and commands to its leader; but he, having encountered them, not many miles from the city, and having lulled their apprehensions by pretending to encamp on the spot, as if to await farther orders, despatched squadrons close on their heels, seized the Coelian and Colline gates, with two detachments, the latter headed by his colleague Pompeius Rufus, the wooden bridge of the Janiculum with a third, and held the main body of his host in reserve without the walls, in person.

Marius and Sulpicius, though terror-stricken, made a desperate effort to defend their usurpation, proclaimed freedom to the slaves, armed them, occupied the capitol in force, and attempted to defend the streets by barricades, and a galling discharge of missiles from the housetops upon the soldiery embarrassed in the narrow thoroughfares.

But Sylla, whose blood was up, and who was thoroughly in earnest, ordered the houses to be set on fire, seizing a torch himself for the purpose, and commanding the housetops to be swept with flights of flaming arrows, soon cleared the streets, forced his enemies to evacuate the town, and causing the *legions* to bivouac in the streets and markets, set watches and instituted patrols to prevent mischief, as if in a captured city.

Order was speedily restored, no violence was done either to person or property, the conflagration was quickly mastered, and on the following morning the senate regularly convened by the consuls, pronounced sentence of death against Marius, Sulpicius, and about twelve others, at the utmost, of the rebels, confirmed Pompeius and Sylla in their magistracies and provincial commands, and resumed their interrupted functions in the state.

The death of Sulpicius, and the escape of Marius to commit fresh crimes and work farther ruin to his country, have been recorded in the life of the great *plebeian*. Few others fell, and none undeservedly or innocent. The soldiers evacuated the city; and, the time of the elections for the ensuing year having arrived, Sylla presided at the consular comitia, and abstained so truly from exerting his power, or even his influence, that he offered no opposition to Lucius Cornelius Cinna, though a close friend and factious partisan of Marius, but suffered him to be elected in conjunction with his own friend, Cneius Octavius, a man of good repute, and a supporter of the constitution; exacting this condition only from the former candidate, that he would attempt nothing against the state or contrary to his proper honour, (*Plutarch*), during his absence from the state.

This praise, therefore, is justly due to him, that he caused not to be shed one drop of civic blood on his own personal account, that he aimed at no personal aggrandizement or gain of wealth, but that, when it was in his power, (*Appian de Bell Civ.*), to render himself absolute monarch, he quietly withdrew from the city, and proceeded to perform the duties of his station, against the enemies of his country in that place to which his country had commanded him.

It was in the close of the year of his own consulship that he was on the point of setting out for Nola, whither his army had returned, after Cinna and Octavius had been elected consuls for the ensuing year, 667 of the city and 81 B.C., when he was once more delayed by the seditious proceedings of the opposite party.

Desperate and defeated, this faction had yet the insolence and influence to procure the shameless aid of one Virgilius, a tribune of the people, who moved to impeach Sylla for the illegality of his late proceedings, hoping thereby to prevent his assumption of his command against Mithridates. But Sylla, though the illegality of his course is undeniable, legally disembarrassed himself of this factious annoyance, taking advantage of the Memmian law, which forbad proceedings against persons setting forth on military service. Then putting himself at once at the head of his five *legions*, in addition to some supernumerary cohorts of infantry and troops of horse, he marched through Italy to Brundusium, now Brindisi, the usual port of embarkation for Greece, where he took ship, landed at Dyrrachium, the modern Durazzo, and thence, levying contributions for the support of his army as he proceeded, descended by Ætolia and Thessaly into Boeotia, which returned to the Romans as easily as it had been before brought over to the king.

At this time Archelaus, the general of Mithridates, held the Piraeus, or port of Athens, one of the most strongly fortified places in the ancient world, being defended and connected with the upper town by the superb long walls, erected by Pericles during the Peloponnesian war, not less than sixty feet in height, wrought in huge blocks of squared stone; while the tyrant Aristion, an Epicurean philosopher by origin, but now a stipendiary of Mithridates, held the city itself, with its Acropolis, heaven-reaching temples, and almost impregnable fortresses, which had set Xerxes himself at defiance. Those in the Piraeus were well supplied with food, provisions and material of war of all kinds; for Mithridates was completely master of the sea, sweeping it in all directions with his victorious squadrons, and shutting up the Rhodians, (*Appian de bell, Mithrid*), now the second naval state of the Mediterranean, in their harbours.

Since the termination of the Punic wars and their relief from all apprehensions on the score of their formidable maritime rivals, the Romans appear to have entirely neglected their marine, and merely maintaining small coasting squadrons to co-operate with their land forces, to have allowed the empire of the seas to fall to whomsoever it would, even to the merest piratical barbarians, who were not reduced without considerable trouble and expense by Pompey the Great, as he was somewhat absurdly styled, and the far greater Caesar.

During the whole summer of the first year of his war, Sylla assailed the Piraeus desperately, but in vain. After attempting escalades several times, all of which failed from the difficulty of procuring ladders of adequate length sufficiently strong for the purpose, and from the extreme height and strength of the works, he fell back, worn out and weary, to Eleusis and the Megarense until he could bring materials of all kinds, iron, cordage, and military machines from Thebes in Boeotia. The beautiful groves of the Lyceum and Academe were felled to supply timber to the besiegers; towers were raised, and a huge mound thrown up, against the fortress, and engines of the largest and most formidable kind were kept constantly playing against the walls.

But, on the whole, little or nothing was effected. A dashing sortie, by which Archelaus, sallying out with his infantry in mass, fiercely assailed the working parties of the Romans in front, while he launched his cavalry to the right and left, in order to overwhelm them, was repulsed. For Athenian partisans of Rome within the walls had contrived to convey information of the intended outbreak to the besiegers, and Sylla had consequently a supporting force, ambushed at hand, sufficient not only to protect his men in the trenches, but to beat back the Asiatics in brilliant style, slaying many and driving more into the sea. Shortly after this failure, however, having erected great internal mounds, and cavaliers overlooking his own defences and the works of the enemy, Archelaus collected fresh powers from Chalcis and the Islands, and armed all the rowers of his fleet; when, being vastly superior in numbers to the besiegers, he again broke out, torch in hand, at dead of night, and cut down, burned, and destroyed all the great assailing works and engines of the Romans.

But so great was the activity and perseverance of the Roman general, that within ten days everything he had lost was replaced; and the enemy was as hard pressed as before, until having erected other counter-works on his walls, and being reinforced by another Asiatic army under Dromichaetes, the daring and energetic governor once more led his whole garrison into the field by all his gates at once, lining his heavy infantry with archery and slingers, and fell so furiously on the Roman lines that he made a serious impression for a considerable time, and was only checked when Muraena brought up the reserves, and rallied the shaken *legions*, not without considerable effort. Fortunately, at this moment a *legion* came up, which had been out wooding and foraging; and this fresh body, supported by the camp-followers, slaves and degraded *legionaries*, renewed the combat so fiercely that the besieged were driven in, with a loss of two thousand men left dead on the field; and that Archelaus himself, fighting desperately to the last, was shut out of the gates, and only escaped capture, being hoisted by ropes over the battlements.

After this bloody but indecisive affair, Sylla drew off his men and placed them in winter quarters, fortifying himself with deep ditches cut from sea to sea, which were intended to prevent the assaults of the numerous and excellent cavalry of the enemy; but, as his men toiled daily at these gigantic works, they were engaged in almost hourly, now about the trenches, now close up to the walls, the Orientals sallying in dense masses and plying them with darts, stones, and vast leaden balls hurled from the catapults. Still, however, the siege continued with unabated fury on both sides. On one occasion, treasonable information from within being conveyed to Sylla, that Archelaus would endeavour to reinforce the upper town and revictual it, being now hard pressed for provision, he was enabled to seize the convoy and cut off the detachment engaged in escorting it.

On another, some Romans having actually escaladed the walls of the Piraeus and effected a lodgement on the rampart, were overthrown by a desperate rally and cast back headlong into their own lines by an attack so impetuous, that the pursuers from the city entered the trenches pell-mell with them, and narrowly missed destroying the remainder of the works and engines of the Romans—a catastrophe prevented only by the arrival of Sylla in person with reinforcements from the camp, who by desperate exertions, toiling and fighting hand to hand through the whole night, like a common soldier, succeeded in re-establishing the combat, and about daybreak repulsed the enemy. Then bringing twenty vast catapults to bear at once on the huge tower of Archelaus, from his own battering tower, he so shook and maltreated the former, that the besieged perforce withdrew it to preserve it from total destruction.

Thus passed the first campaign of the Mithridatic war; and, it may be said, with no advantage to the Romans. Never was place more skilfully or more resolutely defended than Athens; for Aristion, in the upper city, knew that he could hope no quarter for himself or his adherents, and resolved to sell his life at the dearest; while Archelaus, who was a thorough soldier and well aware of the importance of time in war, made a defence such as has never been surpassed in warfare, and which deserved, if it might not command, success.

The city was now sorely pressed by famine; everything edible had been consumed, to the vilest animals, the grass from the ramparts, sword-belts and sandal-leathers, and things obscene and indescribable; yet the feeble and famishing garrison would not surrender to the Romans, too well aware of the nature of Rome's mercy, to come voluntarily into its clutches. With treachery within and Sylla's energy without, no effort of Archelaus, and he tried all, could suffice to throw succours and provisions into the town. All he could do was to counter-plot, and when Sylla, informed of his intentions, ambushed his victualling parties, to sally on his trenches with fire and sword.

Once his works were completely sapped and battered; and the huge walls, being undermined, were supported only by vast props of timber, which were in their turn fired by the besiegers with such masses of pitch, and piles of tow covered with sulphur, that the flames were unquenchable and unendurable. Then the whole immense fabric of Pericles came thundering down, with such a roar and so sudden a ruin, that it appalled the Roman legions, and struck terror to the souls of the garrison, many of whom were crushed and confounded in the downfall. Yet, even under this fearful disadvantage, Archelaus maintained his credit as a general, and saved his post, when all indeed seemed desperate. With several wide and practicable breaches open, he fought so resolutely himself, and animated his men to such stubborn and immovable resistance, that the very ruins were found no less inexpugnable than the uninjured ramparts; and that Sylla was forced, at the sword's point, with his best men, down to the foot of the breach; when most unwillingly he called off the stormers with the trumpet, having undergone a loss at least as great, as that he had inflicted on the enemy.

During the hours of darkness, the noble governor so completely retrenched the breaches, with a new concave rampart, constructed out of the rubbish, that, when on the morrow, the Romans rushed into the *cul de sac*, resolute to win and anticipating little difficulty in battering the soft, new-built masonry, they were overwhelmed by such volleys of missiles from above, in front, and ravaged by such a cross fire of artillery from the flanks, (*Appian de bell, Mithrid*), afforded by the junction of the old rampart with the new retrenchment, as drove them back wholly dismayed and defeated, and compelled their leader to resign all ideas of taking the Piraeus, so defended, by storm, sap, or escalade.

But the fall of Athens was decreed, in spite of the gallantry of its defenders. The spring of 86 B. C, was now far advanced; and the city, entirely circumvallated, and surrounded by deep trenches, had been strictly blockaded for above a year, besides receiving and repelling almost daily assaults from the enemy; when it was reported to Sylla that the garrison were feeding on their own dead, and were so weak, both in morale and physique, that a storm could no longer be supported. To this method recourse was again had, and at length successfully. The walls were carried by escalade, and at the same moment by sap, at the dead of night, Sylla entering, sword in hand, at the breach between the Piraean and the Sacred gate, with wild blasts of trumpets and war horns, and the fierce shouts of the infuriated *legionaries*, rushing unchecked to rape, massacre and pillage. So dreadful was the carnage, that, even to the days of Plutarch, marks were shown on the walls how deep had stood the blood of the victims; that all the Ceramicus, within the gates, was afloat with gore; and that, according to eye-witnesses, the ghastly torrent streaming through the crevices of the portals deluged the barbican and gate-house.

Sylla, it is said, was personally enraged at the scurrile taunts and ribaldry which had been continually launched against him from the walls by the defenders, who did not even spare the name of his wife, the noble Caecilia Metella, and this was his revenge. That he was not a man incapable of taking bloody vengeance for personal insults or wrongs, his subsequent course sufficiently proves, but the unfailing massacre which followed every storm or surrender, when Romans were victors, renders it unnecessary, if not unjust, to ascribe these horrors to the peculiar blood-thirstiness of Sylla, since Scipio the Continent, and Caesar the Clement are equally guilty with him of ruthless and unnecessary carnage.

How many fell in that dreadful night is not recorded, but Plutarch asserts that as many died by their own hands, through despair of receiving mercy and unwillingness to survive their country, as by the swords of the ruthless *cohorts*. It appears, however, that after the sack and first havoc, the city was spared pillage, slavery, or farther dishonour, by the orders of the conqueror, who, if he regarded nothing of living humanity, affected at least to respect the glory of the mighty dead, and the literary splendour of the Athens of other days.

Aristion and his garrison, and all who had held place under him since he first seduced the city from her Roman allegiance, retreated to the citadel, but were speedily reduced by famine, and surrendering at discretion were slaughtered to a man. The remainder of the citizens were pardoned, and permitted to govern themselves, as before, by their own local and municipal laws, and except the Acropolis, which was despoiled at the most of forty pounds weight of gold, and six hundred of silver, the city escaped the systematic Roman spoliation.

Sylla has left it recorded in his own memoirs, quoted by Plutarch, that the city was captured on the first of March, corresponding to the new moon of the Attic month Anthesterion; and, on the very day after its storm, he determined to waste no more time on the blockade of the Piraeus, but to attempt it again with the battering-ram, and to carry it, if possible, by assault, while his men were still flushed with their late success, and confident of victory.

The new retrenchments were the point which he now assailed, and these were soon so much damaged by the ram, and by sappers who undermined the foundations, working beneath the shelter of the tortoise, that large breaches were made again and again, and retrenched only by the besieged, to be once more forced and opened by the besiegers; so that, at length, wearied out, and seeing the inutility of farther resistance, the great king's gallant commander drew off the whole of the Oriental forces, less damaged and less diminished in numbers than the conquerors, and embarking them in his ships, still held the harbour of Munychium, and blockaded Sylla as closely as he had before blockaded the city.

This siege is principally to be considered with a view to the length and obstinacy both of its attack and defence, and perhaps on the whole it reflects more credit on the defender than on the assailant. On both sides, every resource of art, of mechanism, and of engineering, as they were then understood, was brought into play; but it must be remembered, that in no other respect has the modern gained so much on the ancient system of warfare, as in the reduction of beleaguered places. The length of time now required to reduce the strongest place, with adequate breaching batteries, and under ordinary circumstances, has become a mere matter of calculation; and it can be foreseen to a day, by skilful engineers, how soon, if not relieved, the finest first-rate fortress must surrender, or be carried by assault, without a chance of failure.

Before the invention of gunpowder, on the contrary, the art of defence was so far superior and better understood, that many places were utterly impregnable, or reducible only after years of blockade, by means of works so extensive and of such magnitude as to require more toil, time, labour, and materials for the construction, than the fortress they were intended to reduce.

In the siege of Athens, the advantages lay with the occupants of the Piraeus, who having the command of the sea, could not be straitened either of provisions or men, with both of which they were constantly supplied and reinforced, and had always the means of evacuating the place when it was no longer tenable, or desirable to be retained, as they ultimately did, by water.

It must be remembered also, that Sylla had little aid to expect from home at this period; which was probably one cause why his lieutenant, Lucullus, wasted so much time, and so long in vain, seeking to collect a squadron among the islands and shores of the Archipelago, whereby to recover the dominion of the seas, in place of bringing up a Roman fleet from Ostia, Brundusium, or Ravenna. Scarce had Sylla departed from Italy, before his late colleague Pompeius was murdered by his rebellious soldiery; before Cinna, breaking his plighted oath, took arms against the state, recalled Marius and the proscribed exiles, slaughtered his own colleague Octavius, in his robes of office, subverted the Senate, overthrew the constitution, filled Rome with consternation and havoc, and governed it as a conquered country by arms and martial law. During the whole of his Mithridatic campaigns, therefore, he had to rely solely on his own indefatigable energies and resources, on such contributions as he could raise from sterile and oft-wasted countries, on his tact in making war support war, and on such spoils as he might capture from the enemy, for the maintenance of his army and for the materials of war.

He had neither military chest nor magazines, neither provision ships nor transports, neither reinforcements nor whence to raise new levies, while his antagonists had uncounted wealth, dominant fleets, innumerable hosts of men, well provisioned, splendidly equipped and mounted, and amply provided with transports, whereby to transfer the seat of war whither they would, at pleasure. In everything but the quality of the men, and the talents of the general, Mithridates had vastly the superiority, but in both these he was so far inferior that how successful soever behind walls, neither his officers nor his multitudes could avail him much in the open field, against the *legions* led by Sylla.

Notwithstanding all this, he had lost nothing, if he had not actually gained thus far, by the transactions of the first campaign. He had lost no more than a city, which his general had skilfully evacuated only when he cared no longer to retain it, for to him the death of Aristion and his garrison, or the sack of Athens mattered nothing, since by these he lost neither men nor money, in comparison with the time which he had gained, or the use to which his generals had turned it.

For scarcely had the siege ended, when news was brought to Archelaus that Taxilles was advancing in great force, together with a second army under Arcathias, son of Mithridates, by the coast road from Thessaly into lower Greece, and that his co-operation was earnestly required; whereupon he at once weighed anchor, having on board the garrison of the Piraeus, as well as the reinforcements brought to him by Dromichaetes, and landing somewhere on the coast of Boeotia, probably at Chalcis, which was a garrison and naval depot of the king, marched through that country northward, again reducing it to submission; and effected his junction with the grand army at the famous pass of Thermopylae, between the precipices of Mount Œta, and the shores of the gulf of Zituni. Thence, like a mighty inundation, he overflowed the fertile plains of Boeotia with his multitudes, Thracians and men of Pontus, Scythians and Cappadocians, Phrygians, and Galatians, troops from all the newly conquered realms of Mithridates, amounting in all to one hundred and twenty thousand men, while the whole army, which Sylla could muster to meet this mighty power, did not exceed a third of the number.

That general was now himself reduced to considerable straits and had but a choice of difficulties: whether to linger in Attica, where the rocky and uneven surface of the country was adverse to the nature and quality of an Oriental army, the power of which consisted mainly in its cavalry and scythe-winged chariots, but where the poor and sterile country, even in peace, undevastated and in its highest cultivation, was unequal to support its own population, in hopes that the enemy would come in search of him—or to pursue him into the champaign districts of Boeotia, and give him battle on ground of his own choosing.

It was clear, however, that if the war was to be brought to an end at all, it must be through his taking the initiative; and for many reasons he was most anxious to conclude it. For though resolute to postpone the righting his own wrongs, and avenging the crimes of the Marian faction, to his present duty against the foes of Rome, he was yet afire to wreak vengeance on his individual enemies, and to quench in blood the flames of democratic anarchy. He was, moreover, extremely pressed for means of subsistence, as he was still closely blockaded by the king's squadrons, and had exhausted every resource of the unhappy country. Perforce, therefore, he broke up from the city, and entered Boeotia by leisurely advances, retaking and garrisoning the places which had revolted, and cautiously pursuing Archelaus, who fell back before him into the upper country toward the Copaic Lake, where the plains are intersected by many streams and hollow beds of torrents, and broken by isolated knolls, and the projecting spurs of the mountain ridges.

On the northern banks of the Cephissus, or Mauroneri, from its junction with the River Platania, to its embouchure in the marshes and lake of the same name under the battlements of the strong fortress of Orchomenos, are two considerable mountain ridges, Edylium and Acontium, under the lower spur of the latter of which stands the aforenamed citadel. Between these two hills a mountain torrent, the Molus, rushes down from the north-east, having a village named Assia, the modern Karamusu, under the steep slopes of Edylium, situated in the low ground near its mouth. On the extreme northern point of Mount Edylium, a steep, craggy, precipitous hill, above a deep mountain stream, the Assus, now known as the Kineta, stood the ruined citadel of Parapotamii.

To the south of the river lie the open plains of Chaeronea, scene of "that dishonest victory fatal to liberty," which "killed by report the old man eloquent," bounded to the southward by the heights of Thurium, a rugged, pine-shaped mountain, so named from Thuro, the mother of Chaeron, looking down to the westward on the deep rocky ravine of the torrent Morius, which pours its impetuous waters into the Cephissus from the southward, at a point nearly opposite to Assia, about two miles east of the embouchure of the Molus. The distance across the plain, nearly in the centre of which stands Chaeronea, from Assia beyond the river to Thurium, north and south, is about four miles, and that from the Morius, east and west, to the lower waters of the Cephissus, which here makes a wide semicircular sweep, is not much less than five, a beautiful level expanse of meadow and corn-land among the most fertile tracts of Greece.

At a place called Patronis, the site of which has not been identified, even by that enterprising traveller and topographer, Martin Leake, from whose excellent work on Northern Greece, the above details are taken, but which probably lay north-west of Chaeronea, between the Morius and the great valley of the Platania, not far from the opening into that strath of a difficult gorge, above which stands the modern village of Dhávlia, bringing down a wild headlong torrent from the snowy tops of Mount Lycorea, and the loftier cliffs of cloud-capped Parnassus, Sylla came to a stand. Beyond the iron barrier of these huge and toppling mountains, on either side the upper Cephissus, here a pastoral river flowing south-eastward, stretch far and wide the great Elatic plains, at least twelve miles along the river and more than two-thirds that width from the roots of the Parnassian ridge to the great northern chain of Cnemis.

In these Elatic plains, admirably suited to the manoeuvres of his magnificent squadrons of Cappadocian *cuirassiers*, and to the career of his scythed chariots, which required ample space wherein to acquire the velocity needful to their success, lay Archelaus with his mighty host, confident in his vast superiority of numbers, and living luxuriously on the wealth of that fat district, the richest grain and grass country of all Hellas.

Through the difficult hill country to the northwest, Hortensius, the only officer by whom Sylla could be supported, was moving toilsomely up with his heavy reinforcements through the defiles of Parnassus, and the gorge of the river Pindus, which is in fact one of the upper affluents of the Cephissus; and to effect a junction with him was the first object of the Roman commander. At Tithorea, the modern village of Velitza, (*Leake*), on the north-eastern verge of the Elatic plains, and under the base of the great ridges of Mount Lycorea, Hortensius came in contact with the forces of Archelaus. But, although fearfully outnumbered, he chose so good a position, and defended himself with such obstinate resolution against their attacks, which endured through the whole day, that he succeeded in holding them at arm's length until night; when he drew off silently, avoiding the open country, and, through the crags and thickets of Lycorea, made his way to the northern valley of Dhávlia, and thence by the stern ravine of which I have spoken, to the Platania and Patronis, where Sylla awaited him.

Thus reinforced, the Patrician general moved cautiously forward through the pass between the solitary peak of Anemorea and the valley of the Cephissus, running north and south between the cliffs of that rocky fastness and the opposite heights of Edyllium; entered the Elatic plains and made himself master of a beautiful isolated hill, covered with smooth grassy downs and shady groves, having copious springs of pure water at its base, known as Mount Philoboeotus, identified by Leake with a singular insulated conical height, between the river and the modern village of Bissikeni, on which he took post; and extended his lines across the hollow or lap of the plain to another abrupt elevation above the modern village and the bridge of Kervasará; so that his left, as he faced southward, rested on the Cephissus, and his right on the inexpugnable peak of Philoboeotus. Against this formidable position the Orientals drew out their superb array, shaking the plain with the thundrous gallop of their barbed squadrons, and the rolling din of their iron chariots, out-dazzling the sun with the noonday glare of their panoplies glittering with steel and red with gold, and filling the air with their shouts and conclamations.

And it was far from being empty or useless, that magnificence and pomp of martial preparation; for the lightning flashes of their arms and weapons, splendid with gold and silver, and the many-coloured dyes of the Scythian and Median tunics interspersed among the glare of brazen shields and bucklers, as the multitude rocked and rolled like a heaving sea, presented a show so terrible, that the Romans were appalled and cowered within their lines; nor could Sylla, with all the powers of his eloquence, all the prestige of his great and invincible renown, so encourage them as to justify him to himself in giving battle.

Finding it impossible to force him to fight against his will, Archelaus, it would seem, passed the Cephissus near Kervasará, under the face of the Roman left, and leaving a garrison on the craggy knoll of Parapotamii, where were the ruins of an ancient fortress, moved down on both sides of Mount Edyllium by the main river and the torrent Molus, which divides it from the heights of Acontium, and pitched his head-quarters at Assia, whence he extended his line across the open country toward Chaeronea.

Meanwhile, with large detachments of his skirmishers and horse, he cruelly devastated the country, burned Panopaea to the ground, sacked the thriving town of Lebadea, and plundered the rich oracular shrine of Jupiter Trophonius; until, the smoke, rising in columns everywhere throughout the lovely plains, and the scenes of tumult, misery, and slaughter which he could overlook and behold from his rock fastness of Philoboeotus, exasperated Sylla to the point, that he was now as anxious to engage, as he had been before desirous to avoid battle. Still in the present temper of his troops he felt unequal to the contest; and, therefore, took a singular method enough to inspire them with military ardour; for, after reproaching them with their want of courage, and affecting to hold himself insecure, even within his entrenchments among soldiers of such questionable valour, he employed them for several days in the severest labours of fortification and military engineering, compelling them to cut vast trenches across the plain, into which he diverted the waters of the Cephissus,(*Plutarch*), as if to protect his lines, but really in order to enrage the men by such toilsome and degrading occupation.

And therein he succeeded; for on the fourth morning, when Sylla made his appearance from the *Praetorium*, he was saluted by loud acclamations and entreaties to be led to instant action; but he replied only that he knew well their object, which was simply this, not that they did desire to fight, but that they desired not to work; and that in such men he had neither confidence nor hope. Then, on their clamouring more fiercely, that he should let them go, and try them, he answered that, if they indeed meant fighting, they might take up arms on the spot and storm that post—pointing as he spoke to the abrupt and precipitous hill of Parapotamii, divided from the flanks of Edyllium by a deep broken torrent-bed, or *charadra*, and rising from the farther bank of the Cephissus, in scarped and almost inaccessible cliffs and natural ramparts, on the summits of which blazed broadly in the morning sun the brazen bucklers of the royal Chalcaspidae.

On the instant the legions ran to arms, with a mighty shout, forded the river at a rush, and scaled the bold and slippery limestone ledges with such impetuous and headlong spirit, that their charge carried all before it; and that, although stones and trunks of trees were hurled upon their heads as they advanced among a hailstorm of arrows, javelins, and slingshot, they forced their way up passes and over crags, which in cooler moments they could not have carried even unopposed, in spite of every disadvantage, until they reached the summit. Then, charged to the teeth by the long pikes and serried shields of the Chalcaspidae, they went in with the long buckler and short sword with such a will, that they deforced the massy *phalanx* and hurled it down the rocky gorge toward Edyllium, pursuing it with fearful slaughter nearly to its entrenchments at Assia.

Driven down from this fastness, which misadventure in nowise discouraged him or broke his confidence in his numbers, for the Romans were so few in comparison with his armed hordes, that he conceived them wholly incompetent to meet him in the open field, Archelaus made a dash at Chaeronea, which was a town of considerable wealth and magnitude, trusting either to carry it by a *coup de main*, before Sylla could succour it, or, if not, force the Romans to action at disadvantage.

News was brought to Sylla of this movement by some terrified natives of the menaced city, who were serving with his array, imploring instant succour, just as his men, after posting a sufficient force to keep the heights, which they had won so gallantly, were returning, flushed with victory and full of haughty exultation, to their lines. Whereupon, he instantly despatched Gabinius, or, as some say Ericius, one of the tribunes of the soldiery, with a single *legion* to relieve the place; and the men, fired with haughty exultation, made such speed to the rescue, that they actually outstripped the Chaeronean runners, who would have borne tidings of the coming succour, in anticipation of the troops, but could not.

Then was seen the same spirited and thrilling spectacle, which was exhibited by the French and English regiments in the beautiful manoeuvring which preceded the battle of Salamanca; when "those two noble armies marched on parallel heights, within musket shot of each other, in the most perfect array," (*Alison, Hist. Europe, III*), without drawing a sword or pulling a trigger; each striving by dint of the most strenuous exertion, by sheer speed of movement and strength of bodily endurance, to outstrip the other, and gain the spot, for the possession of which they were contending, by celerity and activity of operation.

On either side of the broad and beautiful Cephissus, down the wild valley, thick with the glorious evergreens of Greece, the bay, the daphne, the cypress and the holm oak, now seen, now lost to sight behind the great gray crags, or in the shadowy thickets, the rival troops rushed on, their gleaming panoplies and brazen bucklers now flashing out in the broad light, now quenched in the cool green shadow, vieing, like trained *athletae* in the sportive foot race, the old hills ringing to their emulative shouts and sending back the clash and clangour of their armour in thousands of redoubled echoes. But when they gained the plain toward Chaeronea, the Romans passing the Platania near its mouth and the rocky gorge of the Morius, and the Orientals, the Cephissus in front of Assia, the superiority of the Roman soldier, the trained athlete of Western race, to the more slightly framed natives of the East, was rendered as manifest in his marching qualities as in his fighting capacities. Gabinius with his *legion* entered the town in triumph; and soon the long array of bucklers and massive *pila* lining the walls showed that the *cohorts* were within, and the place consequently secure against any power which should attempt it.

On the following day, well satisfied with his success hitherto, Sylla determined to deliver a general action, having in fact, by his skilful manoeuvres on the preceding days, cramped the enemy up into such a line of country as almost ensured a victory; since the nature of the ground neither permitted of his forming, as it was customary with the ancients to do, a single connected line of battle, nor gave him any opportunity of using to advantage his vast superiority in horse and chariots.

And here it may be well to notice some slight difficulties and discrepancies between the various accounts of this interesting action, the relation of which Plutarch appears to have derived principally from Sylla's own private memoirs, which were extant in his day, as well as a remarkable variance between the narratives and the real nature of the topography, as ascertained by the surveys of Colonel Leake.

In the first place, all the accounts of these operations state Sylla's force to have consisted of five full Roman *legions*, beside some unattached *cohorts*, in addition to Macedonian and Hellenic auxiliaries, and his proper complement of horse; but Plutarch asserts that the Roman army numbered only fifteen thousand foot and fifteen hundred cavalry, which is totally inconsistent with the numerical force of the *legion*. For the latter *legion*, by its form and constitution, never consisted of less than four thousand two hundred foot, with three hundred horse, while generally it greatly exceeded that number. By a decree of the senate, preceding the Battle of Cannae, the *legions* were raised to five thousand infantry, (*Polybius*), soldiers, the cavalry being unchanged. The allied *legions* had the same strength of foot, but their horse was doubled.

When the elder Scipio Africanus carried the second Punic War into Africa, (*Appian Bell. Mith.*), his legions were augmented to six thousand two hundred bucklers and *pila*, with the regular complement of cavalry; and lastly, when Lucius Æmilius Paulus took command of the Macedonian War against Perseus, B. C. 168, the *legions* which accompanied him, (*Livy*), were rated at six thousand shields of infantry, the horse being still kept to the original rate. Nor so far as it appears was this enumeration ever altered; for the Caesarian or imperial *legion* consisted, to the end, of ten *cohorts*, each six hundred strong, the old division by *maniples* being abolished; and the same, it can hardly be doubted, were the *legions* of Sylla, since we find that in his wars the tactic of the *cohort* was already in vogue.

The Roman force, therefore, engaged at Chaeronea, should have amounted to at least thirty-three thousand foot, being five *legions* of six thousand each, and five *cohorts* of six hundred. The horse supposing them to be Roman, would be correctly stated at fifteen hundred; but if they were allies—and after this date the Romans kept no native horse on foot—the number must be doubled, which would raise the whole army to thirty-six thousand men, more or less, exclusive of the auxiliary Greeks, who may have swelled it to forty thousand, or upward, of all arms.

What singularly corroborates this calculation is, the fact, that while Plutarch states the troops of Archelaus and Taxilles at a hundred thousand foot and ten thousand horse, Appian makes them, in round numbers, a hundred and twenty thousand spears and sabres; and declares, in the next line, that Sylla's army had scarce a third of their strength, which corresponds precisely with the above calculation, and with the number of *legions* specified both by himself and Plutarch. The second statement of the latter writer, either arises from his not unfrequent carelessness, or from the fact that he followed Sylla's memoirs, who might have desired to glorify himself by underrating his own command, as compared with that of the enemy, although the real disparity is quite sufficiently to his credit.

The other discrepancy is more curious, for while Plutarch's description of the field of battle is so minute, so lucid, and so correct in its topography, as ascertained by Colonel Leake in his survey, as to all other particulars, that the action might be fought over again without variation; he states that the torrent Assus, which is the modern Kineta, divides the hill of Parapotamii, crowned by an ancient ruin, from the northern point of Mount Edyllium, whereas, in fact, that torrent enters the Cephissus to the northward of the fortified knoll, which is separated from Edyllium only by a rocky hollow, without any stream or watercourse.

These minor points, however, which cannot now be clearly explained, being omitted, it is evident that the army of Archelaus, whose right rested on the fortified village of Assia, where he had drawn a line of strong palisades across the whole space between Mounts Edyllium and Acontium, was *à cheval* on the River Cephissus, extending quite across the open plains, eastward of Chaeronea to Mount Thurium, on which he had stationed his left, on what probably appeared to him an impregnable *point d'appui*. His position formed, therefore, a great hollow semicircle, the chord running nearly north and south from Assia to Thurium, for a distance of about four miles, the city of Chaeronea, held by Gabinius, with one Roman *legion*, being the centre of the whole circle, had it been completed.

On the morning, when he determined to fight, Sylla moved down the gorges of the Kineta and Upper Cephissus, turning Edyllium by his left, until he came directly in front of Assia, where he crossed the latter river exactly at the point where it turns almost at a right angle, eastward; and placed Muraena, with a *legion* and two *cohorts* fronting the lines of Archelaus, near the mouth of the Morius, in command of his own left. Thence he advanced himself to Chaeronea, with the strength of his centre, and having reinforced Gabinius at that point, proceeded to reconnoitre the enemy's left, on the strong height of Thurium, which domineered his right wing, from what appeared at first to be an impregnable point.

By this manoeuvring he had gained everything; he had forced the enemy into the necessity of fighting in a great eccentric circle, among hills and rivers, which prevented his using his fine cavalry, and where he had no means of communication, or roads in his rear, by which to support his own wings or to retreat if worsted, against a concentrated army delivering battle on a convex arc, and therefore entirely manageable and in hand for any emergency.

At the moment when he was in doubt how he should open his attack, he was informed by some men of Chaeronea, that there existed a bye-path among the rocks, unknown to the barbarians, whereby the strongest point of Mount Thurium—on which Archelaus' left stood, in imposing masses of horse, foot, and chariots, crowding the slopes, and ready to sweep the plains below—might be taken in reverse. This would be to master the key of the whole position, by turning the enemy's left, and having beaten him there in detail, forcing him back, with his reserves, as they might successively come up, upon the great lake and mountains, which would then be in his rear, and whence he could have no retreat.

Previously to making this movement, partly, I imagine, to tempt Archelaus to extend his right injudiciously, partly to prevent him from turning his own left, Sylla retired that portion of his line, in some degree, posting Galba and Hortensius on some heights, echeloned to the left of Muraena's rear, so as to overflank, in case of need, any flank movements.

These arrangements made, and the victory being actually won already by the dispositions of the leader, a strong storming party, led by a forlorn hope of Chaeroneans, under Ericius, properly supported by powerful reserves of *legionaries*, made their way silently through the woods by Mount Petrarch us and the grove and temple of the Muses;

and gaining the rear of the enemy's left, turned it completely, stole up the reverse of the crags unobserved, and were in possession of the summit before their presence was suspected. Then, with a shout, which was repeated far and wide by the re-echoing hills, with the stern short blast of the Roman trumpets, and with the clang of blade and buckler, they charged home.

On that height, pre-eminent, and illuminated by the full blaze of the rising sun, they were as a conscious mark for all eyes of both armies; and, as if they felt that it was so, they fought with such prowess that the enemy did not stand their onset, no, not a moment. Deforced from the heights, driven bodily before the compact rush of the *legionaries*, the length of their paces involuntarily increasing as they plunged down the precipitous declivities, they overstrode themselves, lost their footing, and fell, to be spitted on the pikes of their companions in the plain, or broke their necks among the rocks, (*Plutarch*), while the enemy ravaged them with their missiles from above, and smote unsparingly their defenceless rear.

Three thousand fell on Mount Thurium alone; and those who escaped, pressing on the left of their centre, bore it into the position of Muraena, who had wheeled somewhat to his right, and were incontinently cut to pieces. Sylla, meantime, advanced his centre with such vigour, that he fell upon them, while yet embarrassed by the pressure of their discomfitted left, and was hand to hand with their chariots, on which they had placed so much reliance, before the horses could be got to their speed or the impetus acquired, by which alone these terrible engines could be made available. While the horses were rearing and plunging in confusion, in a narrow space, under the lash and shouts of their drivers, they were mastered with such ease by the hardy *cohorts*, who caught them by the heads and cut down the charioteers without quarter, that the thing became ridiculous, and the Romans encored the performance with shouts of laughter and clapping of their hands, as if at the spectacles of the hippodrome.

Thereafter, the main centre of the infantry encountered the best of the enemy's army, being a body of liberated Greek slaves whom the Orientals had emancipated, and who fought in the compact order of the Macedonian *phalanx*, eight files deep, with linked shields and the terrible twenty-four feet *sarissae* levelled. Against these the *legions* charged, sword in hand, without hurling their *pila*, as anxious to come at once to close quarters, and break up their solid array. But the *phalanx* was on favourable ground, without inequalities of surface, which might throw it into confusion; and no impetuosity or persistence, either of desultory fighting or steady attack, could break or disorder their serried advance. The loose lines and short weapons of the *cohorts* availed nothing against them, and it was to no purpose that the Romans hewed at the tough ashen pike-staves with their Spanish blades, or strove to master the round shields with their hands; they made no impression; and had the celebrated Greek tactic been as flexible and handy as it was formidable in direct forward onsets, the action might have been still doubtful.

But though this great solid mass still held its own unbroken in the centre, it was in no condition to improve its advantage, but remained stationary, majestic indeed, and formidable to the eye, like a stranded ship among the breakers, but capable of passive resistance only, until the heavy foot were called off, and reformed by battle-cry and trumpet-blast, while front and flank the skirmishers were let loose on the unwieldly mass, and plied it with sling-shot, arrows, and javelins, until no longer able to endure the incessant volleys, which mowed them down from the head to the rear of their column, and to which they could make no return, they broke, and the sword finished it.

In the meantime Archelaus had fallen into the trap which Sylla had laid for him, but had worked so vigorously with his powerful bodies of *cuirassiers*, that he had nearly counter-balanced the misadventure of his left and centre, by the success of his right, where he fought in person.

Extending himself in this direction entirely round the left of Muraena, who had obliqued, as I have stated, to the right on the oriental centre, he was met midway by the select *cohorts* of Hortensius and Galba, who, bringing up their left shoulders at the *pas de charge*, meant in turn to outflank him. But his two thousand picked *cuirassiers* were too quick for them, and working, as if on parade, actually broke their order, turning them and driving them in upon the hilly ground and the banks of the Morius, toward the spot where Sylla stood with his extreme right, which had not been as yet engaged, observing the chances of the fight.

The battle, it must be observed, had hitherto been fought by the centre and left of the Romans only, the enemy's left having been annihilated by the party detached to the rear, without any movement of the Roman right opposed to them; and this was now brought by the oblique charge of Muraena toward it, nearly into the rear of its own centre, and consequently was only a short distance from the inner arc of its left, which it could easily support by changing its front, and marching .directly forward.

This movement Sylla was in the act of making, when Archelaus, seeing, by the clouds of dust and the consular eagles glittering above it, what succour was at hand, again wheeled off with a still wider sweep, which, could he have accomplished it in time, would have carried him entirely round the Roman lines, almost to the place where his own left wing had been beaten in the morning. At the same instant, Taxilles, with the Chalcaspidae, who alone of the Orientals was disengaged, made a tremendous onset from the right of his centre upon Muraena, who was yet struggling with the slave *phalanx*. The half-won battle might easily have been lost, but Sylla was equal to the emergency.

The shouts arising on both sides, redoubled by the mountain echoes, the great soldier halted for an instant, doubtful where the storm was about to burst; but perceiving quickly that Hortensius was relieved from the pressure, and marking the semicircular sweep of Archelaus, he hurried the former with four *cohorts* to the aid of Muraena, and calling the fifth to follow him, wheeled, as if on a pivot, and was on his ground on his right in time to hurl the enemy back bodily upon Mount Acontius and the lake. Muraena seasonably reinforced, had now carried all before him, and, as Sylla wheeled up faster and faster from his right, converting his whole lines from a convex into a concave arc, and driving the shattered masses of the beaten multitude inward, like fish enclosed in the circular sweep of a seine, they were cut to pieces in the plain, without difficulty or mercy, forced over the river into their original entrenchments at Assia, and, these forced, pent up into the rugged hills, whence there was no escape.

Of one hundred and twenty thousand men, who had swelled the shout for Mithridates, and fought so manfully and with so earnest a resolve to win through that disastrous day, ten thousand only, with their chief, escaped to tell the news at Chalcis to their comrades of the fleet. The remainder fed the vultures of Parnassus, or fattened the corn lands of Chaeronea, which seemed as fatally predestined in those ages to be the scene of gigantic combats, as, in the latter days, the Flemish Netherlands.

Singular to record, in this tremendous and decisive battle, the Roman loss was almost nothing; when the evening rolls were called, after the action, fourteen men only of the *legions* answered not to their names, and of these two were present under arms at the morning roster. Twelve men were the cost to the Romans of this wonderful victory, which cleared Greece of the enemy, as if by a thunder-stroke, and left them, for a time, no one with whom to fight, "unless," to borrow Lord Astley's words to the parliamentarians, "they chose to fall out among themselves." But the time for that, although not far aloof, was not yet.

It would, however, be most unjust to measure Sylla's merit in this action by the amount of his losses. In all the conflicts of the olden day, when fighting was hand to hand, and the sword and pike were the instruments of destruction, the carnage was ever to begin after the strife was ended. In almost all the great pitched battles of antiquity, the loss of the victors was merely nominal—for proof of which, turn to Marathon, Plataea, Cannae—so true it was, under the old tactic and armament, that "daring was a rampart to an army."

For the rest, the battle of Chaeronea was Sylla's, not his army's. It was won, unless spite of incalculable fortune should have snatched it from his hands, before a sword was drawn, by the skilful manoeuvring of the general.

Like all battles of modern times, but few of antiquity, it was a battle of manoeuvres and positions, the centre and wings of the army being spread over wide tracts of country, and unconnected, though in communication, instead of forming on either side one solid integral mass, to be victorious or vanquished at a blow.

The plan of Sylla, acting from a centre by the *radii* on the inner circumference of a great arc, was to double back the left of the enemy before it could be succoured, and that annihilated, to pierce and destroy the centre. In all this he was perfectly successful; but the firmness with which he held his reserved left in hand, the patience with which he awaited the full development of the enemy's last move, the unerring *coup d'oeil* with which he penetrated his final combination, and the rapid and crushing energy with which he launched his reserve and dealt the decisive blow, prove him one of the greatest, if not the greatest strategist and tactician of the Roman school.

In the previous manoeuvring, the countermarching, the mutual struggles to secure commanding heights, and the final victory by the crushing of the centre, it more resembles Salamanca than any other victory, ancient or modern. Nor am I sure that it should not be regarded as the most scientific combat of antiquity.

Immediately after the victory, Sylla pursued his late antagonist to Chalcis, but having no ships, was compelled to suffer his escape, with the relics of his defeated army, to the islands of the Archipelago, where he applied himself with all diligence to the collection of another power. But while there, tidings reached him of such importance from Rome, that he turned on his traces, and passing through Boeotia, entered Thessaly with his legions, and advanced them as far as Meliteia, a city on the Enipeus, not far from the afterward immortal plains of Pharsalia.

Marius, the old blood-gorged lion of the democrats, had died horribly, drunken and despairing; but his party had survived him, full of fiery life and vigour. Cinna had chosen Lucius Valerius Flaccus, a furious partisan, to be his colleague in lieu of the deceased, and appointing him, as his province, to Macedonia and the Mithridatic War, sent him, with two fresh *legions*, to Dyrrachium, under directions to depose Sylla, and take his army under his own command. To meet him, therefore, the proud and vengeful patrician hastened inland, hoping to strike a blow at him, before Mithridates should have gathered fresh head, so that he should not have two enemies on hand at once; for Sylla was not one to be deceived by slight pretexts, and well knew that he was himself the object of Flaccus' expedition, as more detested by the ruling faction at Rome than twenty kings of Pontus, had each been ten times Mithridates. Before the new Consul, however, had penetrated so far into his province, hurried messengers came to Meliteia, with tidings that Dorilaus, another of the king's generals, had arrived at Chalcis, with a large fleet, and there disembarked eighty thousand new troops, the very flower of Mithridates' army, the most soldierly men, the best armed, equipped, and disciplined, and that he gave no heed to the advice and experience of Archelaus, who dissuaded him from fighting the Romans, but was resolved to deliver battle on the first opportunity.

He determined, therefore, to give him the occasion which he desired; hoping to meet and dispose of him before the arrival of his successor, by whom he had no mind to be succeeded. Marching down to encounter him, he fell in with his advanced guard, near the fine spring-head of Tilphossa and the important fortress of Tilphossaeum on the lake shore of the Cephissis, where he maltreated his light troops so severely in the skirmishes which ensued, that he half convinced him of the soundness of Archelaus' councils; so that he was more than a little disposed to decline battle and protract the war, when the extraordinary expenses, difficulty of subsistence, and want of cooperating squadrons on the coast, might do on the enemy the work of the sword.

So soon, however, as they opened the rich and splendid basin of western Boeotia, which consists of the most fertile and glowing plains of that country, unenclosed, level, treeless, except about the sources of the River Melas, close under the steep cliffs and ramparts of Orchomenus. stretching at least twelve miles in length, southwardly, to the lower spurs of Mount Helicon, near Coroneia and Alalcomenae, and not much less westwardly from the marshes and lake Cephissis to the hills beyond Chaeronea, the generals of the king recovered their spirits, and began to contemplate trying once more the fortune of their arms.

Archelaus remembered that, in the other battle which he had lost but a few miles to the westward of that place, the nature of the ground and the broken cliffs, among which he was compelled to fight, deprived him of all service from his chariots, but that still wherever he fought in person with his *cuirassiers*, they made their mark even under the worst disadvantage. Hence he persuaded himself yet that, in these deep, rich, verdant pastures, where there was not a stock or stone for miles, to impede the career of the scythed cars, or the rush of his countless squadrons, he should trample the Romans under foot, in spite of their soldierly qualities and admitted prowess.

Dorilaus had never met European troops in the field, until in the slight irregular fighting of the previous days, and had lost too little of the presumptuous confidence, which is ever the characteristic, as it is the bane, of oriental armies, to hesitate in accepting the altered opinion of his colleague.

Sylla, on the contrary, who, determined as he was, and justly confident in the steadiness and valour of his men, never seems to have left any thing to chance, which prudence could ensure, or to have been induced to that worst military error, the underrating of an enemy, now held somewhat back; fortifying himself with great trenches and field works, and employing his men in cutting canals, easily filled with water in those low-lying and irriguous levels, which should render the firmer and more solid portions of the plain impracticable for the horse, and so deforce them toward the marshes.

But this they were by no means disposed to endure; wherefore, launching their cavalry with spirit, and the men charging home with vigour and decision, though in somewhat loose array, they not only cut to pieces the working parties, but broke and put to flight the supporting cohorts, and threw the Roman force into such increasing confusion, that Sylla leaped from his horse, seized an eagle, and rushed into the densest of the enemy, shouting aloud, so that all might hear him:

> To me it matters not if I die here or elsewhere. But you, O Romans, when anyone shall ask where you left your leader, say, 'fighting at Orchomenus.'—*Plut. vit. Syll.* XXI.

The act and the appeal were irresistible. The centurions and tribunes of the soldiers rushed out to support and rescue their general, the cohorts rallied with a shout, and Sylla, remounting, charged at their head, and shut the enemy up, after heavy loss, within their own palisades.

Nevertheless, neglecting their losses, no sooner did the working parties resume their occupation at the trenches, than the Orientals sallied again in greater force and closer order than before, (*Appian Bell Mith.*), Diogenes, the son of Archelaus' wife, leading them gallantly, till he was struck down, and died literally, within the Roman trenches. His troops, in general, fought desperately, and with a stubborn courage, unusual to the natives of the east, and his archers, more especially; for when they were mixed up, body to body with the Romans, so that they could not use their bows, they grasped their arrows by the middle, in bundles, having no scimitars, and stabbing at the face, inflicted cruel wounds, until at length they were again shut up in their own camp, where they passed the night grievously, sore wounded, and in dismay yet sorer.

No less than fifteen thousand men fell on that day, ten thousand of whom were admirable horse; yet so much alarmed was Sylla, lest the enemy should escape him, as before, by way of Chalcis, to his ships, that he allowed his men no leisure to celebrate the victory, but guarded the whole plain with sentries and pickets, posted at brief intervals, and patrolled it with his cavalry until morning. Then pushing his working parties and engineers up to within a single furlong of Archelaus' camp and palisade, he circumvallated them with a ditch ten feet in width, so that escape was impossible, keeping so large a body, both of horse and foot, under arms, that the king's generals dared not disturb him.

No sooner, however, was this arduous task accomplished, than the great leader, not choosing to waste time in a blockade, when he knew not how soon Flaccus might arrive to supersede him, led out his *cohorts* to assail the works, and carry the encampment by storm.

The attack, under the eyes of the general, was resolute, and well sustained; but so obstinate was the defence, the men on both sides striking and stabbing at each other through the interstices of the palisade, and shooting over the abbatis, that, although many great and conspicuous deeds of prowess were done, no way was made nor any advantage gained, until, at length, the Romans, forming the *testudo* of shields above their heads, tore down the palisades at a salient angle, and the place seemed to be won.

But the barbarians rushed out of the breach, and fought, man to man and sword to sword; and in such a *mêlée* discipline availing nought and swordsmanship much, the Romans were held at bay, and all stood aloof from the fatal gorge, which was heaped with slain, none daring to be the first to rush upon the scimitars.

At length Basillus, (*Appian Bell Mith.*), a *tribune* of the soldiers, and himself commander of the *legion*, went in with such indomitable will, slaying a man at every thrust, that he won the rampart, and defended himself upon the summit until he was supported, when the whole army poured in, and the gallant defence was over. The carnage was incalculable—there was no retreat—and all who were not butchered without mercy, calling piteously in their unknown barbaric tongues, for quarter, to their slayers, were forced into the marshes and lake, and either drowned or miserably stifled in the mud of the morass.

Archelaus remained for two days concealed amid the great reeds and lotuses which grow in these morasses, similar to those of Egypt, especially about the junction of the Melas and Cephissus, (*Plutarch*), until he was so fortunate as to find a skiff, by means of which he got himself safely off down the lake to the sea-shore, and thence to Chalcis, whither he speedily collected such miserable relics as could be recovered of that once royal army.

On the following morning Sylla crowned Basillus as the best doer in that day's conflict, and gave up all Boeotia to be pillaged by the army, in consequence of the inveteracy with which they revolted from the Romans to every new enemy.

Never was battle more decisive or more bloody; not a living enemy was left in Boeotia—this for the second time in a single campaign—the marshes were afloat with blood and the lake choked with corpses; and Plutarch bears testimony, that in his time, nearly two hundred years after the battle, barbaric bows, helmets, fragments of steel corselets, and swords were found buried in the mud, in such quantities as to prove the number of the wretches who there found living graves.

After rewarding his army, Sylla went into winter quarters in Thessaly, at some point on the sea-coast, waiting for the arrival of Lucullus with ships; and, being in complete ignorance where he could be, or what doing, since the enemy were still masters of the sea and no advices reached him from Rome, owing to the dominance of the Marian faction, he applied himself to build ships on the spot, and endeavoured to create a new fleet.

During this period, while Sylla was defeating his country's enemy with unheard of zeal and success, strange and abominable things were in process at the seat of government. Cinna and Carbo—the latter of whom had succeeded Flaccus, when he was dispossessed of his command, his army, and his life by Fimbria, a subaltern who quietly usurped his consular *imperium*—were filling Rome with anarchy, havoc, and consternation; murdering this man for his wealth, that, for his noble birth; this, for his enmity to Marius, that for his favour with his rival; until all good citizens and upright men fled from the city, as from, a place infested with pestilence, and doomed to ruin.

At the very time when the great patrician chief, by his last action, was accomplishing the perhaps unrivalled feat of destroying in a single campaign, with a single army, which never had exceeded forty thousand men, which had received no reinforcement or supplies, except such as it could collect for itself, two separate hosts numbering in the aggregate, two hundred thousand men—and that so completely that ten thousand of them were never again present under arms against Rome—these factious fire-brands, self-elected despots of the republic, were slaughtering the friends, devastating the estates, burning the dwelling-houses of the strong and stern commander, who would not even think of his own wrongs, until he had redressed those of his country.

At his winter-quarters in Thessaly, his wife Metella came fleeing to him for protection, having narrowly avoided death or worse dishonour when her house was burned over her head, bringing her children with her, happily saved likewise, and escorted by such a band of nobles, magistrates, senators, and men of consular dignity, that the camp, on the wild storm-beaten shores of Thessaly, could show as noble and a purer senate than that which sat in the temples of Concord or Peace, on the dishonoured capitol.

When spring broke, while Sylla was in doubt how to act, being anxious to return to Italy, and at the same time resolute to conclude the war himself, partly from patriotic motives, partly from personal ambition, a message was brought to him from Archelaus, which led him to believe that he could gain his end by negotiation, more readily than by arms. He took ship, therefore, to Delos, and had an interview with the king's general, in the temple of Apollo, where, to his surprise, he was encountered by proposals from Mithridates, who was, it would seem, thoroughly cognisant of the affairs of Rome, to the end that he should conclude a private peace with him, giving up Pontus and all Asia to his sway, in consideration of which he should be furnished with a royal fleet, treasures and forces, to whatever amount he should judge necessary, for the reduction of the democrats and the subjugation of Rome.

This well-timed and politic attempt at corruption, he met with a counter proposal to Archelaus to betray the despot, and surrender his fleet, in consideration of which he should be raised to the throne in lieu of Mithridates.

It is here, perhaps, worthy of remark, that during the existence, even nominal, of the republic, though the instances of Roman citizens treasonably aiming at sovereign power, bearing arms against the state, and committing every imaginable crime against the government, under their own standard, for their own hand, as Harry Wynd fought, and to promote their own ambitious views, are of constant occurrence,—there does not exist one, through the whole history of the commonwealth, wherein an officer betrayed his trust to a foreign enemy, took arms against Rome in a foreign service, or in any way gave fealty to a crowned head, or tampered with the stranger, even for his own advantage, to subvert the commonwealth.

This is the more remarkable, that of the Greek leaders and statesmen, who are generally regarded by us as more determined friends of liberty, because more ultra-democratic than the Romans, there is scarce one who did not tamper with the kings of Persia, take bribes from them, serve them in arms against their native cities, accept their aid for the subversion of Greek liberty, or do some foul indirection in their behalf, even when internecine war was raging between Hellas and the East.

With the Roman, Rome was all in all, even if he might choose himself to make it his own property, or to trample it under his feet, rendering himself, by the traitorous deed, only so much the more Roman. To the Greek, Greece was nothing, or at the best a mere abstraction, for he was himself not so much a Greek as an Athenian, a Spartan, an Argive, or a Theban, and could always fall back on his special state individuality against his national generality, as honestly as could Sir Ralph de Vipont, who on being appealed to as a crusader, could remember only that he was a Scotchman before he was a Christian.

Be this as it may, the haughty Roman, burning to slake his thirst for vengeance in the dearest blood of Rome, scorned the proffer. Perhaps he thought that the very vengeance, which he would wreak on Rome, would be incomplete if it were shared by any but a Roman. He contented himself with this reply:

> So you, Archelaus, being a Cappadocian, and a slave, or if you will, a friend of a barbarian king, cannot endure such baseness, even for such reward; and yet to me, who am a Roman general, and whose name is Sylla, you dare to propose treason! as if you were not that same Archelaus who escaped alone, the other day at Chaeronea, out of twelve myriads, and hid yourself two days in the marshes of Orchomenus, leaving Boeotia choked by the multitude of your own dead.—*Plut. vit. Syll.* XXII.

To this there was no reply, nor any course for Mithridates but to yield. Yet Sylla needed the ships and the treasures, and that too for the very end to which they had been offered, and would have them. Yet he would have Rome satisfied first, before he would satisfy himself.

A treaty was therefore concluded, by which Mithridates should withdraw from all Asia Minor, should surrender Bithynia to Nicomedes, and Cappadocia to Ariobarzanes—these being the ends, to gain which war had been declared—and should also pay down two thousand *talents*, equivalent to about eight hundred thousand pounds sterling, and deliver up seventy brazen-beaked ships of war to the Romans, as represented by Sylla—these being the ends, for which peace was now concluded.

Some delay occurred before the articles could be arranged; and Sylla having advanced so far as to the Hellespont, or Dardanelles, returned through Maedica, which he cruelly devastated, into Macedonia, where he was soon after visited by Archelaus, inviting him to a personal interview with Mithridates. For the king was now ready to yield all, being much alarmed by the ravages of Fimbria, the successor of Flaccus, throughout Asia Minor, and considering him a foe more easy to be dealt withal than Sylla. An interview was arranged to take place at Dardanus, in the Troas, and thither came the king, with two hundred ships of war, twenty thousand infantry, six thousand horse, and a heavy force of chariots, and the Roman, with four *cohorts* and two hundred cavalry.

The conference was marked by barbaric arrogance on the part of the king, and the traditional Roman haughtiness on that of Sylla; and the latter is said to have replied to the question of Mithridates, what would be left to him if he should surrender Asia Minor, Bithynia, and Cappadocia, and give up his fleet and treasure?—"The hand, with which you slew a hundred thousand Romans in a single day."

From this M. Michelet argues that he betrayed Rome, and that Fimbria, the mutineer and murderer of his general, would have obtained better terms for the state. But of this I can discover nothing; Sylla gained all for Rome that she had ever demanded, and the means, moreover, of ejecting the bloody faction which illegally held sway in the city, by violence, and of re-establishing, for the last time but one, her ancient constitution.

Flaccus himself, the late consul, was the illegal nominee of an usurper, and Fimbria, his murderer and successor, a mere mutineer, to put down whom it was no more than the duty of any Roman officer. That Sylla was a regularly constituted Roman officer, and the legitimate leader against Mithridates, cannot be denied, up to this moment; and much later, I can discover nothing in his conduct beyond the line of a citizen's and a soldier's duty. For the evil he did afterward, he will be answerable. It and the reproach thereof, are heavy enough, without exaggeration.

But for the fact—the treaty was concluded, the money paid, the fleet and five hundred archers given up, and, the stipulated countries being ceded, Mithridates was confirmed in his ancient hereditary dominions, and declared a friend and ally of the republic. A few days afterward, the army of Fimbria, who lay at Thyatira, now Ak Hissar, in Anatolia, being summoned, deserted their leader—who fell by his own hand—and came over to Sylla, who at length released from the bonds of foreign duty, hastened to his appointed work of retribution and revenge.

Having now arranged everything in Asia, he at once set sail in his newly acquired fleet, for the Piraeus; and, on landing at Athens, is said to have plundered the city of many works of art, among others, the fine library of Apellicon of Teos, containing the works of Aristotle and Theophrastus, which being conveyed to Rome, came under the supervision of Tyrannion the rhetorician, and through him were thrown open to Rhodius Andronicus, who thus compiled his edition of those great masters.

So strangely is the history of art and science, and even of the preservation of letters, blended and confused with records of the wildest passions and blackest crimes of humanity.

Being in ill-health at this time, he proceeded to Ædepsus, now Dipso, in the Histiaeotis, famous even then for its medicinal thermal waters, and to this day the most celebrated watering-place in Greece, where he passed the season in a mixture of licentious luxury, with mimes, buffoons and jesters, as if he had no business of moment on hand, nor anything beyond present amusement on his mind.

Yet at that moment the doom was sealed of thousands, who unconsciously awaited the hour and the man, which coming they must die. And those were now both nigh at hand; for, in the summer of the year of Rome 670, B. C. 84, Sylla having previously exacted an oath of fidelity from his soldiers, crossed over from Dyrrachium to Brundusium with one thousand two hundred ships of war and transports, as he states in his own memoirs, cited by Plutarch, carrying with him five Roman *legions*, six thousand horse, and some Macedonian and Peloponnesian auxiliaries, (*Appian Bell Mith.*), mustering in all, forty thousand men, and this, as he states himself, against fifteen hostile leaders, commanding not less than four hundred and fifty *cohorts*, making an aggregate of at least two hundred and seventy thousand rank and file.

Had the fierce civil wars which followed, been the result merely of personal ambition between the chiefs, involving no constitutional or national question, I should have passed them over as briefly as possible, but I find—a fact which seems to have strangely escaped preceding writers—that these were, in fact, but the termination of the great social struggle between the confederated Italian states and Rome, which should have the mastery. In other words, whether the whole of Italy should become a Roman unity, or the city of Rome be merely the head of an Italian republic—or, once more, whether thereafter Rome was to rule Italy, or Italy, Rome.

Marius, as we have seen, being an Italian by birth, though a Roman magistrate, had shunned his duty in the first social war, and favoured the allies in the field, so evidently that he was forced to resign his command, and to fly the country. During Sylla's absence, the democratic party obtaining a temporary ascendancy, would have confirmed that ascendancy by introducing at once into the old tribes such an overwhelming multitude of Italians, as would at once give the majority to the strangers and aliens, involving the absolute control, and, in fact, the nationality of Rome.

It was for this, then, that the Marian party were in arms—to render Rome the head of an Italian confederacy, destroying her time-honoured nationality and name, in order that, as Italians, they might preserve that power and *imperium* in the new Italic league, which they had usurped, and felt that they could not retain, in the old Roman republic.

It was against this project, or principle if you will, that Sylla had hitherto contended, and was now about to fight. The son and soldier of the ancient commonwealth of Rome, it was not for him to ask whether the abstract right was with the confederates or with the state, but to defend the cause, uphold the supremacy, and maintain the integrity of his native city.

A Roman, he upheld his country; a noble, he upheld his caste, against innovations upon both, which he undoubtedly believed to be uncalled for and unjust, which time proved to be ruinous to liberty and law, and which, after a little while, erected on the ruined altars of freedom, the blood-cemented throne of the imperial Caesars.

For this, who shall blame him? His after cruelties, the horrible deluges of blood, righteously or unrighteously shed, in which he baptized the new constitution, the proscriptions, the confiscations, the dictatorship, assumed only to be cast aside, the newness of its gloss scarce tarnished, in scorn ineffable!—These are another question. For these, let who may justify him or apologise. Of a surety, that shall not! But they reach not, affect not, the previous question, as to the origin of this civil war—and on that point I take issue, that Sylla, the regularly constituted officer of the republic, while the republic yet was, did well and rightly in bringing Roman *legions* to the rescue and renewal of that republic, against self-constituted usurpers, calling themselves Roman consuls, while fighting at the head of Marsic and Samnite armies, against the integrity and empire of Rome.

When he had won the battle, and beat down the rebel leaders of the treason, had he left the punishment, where it should have been, in the hands of the true, re-constituted powers of the state, he had done his work thoroughly and nobly, as a conservative, for the ancient and honoured constitution; as a noble, for his order; as a man, for his native land.

Resentment and revenge, pride and scorn and undying-hate, blinded his better vision, hardened his heart, turned his hand to iron; and he bartered his birthright of immortal glory for a debauch of blood, and a dictator's fasces.

No opposition was offered to Sylla on his landing, by the people of Brundusium, for which, in after times, he rewarded them by immunities, which they still enjoyed in the days of Appian. Shortly after his landing, he was joined by Quintus Caecilius Metellus Pius, who had been exiled from Rome by Marius and Catulus, and Cneius Pompeius, who was afterward surnamed the Great, son of Pompeius Strabo, who had served with Sylla in the social war, and was killed by lightning in his tent. This young man, who was destined in after time, to play a conspicuous and unfortunate part, far above any pretensions to which his merits could entitle him—for he was but a vain, vacillating, common-place man, and a mediocre soldier—brought with him a single *legion*, and shortly levied two others, with which Metellus and Sylla, both legally invested with proconsular dignity, advanced into the country.

The democratic rabble of Rome, deserted by the nobles and the flower of the middle classes, regarded victory or annihilation as their only choice, remembering what they had done against the family and friends of Sylla, while he was absent, serving his country in the field, and were almost palsied with excessive terror. Yet they gave instructions to their partisan consuls to attack the aristocrats on the instant, and spared neither energy nor devotion to collect means and men, and to raise auxiliaries of the Italian faction, throughout all parts of the peninsula.

But nothing could check, though it might delay, the advance of the conqueror. The first meeting of the hostile forces was near Capua, in Campania, where Sylla, in person, encountered Norbanus, one of the consuls, with the younger Marius, defeated them with the loss of six thousand killed and many wounded, at the expense of seventy killed of his own party, and shut up Norbanus within the capital of Campania. Not many days after this, the proconsuls advanced to Teano, and Lucius Scipio, the consul, who had succeeded Cinna, murdered by his own soldiers, moved against them with a second army, superior to theirs in numbers, but dispirited, disaffected, and anxious only to obtain peace.

This army was easily brought round, during some conferences relative to an armistice set on foot with that intent, pending which the privates from both camps intermingled freely; and on a concerted day the consular forces went over in a body, with their arms, officers, and standards, leaving the consul, with his son Lucius, alone in their pavilion, ignorant of what was in process—a thing, as Appian observes, not very creditable to a general, that he should be alone ignorant of so general a feeling in his own command.

Him and his son Sylla dismissed unhurt, for he neither chose to trust nor to punish them; and then having endeavoured, in vain, to treat with Norbanus, who was still shut up in Capua, pressed forward, burning and devastating, as hostile, all the Italian country.

About this time the capitol of Rome was consumed by fire, and this calamity, which was regarded with superstitious consternation on all sides, was attributed alternately to Norbanus, Carbo, and the delegates of Sylla, without any evidence to shew which, if any, was to blame. Probably it was the result of accident; but it is useful to the reader of history, for it marks a date; having occurred on the first day before the *nones* of Quinctilis, (*Plutarch*), corresponding to the sixth day of July, of the year of Rome 670, the first year of the one hundred and seventy-fourth Olympiad, (*Appian*), and the eighty-fourth before the Christian era.

No farther action of moment occurred during the remainder of this campaign, both parties being occupied in exerting every method to augment their armies, the democratic consuls recruiting throughout the Italian states, and even into the Gallic settlements of the Transpadane, and Sylla collecting to his standards all, whom he could find friendly to Rome.

The season of inaction was protracted by the extreme inclemency of the weather, and the following campaign did not open until late in the spring of 83, B. C., Papirius, Carbo, and Marius the younger, nephew of Caius, being the consuls of the year, the latter but twenty-seven years of age. The first action was fought near the River Æsis, now the Esino, in the Picene country, between Metellus and Carrina, one of Carbo's generals, in which the latter was defeated with great loss, when all the surrounding country came over to Metellus; but Carbo came down on the victor in force, and shutting him up in his entrenched camp, besieged him closely, until tidings of a desperate defeat which had befallen his colleague, near Praeneste, obliged him to raise the siege and consult for his safety by decamping toward Ariminum, during which operation Pompeius overtook his rear guard, and threw it into great confusion.

The defeat of Marius was in this wise; Sylla had taken Setia, a town of Latium, not far distant from the port and city of Antium, when Marius, who was encamped near him, fell back to a place called Sacriportum, where he prepared to deliver battle, and at first made some good fighting. But his left wing giving way a little, five *cohorts* of foot and two of horse threw away their standards, and hurrying across the plain, ranged themselves on the side of Sylla. Then commenced a fearful route. The whole army, panic-stricken, fled headlong, the enemy doing terrible execution on their rear, until pursuers and pursued, pell-mell, arrived at the fortified and reputed impregnable stronghold of Praeneste.

The foremost fugitives were admitted into the walls, but as the enemy was mixed confusedly with their friends, the citizens closed the gates and Marius himself was drawn over the battlements with ropes, in time only to escape the after carnage. No quarter was given, for the fugitives were Samnites and Italians, and of them Sylla took no prisoners, but put all to the sword, in reward of their unvarying enmity to Rome. In this action he killed twenty thousand of the enemy, his own loss being twenty-three.

Simultaneously with this defeat, Metellus conquered a third army of Carbo's, five *cohorts* having deserted to him in like manner, in the heat of battle; and Pompeius beat Marcius near the city of Sienna, and plundered the town; while Sylla having circumvallated Praeneste, left the blockade to Lucretius Ofella, intending to let famine do its work in preference to the sword.

From this time, fortune smiled no more on the Marian party; wherever they met the constitutionalists, they either lost their armies by total or partial defection, or were defeated and dispersed irretrievably, with mere nominal loss on the part of Crassus, Pompeius, Metellus, Servilius or Sylla, in person, not one of whom encountered a check, much less a defeat, but pushed forward steadily, step by step, taking possession of the whole country as they passed on, until the walls of Rome, and the Campus Martins, and the Colline gates, against which Hannibal is said to have hurled his javelin, were in full view, and the reward of all their toils and perils appeared doubtless to be won.

But there was yet one more struggle. For Pontius of Telesia, personally and hereditarily the deadliest enemy of Rome, with Lamponius the Lucanian, and Damasippus, and Carrina, with immense levies, had made a desperate effort to raise the siege of Praeneste and liberate Marius; but being frustrated in this attempt by the arrival of Pompey and Crassus, with the advanced guards of Sylla, they made a sudden movement on Rome, hoping to carry it by a *coup de main*, and narrowly missed their object.

All was confusion within the walls; and the cries of the women, running about, tearing their hair and shrieking, as if the city were already taken by assault, were heard far and near, when Sylla's light horse came in sight, and, halting long enough only to wipe the sweat from their chargers and sponge out their nostrils, fell on with spirit, and so opened the fiercest action of the war.

As fast as Sylla's men arrived on the ground, despite the remonstrances of his lieutenants, who deprecated his carrying troops, directly off so severe a forced march, into action, they were hurried, *cohort* after *cohort*, into the conflict, without a moment's delay; and, after a most appalling straggle, conquered. Never, however, did Sylla so nearly lose a battle. It was nearly three o'clock in the afternoon of a hot summer's day when the first charge was made, and the constitutionalists had been marching in their heavy armour, and in close order, in pursuit, through clouds of dust, and under a fierce Italian sun, since daybreak.

The right wing, commanded by Crassus, from the first onset, carried all before it; but the left, which came straggling into action, was taken in detail, and so severely handled, that it was on the point of giving way, when Sylla came up to its support, galloping along the front, on a white horse, conspicuous for its speed and spirit, cheering his men with word and gesture, and rallying them to the action. Well known to all on both sides, so desperate an exposure of his person could not but induce the last danger. He was marked by two of the enemy's horsemen, who rode at him with their javelins levelled, as he careered along the front unmindful of them and intent only on reforming his wavering and dispirited lines, and hurled their weapons, with aim so correct, that they would both have taken effect on his person, had not his groom, who rode close at his heels, lashed his charger so suddenly and severely from behind, that he made a great bound forward, and the spears actually passing through his tail, stood quivering in the ground.

Nevertheless, in spite of all his exertions, all his entreaties and supplications to a small golden Apollo, whom he ever carried in his bosom in his battles, and whom he now implored, with kisses and almost with tears—

> To aid his ever fortunate Cornelius Sylla, whom he had raised to splendour in so many battles, nor to suffer him to perish here, at the very gates of his native city, utterly disgraced and ruined amid the ruin of his fellow-citizens.

He could not on his wing retrieve the fortunes of the day, On that flank the day was irretrievably lost, and the great leader was himself borne back by the rush of his own fugitives into his own camp, which he fortified as best he might, supposing that the tide of fortune had changed altogether, and that the battle had gone against him. He lost many of his men, it is true, and numbers of the citizens of Rome of his party, who had come out to see the battle, were slain and trampled under foot by the Italians; nay, the siege of Praeneste was almost raised, and Marius allowed to escape, for such a crowd of fugitives who had fled even to that place, rushed into the lines of Lucretius Ofella, crying out that Sylla was slain and all lost, that it required the utmost firmness and decision in that officer to resist the panic and maintain the blockade.

In the dead of night, glad tidings came to Sylla, as he sat alone in his tent disconsolate, for the first time in his life believing himself to be a beaten soldier—messengers from Crassus, who had entirely conquered the left and centre of the confederates, killing Pontius Telesinus and Albinus on the field, and chased the disorganised relics of what was no longer an army, so far as to Antemnae, where he had pitched his bivouac, and whither he now requested Sylla to forward supplies for himself and his *legions*, since they were weary, supperless, and hungry.

In this final action about fifty thousand men, on both sides, were left dead on the field of battle; eight thousand were taken prisoners, chiefly Samnites; and of these six thousand, together with Marcius Damasippus, and Carrina, their leaders, were shut up in the hippodrome and butchered by volleys of arrow-shot and javelins, while the conqueror was calmly addressing the senate, whom he had convened in the temple of Bellona. The hideous clamour of the wretches, howling in their hopeless agony, within so small a space, and that little removed from the shrine in which the senate were listening to the graceful and polished orator, whose rounded periods fell from the lips which had so recently issued those bloody orders as if they had been the tidings of salvation rather than the doom of thousands, shook the equanimity and distracted the attention of the senators.

They rose to their feet, gazed uncertainly about them, and, negligent of the speaker, spoke to each other in whispers; nor did it greatly reassure them, or tend much to allay their apprehensions, when with a calm and unmoved countenance the consul requested them to give their attention to the matters before the house, and to pay no heed to what was going on without, for it was but a few of the guilty who were undergoing punishment by his orders. In the like spirit he gazed on the head of the younger Marius, who died by his own hand, when

Praeneste was surrendered, with a quiet philosophizing smile, as it was laid before him in the crowded forum. "Ha!" he said quietly, "the young man should have learned to pull at the oar, before he aspired to steer the ship."

And this spirit it is, which rendered his massacres and proscriptions so terrible to the Romans; Marius, they said, slaughtered through cruelty, through hatred, through furious passions, through blind lust of blood, like an insane wild beast; but Sylla kills with a cool pulse, an unmoved countenance, a quiet voice, like an impassive calculating machine.

Both, unquestionably, were utterly reckless of human suffering or death; but, perhaps, it was that Marius loved blood for its own sake, and that Sylla had no sympathy with mere life, when anything was to be gained by the taking it. And in this consideration, it is not unworthy of remark, that Caius Julius Caesar, himself a member of the democratic faction, and himself, as some say, having barely escaped Sylla's proscription, spoke some years afterward in full senate, when pleading against the execution of capital punishment on the Catilinarian conspirators, in these memorable words:—

> Even within our own memory, when victorious Sylla commanded Damasippus and many others of his gang, who had grown great by public wrong, to be slaughtered, who did not rejoice? All said, that those factious and infamous men who had cruelly tormented the commonwealth by their seditions, well deserved to die.—*Sallust Catiline*

And if such be the deliberate testimony of a contemporaneous Roman, of the hostile faction, while pleading for the life of traitors, how can we doubt that it was indeed a horrible truth—that, during those long years of rebellion, treason, plunder, assassination, butchery, the gangs of licensed murderers had so grown and become so thoroughly engrafted on the state, as to require a stronger hand, and a will more resolute than that of the ordinary magistrate, a keener eye to detect, and a sharper sword to punish guilt, than those of the tardy and blindfold goddess, justice.

On this odious topic, it is alike repugnant and useless to dwell. I am not, as I have said, about to become an apologist for aristocratic, more than for plebeian, cruelty, much less to acquit the great captain of unnecessary bloodshed and unlicensed vengeance.

He first set the awful example of licensed murders and legitimate proscriptions, and the consequences of the accursed precedent which he introduced, perhaps believing that he was executing only unbiased and unpitying justice, fell with unmitigated weight on the heads of his own party; and the counter-proscriptions of the future triumvirates, by extirpating all the purest and most virtuous citizens of Rome, robbed the republic of its only true defenders, and laid the foundations for the iron empire.

Of this, at least, he cannot be held innocent. His reforms, his reorganisation of the republic, his renewal of the old constitution, passed away and perished, because there was no soil left wherein the seeds of regeneration might take root and germinate. But the terrible examples of his civic conquests, civic slaughters, and civic usurpation did not pass away or die fruitless; for in the vicious, the ambitious, the perverted heart of man, there is ever soil wherefrom to ripen the germs of cruelty and lust of power.

But it must be said of him, that when he had constituted himself perpetual dictator, he held that dictatorship only, until he had completed his punishments, his reformations, his reestablishment of what certainly he did believe good and right; and cast it from him scornfully, neither caring to derive personal aggrandisement from its retention, nor fearing personal danger from its abdication.

It must be remembered, that as a soldier, in which view above all others, I have to deal with him, he was the greatest of his time, of his name, and among the first, if not first, of his nation; that as a reformer, he was not a mere puller down, but a builder up, and regenerator likewise; that, with more enemies than any man in Italy, he lived peaceably and in solitude in his beautiful home at Cumae, or walked unguarded and unarmed through the crowded streets of Rome, with no dagger lifted against him, and what is more, with no fears in his secret soul to give the dagger edge. It must be remembered, that when he died calmly in his bed, of a horrible and loathsome disorder, never such a concourse followed the corpse of any Roman to the grave, as pursued, not with curses, but with offerings and honours, and the groans and libations of men, the tears and rich funeral gifts of women, the body of Cornelius Sylla.

It must be remembered, that, when Nero died, if some affectionate hand hung daily flowers upon the urn of Nero, it is that there was even in Nero something which had excited, something which had deserved human affection.

His character is, perhaps, the best summed up in the epitaph, said to be of his own composition, which was engraved on his urn:—

> LUCIUS CORNELIUS SYLLA, FELIX;
> WHOM NO MAN EVER OVERCAME,
> IN THE GOOD DONE TO HIS FRIENDS,
> OR THE EVIL TO HIS FOES.

6

Caius Julius Caesar
Five Times Consul, Perpetual Dictator

Anid Crassos, quid Pompeios evertit? et illum
Ad sua qui domitos deduxit flagra Quirites?
Summus nempe locus, nulla non arte petitus,
Magnaque numinibus vota exandita malignia.
Ad generum Cereris sine csede et vulnere pauci
Discendunt reges, et sicca morte tyranni.

This great soldier and extraordinary man, who presents in many instances an almost perfect ante-type to the yet greater soldier and more extraordinary man, who played a part almost similar to his own, in the commencement of the nineteenth century, first springing, self-made, into light, among the throes and struggles of a convulsed and tortured republic, to which he was destined to deal the deathblow, and on the ashes of which to build the throne of an imperial dynasty, was born in the six hundred and fifty-fourth year of Rome, B. C. 100, in the sixth consulship of Gains Marius, to whom he was connected in the female line, on the tenth day of the month Quinctilis, the name of which, at a later date, was, in honour of him, changed to Julius, and so remains, under a different and more advanced civilization, to the present day.

He was descended, as his gentile name indicates, from the ancient and noble Julian house, which affected to trace its hereditary descent to Julius, the son of Æneas, and founder of Alba Longa; but which, without calling into account the legends of mythical traditions, had sufficient title to its honourable antiquity in the fact, that it gave to the republic, within the first century of its existence, thirteen officers of the highest grade, ten consuls or military *tribunes*, one *decemvir*, one dictatorial master of the horse, and one censor, the highest dignities, without exception, in the gift of the state.

It is true that the family name of Caesar does not appear as one of the branches of this distinguished clan, but that in no wise goes to discredit the descent; since, as has been demonstrated above, (*Marius*), the names of families frequently originated in some personal characteristic or quality of the first founder, and this is said to have been the case in the present instance; three different accounts being given of the derivation of this name and title of Caesar, thereafter to be recognised as imperial, through so many centuries and over so many realms, one of them[1] at least far beyond the *ultima* Thule, and not yet included within the *terra cognita* of antiquity. According to Pliny, the first of the house who bore this *cognomen*, took it from *coedo*, to cut, because he, like Macbeth,

Was from his mother's womb
Untimely ripped.

Others derive the appellation from *coesaries*, as if he had been born with long flowing hair; and others, yet again, from *casa*, alleged to be the Punic word signifying elephant, as if the founder of the house had been the Roman who slew the first elephant in the Italian campaigns of Pyrrhus, when his countrymen became acquainted, for the first time, with that prodigious animal. The last derivation rests itself on a problem, it no where appearing that the word *casa* does signify elephant, either in Punic, an absolutely extinct language, or in any other tongue. The second explanation has been rejected by all authorities, and that of Pliny received the general sanction of his contemporaries, if not of oral tradition.

It affords, however, the strongest corroboration to the accredited pedigree of the house, that the same *praenomina*, answering to the modern Christian names. Gains and Lucius, were peculiar to members of the Julian clan, from the first consul of the name, in the twentieth year of the republic, to the kinsmen of the object of this memoir, murdered by Marius and Cinna during their brief and bloody ascendancy, his father and himself, in its seventh century, and but shortly before its dissolution.

Caius Caesar, himself a man of praetorian dignity and considerable wealth and influence in the state, married Aurelia, a sister of the celebrated Marcus Aurelius Cotta, a lady of the noblest Roman birth,

---

1. Russia. Tsar, *quasi* Caesar.

and his sister Julia was married to the elder Marius, so that his son, of whom I am now writing, was nephew, by courtesy, to that great demagogue, and first cousin to his heir and successor in treason, if not in power.

I have dwelt somewhat more particularly on this point than I should otherwise have deemed necessary, inasmuch as the circumstances of his birth and of his political predilections and career, completely countering his aristocratic origin, throw much light on his particular character, motives and aspirations, from the earliest, and confirm, or, I might say, prove the position taken in the sketches of Marius and Sylla, in relation to the nature of the later civil contentions in Rome—whether there was any real conflict of democratic and aristocratic principle involved in the struggle between what were called the democratic and aristocratic parties—or whether the strife lay not between a faction of able, irresponsible, dissolute men of all origins, castes, and conditions, bent on securing absolute dominion, through the introduction of a foreign element into the state—in fact through anarchy itself—and the defenders of the ancient representative republic, now denounced by the ultraists as aristocratical, and worn out.

This question will solve itself as we proceed, to the understanding of any who will examine the singular combination of desperate men, members of all the different extinct parties who henceforth banded themselves together against the constituted republic, with its representative forms, its senate, and its legitimate authorities; having no seeming link of union beyond hatred to the existing condition of things, and a leaning toward aliens and foreigners of all nations, however barbarous or brutal, whom they persisted to introduce into the state, for the purpose of overwhelming the Roman vote and annihilating the nationality of the city I shall therefore allude to it no farther until events bring it distinctly before us, but shall proceed directly to the facts of his life and career; premising only that my readers must not look for so close and elaborate an examination of every several skirmish and action of a general, whose public life covered a space of thirty-five years, almost every year of which was a campaign, as they would rightfully expect in the case of a strategist, whose claims to consideration rest on two or three well-executed and conceived campaigns, two or three well-delivered or well-fought battles.

Planets are measured by distances, comets by epochs; ordinary men and good generals are judged by their actions, great geniuses, whether good or evil Caesars, Alexanders, Napoleons, Washingtons, by the results and consequences of what they have done.

In the sixteenth year of his age, (*Surtonius 1*), he lost his father, and being appointed Flamen Dialis, high-priest of Jupiter, he put away Cossutia, a rich girl of equestrian family, to whom he had been betrothed before he had assumed the garb and privileges of manhood, and married Cornelia, the daughter of Cinna, the leader of the popular, or as I shall henceforth designate it, the Italian party after the death of Marius, at that time serving his fourth consulship.

This may be regarded as the first step of his life, an act clearly of his own doing, indicating the course he intended to pursue in the politics of the state, as it involved his abnegation of the traditional principles of his house, two of the most distinguished members of which, Lucius Julius Caesar, the conqueror of the Samnites during the social war, and Caius Julius Caesar, his brother, a celebrated wit and orator, were murdered by the orders of Marius and the very man whose daughter he now espoused. Henceforth, therefore, he was regarded as probably he intended it, as having embraced the principles of the revolution, and linked his fortunes with those of the Italian, anti-Roman party, to which may be ascribed all the troubles which thereafter agitated the state, until the convulsions of the dying republic subsided into the still sleep of centralised despotism.

But Caius Caesar—for as such, and never as Julius Caesar, was he known to his contemporaries—was by far too clear-headed and clear-sighted a man to attach himself to any party or person, longer than it suited his own prospects and subserved to his own ascendancy. Never, during his long meteoric career, did he ally himself to any person, whom he did not turn wholly to his own uses, whom he did not sacrifice instantly when he could no longer be rendered useful, or when his own advancement rendered his ruin necessary.

In addition to wonderful abilities, extreme learning, eloquence second to no one, save Cicero, of his own day, perfect mastery of all martial and athletic exercises, boundless liberality, whether of his own or of other's affluence, rare address, deep dissimulation, undisturbed affability, an address the most conciliating, a will of adamant, and a heavenreaching genius, he possessed this advantage when it came to the struggle, over all his antagonists—that while they were divided between counsels, actuated by many principles, not a few self-conflicting, and aiming at many ends, he had, from the beginning, one principle, one end—to advance himself by all means, risks, sacrifices, to supreme dominion. They were divided, whether as his friends or his foes, and, taken in detail, busied each about his petty several ends, fell one by one. He was himself alone his own counsellor, intriguer, actor; and pressing resolutely, silently, immutably, alway onward to his one grand object, from which his eagle eye never swerved for a moment, of course won it.

From this day forth, when he fixed his prophetic gaze upon " that more than mortal crown, the dictatorial wreath," resolved to shadow his brows, prematurely bald, with the perpetual crown of unfading bays, he never hedged aside from the direct road, no, not a single pace; he never hesitated, never shook. No danger appalled, no infamy deterred, no friendship dissuaded, no love distracted, no sacrifice revolted him—whether of friendship, love, life, virtue, honour, from winning what he had resolved to win, when but a beardless boy.

Almost simultaneously with his marriage, his father-in-law, Cinna, was murdered by his soldiery, whom he had so thoroughly indoctrinated in rebellion, that they rebelled once too often, even for him, arch-rebel.

Sylla, the avenger of noble blood, landed at Brundusium; and, army after army either slaughtered in the field or seduced from their leaders, the host of the anarchists, the four hundred and fifty *cohorts* and their fifteen generals, melted like wax before the fire, in the fierce heat of the Patrician victor's progress.

In the last bloody and long-disputed battle, before the Colline gates and under the very walls of Rome, fell Pontius Telesinus, fell the last and best army of the true Italians; and never again, though factions might rally to the standard of their cause, and ambitious men use their name as the stepping-stone whereby to stride to empire, did they revive as a genuine party, or play a national part in the game of politics or war.

It is evident that the ambitious and precocious boy had already the shrewdness and foresight to discover, that adherence to the traditional policy of his house, and adoption of the aristocratic, or conservative Roman party, could, at the utmost, promote him only to be one greater among many great, could only elevate him to the highest offices under the republic—while, by mounting the ladder, constructed from the fragments of the old agrarian and new Italian factions, he might raise himself to be, what he aspired, the greatest, and grasp the one authority, above senate, commonwealth, and country.

Sylla entered Rome, as we have seen; massacres and proscriptions followed, blood flowed like water—and boy as he was, Caius Caesar attracted the deadly glare of those green eyes of Sylla, which, tiger-like, for the most part, marked only to destroy. He received orders, as the condition on which he might live, to repudiate Cornelia, whose paternity rendered her hated at once and suspected by the vengeful dictator.

But the boy's advancement rested on his adherence to the forbidden wife and the proscribed party, and he saw it—otherwise he had sacrificed both to the star of his ascendancy.

As it was, he defied what few defied and lived—the dictator's wrath. He was deprived of his priesthood; his wife's dowry was confiscated; a price was set on his head, and he escaped only by hiding himself among the hills and woods of the Sabine country, and on one occasion by bribing the officer of a detachment which actually apprehended him, while suffering from an attack of *quartan ague*, to which he was ever subject, as he was shifting from one lurking-place to another in the gloom of a starless midnight.

According to Suetonius, he obtained his pardon in the end, at the intercession of the vestal virgins, of Mamercus Æmilius, and of Aurelius Cotta, his kinsmen, members of the highest and strictest senatorial party; but, as Plutarch says, he got down unobserved to the sea shore, where he found a ship which conveyed him in safety to the court of Nicomedes, king of Bithynia; a retreat more conducive to his personal impunity than to his personal reputation; for reports, too abominable to be written down, prevailed, concerning his intimacy with that monarch, which he never outlived in all his greatness.

It is of this time that the story goes, concerning the reply of Sylla to the intercessors for the life of Caesar, which is related both by Suetonius and Plutarch, though the latter, to colour his version of the event, converts it into a positive refusal to pardon. "For," he said, "he could perceive many a Marius in that dissolute boy."

More stress has been laid on the anecdote than it is really worth, and the whole story has been decidedly negatived as impossible, as if Sylla were incapable of discharging a person of whom he entertained such an opinion. A better reason for declining it, is the total lack of grounds whereon Sylla should have formed or expressed such a judgment. If he did use the expression, it was probably a half sarcastic, half genuine sentiment, elicited from him by the young man's obstinacy, which had no real meaning, and was forgotten as soon as uttered.

It is not a matter of much importance either way, but it is more probable that he was pardoned, than that he was a mere fugitive from justice, since we find him in the employment of Minucius Thermus, who was sent by Sylla to the assistance of Nicomedes against Mithridates, and gaining under his command the honour of a civic crown during the blockade of Mitylene, for saving the life of a Roman citizen; things not likely to have occurred had he been at that time under proscription and the dictator's ban.

In the following year he served part of a campaign in Cilicia under the consul Servilius Isauricus, but speedily resigned and returned home, for the death of Sylla had produced a change in affairs, and there appeared some probability that the anti-Roman party might again gain the ascendant.

Marcus Æmilius Lepidus, a man of mean capacity but profligate ambition, (*Ferguson's Roman Rep. III*), had been elected consul by the relics of the Marian party, in the year of the city 676, B. C. 78, and had relieved Cisalpine Gaul as his province, whence he marched with his army upon Rome, intending to play again the game of Marius, but his abilities were utterly unequal to his aims, and he was entirely defeated in the Janiculum, by his colleague Quintus Lutatius Catulus. His party was dispersed, and he shortly afterward died in Sardinia, broken-hearted.

It was to be on the spot, and in readiness to take advantage of any favourable opportunity, that Caesar had returned to Italy, but his keen eye soon perceived that the elements of success were wanting to this vain and weak attempt, and that the reconstituted republic, since the reforms of Sylla, stood on too firm a base to be shaken from without, until its foundations should be sapped insidiously from within.

In truth, after the death of that great and politic usurper, the commonwealth was restored almost to the condition in which it stood at the moment when Hannibal was driven from Italy. The magistrates were elected by the same regulated assemblies; the senate, long before shorn of all excessive privileges, or powers dangerous to their countrymen, possessed the same authority which it had used so nobly in the Punic Wars; the *tribunes*, stripped of the enormous prerogatives which they had usurped, constituting them almost omnipotent for good or for evil, were restricted to the functions for which they were created, in repressing inconsiderate legislation, and putting their veto on unconstitutional or illegal acts of the executive.

But, above all, the treasonable wickedness of Marius in altering the formation of the *legions*, admitting into them proletarians, aliens, and freedmen, was in some considerable degree counteracted by the sound policy of the dictator in planting the veterans of all the armies as military colonies in the towns, boroughs, villages and districts which had been confiscated from the inhabitants, dispossessed in consequence of their participation in the Italian rising against Rome. By this act, from penniless desperadoes, with no stake in the well-being of the country, ready to follow the first lucky leader who could promise them pay and plunder, they were converted into citizens and freeholders; they had homes, and speedily acquired family ties and all those home affections, which bind men to the soil beyond loyalty or law; and though, in his account of the Catilinarian conspiracy, Sallust, who was a well-wisher to that nefarious plot, if not directly a partisan, represents those conspirators as resting their hope of armed support on a rising of the veterans of Sylla in their favour, no such occurrence took place, nor does it appear that the military colonies ever forsook their allegiance to the Republic. At least it was not they, but a mixed horde of Gauls, Ligurians, Germans, ruffians and runaways from all nations, banded under the desecrated eagles of Caesar, who struck down the standard of the republic at Pharsalia, and extinguished the last sparks of liberty in the blood of Brutus at Philippi.

Of all these facts Caesar was far too subtle not to be thoroughly aware; and consequently, although earnestly solicited to join the movement, he held aloof, and saw his associates perish by the sword of Catulus or the axes of his *lictors*, with unmoved philosophy.

Nevertheless, after the extinction of this conspiracy, he made a move, in attempting to procure the impeachment of the ex-consul Cornelius Dolabella, which proved so far premature, that, on failing, he found it prudent to withdraw for a while into private life, and retire to the island of Rhodes, where he assiduously applied himself to the study of rhetoric and oratory, under Apollonius Molo, one of the most distinguished masters of the day. On his way thither, occurred an incident worthy of notice, as showing the indomitable will and unflinching determination of the man, even in his early youth, no less than the small regard he paid to the authorities, when they conflicted with his pleasure.

Being taken by pirates near the island of Pharmacusa, he was detained by them for forty days, though treated with all honour, until he should pay a ransom of fifty *talents*. When he had succeeded in obtaining this sum, he was landed, with his suite, on the sea shore, and, immediately raising a squadron, and equipping it at his own expense, sailed in pursuit of his recent entertainers, forced them to action, sunk or took all their vessels, and, having constantly, while in their power, threatened them jocosely that he would one day crucify every one of them, kept his word in a manner which they found anything but jocose—for so soon as he had them all in chains, he landed and proceeded to Junius Silanus, the proconsul of Bithynia, of whom he sought an order to execute his prisoners; but this request being refused, as he was in no authority, nor held any office under the government, he made all haste back to the place where he left them, and before any instructions to the contrary could reach him, made his promise good, by nailing the whole number of them to crosses, along the sea-shore.

Shortly after his return to Rome, he was elected a tribune of the soldiers, and in that capacity exerted himself with the greatest success in procuring the restoration to the tribunes of the people, of those odious and aggressive powers of which Sylla, to the eminent good of the republic, had deprived them. And this done, by their aid ever ready in behalf of the mutinous and ill-disposed, he procured the recall, by the Plotian law, of Lucius Cinna, his brother-in-law, and the other traitor refugees, who had fled for safety, after the discomfiture of Lepidus, to the camp of Sertorius, who still held out in Spain for the Marian faction.

Succeeding to the office of *Quaestor*, he made himself notorious by delivering two orations in honour, the one of his aunt Julia, the widow of Caius Marius, and the other of his own wife, Cornelia, the daughter of Marius' colleague, Cinna; and thereafter had the courage to restore the statues of Caius Marius conquering Jugurtha, and leading captive the Teutons and Cimbri. The nobles were greatly annoyed at this show of reckless defiance to the acts of the senate under Sylla's rule; but the mass of the people were yet more intoxicated by the daring of the deed, and by the gratification of once more beholding the trophies of their favourite adorning the public places, whence they had so long been banished.

As *quaestor*, it does not appear that he had any foreign jurisdiction, or any opportunity of distinguishing himself except by these invasions on the integrity of the state and influence of the senate; but during his occupation of the magistracy he married Pompeia, the daughter of Quintus Pompeius, and grand-daughter of Lucius Sylla, whom he afterward divorced, on suspicion of adultery with Publius Clodius, (*Suetonius 1*), who introduced himself into his house in female attire, during the celebration of the mysteries of the *Bona dea*—a sacrilege, which was afterward made the subject of a public prosecution before the senate.

Up to this time he had led a life the most licentious and debauched that can be conceived; and so profuse was he of his largesses and reckless liberalities, that when he attained to the office of Curule Ædile, the next in rotation to the *quaestorship*, he was already indebted to various creditors in the vast amount of thirteen hundred *talents*, a sum equal to above three hundred thousand pounds sterling, or a million and a half of dollars; (*Plutarch*), and to this enormous debt he added fresh burdens, by the magnificent games, pomps, banquets and processions, which he exhibited—not the least of these being a combat of three hundred and twenty pairs of trained gladiators—during his tenure of that office.

It would appear, that in the year before he was appointed to the *ædileship*, the Latin colonies were again in a state of violent agitation on the old question of obtaining the full Roman *franchise*; and the whole revolutionary faction was busily at work, Caesar among the rest, secretly undermining the foundations of the commonwealth, and stimulating them to rise in overt rebellion, which they would unquestionably have done had not the consuls kept the *legions* in hand, which had been levied for the Cilician war, and thereby frustrated the attempt.

A few days, certainly, (*Suetonius 1*), before he entered upon his *ædileship*, the gravest suspicion arose, that he was engaged in a conspiracy with Crassus, the richest man in Rome, of consular dignity, and the two consuls of the year, Publius Cornelius Sylla and Lucius Autronius Paetus—both recently ejected from office for bribery—to massacre the senate in the Campus Martins, on a given signal; declare Crassus dictator, with Caesar for his master of the horse; and to proclaim the Italian republic, with Corfinium, instead of Rome, for its head. From fear, or that his heart failed him, Crassus was not on the spot when the appointed time arrived; and Caesar, in consequence, failed to give the signal which had been agreed on, by letting his *toga* slip from his shoulder. The rich man's hesitation, caused probably by his apprehension that his property, much of which lay in city tenements, would suffer in a plot, which involved conflagration as a part of the design, preserved Rome.

This was the first germ of the more celebrated Catilinarian conspiracy, which matured three years later, and was suppressed in the consulship of Cicero and Antonius; and to both these the key is the elevation of the Italian confederacy on the ruins of Rome. To their non-perception of this fact, it is to be attributed that many able and well-informed historians have doubted the reality of any such conspiracy, involving the total destruction of Rome and the annihilation of her power, by the hands of her own citizens, as a thing absolutely incredible, owing to the absence of motive. But motive is not absent, when it is considered that the project embraced the organisation of a yet vaster and more powerful republic, even the whole peninsula, of which every Italian should be a freeman, and the parricides of Rome the lords and *imperators*.

After the explosion of this abominable plot, (*Sallust Bell*), another appears to have been organised, with a view to transferring the seat of the first outbreak to Spain; where, Piso going to the province with an army, as *propraetor*, should rally the old Sertorian and Marian party upon himself, and raise the standard of rebellion, which would be seconded by a revolution in the city, to be headed by Crassus and Caesar.

This, like the preceding plot, fell through; Piso being murdered on the route to his province, for his cruelty, by some Spanish horsemen, said also to be old clients still in the pay of Cneius Pompeius, afterward surnamed the Great who moved alike by enmity to Crassus and regard for the constitution, took this strong method of ridding the one of an unscrupulous tool, and the other of an inveterate enemy.

Frustrated thus of any occasion, for the present, of gratifying his lust of power—thirst of blood, unlike the others, he had none to gratify, for he was a good-tempered, easy man by nature, and would rather have preferred not to shed blood at all, provided he could have gained his ends without it, though entirely careless what oceans should flow if necessary to achieve those ends—he had no other way of passing his *ædileship* than in sumptuously beautifying the *comitium*, and forum, the *basilicas*, the Appian way, and the capitol, to the burning of which, he had but a few days before been consenting, by *porticoes* and other edifices of such cost as added vastly to his already gigantic encumbrances.

His next step was a bold one—no less than to aspire to the office of Pontifex Maximus, the most honourable and reverend dignity in the gift of the republic, conferring no power, indeed, or privilege on its holder, but investing him with such sanctity, and so elevating his personal character, as to be sought after only by the most considerable persons, and never before granted to any but men of probity and weight.

It was now vacant by the death of Quintus Caecilius Metellus Pius, the most virtuous and generally respected citizen of Rome, and was the subject of aspiration to two candidates, worthy, by their families and their own precedents, of that high dignity. These were Publius Servilius Vatea, Isauricus, and Quintus Lutatius Catulus; and against these, having no qualifications to show except a fortune and a character broken by licentiousness and riot and a career tainted by suspicions of the blackest treason, he had the effrontery to offer himself competitor.

Unblushing corruption carried the day, and so extraordinary, it is said, was the extent to which he carried his briberies, that he was himself staggered by the amount of his liabilities; and, when his mother kissed him and wished him good speed, as he left his house on the morning of the canvass, replied, "I shall either return home Pontifix Maximus, or not return at all." He did return, however; for, so far did effrontery and bribery carry it above age, dignity, desert, service and virtue, that he actually gained more votes in the particular tribes of his competitors than they in their whole canvass.

At the ensuing elections, which were in the six hundred and ninetieth year of the city, B. C. 64, when he was thirty-six years old, he was chosen praetor for the ensuing year, that wherein the conspiracy of Catiline finally came to a head, and was suppressed. There is not a shadow of doubt, that both Crassus and Caesar were deeply compromised in this matter; but the latter had probably satisfied himself by this time, that the Italian element in this great conspiracy was too much broken and dispirited to be of any practical value; that the true old plebeian party of the Gracchi did not care to move, the issues being entirely altered since their struggles; that the colonized veterans were looking rather to the domestic comforts of their newly-acquired homes, than to the brewing of fresh plots; that the only persons truly to be depended on, were a small knot of desperate, dangerous, ruined nobles, capable in will and wickedness of doing anything, but incapable, for lack of men and means, of success—in a word, that neither the time nor the persons, for dismantling the commonwealth, had arrived.

His sagacity, doubtless, kept his weaker-minded confederate, Crassus, as superadded to his fears on account of his property, from showing his hand prematurely. And they both remained tranquil and apparently undisturbed among the fierce dissensions, of which, had there appeared a probability that they could succeed, both would have taken quick advantage.

It must have required rare subtlety to play that game—to avoid the awakened suspicions of the senate, with Cicero and Cato at their head—to avoid the jealousy of such men as Lentulus, Cethegus, Catiline, who, should they imagine themselves deserted or betrayed by their fellows, were certain to denounce them, if for the mere pleasure of involving them in a common ruin. It must have required rare audacity.

But to this extraordinary man, neither subtlety nor audacity were wanting, and the game played itself into his hands, where the cards with which to win were wanting.

Cicero, and Cato, and probably Cneius Pompeius, at this time antagonistic to Caesar, undoubtedly were aware of the complicity of both these men, but probably did not possess irrefragable evidence to convict, and, if they did, dared not array against themselves, in addition to the known strength of the conspiracy, the unknown powers, bought by the wealth of Crassus, and won by the address of Caesar, which would be thrown into the balance against Rome, on the first attempt to implicate them in the charges.

This point in the game was not, one may be sure, lost upon Caesar, who saw that, so long as he remained impassive, he had nothing to fear from the government, and that all that remained to parry was the jealousies, the resentments, the revenge of the ruined traitors.

Nor, however deeply one may detest and loathe the duplicity and treachery of this false and recreant noble, false to the honours of his house, false to the principles of his caste, false to the trust of his country, can he but admire the magnificent effrontery, the calm, sublime audacity, with which Caesar arose, conscious of equal guilt, in presence of his arraigned confederates; conscious of detected crime, in the presence of the indignant judges, and delivered an oration in their favour, and against the capital sentence, so closely logical, so admirably sophistical, so cogent and so eloquent, that it changed the hearts of more than one of the assessors, and filled the souls of the prisoners with renewed hope of life, and with gratitude for him who had risked so much to save them.

He did risk much; for, after Cato had replied, carrying conviction on every word he uttered, and the prisoners were led to the Tullianum, and the death by the hangman's noose, such was the indignation raised against him, that the equestrian order, who had rallied strong in arms about their equestrian consul, drew their swords on him, as he issued from the senate house, and would have slain him there, had not Curio cast the skirt of his toga over him, and Cicero and Cato exerted themselves to the utmost to prevent another act of violence, which, however just in itself, would but have added another brand to the burning.

And this is the man who died "The Father of his country," and dead, was worshipped as a god by Romans.

From this day Caesar renounced conspiracies; from this day he had no confidants, no assistants; ignorant and blind tools only, by whom to work out his own inscrutable will. And again, fortune favoured him. The senate, aware how dangerous he was at home, and entirely unsuspicious of his possessing almost unequalled military talents, thought they did well and wisely in sending him far off, on an honourable mission, to take the government of a remote, wild, half-conquered province, and the command of a turbulent and seditious army. So they gave to him, as *propraetor*, the government of farther Spain, hoping, it is like enough, that he would share the fate of Sertorius, of Piso, and of so many other officers, who in these infamous times perished by the hands of their own lawless soldiers or mutinous subalterns.

His debts still stood in his way; and so vast had they become, and so hopeless were his creditors of ever being paid, even by the fruits of the utmost extortion which a Roman *praetor* could apply to his province, that they served process upon him, forbidding him to quit the city. Nor could he have availed himself of this his first opportunity of acquiring either renown or wealth, had not Licinius Crassus become security for him in the sum of eight hundred and thirty *talents*, or about one million of dollars.

It is possible that this act of munificence on the part of Crassus, who was ordinarily esteemed no less avaricious than wealthy, had its origin in gratitude for the beneficial influence Caesar had exerted on him, in preventing his farther complication in the conspiracy of Catiline. It is more probable, that he, also, desired the absence of his brilliant, versatile, and dangerous companion.

In the thirty-eighth year of his age, therefore, he set forth to that strange and inexplicable country, which has afforded the school to more great generals of other countries than any other portion of the world, while it has produced few, if any, in the first class, of its own— to Spain, the then El Dorado of the western continent, to whom her own gold and silver mines brought the same misery and ruin, which she herself for the like treasures wrought on the softer savages of a new and richer Spain beyond the utmost ocean.

It must be remembered that when, at this period, Caesar took his first military command, and set forth with as high ambition as ever fired a mortal breast, with as stern necessities to spur him to exertion as ever made a hero, himself an adventurer, possessing nothing but his sword, his debts, his iron will, and his consciousness of unrivalled talents, two others, but a few years older than himself—one destined to be his rival and antagonist through life unto death, who had started, but a distance before him, in the same race for honours and distinction—had reaped, already, such harvests of glory, and stood so high in the esteem and admiration of their countrymen, that any effort to equal, much more to surpass their glory, seemed but the vanity of vanities.

Lucius Licinius Lucullus, and Cneius Pompeius Strabo, already named the Great, had both served as consuls, had both commanded armies, won great battles, and acquired influence and honours, while Caesar was yet known, at the best, as a wild, dissolute, daring youth, of talents worthy better things, of energetic will and heaven-reaching courage; at worst, as a bad citizen, a factious magistrate, in short, all but a traitor.

Pompey, but six years older than himself, had commanded armies and set *batallia* in the field before he had changed the boy's *bulla* and *praetexta* for the robes of manhood; had filled the place of consul, before he was elected to his first civic office; and now, when he was setting forth on his first military mission, had reduced the pirates of Cilicia and the Isles, had conquered Mithridates, overrun Pontus, Paphlagonia, Colchis, Armenia, Syria, even Judaea; had besieged and stormed Jerusalem, had entered the temple of the Most High God; had carried the eagles of Rome in unabated triumph, from the Atlantic coasts of Spain and the boundaries of Numidia, to the shores of the Euxine and the vicinity of the Caspian sea, to the mighty waters of Euphrates, the clear rivulets of Damascus, and "Siloa's brook that flowed

Hard by the living oracle of God.

He had taken a thousand fortresses; reduced nine hundred cities. Eight hundred ships of war, two millions of captives, and twenty thousand *talents*, borne to the treasury, were his trophies; kings and the sons of kings followed his chariot wheels, in troops; and such a triumph as he carried up the sacred way, in the same year which saw Gains Caesar a poor *propraetor* in the farther Spain, Rome had not beheld in her seven centuries of glory.

Yet this was the man, to surpass and conquer whom he had girded up his loins, and gone forth in that self-confident resolve which ensures, if it is not, victory.

His purposes thus fully determined, he took his way to his seat of government, which he found in a state of absolute tranquillity, so far as subjection to Rome was concerned, and but slightly agitated internally by the feuds and forays which are the constant occupation and delight of all the Celtic races, with the blood of whom the early Spaniards would appear to have been largely tainted. This readily afforded a pretext and occasion to the magistrate, who entered his province with the almost avowed object of gaining wealth and military distinction at the expense of the miserable inhabitants, who, if he would have allowed them, were content to be the most tranquil and obedient of subjects.

It is on his march to this his first government, that the circumstances are said to have occurred, which gave origin to two most characteristic anecdotes, which, if not actually true, are so consonant with the spirit and temper of the man, that they should not be passed over—the one, that in passing through a small and miserable village among the mountains, he exclaimed: "I had rather be first in that hamlet, (*Plutarch*), than second in Rome,"—the other, that on seeing a statue of Alexander the Great in Cadiz, he shed tears at the thought, (*Suetonius 1*), that the Macedonian hero had conquered a world, done his work, and fallen asleep in everlasting glory, before he had won a single trophy.

A fault he was soon about to rectify; for scarcely had he reached his seat of government, before he grasped at the pretext given him by the *praedatory* excursions of a tribe of mountaineers, who inhabited the gorges of the Mons Herminius, (*Dio Cassius*), the Villuerca or Toledo mountains, lying between the Guadiana and the Tagus, and whom he commanded to abandon their hill dwellings and betake them to the plain, as if to put a stop to their forays, but in reality to force them to arms.

To anyone acquainted with the character of Highlanders, no more need be said. The infamous scheme was successful; the mountaineers sent their wives and families, and all the most precious of their possessions, beyond the Douro, into the northern parts of Portugal, and made a strenuous but ineffectual resistance to the robber Romans. The science and discipline of the *legions* easily prevailed; the Herminii were driven from point to point, until deserting the mainland, they betook themselves to certain islands on the coast, whither they fancied that Caesar, having no squadron at hand, would not care to pursue them. But they little knew with whom they had to deal. In the first heat of blood he caused rafts to be made, and embarked a detachment on such frail support to storm the islands; but the rafts grounding on a reef at some distance from the rocks on which were crowded the unhappy barbarians, with deep water between; the *legionaries* attempted to ford or swim the strait, and, their leader being carried away by the undertow and so drowned, all perished, either in the waves or by the missiles of the Spaniards, with the exception of one Publius Scaevius, who having lost his shield and received many wounds, swam back to the mainland, and so escaped with his life.

On the following day, Caesar sent for ships to Cadiz, and passing over his whole army into the island, reduced the mountaineers, who were starving, to unconditional surrender. Thence he navigated all the seas adjoining the western coast of Spain, so far as to Brigantium, the modern Corunna, where the unfortunate natives, never having seen a ship, were so terrified at their approach, with the white foam curling about their beaks and oar-blades as they came on with all sail set, that they were overthrown, and their town destroyed, without the slightest difficulty, as without the smallest provocation.

This cowardly, savage, and intrinsically piratical action having been performed by a man whom his flatterers have represented, and been followed by most historians in representing, as the most humane and kindest hearted of men, one constitutionally averse to the sight of cruelty or blood, was followed up, through his whole career, by similar acts of wanton barbarity and spoliation, wherever it suited his pecuniary or political exigencies to slaughter a few hundred thousand half-armed barbarians, in order to give the Romans a triumph and a holiday, or to plunder a few hundred towns, respecting neither public nor private property, in order to pay his debts, or propitiate his greedy soldiery.

In the present instance, he aimed at four different ends by this butchery of unoffending Roman subjects; for Farther Spain was, at this time, a regularly constituted province of the Republic, and its inhabitants were as much entitled to his protection in his quality of *propraetor* and governor, as were those of Latium, or the Sabine country to that of the senate and consuls. Those ends were the payment of his debts, the gratification of his *legionaries* by vast largesses, a triumph, and the consulship. Of these ends he gained three, for the taxes which he imposed on the wretched provincials were so exorbitant, that while he indulged the soldiery, almost beyond their desires, he enriched himself to such a degree, that on his return to Rome he found means to pay off a considerable portion of his debts, and to establish such a credit as lasted him until he had secured himself in a position which supplied all the ends of wealth without either moneys or credit; and, though he missed the triumph, obtained the grand object of his ambition, the consulship.

His return was no less illegal and unconstitutioual, than had been all his proceedings during his sojourn; for, neither waiting to be recalled himself, nor to hear that his successor was appointed, he hurried with indecent haste to Rome, and, remaining, according to custom, without the gates, as retaining his *imperium* and the standards and other insignia of his military rank, sought permission of the senate to enter the walls and canvass for the consulship as a private person, while soliciting a triumph at the same moment as *propraetor*.

The nobility, at the head of whom were Cicero and Cato, supported or impeded—according as one may view it—by the exalted name, extended popularity, honourable principles, but vacillating, unstable temper of the vain and mediocre Pompey, were now fully aroused to the real nature of the new candidate's views, purposes, and character. They knew him the vigorous, though uncommitted ally, comforter and suborner of all dangerous plotters against Rome—they knew him the bitterest maligner of the aristocracy, and the loudest inveigher against the corruptions and crimes, in which he himself, one of their number, far surpassed the most guilty of his order. They knew him the faitour, flatterer, pandar of the populace, the cold-blooded agitator of the democratic whirlwind, on which he hoped to ride to sublime dominion. But they understood not at all, either the depth and force of his wonderful genius, or the unity of purpose with which he persisted ever to his one object.

A triumph was the grand aim of the Roman general's ambition, before which all other honours paled their ineffectual light; it was the end for which men sought *praetorships*, provinces, consulships, command of armies; for which they "shunned delights and lived laborious days;" it was the one thing which Juvenal himself admits to be next to the beatitude of the gods, to be seen—

curribus altis

Extantem, et medio sublimem in pulvere circi
In tunica Jovis, et pictae Sarrana ferentem
Ex humeris aulaea togae, magnaeque coronae
Tantum orbem, quanto cervix non sufficit ulla?

It never occurred to one of them, therefore, that the pale, prematurely aged, ague-stricken *debauchee*, who had displayed so fitful and ill-regulated an ambition, would scornfully turn aside from the fruition of this greatest of Roman splendours, to embrace the mere chance of attaining a consulship, which most men regarded but as the first happy step by which to climb to the last, highest point—the triumph.

Therefore, after debating on his petition, while they held out to him fair hope that his claims to the triumph would be favourably considered, and in fact gave him secretly to understand that it would follow the *comitia*, they refused him permission to enter the city, in order to canvass for the consulship; since, they said, it was contrary to all precedent, and, if granted, would form a most dangerous example, that an officer, while in command of an army, having his banners displayed and his troops mustered before the gates, should enter the city in military array on a civic errand. Alas! the precedent had been set, and the example too well followed, within the last half century. Not only had generals entered the gates in their garb of war, but their armies had followed them with sword and fire-brand; and banners, more fatal than those of Hannibal to the life of Rome, had been seen pitched, where he had vainly sworn to pitch his own, in the midst of the Suburra.

So little did even Cato yet know Caesar, that he supposed "this weak invention of the enemy" would suffice to detain him, at least that year, from the office, they so much dreaded his attaining.

What then must have been their astonishment and dismay, when on the day previous to the elections, they saw him enter the gates, having laid aside the sword, the *sagum* and the crested casque, having sacrificed all aspirations after the tunic of Jove and the triumphal laurels, clad in the whitened *toga* of the candidate, and soliciting, as a citizen, the votes of his fellow-citizens for the first office in their gift, the chief-magistracy of the commonwealth.

What to others would have been the end, to him was the beginning. A consulship—a province—a war! Out of a war, armies, armies of his own creation, instruments of his own forging, weapons for his own purposes—conquests—Rome—the World! Such were the visions that already filled his soul—such the stakes for which he played in that canvass, losing the trump, to win, literally, with the king.

If the senate were alarmed when they discovered how their wretched stratagem had resulted, and saw that their dreaded enemy had boldly taken the initiative, what must have been their consternation and unmixed confusion, when they learned that the plausible, sweet-tongued, pliant, courteous demagogue had won away from them their surest and most trusted champion, the pillar of the aristocracy, the column of the constitution, the "*hominem severum et castum et integrum et gravem*," the very converse of the licentious, dazzling, daring spendthrift, with whom he was now connected by the closest ties of personal friendship, was soon to be connected by the closest ties of consanguinity.

Crassus and Pompeius, the wealthiest man and the most honoured man in Rome, had hitherto been at variance, favouring different parties, and jealous each of the other's advancement. To these, now united by his specious artifice, was added the ablest man, not in Rome only, but, at that day, in the world. The union of the three was irresistible as against Rome, and so the ablest of the senators felt and foresaw it. The union was cemented by the marriage of Pompey, who had lost his first wife Æmilia, to Julia, Caesar's daughter, grand-daughter of Cornelius Cinna. This was the first *triumvirate*. So the lampooners and wits of Rome named the cabal with laughter; as if they had been, indeed, three *triumvirs*, appointed to lead out colonies, or make partition of the conquered domains of the republic.

But the partition, which they did make, was of the republic itself; and it was with tears, not laughter, that the city marked the progress, the dissolution of that first *triumvirate*.

Caesar had played high, but won more high; his *praetorship* was bought by a debt of a million and a half of dollars—the consulship cost him less, his daughter's hand. History leaves us to conjecture, whether that was a sacrifice. In one thing, Julia was happy, she died childless, before her father wept Egyptian tears over the headless trunk of him whom he on that day called son.

It was in the year of Rome 695, and the fifty-ninth before the Christian era, that Caius Julius Caesar obtained the consulship, the prize for which he had been so many years contending through every species of intrigue, indirection and infamy. The means by which he obtained it, the transference of his beautiful daughter, Julia, from Servilius Caepio, to whom she had been promised as a bribe, and whose adherence against Bibulus the expectation of her hand had purchased, to Pompey, were not more creditable than the use which he made of the office when gained, or the other matrimonial arrangements by which this compact of sedition was ratified.

Servilius was to be recompensed for the loss of Julia by gaining Pompey's instead of Caesar's daughter—hearts were things of no more consideration then, than under the ancient regime of France—and Caesar himself, doubly widowed, once by death, once by divorce, espoused the daughter of Calpurnius Piso, consul with Gabinius, both tools of Pompey, for the ensuing year, and so bought their suffrages.

This triple alliance it was, which gave rise to Cato's famous expression, "that it was intolerable that provinces, armies and governments should be bartered for women, and that the empire itself should be offered as a bribe for their prostitution" (*Plutarch*)—but the saying injured Caesar nothing. For during his consulship he used his power so adroitly in conciliating all classes—the lower orders by enacting a new agrarian law, which provided lands in Campania for twenty thousand indigent citizens, without invading private property or infringing on vested rights, since the territories distributed were either wastes or public property—the equestrian class, whom he had offended in the matter of Catiline, by a remission of the third part of their rents as revenue farmers in Asia—and the better class of citizens by sundry salutary and equitable laws, which he procured to be passed, in regard to the method of balloting in the public elections, to the challenge of judges and jurors, to the increasing the penalties of persons convicted of treason, and to the placing farther restrictions on governors of provinces, so as to prevent extortion, facilitate justice, and compel restitution—that he procured from the popular assembly all that he most ardently desired.

This was a province for a term of years, (*Suetonius 1*)—amounting, in fact, almost to a tenure of it in perpetuity—with the command of an army, in the very jaws of the republic, overlooking the walls of Rome from the summits of the upper Appennines, commanding the city and overawing the senate, and assuring him of the future means, whenever the pear should be ripe, of conquering the one and subverting the other.

There was abroad at this time a rumour, that the Helvetii, the fierce mountaineers of the Alpine valleys of Switzerland, a people second only in valour, fierce barbarism, and the terrors they inspired, to the Teutons and Cimbri, whose destruction had given immortality to Marius, were moving among their misty pasturages in the Grisons, and in the dark pinewoods of the forest cantons, and preparing to emigrate with the whole population of four cantons into the Roman province of Gaul, or the countries of the Allobroges and Sequani, immediately adjoining it.

On this pretext, for nothing so surely excited alarm and induced extraordinary measures at Rome, as tidings of a Gallic tumult, at Caesar's instigation a motion was made by the *tribune*Vatinius that the people should set aside the Sempronian, (*Ferguson's Rom. Repub. II.-III.*,), laws of Caius Gracchus for the regulation of the provinces—by which the appointment of all officers was left to the senate alone, and was to be made annually before the election of the consuls—and that Caesar should be appointed to the provinces of Cisalpine Gaul and Illyria, for a term of five years, with an army of three *legions*. The senatorial party was at first greatly alarmed at this arbitrary stretch of power, and would fain have opposed it; but, seeing that it was useless to attempt to stem the tide, apprehending that farther powers would be granted to him by the populace, and either vainly hoping to involve him in foreign wars and conquests, and so keep him at a distance, or yet more vainly thinking to conciliate him to their party, ultimately increased the popular grant, by adding Gallia Comata, the barbarous, unshorn. Transalpine Gaul, to his province, and another legion to his army.

When Cato heard these tidings, he remarked that the "Senate had elected their king, and planted him with his body-guard in the capitol," (*Plutarch*), and it cannot be doubted that he spoke truly, and that Caesar—but probably Caesar alone, for he had no confidants, but only instruments in his designs—so regarded it.

It must be remembered that it had been the invariable, traditional policy of Rome, never to keep an armed force on foot, even of a hundred men, in time of peace, within the bounds of the republic—not a soldier could enter the gates as a soldier; and though their civic magistrates were, *exofficio*, their military leaders likewise, the double functions were so arranged, that when one commenced the other ceased. No sooner had the consul donned the *sagum* and carried his *imperium* beyond the gates and his fasces to the head of the *legions*, than he ceased in all respects to be a civil magistrate, nor could he re-enter the walls, even to visit his family or to address the senate, until he had resumed the *toga* and abdicated his military command.

The two nearest provinces, both of which involved the command of a standing army, were Cisalpine Gaul—that is to say, all the country from Lucca, the northern Appenines, and the little river Rubicon, now Fiumicino, to the Alps—and Sicily. The former was within easy striking distance, not exceeding one hundred and twenty miles, of the capitol itself; while the second lay at the extreme end of the whole peninsula, and was farther separated by the channel of Messina, narrow, it is true, and easy of transport, but still not to be traversed without a fleet.

The state, it must also be observed, had not even that indirect and constitutional force of household troops, burgher guards, or even organised police, whereon to rely on occasion of foreign invasion or domestic dissension; and this fact must have often struck every intelligent reader, on observing, that on the occurrence of the most dangerous seditions and tumults, the senate, or the consuls, armed by them with dictatorial power, had no means of putting down disturbance and re-establishing order, but by the arming of volunteers, the equestrian class and the younger senators, for the protection of the state.

Italy, it is true, was the mother and nurse of the *legions*, but since war had been long banished from her shores, she was no longer a school for arms, or an exercise ground for the formation of soldiers. In the early ages of the republic, before the men were paid, when the whole army was in fact the whole body of the landholders, and they a feudal agricultural militia, every citizen was a soldier, and the term of the enlistment was the duration of the campaign; but as military science advanced, and discipline, skill, and the habit of acting together, were found entirely to supersede bravery, strength, and patriotism, soldiership became a profession, soldiers a class, and service regular.

Legions were raised for terms of years—we find many mentioned in the later times of Rome who had served ten years and upward in succession; the *legions*, disgraced at Cannae in 216 B. C. were the same which under Scipio conquered at Zama, after a lapse of fourteen years; and the eleventh legion in Caesar's Gallic campaigns was put on active duty, out of the regular routine of service, because it was considered yet inferior in discipline, though it had been for eight years constantly in the field before an enemy.

Macedonia, Numidia, Spain and Gaul had been for many years past the school both for soldiers and officers; and the consequence of these changes in the art of war, as well as of the recent alteration in the constitution of the legions, by which the camp was made the home and country of the proletarian or barbarian soldier, was to bring about a state of things similar to that existing in modern Europe; where one regiment of trained soldiers is equal to five thousand undrilled clowns, and where a country, however populous or however brave its inhabitants by nature, if it have no regular disciplined troops, is delivered over, literally bound hand and foot, to the first invader who passes its frontier with an army of twenty thousand veterans.

The difference was no smaller between the legionary and the ordinary citizen of Rome; and the officer commanding half a dozen *legions*, perfect in the practice of war, and devoted to his person, within a hundred or two miles of the gates, was as much master of Rome as if she had named him her king.

For some time after the appointment of Caesar to this extraordinary command, though he had quitted Rome, raised his forces, and thus disqualified himself from taking any share in civil affairs, he yet tarried in the suburbs to observe the proceedings instituted against Cicero by the tribune Clodius, to which both he and Pompey were privy, and which terminated in the exile of that consistent patriot and virtuous citizen.

In the opening, however, of the year 58, B. C, he proceeded to his province, where he immediately found that the report, concerning the danger from the Helvetii, was by no means exaggerated, and that the swarms of those bold and hardy barbarians were already in motion.

And here, in fact, commences that long series of splendid campaigns, of irresistible progresses in the teeth of almost insuperable difficulties, of enterprises which would have been pronounced absurd, had not success proved their soundness, of conquests won by deluges of innocent and unnecessary blood, of victorious wars uncheckered by a single defeat, which carried him to the summit of his aspirations, a throne, and thence, as a consequence, to a bloody and unhonoured grave.

Suetonius says:

> During these nine years, these for the most part were his actions. He reduced all Gallia within the Alps and Pyrenees, the Cevennes, the Rhine, and the Rhone, allied and friendly nations alone excepted, a circumference of twice three hundred miles, into the form of a Roman province, and exacted from it, annually, in the form of a tribute, four hundred millions of Roman money. Having attacked the Germans who dwell east of the Rhine, by means of a bridge, the first Roman who crossed

that river, he inflicted on them terrible defeats. He invaded the Britons, a people previously unknown, and having overcome them, received moneys and hostages at their hands. In the course of these signal successes he incurred but three losses: the destruction of his fleet by a storm on the coasts of Britain; the defeat of a *legion* entirely cut off at Gergovia, in Gaul; and the loss in Germany of his lieutenants, Auruneuleius and Titurius, who were drawn into an ambush, surrounded and put to the sword.

In a sketch of the nature of the present work, it is of course impossible to give more than a synopsis of these brilliant and masterly campaigns; for to follow every incident, and describe in detail every battle, siege, march, and operation of each—so full are they of incidents—would require a history in itself, as is sufficiently evident from the fact that his own commentaries occupy, in themselves alone, five hundred pages. Nor indeed do they, in my opinion, merit such a scrutiny; for, as I view it, Caesar's great merit, as a general, lies in the comprehensiveness, the vastness, the audacity of his gigantic schemes, the irresistible energy and impetus of his execution, and the never-failing success, which crowned his every enterprise—not in the detail or manner of his operations.

Nothing deterred him, nothing caused him to hesitate, nothing stopped him, when he was once resolved. Distance and time seemed to be annihilated by the gigantic strides with which he scaled mountains, bridged unfathomed rivers, traversed unexplored forests, pathless morasses, stormy oceans. The deepest snows of the most horrid winters, the scorching heat of the most inclement summers, detracted nothing from the certainty, the celerity of his operations. We find him in a single campaign traversing and re-traversing the length and breadth of Gaul; annihilating German hordes in the marshy woodlands and aguish morasses of the Scheldt and Waal; thunder-striking the rebellious tribes of Brittany and the Norman shores; desolating the rich valleys of Auvergne and Languedoc, and hunting the painted Britons to their fastnesses beyond the silver winding Thames, amid the forests of Kent and the fens of Cambridgeshire and Ely.

Nothing so appalled his enemies, nothing so roused his soldiers to a belief that he and they were invincible, as this apparent ubiquity. No sooner did a savage tribe revolt from his hardly endured dominion, among Druid-haunted oaks or blasted heaths, unknown and almost inaccessible, than, as if the birds of the air or the viewless winds had carried him the tidings of their half-formed insurrection, the Roman and his *cohorts* were upon them. No sooner was a *legion* hemmed in and beset in some isolated forest-girdled camp, hopeless of relief, and miles away from Caesar and his unexpected succours, than his trumpets woke the echoes of the wilderness, and the leaguer was raised almost as soon as commenced, and the besiegers scattered, as if by lightning.

Never, except the greatest of all soldiers, did any leader so utterly set at nought all rules, all maxims, all *formulae*; so thoroughly overcome all obstacles of nature, climate, ground, space, and time. With him to will was to execute; to undertake was to succeed.

Means appeared to make themselves to his hands, so inexhaustible were his resources. In his campaigns he almost realized the reply of the French minister to his unhappy mistress; "If it be difficult, it shall be done; if impossible, it is done already." No idea of failure ever seems to have entered his mind—no enormity of carnage, no extremity of human misery, to have formed an item in his calculations.

To succeed, if success could be had only by extermination; to succeed by fraud, by treachery, by slaughter; to succeed in the despite of honour, honesty, religion, mercy, all bonds, human or divine; only to succeed was his rule in policy and in warfare.

Curio, in after days to Cicero, said:

> Think not, that his not being cruel is a consequence of will or disposition. He is clement only because he believes clemency to be popular; let him once lose the desire to court the popular favour, he shall be as cruel as the bloodiest.

Two millions of men were slaughtered in battle, massacred in their sacked villages, butchered as gladiators, after being made prisoners, in the arena; whole detachments were slaughtered in cold blood, after surrender; whole tribes were surrounded and put to the sword, unsuspicious, during the existence of undenounced armistices; the entire population of a large city, which surrendered at discretion, were maimed by the amputation of their right arms, to deter others from the like crime of defending their homes and hearthstones against a merciless and unprovoked invader.

And this, in Caesar, is called mercy. Because he did not massacre his political enemies, like Sylla and Marius, by wholesale proscription; or, like that cold-blooded butcher, his successor, the august Octavius, by the prostituted axe of justice, the Romans wondered at his mercy, and historians have been found from his own time to the present day, to harp upon the parrot strain, celebrating, even to loathing and disgust, the clemency of Caesar.

The same disgusting process has been repeated, even more outrageously, in the case of the elder Napoleon, concerning whom and whose character, as for cruelty or mercy, the questions of the Duke of Enghien's execution, the massacre of the Arnaouts at Acre, and the poisoning of the plague patients at Jaffa, have been argued *ad nauseam;* as if the blood of a few isolated individuals could form an item in the account of one, who sent seven millions of immortal souls before the judgment seat, to gratify his own inordinate ambition.

The blood of Gaul, of Germany, of Britain, was necessary to Caesar, as the purchase money wherewith to buy the throne of imperial Rome, and the wreath of perpetual laurels; and he was profuse of it, as he was of the gold of others.

The blood of Romans was not necessary to him, perhaps the reverse, since it was his policy to be called the Clement Caesar, but had he deemed it needful to his purpose, the kennels of Rome would have run with as red a tide as drained from the morasses of Hainault into the polluted channels of the Sambre and the Meuse.

It is of this man that M. Michelet writes, in his fantastic *History of the Republic:*

> In good and in evil Caesar was the man of humanity!

In the name of all that is just and holy, what then is cruelty?

A brief sketch of the nine wonderful campaigns of Gaul will show the characteristics which I have mentioned, as the peculiar excellencies of Caesar's system of war.

Ferguson has admirably hit off, in his fine and philosophical History of the Roman Republic, one of the peculiar points in this extraordinary man's almost unrivalled genius, in the following sentence:—

> Caesar's own disposition of his forces, as has been already mentioned, in assigning what appeared to have been the reason of his conduct, had been made with the greatest ability; and the more, that they gave him the appearance of a person acting without design, and suddenly forced to the measures which he embraced. In talking of ordinary men, we may err in imputing too much to design and concert, but with regard to Caesar, the mistake to be feared, is not perceiving the whole extent of his foresight or plan.

So true is this remark, that it were dangerous even to assume that Caesar at times pushed his extreme audacity to the length of unauthorized rashness, and that some of his operations were more showy than sound, and were consequently not only fruitful of the greatest risks to his army, but deficient of immediate and perceptible results—for it is possible that these seemingly rash and inexplicable enterprises were, in truth, the result of deep calculations, and were planned to produce ends which we cannot now easily discover, and which may have been effected by movements apparently inconsequential.

In warfare against barbarians, it is no inconsiderable point of the game to cause them to believe in the omnipotence, infallibility, and invincibility of the civilized soldier. To make them consider nothing too great for his audacity, too difficult for his enterprise, impossible to his genius. And it may be that some of his wildest and most dazzling exploits, such as his bridging the arrowy Rhine, and carrying his eagles across the dark and misty channel of the Morini, to swoop upon the sacredest and most sequestered haunts of Druidism, had thus an effect, superior to what appear their results, in quenching the hearts and palsying the hands of the fierce savages.

Still one must say, that not a few of his daring strokes appear to have been calculated rather for theatrical effect, and intended to dazzle the imagination, catch the applause, and fire the national spirits of the plebeians in the Suburra, than to facilitate the prosecution of the war, or bring it to a close. In this connexion another point may be insisted on with justice, that to conclude the war too speedily was neither his policy nor his design. Gaul was to him as a preserve to a sportsman, and the Gauls his pheasants, to be killed off, as the exigencies of the market and the state of demand at Rome might require. But the warlike race itself was to be sedulously maintained, and the war itself fostered," for the purpose of making perfect soldiers, to whom it was a school of discipline, valour, and endurance, of keeping them ever ready in arms, ever dependent on their general, ever in exercise, employment, and good humour, until the moment and the opportunity should arrive for launching them into a mightier conflict and for a grander prize.

Still one must admit, that as a general he was more showy than safe; that the risks he ran were often immense, and that at times, and that not seldom, he was forced, as a forlorn hope, to extricate himself from difficulties seemingly insuperable, by delivering battles at the last disadvantage, which he gained only by the desperate bravery and unflinching devotion of his soldiery.

Although he never actually lost a battle, in which he commanded in person, no general ever was compelled so often to fight hand to hand in the ranks as a private, ever restored so many half-lost combats, or won so many victories, when defeat seemed certain. His raising the siege of Gergovia in his seventh campaign, and all his subsequent operations between the Allier and Saone, and the mountains of Auvergne were so dangerous and disastrous as to have nearly occasioned the annihilation of his army, which was relieved only by the arrival of a reinforcement of Germans, whose headlong valour won a hard battle and restored the campaign.

For the rest, the men against whom he fought were undisciplined barbarians; and, though the bravest, fiercest, and most fiery of men in temper and spirits, the hardiest in habit, and the strongest and largest in stature and in limb—so much so that they derided the *legionaries* as *homines pusilli*, dwarfs and weaklings—they knew nothing of war as an art; were incapable of combined movements or manoeuvres; and were, moreover, as all savage armies are, Celtic savages especially, liable to sudden panics, by which all power of systematic resistance is lost, when indiscriminate carnage and absolute rout follows the first motion toward retreat.

As to generals, in his Gallic campaigns, Caesar never met anything worthy of the name, the Ariovisti, Vercingetoriges and Divitiaci were mere chiefs and leaders, whose sole ideas of a general's duty were to be foremost in attack and last in retreat, and whose utmost strategy was limited to the warfare of ambushes and sudden unexpected attacks, which are the ordinary operations of all savages, particularly those of forest or mountain regions.

Yet even against these he prevailed almost invariably by sheer force, by the superior fighting qualities of the legions, their singular manageableness under arms, and their admirable armature and equipment, rather than by any peculiar talent of his own, or by any operations which secured victory as the necessary consequence of the manoeuvre.

Unequalled in his disposition and managery of vast bodies of forces, scattered, apparently unconnected, but really supporting each the other, over wide tracts of country, admirable at knowing when and where to deliver his attacks, rapid as lightning in the development and execution of his projects, terrible as the thunder-stroke in following up and crushing the last spark of life out of a defeated and discomfited enemy, prodigious in resources, a giant in his conceptions—for in all these dazzling and decisive qualities he fully equalled the great Napoleon—in one essential point he fell far behind not him alone, bat scores, nay hundreds of far inferior captains.

As a manoeuvring general I cannot rate him even as a second-class commander. I do not know a single action which he fought either against barbarians with Romans, or against Romans with barbarians—for of these were the *legions* constituted with which he conquered Pompey and his successors—in which he prevailed by any movement, or system of operations, ensuring or even facilitating success. In his operations at Dyrrachium he was completely outmanoeuvred, outgeneralled, beaten, and might have been destroyed, by Pompey, had that officer shown as much ability in completing as he had exerted in opening the battle. In the subsequent operations through Thessaly and Macedonia, Pompey had by far the best of him in strategy; as with all his efforts Caesar entirely failed to force him to give battle, and, could the petulant patrician army of the republican general have been restrained from fighting, the campaign, and probably the war, would have terminated in favour of the commonwealth. Battle once joined on fair ground, the admirable quality of Caesar's *legions*, combining the vigour of bone, boundless contempt of life, and fierce impetuosity of barbarians, with the iron discipline and perfect tactics of Roman veterans, rendered the victory easy and certain.

Yet Pompey himself had no claim to rank, nor ever has been ranked as more than a second, or perhaps third, rate commander; and his greatly lauded and greatly exaggerated victories in the east, were rightly designated by Cato, his own friend and partisan, as victories won by men over women.

At Ruspina, in Numidia, he was surprised and overreached, and extricated himself by the superiority of his *cohorts* over the light troops and Numidians of Labienus and Petreius. From the siege of Uzita he was forced to make a perilous retreat; in the battle of Thapsus the victory was carried by an impetuous onslaught of the *legions*, not only without orders, but literally contrary to them, though Caesar followed it up and crushed the relics of the fight with his usual vigour and determination. In the Battle of Munda, his last and crowning victory, so far was he from owing his success to his conduct as an officer, that he was fighting as a private *legionary*, with sword and buckler in the ranks, when a mere accident turned the fortune of the day, and converted what was almost a defeat into a complete victory.

In his powers of forming troops, both as to their physique and their morale, he has no superior, ancient or modern. In fair fight his men were never beaten by any superiority of numbers, and their confidence in their chief was so boundless, that when he was at their head they held themselves invincible, and victory over an enemy certain. He was bounteous to them in the extreme, affable and familiar, knowing his veterans by name, and having the Napoleon's faculty of making them rush upon death for a word of applause, dearer than any decoration or reward. He marched on foot, at their head, through deep snows and driving rains; rode on horseback through the scorching noonday heat, while his secretaries were carried in litters, writing letters from his dictation, in four or five different languages at once; swam the most rapid rivers, braved every peril, endured every hardship, in defiance of the terrible disease of epilepsy to which he was constitutionally subject, and of a frame naturally delicate, and shaken by excesses and debauchery.

Had he been equal in his method of handling soldiers in the field, to himself, in forming them for their profession, in conceiving campaigns, and carrying all before him by the impetuous rush of his energetic genius, he would have been the greatest general the world has ever seen. But he was not so; and in my opinion, notwithstanding his infinite and over-mastering genius, which, like that of Napoleon, was not sublime in one line, but supreme in all, turning everything which he touched into gold, must rank far below such soldiers as Epaminondas, Xenophon, Alexander, Hannibal, or of moderns— Frederick the Great, Marlborough, Turenne, Wellington, or greatest, though last. Napoleon.

On the twenty-fifth of March, of the year of Rome 696, B. C. 58, learning that the Helvetii had broken up[1] from their own country, burning their towns and villages, and had set out on their migratory expedition, three hundred and fifty-eight thousand souls in all, of whom ninety-two thousand were warriors, or men capable of bearing arms, he set forth to the scene of war. This vast multitude, on Caesar's arrival at Geneva, were pouring down toward that town with the intention of passing by the defiles, between the Jura and the Vuache, into Gaul, journeying down the Rhone, in the direction of Lyons and the Roman province. This he determined to prevent, and having gained some time necessary for bringing up his troops, by pretended negotiations, broke down the bridges, fortified the banks of the Rhone and the mountain passes with works, consisting of a wall sixteen feet in height, and a corresponding ditch, nineteen miles m length, from the lake to the cliffs of the Jura, and then to the request of the Helvetii, to be allowed a free passage on condition of abstaining from all hostilities toward the Romans or their allies, he returned a positive refusal, accompanied by a peremptory command, that they should return to their own cantons, and disturb the peace of the world no longer.

This done, he left the lines in charge of Labienus, with the only legion then in Gaul, and, himself hurrying into Italy, levied two new *legions*, and brought up three others of veterans, which were lying in winter-quarters at Aquileia, under the Carnian Alps. This force he led in seven days from Ocelo, in the Cisalpine province, across the Pennine Alps, probably by the pass of Traversette, under the Monte Viso, not without some hard fighting, into the country of the Allobroges, and thence to Geneva, where he found that the enemy not daring to attack his lines, had fallen back along the lake, and turning the Jura by its eastern extremity and the banks of the Rhine, had entered France, and were marching into the heart of the country, by the valley of the Saone, threatening the Sequani and Ædui, tribes in the neighbourhood of Doubs and Chalons, who were allies of Rome, and implored her aid against these formidable armies.

On receiving the deputies of these cantons, Caesar determined to pursue the enemy, which he did with his usual energy and speed, and overtook them as they were in the act of passing the broad and deep but sluggish stream of the Saone. Three of the four cantons into which the whole people of the Helvetii were divided, had crossed over; but the Tigurini, supposed to be the men of Zurich, yet lingered on the hither bank. This was the canton which in the commencement of the Cimbric and Teutonic campaign had slain the consul Cassius and sent his army under the yoke. On these sallying from his camp shortly after midnight, he fell with incredible fury at the head of three *legions*, and put the most of them to the sword, a few miserable relics only escaping into the neighbouring forests.

This done he bridged the Saone in a single day, which struck more terror into the minds of the Helvetii than the slaughter of their brethren, for they had passed twenty days in crossing a river which he passed in less than as many hours; so that they attempted to treat; but as Caesar would hear of no terms short of their return to Switzerland, they continued their march, and he his pursuit toward the town of

---

1. This and all the following details are from *Caesar de Bello Gallico, X, et seq. Dio Cassius, XXXVIII. 31 et seq. Plutarch vit. Caesaris,*

Autun. Once his cavalry, which was entirely composed of Gauls under Roman officers, pressing too hardly upon their rear, they halted, and repulsed them with considerable loss, which emboldened them so much that they resolved to give battle. Caesar, however, having sent Labienus to turn them, and occupy a hill in their rear, they took the alarm, decamped, and pursued their march before the attack could be commenced; but two days after, the *legions* having turned off from the direct line of pursuit toward Autun for convenience of foraging, the Helvetii learning the movement from some Gaulish deserters, fancied that Caesar was retreating, and turning on their traces attacked him furiously.

The battle was long and obstinate, and once the Boii and Tulingi, some fifteen thousand strong, having wheeled round a hillock, and fallen on the flank of the legions, the issue was doubtful, but discipline and Roman valour prevailed; and after fighting from one in the afternoon until nightfall, victory declared itself for Caesar. Out of all that great host, one hundred and thirty thousand persons only escaped, and by forced marches gained four days on the Romans, who were compelled to halt three days to care for their wounded and bury their dead.

On the fourth day, as Caesar was breaking up his camp, messengers came from the Helvetii, offering to surrender, for that they were starving; on which they were commanded to give hostages, restore all the fugitive slaves who had joined them, lay down their arms and await the general's pleasure. All complied except six thousand men of the canton Verbigenus, who fled by night, but being pursued by the Roman cavalry, were brought back and treated as enemies—in other words, cut to pieces. So much for the clemency of Caesar.

The remainder, Helvetii, Latobriges, and Tulingi, were compelled to return to their own cantons among the mountains, and to rebuild their towns and villages which they had burned; but as they had consumed all their grain, the Allobroges, or people of Savoy, were ordered to supply them with food, and seed corn for the ensuing season. The Boii only, being men of surpassing valour, were allowed, at the request of the Ædui, to remain in that country, and were incorporated in the clan.

So soon as this conflict had decided the question as to the Helvetic settlement in Gaul, the Sequani and Ædui asked permission of Caesar to hold a general assembly of their allies and all the Gaulish tribes and clans in general, at his headquarters; when it speedily appeared that these unfortunate people, liberated by the Roman victory from one fearful impending calamity, had made up their mind to implore assistance against another enemy more dangerous, because already naturalized and allocated in the land.

Some years before, it would appear, that being hard pressed in a local war with their neighbors the Ædui, the Sequani and Arverni—the latter inhabitants of the beautiful districts of Auvergne—they had invited the Germans to their aid, fifteen thousand of whom had crossed the Rhine, with their chief, Ariovistus. That war ended, the Germans not only remained in the country, grievously oppressing their late allies, and forcing them to give up to them a third part of all their lands, but had been continually calling reinforcements from beyond the Rhine, until they now numbered one hundred and twenty thousand men, instead of the fifteen thousand who had first issued from the dark gorges and shadowy dingles of the black forest. Thus augmented in numbers, their demands augmenting in like ratio, they threatened all Gaul with ruinous occupation, and against these, the yet more rugged barbarians of the north, the semi-civilised Gauls, on the frontier of the province, claimed the aid of Italian skill and prowess.

Than this Caesar desired nothing better, for he secured at once a legitimate cause of war, and allies on whom to base his operations. Accordingly deputies were sent to Ariovistus, demanding that he should render himself to Caesar's headquarters, where to hold a solemn conference. But the hardy barbarian replied that he had no occasion to confer with Caesar, but that if Caesar wished to talk with him, he might come and find him.

> That he would neither trust himself alone in the camp of the Romans, nor be at the trouble of raising an army to protect himself.

On receiving this reply, Caesar collected grain and forage sufficient for the enterprise, and marched with extreme rapidity to Besançon, a strong and well fortified place, nearly surrounded by a semicircular reach of the River Doubs, of which he had information that the German intended to possess himself. Here the army first learned that they were to be directed against the Germans, and such a panic fell upon the whole army, that wills were commonly made throughout the camp; and the men were so much dispirited, that Caesar found it necessary to harangue the troops in very severe terms, and state his determination, if all else should desert him, to march, himself, against the enemy with the tenth *legion*, alone. Henceforth it is not difficult to understand why the *tenth* legion loved Caesar, and dared and did all things to deserve and retain his good opinion. The spirits of the soldiers thus restored, taking with him the Druid Divitiacus as a guide; Caesar advanced, till he was informed by his scouts that Ariovistus lay within four and twenty miles, when he halted, and fortified his camp. The German now proposed a conference, both parties to be attended by their cavalry, but neither to bring any footmen.

Caesar accepted the proposal, but having no Roman horse, and not choosing to trust himself to the guardianship of the Gaulish cavalry, mounted the tenth *legion* on the troop horses of the Æduan contingent, by which he still further won their affections, repaired to the place appointed for the interview, which was a knoll in the centre of an extensive plain.

The conference had of course no results, and was broken off by indications of treachery on the part of the German horse, who began to ride up in great force to the knoll, and throw their darts, whereupon Caesar declined farther parley, and returned to his camp amid the indignation of his soldiers, who clamored to be led against the treacherous enemy. A second request of the king that deputies should be sent to arrange a truce with him, was met by the dispatch of Caius Valerius Procillus and Marcus Mellius, both bound to the German by ties of the closest hospitality, both of whom he affected to consider spies, and threw them into chains.

Nothing now was left but to prepare for battle. On the second day Ariovistus advanced to within six miles of Caesar's camp, fortified himself, and sat down at the foot of a strong mountain; the day following he marched past Caesar's entrenched camp, and posted himself two miles in his rear, in a strong position, with a view to cut off his supplies of grain as they came up from the Ædui, and to straiten him for the want of provisions. Caesar instantly drew out his *legions*, formed his lines, and offered battle; but Ariovistus would not fight, but kept his infantry within their entrenchments, and skirmished daily with his horse. From some captives Caesar learned that the German women had forbidden them to fight, on pain of defeat, until the full of the moon, when they promised victory; whereupon he determined to anticipate that day, so as to deprive them of the aid and encouragement of their national superstition.

By dividing his forces and palisading a second camp in the rear of the Germans, as if to secure his allies, he drew them to risk an attack, which being bloodily repulsed, he drew out all his force, formed it in the plain, and advanced, as if to storm the camp of Ariovistus, when the fierce barbarian made *a sortie en masse*, and delivered battle in the open ground, having his rear blockaded with his *wains* and cars, both as a fortification and as a prevention against flight. The battle was obstinate and fierce. On the right wing, where Caesar led in person, the *legions* cast away their *pila*; went in, hand to hand, with sword and buckler, with a rush that carried all before it, and their superiority at those weapons secured and fixed the advantage. On the left wing, however, the numbers of the enemy told with fearful effect, and the action laboured and went doubtfully, until young Publius Crassus, who commanded the horse, galloped like lightning to the rear, brought up the reserves of the *triarii*, restored the fight, and turned it into a complete victory.

The enemy were slaughtered by the horse without mercy or relaxation, till the Rhine, fifty miles distant, put a stop to the pursuit but not to the carnage, for a few only of the strongest could swim across the violent river, and fewer yet found boats in which to pass it. Of these, one was Ariovistus; all the rest perished by the sword, women and children not less than armed warriors. Two wives of the king were slaughtered in the chase, one of his daughters likewise—the other, less fortunate, was taken. The captive deputies were recovered, and nothing marred the rejoicings for this great victory.

On the news of this victory the Suevi and Ubii, two fierce Germanic tribes who had marched down to the Rhine, in readiness to pass it, and join their countrymen, fell back into their forests. Leaving his army in winter quarters, near the Saone, under Labienus, Caesar returned into his province of hither Gaul, to hold the assemblies and preside over its civic government. He had finished two great wars in one, his first, campaign, had taken the lives of three hundred and forty-eight thousand human beings, who had done no wrong to himself or his country, and might have claimed a triumph, but his thirst was not yet half slaked, either for blood or glory.

In the ensuing spring, B. C. 57, he was aroused, at the very opening of the season, by a report that the Belgae, reputed to be the hardiest and bravest race in Gaul, of distinct blood from the purely Celtic tribes, who inhabited all the north-east of France and the Netherlands, including Holland and Alsacia, from the Rhine to the Saone and Seine, and from the Marne to the British channel and the North sea, were combined in a general league against the Romans, whose continued occupation of Gaul disturbed them, and whose intentions they began to suspect.

Again an occasion had made itself to his hands, and as if he had been already a crowned head instead of the responsible magistrate of a republic, setting at nought the ordinance of the senate, which limited the establishment of his province to five *legions*, having already six in winter-quarters on the Saone, he at once raised two more, one entirely of Celtic Gauls of the hither province, which received the title of Alauda, or the *legion* of the lark, from a tuft of plumes resembling the crest of that bird which they wore in their casques. This *legion*, which ultimately became one of the most distinguished in the service, he sent on, with the other new levies, to the seat of war, under Quintus Pedius, one of his lieutenants, or as we should rank them, generals of division, while so soon as the crops were green and ready to supply forage, he followed and joined the army.

Advancing into the enemy's country, he soon learned that the confederates amounted to two hundred and fifty-eight thousand men, to whom he could oppose eight *legions*, beside Cretan, Barbaric, and Numidian light troops, with the large contingents of cavalry furnished by the Gaulish allies. Allying himself to the Remi, whose country is in the neighbourhood of Rheims, lying between the Aisne and Vesle, the confluence of which forms the Oise, he sent a strong division of the Æduans into the Beauvoisis to plunder the country and make a diversion, while after garrisoning Bibrax, a city of the Remi, with his light troops and foreign archery, so as to render it proof to any *coup de main*, he pitched his camp in a very strong position, having his left covered by the Aisne, having a bridge defended by a strong *tête de pont*, in which he posted Quintus Titurius Sabinus, another of his lieutenants, with six *cohorts*. The other flank of his camp rested on a hill, defended with strong field works, from either extremity of which he cut two deep, diverging fosses, with a redoubt at the outer extremity of each, well garrisoned with artillery, to cover his flanks, apprehending that the enemy, with their vast superiority of force, might endeavour to turn him.

Having attempted Bibrax and sustained a sharp repulse, the Belgae now advanced in force, and sat down at about two miles from Caesar's camp, their bivouac, as indicated by their line of fires, extending over a front of above eight miles. As soon as it was light, Caesar, leaving two *legions* in his entrenched camps, and leading out the rest, offered battle, both his flanks being covered by his ditches and redoubts. A small swamp, however, lay between the two positions, and neither party chose to attempt it, being aware that they should be attacked to disadvantage in the broken ground of the morass; so that after a smart cavalry action, in which the Romans had some advantage, both parties retired to the camps. On the following day the Belgae passing the Roman camp, probably by the right, attempted to ford the river, in order to attack the *tête de pont* defended by Titurius in reverse, and to take the Roman lines in the rear.

So soon as this movement was developed, Caesar passed all his cavalry, light-armed Numidians, archery and slingers, over the bridge to the aid of his lieutenant, and these falling strenuously on the enemy while entangled in the fords, slew vast numbers of them, surrounded and cut off those who had already passed with the cavalry, and drove back the rest, who strove audaciously to march over the bodies of their own dead, which bridged the river, by sustained volleys of their admirable missiles.

Foiled in their attempt on the city of Bibrax, and defeated in the fords of the Aisne, the Belgae now lost heart, and decamped by night, but with so much noise and confusion, that Caesar apprehending an ambuscade, declined the attack, and kept his men on hand. On the following morning, however, finding that the camps were really vacated, he launched all his cavalry under Quintus Pedius and Aurunculeius Cotta, with three *legions* in reserve, commanded by Titus Labienus. These hewed down and trampled under foot thousands and thousands of the fugitives straggling and mobbed together, without resistance, before they reached the solid and compact rear guard, which stood firm and fought till it was wholly cut to pieces; those in the van flying headlong as they heard the tumult, and leaving their comrades to their fate.

After prodigious slaughter the pursuers returned to the camp, and on the next day giving the enemy no time to rally or recover from their panic, Caesar entered the country of the Suessones, and besieged their capital, Noviodunum, now Soissons, with such vigour, that terrified at the effect of the Roman engines, they surrendered at discretion, and were spared on the intercession of their neighbours the Remi. Thence he penetrated the Beauvoisis, and received its submission; but, not content with such partial success, and resolute to subdue the whole of this obdurate race, he forced his way, axe in hand, felling the dense woods, and causewaying the morasses, through the vast virgin forests to the river Sabis, now the Sambre, beyond which he learned that the

Nervii, the fiercest and hardiest of all the Belgic family, were in arms with the Veromandui and Atrebates, and prepared to give battle.

These barbarians had learned, it appears, from deserters, that the march of the Roman armies was conducted by columns of *legions*, a great space being left between the columns, which was occupied by the baggage, and it was their plan of battle to let the first *legion* pass their ambush, fall on it and destroy it while the bulk of the army was yet at a distance, and to overpower the rest in detail as they came, one by one, into action. Casually, however, Caesar had altered his order of march, in consequence of the vicinity of the enemy; and the van consisted of six entire *legions*, with all the light troops and horse, then the baggage of the whole army, and the two *legions* last levied in the rear, as a reserve and baggage guard. This disposition, though made in ignorance of the enemy's plan, saved the army; but the action which ensued was the best contested that had yet occurred in Gaul, and the legions were all but defeated.

On reaching the Sambre the enemy's horse made some demonstrations of attack, no infantry showing themselves, but were speedily dispersed by the archery and slingers, supported by the cavalry, who charged across the river and drove the Nervii into the cover of the woods. Thereupon the six *legions* laid aside their arms, and began to fortify their camp, undisturbed, and not imagining the enemy to be in the vicinity, so perfect was the solitude and silence of the forests. But no sooner did the first baggage wagons appear, which was the moment agreed on by the Gauls, than the enemy were everywhere at once, as if by magic. The woods, the river, the hills were full of them, and at the same time they were hand to hand with the men, before they could get on their helmets or uncase their shields, much less effect any formation. For a time all was desperate confusion, but the men and the officers all knew their duty, and, without waiting for Caesar's orders, fell in as best they might, fighting all the while hand to hand, and at length got into array of battle.

On the left wing the ninth and tenth *legions*, who were the first to form, received the Atrebates with such a hurtling volley of their *pila*, that they broke them, and charging home with their swords, drove them across the river, where they rallied and fought hard, only to be again routed. In another part of the field, for the *legions*, as surprised, necessarily fought unconnectedly, and without concert, the eleventh and eighth beat the Veromandui, who were opposed to them, and drove them into the bed of the river from the upper ground, where there was again severe fighting. But the advance of the ninth and tenth had uncovered the left of the centre and the half-fortified camp, in defence of which fought the twelfth and seventh; and on these fell the brunt of the attack, for the Nervii fell upon them in solid column, front and flank at once, led by their king, Boduognatus, and they were outnumbered and almost deforced from their ground.

At the same moment, the cavalry and light troops returning from their easy victory of the enemy's horse, and all the camp followers and horse boys, who had gone out from the rear of the camp to plunder, fell unexpectedly into the main body of the Gauls, and were so totally routed and dispersed, that the auxiliary mounted troops from Treves, who stood well for courage and conduct, fled, without drawing bridle, at speed to their own country, some fifty miles distant, and reported that the Roman Army was annihilated. And in fact little was wanting to make it so. The fourth *cohort* of the twelfth had lost all its *centurions*, its standard-bearer and its eagle; scarcely an officer in the whole *legion* but was killed or wounded, and the men were dropping away from the rear singly or in knots, when Caesar coming up, snatched a shield from one of the privates, and rushing to the front, ordered the ranks to open and charge hand to hand with sword and buckler.

The seventh *legion* being equally pressed and reduced in numbers, he commanded the tribunes to form it into one body with the twelfth, and to advance. The battle was thus somewhat restored, but things looked ill until the two *legions* of the baggage guard, hearing the din of conflict, were brought up at double quick time and carried into action gallantly by their officers, while Titus Labienus perceiving, from the higher ground on the left to which he had chased the Atrebates, how things went in the centre, detached the tenth *legion* to its succour. That was the crisis of the day. The tide was turned, and the cavalry, rallying and eager to recover lost credit, charged with such vigour that the day was won.

The Nervii fought to the last and died, almost to a man. That day closed the existence of the Nervii, as a nation. When, a few days later, the women and old men came in and sued for mercy, which strange to say, was granted; they reported, that of six hundred chiefs of their tribe, three had escaped the carnage, and of sixty thousand men, scarcely five hundred capable of bearing arms.

The Aduatuci, whose contingent had not arrived in time to share the battle, and who were no others than the relics of the great Cimbric and Teutonic host, who were destroyed by Marius, were next to be reduced. They had been received into fraternity by the Belgic tribes, who were probably of Cimbric blood, and had obtained from them a town and fortress, supposed to be impregnable, not far from the modern city of Tongres. At first, these people offered to surrender and give up the greater part of their arms, which they threw over the walls, so that they actually filled the ditches, and nearly reached the level of the ramparts; on the following night, however, doubting the good faith of the Romans, they armed again, sallied at midnight, and furiously assaulted the camp. There was hard fighting all night, but at daybreak they were beaten back with the loss of four thousand men, and shut up in the city, when the gates being forced, fifty thousand souls of the inhabitants were sold as slaves.

In the meanwhile, Publius Crassus, who had been detached with a *legion* to reduce the clans on the sea coast, reported that all the nations had submitted to the Roman authority, so far as to Vannes in Brittany, along all the shores of the channel, and down the coast of the ocean so far as to the embouchure of the Loire. Thereupon Caesar cantoned the *legions*, for their winter quarters, about the cities of Angers, and Chartres on the lower Loire and in the district of Touraine, bordering on the countries last conquered, and this done returned into Italy and Illyria. Thus ended his second Gallic campaign. The carnage of this year amounted to about one hundred and fifty thousand Belgians, sixty thousand Nervii, and four thousand Aduatuci, put to the sword, and of the last unhappy people, fifty-three thousand sold into perpetual slavery. For this good service the senate voted to Caesar a thanksgiving to the immortal gods for fifteen, (*Caesar de Bello. Gall. III.*), consecutive days, an honour granted to no one previously.

During this winter, Cicero was recalled from banishment, and joined the Pompeian party; Pompey was appointed to proconsular power over all the provinces, to superintend the supply of corn to Rome, with the power to appoint fifteen lieutenants; Clodius, the great disturber of public order was, for the time, reduced to quiet, if not to peace; but what is far more important to the fate of Rome, Crassus and Pompey visited Caesar in his quarters at Lucca, and it was agreed among them that Crassus should have Syria, and Pompey Spain, as his province, each with a large army, Caesar to retain his own for five years longer, with his present complement of eight *legions*, with their contingents of auxiliaries and irregulars—to such a vast amount had the original grant of the people of three *legions* swelled.

The second campaign of Gaul, B. C. 56, had ended with the despatch of Galba with a legion into the higher Alps from the lake of Geneva and the Rhone to the upper passes, for the purpose of opening and securing the mercantile roads from Italy, by Switzerland, into France; and he, after building forts and clearing the defiles, wintered on the ground. The third campaign opened by the rising of all the mountain tribes at once, with the intent to cut off the Roman detachment, but they were defeated with tremendous losses, and the roads were permanently opened, and kept open by garrisoned posts.

In the meantime all the seacoast nations rose in arms again, to shake off the Roman yoke, half imposed during the past campaign, and especially the hardy and half maritime inhabitants of the coasts of Brittany and Morbihan. At the same moment tidings arrived that the Belgians were again stirring, and that large German reinforcements were moving down toward the Rhine. Publius Crassus was detached with twelve *cohorts* and a strong force of cavalry to pass the Loire into Aquitaine, and hold the nations of the south in check, so that they should render no aid to the Britons; Titus Labienus was sent with the cavalry to Treves, to keep the Belgae quiet and protect the Rhine frontier; Titurius Sabinus, with three *legions*, entered Normandy to intimidate the inhabitants, from Cap la Hogue and Cherbourg to Lizieux at the mouth of the Seine; Decimus Brutus went south to Poitou and Saintonge to collect all the vessels he could find along the shores from the Garonne to the Loire, and bring them up to Morbihan, whither Caesar proceeded in person, with all his infantry.

Everywhere the operations were perfectly successful, though not without severe and well-sustained resistance in the west and south. Sabinus was so strong in Normandy that little effective opposition was made to him; Labienus also had sufficient force to overcome the Belgae, and no attempt was made on the Rhine. At Vannes several sharp actions on land occurred, and no permanent effect was produced until ships were collected, when a fierce naval combat was fought, the people of Morbihan totally defeated, and the whole of that district and coasts permanently subdued.

Crassus swept the whole country, from the Loire to the Garonne, and crossing that river to the Pyrenees, where he stormed several cities, fought a hard battle with the natives, aided by the Spaniards, veterans of Sertorius' old armies, and, gaining a decisive victory, opened a communication between the Roman province of Narbonensis in the south and Caesar's new conquests in the north and west; an attempt, not wholly successful on the Morini and Menapii, from Calais to the mouths of the Scheldt and Rhine, whose forests protected them, closed the campaign. The army went into winter-quarters in Normandy and Bretagne from Lisieux to the Loire.

In the next year, B. C. 55, the Usipetes and Tenchtheri, two powerful migratory German tribes, crossed the Rhine near its mouth, into the country of the Suevi, utter barbarians, ignorant of agriculture, living on the milk and flesh of their herds, which they drove with them, touching no wine nor cooked food, wearing no garb but skins, breaking the ice in mid winter to bathe in the rivers; large-boned, weather-proof, strong, ferocious barbarians.

These men, the rude children of nature, were unable to compete in villainy, in treason, with the polished, subtle, smooth and villainous Italians. Caesar treated with them, proclaimed an armistice, attacked them unawares, butchered them unresisting, chased them, slaughtering all the way, to the confluence of the Rhine and Meuse, into which they were driven, so that all who escaped the sword perished in the waters.

No one of the Romans was killed, and very few were wounded. Of the enemy, who numbered four hundred and thirty thousand, none escaped. Some five thousand horse only, of this ill-fated horde, who had been foraging beyond the Meuse at the time of the butchery, escaped across the Rhine, into the country of the Sicambri, below Cologne; and Caesar sent a deputation to this powerful tribe, demanding their immediate extradition. This demand, being as he expected, peremptorily refused, he immediately applied himself to bridge the Rhine, a feat which he accomplished, from the felling the first timber to the transportation, to the German soil, of the last baggage wagon, in the extraordinarily short period of ten days. The expedition had no effect, whatever, unless to intimidate the barbarians at the wonderful power and audacity of Romans, and to furnish subject for the self-gratulation of the mob of the capital.

Having marched across the bridge and up the Rhine, he marched down and back again, and after burning a few wretched villages and wasting the half-cultivated fields of the Ubii, returned into Gaul and broke down the bridge, having gained nothing for himself or for his country, except the empty renown of being the first Roman who had set foot on German soil with an army. Late as it was in the season, he was yet eager for more display—for it can be called nothing else—and collecting ships, passed over the channel, landed on the coast of Britain, gained some advantages in skirmishes over the barbarians, whom he drove into the forests, and then, to conclude, after nearly losing his whole fleet on the rocky coasts between Beachy head and Dover, during the neap tides of the equinox, returned as he went, but for the same empty honour of being the first civilized man who had invaded the sacred isle of Britain in the unknown sea.

The reward of this fourth campaign was a thanksgiving to the gods of twenty days, and the adulatory exclamation of the weak and subservient Cicero, "When compared with the exploits of Caesar, what has Marius done?" The honest Cato spoke of the dishonour brought upon the Roman name by the base treachery and broken armistice, in the case of the Germans, as it became a Cato to speak, and moved the senate that Caesar should be delivered up to the Germans, as a traitorous offender against the law of nations. But if Cato were honest, Rome was so no longer; and his motion had no more effect than Caesar's Britannic conquest.

In the next year, the 700th of Rome, B. C. 54, Pompey, while maintaining a vast army in Spain under his lieutenants, resided in princely pomp in his villas, in the neighbourhood of Rome, actually governing the city by intrigue and through the medium of his friends; Crassus repaired to his Syrian province, pillaged the temple of Jerusalem, and invaded the country of the Parthians; Caesar again crossed the channel with six hundred transports and twenty-eight ships of war, landed, probably near the mouth of the Stour; fought several actions, in all of which he defeated the enemy; advanced as far as the Thames, which he forded somewhat between Kingston and Brentford; chased Casivellaunus, the king, from forest-hold to forest-hold, seizing his flocks and herds, which were the only riches of the land, and, after being compelled to defend his own ships and the retrenchments which covered them as they lay drawn upon on the sand, returned into Gaul, receiving a nominal submission and imposing a nominal tribute on the tribes south of the Thames.

Such was his far-famed conquest of Britannia. During his absence his daughter Julia, the wife of Pompey, died; and the first connecting tie was rent between the two real enemies and rivals, who had been kept together only, in spite of clashing ambitions, jarring interests, deadly jealousies, by the thinnest web of policy, to scatter which to the four winds of heaven, both waited but the best occasion. Crassus yet lived, and preserved the balance; but not for long; he gone, the last link was broken.

During this winter, contrary to his usage, he was compelled to remain in Gaul, for on his return from his vainglorious expedition to Britain, he found that the country was utterly exhausted and unable to support the array, united in a single body. He was obliged, therefore, to separate his force, and disperse his posts through the country, unconnected and unsupported, from the mouth of the Rhine to the vicinity of Treves, through a country of impenetrable forests and impassable morasses. Labienus with one division was detached to the Moselle, near its junction with the Rhine; Sabinus was quartered on the Meuse, near Liege; Quintus Cicero on the Sambre in Hainault; Caesar himself was in force at Samarobriva, now Amiens.

This disposition inspired Ambiorix, a Belgic chief of the tribes inhabiting the country about the confluence of the Seine and Meuse, with the idea of attacking and cutting off all the Roman posts in a single day, without allowing them an opportunity of communicating with one another. The scheme was executed with singular ability; Sabinus in an attempt to effect a junction with Cicero was cut off with a whole *legion* and five *cohorts*; Cicero and Labienus were attacked, blockaded and surrounded by lines of circumvallation, by not less than sixty thousand men each. Tidings were conveyed to Caesar with much difficulty, and with his usual celerity, taking with him but a single *legion*, he marched day and night, raised the sieges, fell on the enemy like a thunderbolt, liberated his divisions, and won a complete victory.

The following season, his sixth campaign, he devoted solely to the task of punishing these revolters by devastation of their country, and utter destruction of their tribes. He again bridged and crossed the Rhine, brought the Ubii and other German clans to give hostages, and forced them to assist him with auxiliaries in the work of blood, which he meditated. Then he turned on his steps, parted his army into three divisions, invited all the neighbouring nations to join in the slaughter and the spoil, and beat the whole country, as if with a band of hunters in pursuit of game, putting all whom he encountered to the sword. In seven days the three divisions united at a pre-appointed rendezvous, and their work was done. The country was a desert in which men could not subsist; the miserable fugitives, who escaped the butchery, took refuge in the morasses, or hid themselves among the neighbouring tribes. In Belgic Gaul the war was ended. He had made a solitude and called it peace. So much for the clemency of Caesar.

On the conclusion of this campaign, Caesar returned into Italy, where had arrived the tidings of the defeat and death of Crassus, and there was much to be done politically to secure his own continuance in power. During this winter popular tumults rose to such a height, that it was judged necessary to appoint Pompey sole Consul in order to restore tranquillity, and it must be admitted, that this singular man, who was ever intriguing for illegitimate and extraordinary powers, yet never using them when gained except for purposes of vanity and show, did not exceed his authority or abuse the trust reposed in him. Clodius had been slain on the high road by Milo, and Pompey was affecting the state, and using more than the arrogance, of a king, while acting with the Senate, observing the forms of the government and ruling in accordance with the laws.

During this winter also, as a counterpoise to Pompey's sole consulship, Caesar was allowed the right of suing for the consulship in his absence, as his command was soon to expire, and so long as he retained his *imperium* as a general he could not enter the walls. Contented with this permission, he left Pompey in the temporary possession of the state, confident in his own power and resource to overturn him, when he chose, from his vainly-usurped and weakly-used dominion.

But he was now called back to his province by the greatest danger that had yet threatened Gaul. Irritated beyond measure by his barbarities in the last campaign, the whole of Gaul rose as a single man, and determined to extirpate the Roman race by a war of extermination, a war to the knife. In the city of Genabum, now Orleans, all the Roman residents were massacred in a single night, and the tidings conveyed by the human voice, man shouting to man, across field and flood, fell and forest, so that they were known everywhere through the country over a tract the diameter of which is three hundred and twenty miles, before sunrise. All Auvergne sprang to arms, and the Narbonense, the Roman province itself, was seriously endangered.

But Caesar was equal to the crisis. He was in the province almost before it was known to be threatened; he rallied whatever forces lay in those districts, secured all the towns, garrisoned all the forts, put the province in a perfect state of defence, and then launching his cavalry into Auvergne to burn, waste and destroy, and so create a powerful diversion, he crossed the Cevennes, then six feet deep in snow, reached Vienne on the Rhone, where he procured an escort of cavalry, and reassembled his *legions* which had wintered on the Seine, before the enemy knew that he had left Auvergne.

Then rushing impetuously without a check through the country, he entered Genabum and put every living thing to the sword, the Gauls retiring before him, wasting the country and burning their own towns and villages, all but Avaricum, the present town of Bourges, which being very strong, they spared contrary to the opinion of their leader. This place he besieged in form, and, after a desperate resistance from within and the most resolute efforts to relieve it from without, carried it by escalade in a night of darkness and tempest.

Of forty thousand persons, who composed its population, eight hundred escaped alive. After this followed some intricate manoeuvring, marching and countermarching between the Allier and the Loire, in which the Romans gained, to say the least, no advantage. The siege of Gergovia failed—this place is supposed to be in the vicinity of Clermont of Puy de Dome in Auvergne—and Caesar actually doubted whether he should not abandon Labienus, who was besieging Lutetia, which is now no less a place than Paris, to his fate, and retreat into the province. Happily for his fame he succeeded in forcing a ford on the Allier, hurried toward the Seine, effected his junction with Labienus near Melun, and having obtained reinforcements of German horse, was once more in condition to meet the *Vercingetorix*, which is clearly a title, not a name, in the field, (*Ver-cinn-cédo-righ* Great captain *generalissimo.* Thierry, *Hist. Gaul, III*),

In a smart cavalry action the German horse of Caesar turned the day, and the *Vercingetorix* dismissing his cavalry, took post at Alesia, a strong town at the confluence of the Seine and Marne with eighty thousand men and thirty days' provisions, trusting to be relieved by a Gaulish levy *en masse*, if Caesar should dare to besiege him.

That Caesar did; and, in an incredibly short time, surrounded the city with an inner line of circumvallation, and his own camp and entrenchments with an outer line of countervallation, embracing continuous ramparts of more than fourteen miles' circumference, fieldworks, redoubts, fosses, inundations, with outer palisades, abattis, and pitfalls, with crowsfeet to receive cavalry, which rendered his own camp perfectly secure, and the position of the enemy desperate.

The fighting was tremendous; the besieged were pressed by famine, and in order to make their provisions last as long as possible, drove out all the non-combatants, old men, youths, women, infants at the breast, and as Caesar would not allow them to pass the lines, they all perished, in sight on the one hand of their friends and countrymen, on the other of their merciless invaders.

In the meantime an immense force, said to have amounted to two hundred and forty thousand foot and eight thousand horse, was collected to raise the siege. From within and without, the lines were assailed with equal fury and determination. Once the exterior lines were forced, when Caesar sallied, took the storming party in the rear, threw his whole force into the plain, making the action general, and bringing it to the sword and buckler work, in which, over barbarians, the *legionaries* never failed to conquer.

The relieving army fled and was pursued, as usual, to extremity by the victorious horse, until dispersing they saved themselves in the woods and marshes, which were now their only refuge. Deprived of their last hope of relief, the people of Alesia now surrendered at discretion, their Vercingetorix giving himself up first, if thereby he might mitigate the doom of his own people. Of his fate no record survives; but, to the reader of Roman history, it is in no wise doubtful—long captivity, the procession at the chariot wheel, the Tullianum, and the *lictor's* scourge and axe. The people were sold into slavery.

So fell Alesia, and so closed the seventh and most critical of the Gaulish campaigns. The *legions* went into quarters, partitioning the whole country as if already conquered, on the Meuse, the Marne, the Seine, the Saone, the Garonne, garrisoning all France without the Roman province with an impregnable line of military cordons. From this day the war was in truth ended, though it suited the general, for the gratification of his troops, for the entire annihilation of all national spirit in Gaul, and to gain time, to protract it through one more campaign of cruelty and wrong.

During the winter, which followed this campaign, Caesar remained tranquilly in Gaul, affecting to take no heed of events which were passing in Rome, while in reality by his agents, one of whom was the consul Sulpicius, with the assistance of three or four *tribunes* of the people, he contrived that everything should so far be regulated according to his pleasure, that no decree of the Senate should stand, to his detriment.

His principal object would now seem to have been the gratifying and gaining to his own personal uses the flower of the legions, and to pacifying his province by any means. For the first purpose, therefore, and also, it may be, to prove to the adverse party in Rome that the war was not ended, so that his presence or command in the province could be dispensed with, he called out two *legions*, the eleventh and twelfth, and employed them in devastating the country of the Bituriges, south of the Loire, whose capital was the unfortunate city of Avaricum, so mercilessly dealt withal in the late campaign, on the pretext that they were again moving.

For this service, as it was irregular, being performed in the dead of winter, and produced no booty, he himself gave a private bounty of two hundred *sesterces* to each of the privates, and ten times that sum to every centurion. No sooner had these troops returned to their quarters than he in turn called out two other *legions* and employed them on similar duty, with a like reward, in the country of the Carnutes, about the ruins of the wretched Genabum.

In the spring of the year 103 of Rome, and 51 B. C, these severities again had the desired effect. The people called Bellovaci, in the Beauvoisis, judging from the fate of their neighbours on the Loire, despaired of safety from friendship or fidelity to Rome, and took up arms for their own security. But arms were no stronger defence to them, than innocence. Caesar marched with the eighth, ninth, and eleventh *legions*, the latter out of its turn of duty, because it was supposed, although now in its eighth year's service, to be inferior in discipline, and partly by skilful operations, partly by a successful and destructive action, compelled them to surrender at discretion.

This done and the Belgic nations once more subjugated, he detached Fabius with twenty-five *cohorts* to operate on the left of the Loire, sent the twelfth *legion* toward the sources of the Garonne in order to cover the province from the consequences of any risings which might arise from his intended cruelties in the north, and then with Marc Antony and Labienus, returned toward the Scheldt and Meuse, to renew the barbarous executions of his sixth campaign.

The inhabitants of that wretched devastated district had gradually crept back to their ancient homes, the fields were once more cultivated, the villages again becoming populous. Ambiorix had resumed his government, and thinking of nothing less than war, was striving to heal the bleeding wounds of his country. But it was necessary to prove to all Gaul that Rome, or Caesar, never forgave one who strove against her for freedom. The fields were again wasted with fire and sword, and military execution done on all who were found in the country, without discrimination of age or sex, till that rich district of the low countries was reduced once more into a howling desert.

Thence, like a vulture, lured by the prescience of carnage, and with speed equal to that of the vulture's wing, he swept back with terror in his van and desolation in his rear to the beautiful plains of the Loire and Garonne, where Fabius his worthy lieutenant had by his oppression fanned the last spark of sedition into flame. Drapes, the prince of that country, had raised an army and, when defeated, had taken refuge in Uxellodunum, a strong place supposed to be Cap du Nac, in Quercy, where his defence was so resolute as to raise the hopes of the neighbouring nations. Hither came Caesar, and hope fled with mercy, from before his footsteps. His masterly and rapid operations soon reduced the last fortress of Gaul to a surrender at discretion, and Caesar wrote in indelible characters his title to the name of clement, by the deed which followed that rendition; he struck off the right arms of all the males who had borne arms in Uxellodunum, for the intimidation of all evil doers who should presume thereafter to strike for liberty or country.

Thus terminated the war in Gaul. Treason in Italy was to follow. Caesar had now gained all his objects. He had a large rich country utterly prostrate at his feet, capable, so soon as its wounds should be a little healed, of furnishing him ample resources either to conquer or to purchase Rome —he had an army of twelve legions, beside auxiliaries of every arm, probably the best troops the world had ever seen, thoroughly devoted to his will, *echelloned* with admirable skill across the whole of France, from the borders of his original province, not far from Toulouse, to the Scheldt and Meuse in his new conquests. He now wanted only a pretext, nor was he long in finding that.

Another year passed, and, still residing in the low countries, he had assumed for a time the reality of mercy; he conciliated the temper of the nations, preserved admirable order and tranquillity in his province, administered justice candidly, and, instead of the merciless general, showed himself the mild, liberal, impartial, popular magistrate.

Golden opinions he won from the provincials, from the army; while he never ceased for a moment to collect money, arms, materials, to exercise his legions, as if for a mighty war—truly it was the mighty war, for which all the past service, all the past toil, all the past bloodshed, had been but boy's play of practice and preparation—never ceased to agitate, to manage, to buy Rome by his agents, of whom Marc Antony was the ablest and most unscrupulous, by his intrigues, by his wealth, which was now as overgrown and enormous, as his debts had been formerly extraordinary.

Still he affected to preserve the utmost veneration for the Senate, and to hold his loyalty and obedience to its orders unbroken. When he was called upon to restore two *legions*, which he had borrowed from Pompey for the prosecution of the war, he restored them almost before the mandate was received—two which he knew thoroughly devoted to himself, and from which he could expect better service, when amalgamated with the troops on whom Pompey could depend, than when mustered with his forces. He even proposed to resign his command if his rival would do so likewise. Of that he knew there was no danger.

It was now the winter of the year of Rome 104, 50 B. C, and the ninth that he had been engaged in active hostilities. This winter he resolved to spend in Italy, but with his usual caution, he left all his army, except the veteran thirteenth *legion* which he had stationed at Placentia, cantoned in France, four *legions* on the Scheldt and Meuse, four at Autun between the Saone and Loire.

His reception in Cisalpine Gaul was a triumph, and his approach, even without an army, struck terror to the Senatorial party and was regarded almost as a declaration of war. But he was resolved not to stir without a pretext of law, and that his partisans obtained for him. In the opening of the year 705, the Consuls Marcellus and Lentulus moved that prior to any other business, the matter of Caesar's province and command should be considered, and on the seventh of January a resolution passed, ordering Caesar to dismiss his army and retire from his provinces within a certain day, and, in case of disobedience, declaring him an enemy to his country, (Ferguson, *Rom. Rep. IV.*).

Antony and Cassius interposed their *veto*, and, when the Senate invested the consuls with dictatorial power by the charge "that they should see that the republic took no harm," affecting to believe that their lives were in danger, fled to the camp of Caesar for protection. The time had come, and the man was ready. Now was the hour for which he had so toiled, so steeped his soul in bloodshed. They say he hesitated. As much as the hungry tiger hesitates to spring on its defenceless victim. He harangued the thirteenth *legion*, sent orders into Gaul to the twelfth *legion*, which was already under marching orders to join him, advanced upon Ariminum, crossed the Rubicon, and was at war with Rome.

Everywhere the people fled before him, everywhere the soldiery joined him, the eighth and twelfth *legions* and twenty-two *cohorts* of new levies overtook him from Gaul as he pressed forward in pursuit of Pompey, who found that the army which, he had boasted, would arise from the soil of Italy, at the first stamp of his foot, was not of flesh and blood, nor likely to withstand the half-barbarian *legions*, inured to discipline and danger, and drunken with the blood of Gaul, who rushed like a torrent at the heels of his dreaded rival over the prostrate plains of Italy.

After a fruitless stand at Brundusium, until Caesar was thundering at its gates and planting his ladders against the walls, Pompey evacuated the country, took ship with such soldiers as adhered to him, and half the aristocracy of Rome, and fled to Dyrrachium in Epirus, whence to renew the war, and meet his destiny, and that of the Republic, at Pharsalia. In sixty days he had cleared Italy of every enemy, and every soldier who had been raised against him was mustered under his eagles. Entering Rome, he assumed the control as an absolute master, though he affected clemency, made no threat of violence or proscription toward the friends of Pompey, and even performed the farce of deferring to the will of the Senate. The value of this deference, however, was soon proved, when on moving the Senate to appropriate the moneys in the public treasury to the prosecution of the war, the *tribune* Metellus Celer opposed him.

Then the spirit of the tyrant spoke in the voice of the gladiator. He threatened the honest magistrate with immediate death, adding the words, "this is easier for me to execute than to utter." The menace was enough, the doors of the treasury were forced, the moneys, which had been hoarded there, since the destruction of Rome by the Gauls, in readiness for some last emergency and deadliest need of the republic, untouched during all the dark trials of the Punic war, when Hannibal was threatening annihilation to the very name of Rome, were seized by the usurper, to be used as the best weapon against the last stay of the commonwealth.

Almost before Pompey was in Macedonia, Caesar was in Gaul besieging Marseilles, into which Domitius Ahenobarbus had thrown himself with the crews of a squadron, and raised the population for Pompey and the Republic. The siege of this rich and strong town, by sea and land, Caesar committed to Trebonius and Decimus Brutus with three *legions*; and, having received tidings, which proved false that Pompey was in Numidia on his way to Spain, where he had a regular army of seven Roman *legions*, five thousand horse and eighty *cohorts* of provincial foot, ordered Fabius from the Garonne through the Pyrenees into Spain with the four *legions* which he commanded, and himself followed him at full speed, and overtook him with an escort of nine hundred horse only in the neighbourhood of Lexida, and in the face of an overwhelming superiority of the enemy.

The campaign which followed was one of incessant marching, manoeuvring, intriguing, and but little fighting. Generally speaking Caesar was out-generalled, and in some instances out-fought, but the superior qualities of his soldiers stood him in stead, and his own marvellous tact and mastery over men's minds converted all his losses into gains, all his disadvantages into absolute success. Petreius and Afranius narrowly escaped being delivered up by their troops, and at last their whole army was reduced to surrender at discretion without striking a blow. From Spain he returned victorious to Marseilles, which had resisted gallantly, till it heard of Caesar's return, when it implored mercy and surrendered; that crafty and politic man, whose game now was mercy, as it had been in Gaul ruthless execution, receiving its submission without an expression of anger or resentment.

While in Marseilles, he learned that he had been dignified in Rome with the office of Dictator, between the active energy of his own partisans and the timidity and torpor of the opposite faction, and hurried at once to the city, eager to be invested with a legal authority, however illegally obtained, which might justify his unconstitutional and treasonable acts. Stopping a short time at Placentia he checked a dangerous mutiny of the *legions*, executed the ringleaders, dismissed the ninth legion bodily from the service, proceeded to the city, was invested with the authority, and decorated with the twenty-four *fasces* of dictator. This high trust he instantly violated and disgraced by creating at a single blow all the inhabitants of Cisalpine Gaul, those semi-barbarians, whose least rising under the name of a Gallic tumult had been used to make all Rome throw off the *toga* and assume the *sagum*, free citizens of the Republic; and by procuring an indemnity for all the criminals, Milo the slayer of Clodius alone excepted, who lay under sentence of the law, or who were in exile for political offences, at the commencement of the war. This closed the tenth campaign, and eleventh year of command, of this most wonderful man, this most dishonest citizen and plausible usurper.

From this day he was—as the vision is said to have prophesied to Cromwell—if not king, the first man in Rome.

From this period of his life to the end, all is one rapid rush of meteoric splendour and success, until all is darkened for ever, but, beyond a mere summary of the events, little is needed.

It will not do to say that a man who won every battle that he fought, displayed no generalship; still less will it do to say that the victor was in truth beaten, but that he and his army could not find it out and therefore beat the beaters. Yet it is certain that, throughout all the operations about Dyrrachium, through Macedonia, and before Pharsalia, he was completely outgeneralled, outmanoeuvred, once defeated, and that he must have been annihilated but for the undue caution and remissness of his adversary. His victory over Pharnaces and his Alexandrian tumults were mere child's play, scarcely affairs of outposts, and unworthy of notice in a dispatch, to a man who had gone through the gigantic combats of the Helvetii, the Nervii and Alesia. His *Veni, vidi, vici*, was an empty boast, intended rather, I believe, to represent his scorn for the triumphs of Lucullus and Pompey, than to express pride at his own exploits.

His campaigns in Africa and Spain present nothing whatsoever to increase his fame as a strategist, or to gain him any reputation beyond that of an invincible fighter.. Labienus and Petreius surprised, and ought to have defeated him at Ruspina; Scipio frustrated all his endeavours to force him to give battle at Uzita and obliged him to raise the siege; at Vaga, Sarsura, and Tysdra he was foiled; at Tegea he was worsted in an affair of horse, and, if he won at Thapsus, it was by the impetuosity of his irresistible soldiers, and neither by his own dispositions, nor by his own orders.

In his last Spanish campaign, the most rapid, dashing and decisive of all, the fate of the war was set on the hazard of a die in the single action of Munda, the only action probably in the whole war in which his troops encountered their equals in spirit, in discipline, in physical force and moral courage, and this battle was won by the consequences of the merest accident.

A Numidian partisan with a few squadrons of irregular horse, made an unmeaning and unauthorised dash at the camp of the Pompeians; Labienus, deceived by the movement, wheeled to repel the attack, and the whole army, which had hitherto fought with advantage and were gaining ground on all points, instantly broke and fled. Such a victory is indeed the fortune of war, and were I called upon to name a general, who was especially entitled to be named the fortunate, it would not be Sylla, but Caesar.

He certainly never met a general of above second or third rate ability, yet he was constantly foiled and outmanoeuvred in the field, and more than once must have been beaten but for the gross misconduct of his enemies, or the egregious excellence of his own soldiers. Once or twice, in spite of the immense superiority arising from the quality of his command, and the confidence reposed therein, he was nearly destroyed by untrained barbarians.

As a manoeuvring general, or captain in the field, I cannot rate him very high; but in the cabinet, for combining his plans, concerting his operations, calculating his means, disposing his powers, so as to render defeat impossible and victory certain, he probably never had an equal, certainly never a superior.

As a creator of armies again he stands unrivalled; and he is no mean master of the art of war, or of the world's wisdom, who can make of men machines, with which he can, beyond a peradventure, calculate on conquering a world.

In a word he must be held a great general who never lost a battle or failed in a campaign, even as he must be admitted a great man, who creates his own occasions out of which to work his own will—especially when that will outsoars all scope of the most mounting ambition, all reach of human calculation, all limit of what may be called human possibility.

Morally, as a man, no one could be worse than Caesar—he had no hue or blush of principle, honesty, honour, decency, consistency or humanity. Interest was his only guide, self his only God. He loved nothing, honoured nothing, feared nothing, and he died, feared indeed, but neither loved nor honoured.

Politically, as a citizen, no one that was ever born can compete with Caesar for deliberate, cold-blooded, calculated treason. Thirty years before, when the commonwealth was tranquil, at peace at home and abroad, perfectly free, moderately well governed, and in danger of no present convulsion, he deliberately resolved to subvert the Constitution, cheat the people, destroy the Senate and make himself king. By feigning an excessive zeal for even ultra liberty he convulsed the state, sapped the foundations of law and order, and prepared the way for revolution. By immeasurable hypocrisy he undermined and ruined every friend and defender of the constitution. By incalculable bloodshed he made to himself an invincible machine for defence or aggression, and, when the moment came, turned it against his own country and destroyed her.

He has no plea of party, for he had no party, except whichever he chose for the moment to make his tool. No excuse of creed, for he believed in nothing, aristocracy or democracy, senate or tribunes of the people, equally rotten and contemptible to his cold sarcastic eye. No apology of fanaticism, for he was not a fanatic—no not even of glory.

He made himself absolute hereditary monarch, if he did eschew the name king—and even this seems doubtful—of a free Republic,—if, as I take it, the power to make and execute the law, the power of life, the possession of the purse and sword, constitute absolute monarchy, whether the man wear a wreath of laurel or a diamond crown, whether he wield a sceptre or a sword, whether he call himself dictator, king or president.

Strange to say, having the substantial power, having even the frippery and tinsel, the palmated tunic and purple *toga*, the gilded laurels and the *curule* chair, he coveted the empty title—craved to be called king.

Therefore he perished, not that he *was* the actual thing, but that he coveted the unreal name. So inconsistent are men, even the lovers of immortal liberty.

I may not justify nor even palliate assassination, but I must coincide with the *dictum* of the senate, "*Jure Caesus habeatur!*" Let him be accounted justly slain! he and all they who do likewise!

With Caius Julius Caesar, ends the list of the Captains of the Roman Republic; as in fact with him ends the Republic. He was the first emperor of Rome, and the founder of her first dynasty. If a few months of doubtful strife followed his fall, if a few spasmodic efforts at liberty convulsed the corpse of the expiring republic, they were the effects of departing, not of returning, life. If it did require the holy blood shed at Philippi to consummate the sacrifice of freedom, if it did require the shameless flight of the wild Antony at Actium to consolidate the despotism which endured for centuries unchanged, until the years had elapsed predicted by the mythic vultures seen from the Palatine by Romulus and Remus, and Rome sank from the arbitress of nations and the mistress of the world to be the slave of the barbarian, and the handmaid of the priest—still with the fall of Caesar fell the Republic of Rome, never it may be feared to know liberty again, until the end of all recorded time.

ALSO FROM LEONAUR
AVAILABLE IN SOFTCOVER OR HARDCOVER WITH DUST JACKET

THE FALL OF THE MOGHUL EMPIRE OF HINDUSTAN *by H. G. Keene*—By the beginning of the nineteenth century, as British and Indian armies under Lake and Wellesley dominated the scene, a little over half a century of conflict brought the Moghul Empire to its knees.

LADY SALE'S AFGHANISTAN *by Florentia Sale*—An Indomitable Victorian Lady's Account of the Retreat from Kabul During the First Afghan War.

THE CAMPAIGN OF MAGENTA AND SOLFERINO 1859 *by Harold Carmichael Wylly*—The Decisive Conflict for the Unification of Italy.

FRENCH'S CAVALRY CAMPAIGN *by J. G. Maydon*—A Special Correspondent's View of British Army Mounted Troops During the Boer War.

CAVALRY AT WATERLOO *by Sir Evelyn Wood*—British Mounted Troops During the Campaign of 1815.

THE SUBALTERN *by George Robert Gleig*—The Experiences of an Officer of the 85th Light Infantry During the Peninsular War.

NAPOLEON AT BAY, 1814 *by F. Loraine Petre*—The Campaigns to the Fall of the First Empire.

NAPOLEON AND THE CAMPAIGN OF 1806 *by Colonel Vachée*—The Napoleonic Method of Organisation and Command to the Battles of Jena & Auerstädt.

THE COMPLETE ADVENTURES IN THE CONNAUGHT RANGERS *by William Grattan*—The 88th Regiment during the Napoleonic Wars by a Serving Officer.

BUGLER AND OFFICER OF THE RIFLES *by William Green & Harry Smith*—With the 95th (Rifles) during the Peninsular & Waterloo Campaigns of the Napoleonic Wars.

NAPOLEONIC WAR STORIES *by Sir Arthur Quiller-Couch*—Tales of soldiers, spies, battles & sieges from the Peninsular & Waterloo campaigns.

CAPTAIN OF THE 95TH (RIFLES) *by Jonathan Leach*—An officer of Wellington's sharpshooters during the Peninsular, South of France and Waterloo campaigns of the Napoleonic wars.

RIFLEMAN COSTELLO *by Edward Costello*—The adventures of a soldier of the 95th (Rifles) in the Peninsular & Waterloo Campaigns of the Napoleonic wars.

AVAILABLE ONLINE AT **www.leonaur.com**
AND FROM ALL GOOD BOOK STORES

ALSO FROM LEONAUR
AVAILABLE IN SOFTCOVER OR HARDCOVER WITH DUST JACKET

ZULU: 1879 *by D.C.F. Moodie & the Leonaur Editors*—The Anglo-Zulu War of 1879 from contemporary sources: First Hand Accounts, Interviews, Dispatches, Official Documents & Newspaper Reports.

THE RED DRAGOON *by W.J. Adams*—With the 7th Dragoon Guards in the Cape of Good Hope against the Boers & the Kaffir tribes during the 'war of the axe' 1843-48'.

THE RECOLLECTIONS OF SKINNER OF SKINNER'S HORSE *by James Skinner*—James Skinner and his 'Yellow Boys' Irregular cavalry in the wars of India between the British, Mahratta, Rajput, Mogul, Sikh & Pindarree Forces.

A CAVALRY OFFICER DURING THE SEPOY REVOLT *by A. R. D. Mackenzie*—Experiences with the 3rd Bengal Light Cavalry, the Guides and Sikh Irregular Cavalry from the outbreak to Delhi and Lucknow.

A NORFOLK SOLDIER IN THE FIRST SIKH WAR *by J W Baldwin*—Experiences of a private of H.M. 9th Regiment of Foot in the battles for the Punjab, India 1845-6.

TOMMY ATKINS' WAR STORIES: 14 FIRST HAND ACCOUNTS—Fourteen first hand accounts from the ranks of the British Army during Queen Victoria's Empire.

THE WATERLOO LETTERS *by H. T. Siborne*—Accounts of the Battle by British Officers for its Foremost Historian.

NEY: GENERAL OF CAVALRY VOLUME 1—1769-1799 *by Antoine Bulos*—The Early Career of a Marshal of the First Empire.

NEY: MARSHAL OF FRANCE VOLUME 2—1799-1805 *by Antoine Bulos*—The Early Career of a Marshal of the First Empire.

AIDE-DE-CAMP TO NAPOLEON *by Philippe-Paul de Ségur*—For anyone interested in the Napoleonic Wars this book, written by one who was intimate with the strategies and machinations of the Emperor, will be essential reading.

TWILIGHT OF EMPIRE *by Sir Thomas Ussher & Sir George Cockburn*—Two accounts of Napoleon's Journeys in Exile to Elba and St. Helena: Narrative of Events by Sir Thomas Ussher & Napoleon's Last Voyage: Extract of a diary by Sir George Cockburn.

PRIVATE WHEELER *by William Wheeler*—The letters of a soldier of the 51st Light Infantry during the Peninsular War & at Waterloo.

AVAILABLE ONLINE AT **www.leonaur.com**
AND FROM ALL GOOD BOOK STORES

www.ingramcontent.com/pod-product-compliance
Lightning Source LLC
Chambersburg PA
CBHW030216170426
43201CB00006B/100